FIRST EDITION

GENDER AND POPULAR CULTURE

A Visual Study

EDITED BY TARA L. WARD

cognella

SAN DIEGO

Bassim Hamadeh, CEO and Publisher
Alisa Munoz, Project Editor
Abbey Hastings, Associate Production Editor
Emely Villavicencio, Senior Graphic Designer
Trey Soto, Licensing Coordinator
Natalie Piccotti, Director of Marketing
Kassie Graves, Vice President of Editorial
Jamie Giganti, Director of Academic Publishing

Cover image copyright © 2012 iStockphoto LP/sturti.
copyright © 2018 iStockphoto LP/IPGGutenbergUKLtd.
copyright © 2012 iStockphoto LP/JOHNGOMEZPIX.
copyright © 2018 iStockphoto LP/The7Dew.
copyright © 2018 iStockphoto LP/Tassii.
copyright © 2018 iStockphoto LP/brusinski.
copyright © 2018 iStockphoto LP/Gearstd.
copyright © 2018 iStockphoto LP/Bilgehan Tuzcu.
copyright © 2018 iStockphoto LP/areeya_ann.
copyright © 2018 iStockphoto LP/LightFieldStudios.

Printed in the United States of America.

3970 Sorrento Valley Blvd., Ste. 500, San Diego, CA 92121

CONTENTS

Section 4: Theorizing Single Gender Cultures 165

Introduction

This text is based on a simple, though often forgotten principle: Academic ideas and everyday life should reflect and enhance each other. If a theory is not applicable to the real world, it is simply mental masturbation. And unless we observe our lives through carefully considered frameworks, we will be stuck in the status quo or worse. This book brings together a series of texts that can help all of us bridge the gap between theory and practice because the particular writings presented here share an interest in questioning and even undermining binary dichotomies, like theory and practice. Starting with the first selection from Simone de Beauvoir's *The Second Sex*, they will look at our culture's propensity to divide things by two's as well as the ways that process creates both ill-fitting categories and inequality. Given this theme, I would recommend making a habit of asking the following questions of each new text:

1. What categories does the author discuss? Think about both explicit and implicit classifications.
2. What or who is left out, mismatched, or forced into these groups?
3. What power differentials exist between the types?

Not only will they help you better understand the writings in this anthology, their repetition will prompt other questions, like why would we do this and what can we do to change it? And those inquiries tend to lead to practical considerations.

The subjects theorized in this book deal with three long-established and pervasive dichotomies: male-female, intellectual-popular, text-image. Since I ultimately hope that readers will come to see these divisions as suspect, I will not attempt to define them. Instead, I ask that we all try to reorient our sense of the relative importance of these categories and to privilege the historically denigrated terms (*female*, *popular culture*, and *image*). This means demanding that theories address, explain, and validate women's and non-binary people's experiences; that conceptual frameworks adequately characterize contemporary popular culture; and that visual phenomena are treated as meaningful conduits of cultural messages. At first, this may seem strange, disorienting, or even wrong; however, those feelings reveal how deeply entrenched inequity is in our thought patterns. It is also worth rearranging any mental hierarchies that you might have amongst the concepts *female*, *popular culture*, and *image*. These kinds of repositionings often help us achieve critical distance and learn to question supposedly natural or universal orders.

That said, gender also adds an urgent political motivation to these questions. All of these texts speak in one way or another to questions that are currently debated in legislatures and chat rooms as well as being subjects of organizing and protest. However, this book does not directly address those activities. Rather it seeks to introduce a series of critical tools that will allow students to consider and reconsider the ways gender functions in contemporary Western and especially American culture. This tactic is in no way a meant to belittle political action; in fact, it aims to bolster and expand it by providing an opportunity take a close look at where our society stands and to imagine what it might look like. In the process, it will repeatedly encounter the fact that feminist theory broadens notions of what counts as political and asks us to question who we really are. As the mantra goes, "the personal is political."

Which brings me to the last foundational principle: The questions asked by the texts in this book demand a lot of self-reflection. To take them seriously is to be not just troubled by the world, but uncertain of one's self. This means that the traditional division between the intellectual and the emotional is untenable. Ideas will affect you; feelings will make you think. As long as that isn't traumatic, it signals yet another binary being dismantled.

HOW TO USE THIS BOOK

There are a lot of different ways to read. We can appreciate the sound of words and the elegance of their combination. We can parse language for facts or terminology. And we can assess an essay for the strength of its argument. All of these kinds of reading are possible with this anthology, but I would suggest that students approach these texts as if they were descriptions or verbal pictures of some aspect of the world. When we read a description, we treat it differently than other forms of writing. However beautiful the prose might be, it must always be compared to what it describes. While descriptions can certainly be wrong, they are rarely totally correct. Something will be left out. You'll see something differently than the writer did. Finally, unlike philosophical arguments, descriptions don't make explicit claims to work for all examples or in all cases. Descriptions are not universal and when they cover groups rather than individual instances, each case must be considered and compared.

This raises the question of what these texts are describing. Well, on the most basic level the answer is your everyday life and the experiences of people around you. To narrow that down a bit, I have provided a list of examples from popular culture after each text. (If there are others that occur to you as you are reading, please email me at tlward@umich.edu). Since these examples are also representations of the world, you might think about whether they are good descriptions and what's missing from them. Throughout the text you will also encounter ideas that are new to you and examples to which you are not normally drawn. In these cases, I urge you to remember that however foreign or different they may seem, they emerged from someone's experience and thus they should not be dismissed until you get to know that person or someone like them.

That idea brings us back to where we began. Academic writing, especially its more theoretical forms, can often seem to exist in an intellectual utopia with its own language and mores. That couldn't be further from the realities in which these texts are produced. Real people with bodies, problems, home lives, bureaucratic duties, and even guilty pleasures produce these theories. The language they use, while sometimes difficult, is intentional. And just as you would make an effort to understand some you met in real life, you should engage with these texts remembering that they were written by people who were trying to describe some facet of their world.

SECTION 1

INTRODUCTION

The Second Sex

By SIMONE DE BEAUVOIR

I hesitated a long time before writing a book on woman. The subject is irritating, especially for women; and it is not new. Enough ink has flowed over the quarrel about feminism; it is now almost over: let's not talk about it anymore. Yet it is still being talked about. And the volumes of idiocies churned out over this past century do not seem to have clarified the problem. Besides, is there a problem? And what is it? Are there even women? True, the theory of the eternal feminine still has its followers; they whisper, "Even in Russia, *women* are still very much women"; but other well-informed people—and also at times those same ones—lament, "Woman is losing herself, woman is lost." It is hard to know any longer if women still exist, if they will always exist, if there should be women at all, what place they hold in this world, what place they should hold. "Where are the women?" asked a short-lived magazine recently.[1] But first, what is a woman? "*Tot a mulier in utero*: she is a womb," some say. Yet speaking of certain women, the experts proclaim, "They are not women," even though they have a uterus like the others. Everyone agrees there are females in the human species; today, as in the past, they make up about half of humanity; and yet we are told that "femininity is in jeopardy"; we are urged, "Be women, stay women, become women." So not every female human being is necessarily a woman; she must take part in this mysterious and endangered reality known as femininity. Is femininity secreted by the ovaries? Is it enshrined in a Platonic heaven? Is a frilly petticoat enough to bring it down to earth? Although some women zealously strive to embody it, the model has never been patented. It is typically described in vague and shimmering terms borrowed from a clairvoyant's vocabulary. In Saint Thomas's time it was an essence defined with as much certainty as the sedative quality of a poppy. But conceptualism has lost ground: biological and social sciences no longer believe there are immutably determined entities that define given characteristics like those of the woman, the Jew, or the black; science considers characteristics as secondary reactions to a *situation*. If there is no such thing today as femininity, it is because there never was. Does the word "woman," then, have no content? It is what advocates of Enlightenment philosophy, rationalism, or nominalism vigorously assert: women are, among human beings, merely those who are arbitrarily designated by the word "woman"; American women in particular are inclined to think that woman as such no longer exists. If some backward individual still takes herself for a woman, her friends advise her to undergo psychoanalysis to get rid of this obsession. Referring to a book—a very irritating one at that—*Modern Woman: The Lost Sex*, Dorothy Parker wrote: "I cannot be fair about books that treat women as women. My idea is that all of us, men as well as women, whoever we are, should be considered as human beings." But nominalism is a doctrine that falls a bit short; and it is easy for antifeminists to show that women *are* not men. Certainly woman like man is a human being; but such an assertion is abstract; the fact is that every concrete human being is always uniquely situated. To reject the notions of the eternal feminine, the black soul, or the Jewish character is not to deny that there are today Jews, blacks, or women: this denial is not a liberation for those concerned but an inauthentic flight. Clearly, no woman can claim without bad faith to be situated beyond her sex. A few years ago, a well-known woman writer refused to have her portrait appear in a series of photographs devoted specifically to women writers. She wanted to be included in the men's category; but to get this privilege, she used her husband's influence. Women who assert they are men still claim masculine consideration and respect. I also remember a young Trotskyite standing on a platform during a stormy meeting, about to come to blows in spite of her obvious fragility. She was denying her feminine frailty; but it was for the love of a militant man she wanted to be equal to. The defiant position that American women occupy proves they are haunted by the sentiment of their own femininity. And the truth is that anyone can clearly see that humanity is split into two categories of individuals with manifestly different clothes, faces, bodies, smiles, movements, interests, and occupations; these differences are perhaps superficial; perhaps they are destined to disappear. What is certain is that for the moment they exist in a strikingly obvious way.

If the female function is not enough to define woman, and if we also reject the explanation of the "eternal feminine," but if we accept, even temporarily, that there are women on the earth, we then have to ask: What is a woman?

Merely stating the problem suggests an immediate answer to me. It is significant that I pose it. It would never occur to a man to write a book on the singular situation of males in humanity.[2] If I want to define myself, I first have to say, "I am a woman"; all other assertions will arise from this basic truth. A man never begins by positing himself as an individual of a certain sex: that he is a man is obvious. The categories masculine and feminine appear as symmetrical in a formal way on town hall records or identification papers. The relation of the two sexes is not that of two electrical poles: the man represents both the positive and the neuter to such an extent that in French *hommes* designates human beings, the particular meaning of the word *vir* being assimilated into the general meaning of the word "homo." Woman is the negative, to such a point that any determination is imputed to her as a limitation, without reciprocity. I used to get annoyed in abstract discussions to hear men tell me: "You think such and such a thing because you're a woman." But I know my only defense is to answer, "I think it because it is true," thereby eliminating my subjectivity; it was out of the question to answer, "And you think the contrary because you are a man," because it is understood that being a man is not a particularity; a man is in his right by virtue of being man; it is the woman who is in the wrong. In fact, just as for the ancients there was an absolute vertical that defined the oblique, there is an absolute human type that is masculine. Woman has ovaries and a uterus; such are the particular conditions that lock her in her subjectivity; some even say she thinks with her hormones. Man vainly forgets that his anatomy also includes hormones and testicles. He grasps his body as a direct and normal link with the world that he believes he apprehends in all objectivity, whereas he considers woman's body an obstacle, a prison, burdened by everything that particularizes it. "The female is female by virtue of a certain *lack* of qualities," Aristotle said. "We should regard women's nature as suffering from natural defectiveness." And Saint Thomas in his turn decreed that woman was an "incomplete man," an "incidental" being. This is what the Genesis story symbolizes, where Eve appears as if drawn from Adam's "supernumerary" bone, in Bossuet's words. Humanity is male, and man defines woman, not in herself, but in relation to himself; she is not considered an autonomous being. "Woman, the relative being," writes Michelet. Thus Monsieur Benda declares in *Le rapport d'Uriel* (Uriel's Report): "A man's body has meaning by itself, disregarding the body of the woman, whereas the woman's body seems devoid of meaning without reference to the male. Man thinks himself without woman. Woman does not think herself without man." And she is nothing other than what man decides; she is thus called "the sex," meaning that the male sees her essentially as a sexed being; for him she is sex, so she is it in the absolute. She is determined and differentiated in relation to man, while he is not in relation to her; she is the inessential in front of the essential. He is the Subject; he is the Absolute. She is the Other.[3]

The category of *Other* is as original as consciousness itself. The duality between Self and Other can be found in the most primitive societies, in the most ancient mythologies; this division did not always fall into the category of the division of the sexes, it was not based on any empirical given: this comes out in works like Granet's on Chinese thought, and Dumézil's on India and Rome. In couples such as Varuna—Mitra, Uranus—Zeus, Sun—Moon,

Day—Night, no feminine element is involved at the outset; neither in Good—Evil, auspicious and inauspicious, left and right, God and Lucifer; alterity is the fundamental category of human thought. No group ever defines itself as One without immediately setting up the Other opposite itself. It only takes three travelers brought together by chance in the same train compartment for the rest of the travelers to become vaguely hostile "others." Village people view anyone not belonging to the village as suspicious "others." For the native of a country inhabitants of other countries are viewed as "foreigners"; Jews are the "others" for anti-Semites, blacks for racist Americans, indigenous people for colonists, proletarians for the propertied classes. After studying the diverse forms of primitive society in depth, Levi-Strauss could conclude: "The passage from the state of Nature to the state of Culture is defined by man's ability to think biological relations as systems of oppositions; duality, alternation, opposition, and symmetry, whether occurring in defined or less clear form, are not so much phenomena to explain as fundamental and immediate givens of social reality."[4] These phenomena could not be understood if human reality were solely a *Mitsein** based on solidarity and friendship. On the contrary, they become clear if, following Hegel, a fundamental hostility to any other consciousness is found in consciousness itself; the subject posits itself only in opposition; it asserts itself as the essential and sets up the other as inessential, as the object.

But the other consciousness has an opposing reciprocal claim: traveling, a local is shocked to realize that in neighboring countries locals view him as a foreigner; between villages, clans, nations, and classes there are wars, potlatches, agreements, treaties, and struggles that remove the absolute meaning from the idea of the *Other* and bring out its relativity; whether one likes it or not, individuals and groups have no choice but to recognize the reciprocity of their relation. How is it, then, that between the sexes this reciprocity has not been put forward, that one of the terms has been asserted as the only essential one, denying any relativity in regard to its correlative, defining the latter as pure alterity? Why do women not contest male sovereignty? No subject posits itself spontaneously and at once as the inessential from the outset; it is not the Other who, defining itself as Other, defines the One; the Other is posited as Other by the One positing itself as One. But in order for the Other not to turn into the One, the Other has to submit to this foreign point of view. Where does this submission in woman come from?

NOTES

1. Out of print today, titled Franchise.

2. The Kinsey Report, for example, confines itself to defining the sexual characteristics of the American man, which is completely different.

3. This idea has been expressed in its most explicit form by E. Levinas in his essay *Le temps et l'autre* (*Time and the Other*). He expresses it like this: "Is there not a situation where alterity would be borne by a being in a positive sense, as essence? What is the alterity that does not purely and simply enter into the opposition of two species of the same genus? I think that the absolutely contrary contrary, whose contrariety is in no way affected by the relationship that can be established between it and its correlative, the contrariety that permits its terms to remain absolutely other, is the feminine. Sex is not some specific difference ... Neither is the difference between the sexes a contradiction ... Neither is the difference between the sexes the duality of two complementary terms, for two complementary terms presuppose a preexisting whole ... [A]lterity is accomplished in the feminine. The term is on the same level as, but in meaning opposed to, consciousness." I suppose Mr. Levinas is not forgetting that woman also is consciousness for herself. But it is striking that he deliberately adopts a man's point of view, disregarding the reciprocity of the subject and the object. When he writes that woman is mystery, he assumes that she is mystery for man. So this apparently objective description is in fact an affirmation of masculine privilege.

4. See Claude Lévi-Strauss, *Les structures élémentaires de la parenté* (*The Elementary Structures of Kinship*). I thank Claude Lévi-Strauss for sharing the proofs of his thesis, which I drew on heavily, particularly in the second part, pp. 76–89.

* *Mitsein* can be translated as "being with." The French term *réalité humaine* (human reality) has been problematically used to translate Heidegger's *Dasein*. TRANS.

DISCUSSION QUESTIONS

- According to Beauvoir, what is a woman?
- What accounts for inequality in Beauvoir's view?
- Can you define the term "other"?

Keywords

A Vocabulary of Culture and Society

SELECTIONS

By RAYMOND WILLIAMS

CULTURE

Culture is one of the two or three most complicated words in the English language. This is so partly because of its intricate historical development, in several European languages, but mainly because it has now come to be used for important concepts in several distinct intellectual disciplines and in several distinct and incompatible systems of thought.

The fw is *cultura*, L, from rw *colere*, L. *Colere* had a range of meanings: inhabit, cultivate, protect, honour with worship. Some of these meanings eventually separated, though still with occasional overlapping, in the derived nouns. Thus 'inhabit' developed through *colonus*, L to *colony*. 'Honour with worship' developed through *cultus*, L to *cult*. *Cultura* took on the main meaning of cultivation or tending, though with subsidiary medieval meanings of honour and worship (cf. in English **culture** as 'worship' in Caxton (1483)). The French forms of *cultura* were *couture*, oF, which has since developed its own specialized meaning, and later *culture*, which by eC15 had passed into English. The primary meaning was then in husbandry, the tending of natural growth.

Culture in all its early uses was a noun of process: the tending *of* something, basically crops or animals. The subsidiary *coulter*—ploughshare, had travelled by a different linguistic route, from *culter,* L—ploughshare, *culter,* oE, to the variant English spellings *culter, colter, coulter* and as late as eC17 **culture** (Webster, *Duchess of Malfi,* III, ii: 'hot burning cultures'). This provided a further basis for the important next stage of meaning, by metaphor. From eC16 the tending of natural growth was extended to a process of human development, and this, alongside the original meaning in husbandry, was the main sense until 1C18 and eC19. Thus More: 'to the culture and profit of their minds'; Bacon: 'the culture and manurance of minds' (1605); Hobbes: 'a culture of their minds' (1651); Johnson: 'she neglected the culture of her understanding' (1759). At various points in this development two crucial changes occurred: first, a degree of habituation to the metaphor, which made the sense of human tending direct; second, an extension of particular processes to a general process, which the word could abstractly carry. It is of course from the latter development that the independent noun **culture** began its complicated modern history, but the process of change is so intricate, and the latencies of meaning are at times so close, that it is not possible to give any definite date. **Culture** as an independent noun, an abstract process or the product of such a process, is not important before 1C18 and is not common before mC19. But the early stages of this development were not sudden. There is an interesting use in Milton, in the second (revised) edition of *The Readie and Easie Way to Establish a Free Commonwealth* (1660): 'spread much more Knowledg and Civility, yea, Religion, through all parts of the Land, by communicating the natural heat of Government and Culture more distributively to all extreme parts, which now lie num and neglected.' Here the metaphorical sense ('natural heat') still appears to be present, and *civility* (**cf. civilization**) is still written where in C19 we would normally expect **culture.** Yet we can also read 'government and culture' in a quite modern sense. Milton, from the tenor of his whole argument, is writing about a general social process, and this is a definite stage of development. In C18 England this general process acquired definite class associations though **cultivation** and **cultivated** were more commonly used for this. But there is a letter of 1730 (Bishop of Killala, to Mrs Clayton; cit Plumb, *England in the Eighteenth Century*) which has this clear sense: 'it has not been customary for persons of either birth or culture to breed up their children to the Church'. Akenside (*Pleasures of Imagination,* 1744) wrote: '... nor purple state nor culture can bestow'. Wordsworth wrote 'where grace of culture hath been utterly unknown' (1805), and Jane Austen (*Emma,* 1816) 'every advantage of discipline and culture'.

It is thus clear that **culture** was developing in English towards some of its modern senses before the decisive effects of a new social and intellectual movement. But to follow the development through this movement, in 1C18 and eC19, we have to look also at developments in other languages and especially in German.

In French, until C18, **culture** was always accompanied by a grammatical form indicating the matter being cultivated, as in the English usage already noted. Its occasional use as an independent noun dates from mC18, rather later than similar occasional uses in English. The independent noun *civilization* also emerged in mC18; its relationship to **culture** has since been very complicated (cf. CIVILIZATION and discussion below). There was at this point an important development in German: the word was borrowed from French, spelled first (1C18) *Cultur* and from 1C19 *Kultur*. Its main use was still as a synonym for *civilization*: first in the abstract sense of a general process of becoming 'civilized' or 'cultivated'; second, in the sense which had already been established for *civilization* by the historians of the Enlightenment, in the popular Cl8 form of the universal histories, as a description of the secular process of human development. There was then a decisive change of use in Herder. In his unfinished *Ideas on the Philosophy of the History of Mankind* (1784-91) he wrote of *Cultur*: 'nothing is more indeterminate than this word, and nothing more deceptive than its application to all nations and periods'. He attacked the assumption of the universal histories that 'civilization' or 'culture'—the historical self-development of humanity—was what we would now call a unilinear process, leading to the high and dominant point of Cl8 European culture. Indeed he attacked what he called European subjugation and domination of the four quarters of the globe, and wrote:

> Men of all the quarters of the globe, who have perished over the ages, you have not lived solely to manure the earth with your ashes, so that at the end of time your posterity should be made happy by European culture. The very thought of a superior European culture is a blatant insult to the majesty of Nature.

It is then necessary, he argued, in a decisive innovation, to speak of 'cultures' in the plural: the specific and variable cultures of different nations and periods, but also the specific and variable cultures of social and economic groups within a nation. This sense, which has become common in C20 anthropology and sociology, and by extension in general use, remained comparatively isolated, however, in all European languages until at earliest mC19 and was not fully established until eC20.

What mainly happened in eC19, under the influence of Herder and many other writers of the Romantic movement, in Germany, England and France, was a social and historical application of an alternative idea of human development: alternative, that is, to the ideas now centred on 'civilization' and 'progress'. This application was exceptionally complicated. It was used to emphasize national and traditional cultures, including the new concept of **folk-culture.** It was used to attack what was seen as the 'MECHANICAL' (q.v.) character of the new civilization then emerging: both for its abstract rationalism and for the 'inhumanity' of current industrial development. It was used to distinguish between 'human' and 'material' development. Politically, as so often in this period, it veered between radicalism and reaction and very often, in the confusion of major social change, fused elements of both. (It should also be noted, though it adds to the real complication, that the same kind of distinction, especially between 'material' and 'spiritual' development, was made by von Humboldt and others, until as late as 1900, with a reversal of the terms, **culture** being material and *civilization* spiritual. In general, however, the opposite distinction was dominant.)

The complexity of the modern development of the word, and of its modern usage, can then be appreciated. We can easily distinguish the sense which depends on a literal continuity of physical process as now in 'sugar-beet culture' or, in the specialized physical application in bacteriology since the 1880s, 'germ culture'. But once we go beyond the physical reference, we have to recognize three broad active categories of usage. The sources of two of these we have already discussed: (i) the independent and abstract noun which describes a general process of intellectual, spiritual and aesthetic development, from C18; (ii) the independent noun, whether used generally or specifically, which indicates a particular way of life, whether of a people, a period or a group, from Herder and C19. But we have also to recognize (iii) the independent and abstract noun which describes the works and practices of intellectual and especially artistic activity. This seems often now the most widespread use: **culture** is music, literature, painting and sculpture, theatre and film. A **Ministry of Culture** refers to these specific activities, sometimes with the addition of philosophy, scholarship, history. This use, (iii), is in fact relatively late. It is difficult to date precisely because it is in origin an applied form of sense (i): the idea of a general process of intellectual, spiritual and aesthetic development was applied and effectively transferred to the works and practices which represent and sustain it. In English (i) and (iii) are still close; at times, for internal reasons, they are indistinguishable as in Arnold, *Culture and Anarchy* (1867); while sense (ii) was decisively introduced into English by Tylor, *Primitive Culture* (1870). The decisive development of sense (iii) in English was in 1C19 and eC20.

Faced by this complex and still active history of the word, it is easy to react by selecting one 'true' or 'proper' or 'scientific' sense and dismissing other senses as loose or confused. There is evidence of this reaction even in the excellent study by Kroeber and Kluckhohn, *Culture: A Critical Review of Concepts and Definitions,* where usage in North American anthropology is in effect taken as a norm. It is clear that, within a discipline, conceptual usage has to be clarified. But in general it is the range and overlap of meanings that is significant. The complex of senses indicates a complex argument about the relations between general human development and a particular way of life, and between both and the works and practices of art and intelligence. Within this complex argument there are fundamentally opposed as well as effectively overlapping positions; there are also, understandably, many unresolved questions and confused answers. But these arguments and questions cannot be resolved by reducing the complexity of actual usage. This point is relevant also to uses of forms of the word in languages other than English, where there is considerable variation. Even within English, 'social anthropology' is normally used in Britain where 'cultural anthropology' would be used in North America. The anthropological use is common in the German, Scandinavian and Slavonic language groups, but it is distinctly subordinate to the senses of art and learning, or of a general process of human development, in Italian and French. Between languages as within a language, the range and complexity of sense and reference indicate both difference of intellectual position and some blurring or over lapping. These variations, of whatever kind, necessarily involve alternative views of the activities, relationships and processes which this complex word indicates. The complexity, that is to say, is not finally in the word but in the problems which its variations of use significantly indicate.

It is necessary to look also at some associated and derived words. **Cultivation** and **cultivated** went through the same metaphorical extension from a physical to a social or educational sense in Cl7, and were especially significant words in Cl8. Coleridge, making a classical eC19 distinction between civilization and culture, wrote (1830): 'the permanent distinction, and occasional contrast, between cultivation and civilization'. The noun in this sense has effectively disappeared but the adjective is still quite common, especially in relation to manners and tastes. The important adjective **cultural** appears to date from the 1870s; it became common by the 1890s. The word is only available, in its modern sense, when the independent noun, in the artistic and intellectual or anthropological senses, has become familiar. Hostility to the word **culture** in English appears to date from the controversy around Arnold's views. It gathered force in 1C19 and eC20, in association with a comparable hostility to *aesthete* and AESTHETIC (q.v.). Its association with class distinction produced the mime-word *culchah*. There was also an area of hostility associated with anti-German feeling, during and after the 1914–18 War, in relation to propaganda about *Kultur*. The central area of hostility has lasted, and one element of it has been emphasized by the recent American phrase **culture-vulture.** It is significant that virtually all the hostility (with the sole exception of the temporary anti-German association) has been connected with uses involving claims to superior knowledge (cf. the noun INTELLECTUAL), refinement (*culchah*) and distinctions between 'high' art (**culture**) and popular art and entertainment. It thus records a real social history and a very difficult and confused phase of social and cultural development. It is interesting that the steadily extending social and anthropological use of **culture** and **cultural** and such formations as **sub-culture** (the culture of a distinguishable smaller group) has, except in certain areas (notably popular entertainment), either by-passed or effectively diminished the hostility and its associated unease and embarrassment.

POPULAR

Popular was originally a legal and political term, from *popularis*, L—belonging to the people. An **action popular,** from C15, was a legal suit which it was open to anyone to begin. **Popular estate** and **popular government,** from Cl6, referred to a political system constituted or carried on by the whole people, but there was also the sense (cf. COMMON) of 'low' or 'base'. The transition to the predominant modern meaning of 'widely-favoured' or 'well-liked' is interesting in that it contains a strong element of setting out to gain favour, with a sense of calculation that has not quite disappeared but that is evident in a reinforced phrase like **deliberately popular.** Most of the men who have left records of the use of the word saw the matter from this point of view, downwards. There were neutral uses, such as North's 'more popular, and desirous of the common peoples good will and favour' (1580) (where **popular** was still a term of policy rather than of condition), and evidently derogatory uses, such as Bacon's 'a Noble-man of an ancient Family, but unquiet and popular' (1622). **Popularity** was defined in 1697, by Collier, as 'a courting the favour of the people by undue practices'. This use was probably reinforced by unfavourable applications: a neutral reference to 'popular ... theams' (1573) is less characteristic than 'popular error' (1616) and 'popular sickenesse' (1603) or 'popular disease' (C17–C19), in which an unwelcome thing was merely widespread. A primary sense of 'widely favoured' was clear by 1C18; the sense of 'well liked' is probably C19. A 1C19 American magazine observed: 'they have come ... to take popular quite gravely and sincerely as a synonym for good'. The shift in perspective is then evident. **Popular** was being seen from the point of view of the people rather than from those seeking favour or power from them. Yet the earlier sense has not died. **Popular culture** was not identified by *the people* but by others, and it still carries two older senses: inferior kinds of work (cf. **popular literature, popular press** as distinguished from *quality press*); and work deliberately setting out to win favour (**popular journalism** as distinguished from *democratic journalism,* or **popular entertainment**); as well as the more modern sense of well-liked by many people, with which of course, in many cases, the earlier senses overlap. The recent sense of **popular culture** as the culture actually made by people for themselves is different from all these; it is often displaced to the past as *folk culture* but it is also an important modern emphasis. The range of senses can be seen again in **popularize,** which until C19 was a political term, in the old sense, and then took on its special meaning of presenting knowledge in generally accessible ways. Its C19 uses were mainly favourable, and in C20 the favourable sense is still available, but there is also a strong sense of 'simplification', which in some circles is predominant.

In mC20 **popular song** and **popular art** were characteristically shortened to **pop,** and the familiar range of senses, from unfavourable to favourable, gathered again around this. The shortening gave the word a lively informality but opened it, more easily, to a sense of the trivial. It is hard to say whether older senses of **pop** have become fused with this use: the common sense of a sudden lively movement, in many familiar and generally pleasing contexts, is certainly appropriate.

READING 2: KEYWORDS

DISCUSSION QUESTIONS

- What kinds of value judgments are connected to the term "popular"?
- How many different uses or definitions of "culture" can you identify in Williams's description?
- Why would historical definitions of words be associated with political change?

The Communist Manifesto

SELECTIONS

By KARL MARX AND FRIEDRICH ENGELS

I. BOURGEOIS AND PROLETARIANS

The history of all hitherto existing societies is the history of class struggles.

Freeman and slave, patrician and plebeian, lord and serf, guild-master and journeyman, in a word, oppressor and oppressed, stood in constant opposition to one another, carried on an uninterrupted, now hidden, now open fight, a fight that each time ended, either in a revolutionary re-constitution of society at large, or in the common ruin of the contending classes.

In the earlier epochs of history, we find almost everywhere a complicated arrangement of society into various orders, a manifold gradation of social rank. In ancient Rome we have patricians, knights, plebeians, slaves; in the Middle Ages, feudal lords, vassals, guild-masters, journeymen, apprentices, serfs; in almost all of these classes, again, subordinate gradations.

The modern bourgeois society that has sprouted from the ruins of feudal society has not done away with class antagonisms. It has but established new classes, new conditions of oppression, new forms of struggle in place of the old ones. Our epoch, the epoch of the

Karl Marx and Friedrich Engels, "The Communist Manifesto," 1888.

bourgeoisie, possesses, however, this distinctive feature: it has simplified the class antagonisms. Society as a whole is more and more splitting up into two great hostile camps, into two great classes, directly facing each other: Bourgeoisie and Proletariat.

From the serfs of the Middle Ages sprang the chartered burghers of the earliest towns. From these burgesses the first elements of the bourgeoisie were developed.

The discovery of America, the rounding of the Cape, opened up fresh ground for the rising bourgeoisie. The East-Indian and Chinese markets, the colonisation of America, trade with the colonies, the increase in the means of exchange and in commodities generally, gave to commerce, to navigation, to industry, an impulse never before known, and thereby, to the revolutionary element in the tottering feudal society, a rapid development.

The feudal system of industry, under which industrial production was monopolised by closed guilds, now no longer sufficed for the growing wants of the new markets. The manufacturing system took its place. The guild-masters were pushed on one side by the manufacturing middle class; division of labour between the different corporate guilds vanished in the face of division of labour in each single workshop.

Meantime the markets kept ever growing, the demand ever rising. Even manufacture no longer sufficed. Thereupon, steam and machinery revolutionised industrial production. The place of manufacture was taken by the giant, Modern Industry, the place of the industrial middle class, by industrial millionaires, the leaders of whole industrial armies, the modern bourgeois.

Modern industry has established the world-market, for which the discovery of America paved the way. This market has given an immense development to commerce, to navigation, to communication by land. This development has, in its time, reacted on the extension of industry; and in proportion as industry, commerce, navigation, railways extended, in the same proportion the bourgeoisie developed, increased its capital, and pushed into the background every class handed down from the Middle Ages.

We see, therefore, how the modern bourgeoisie is itself the product of a long course of development, of a series of revolutions in the modes of production and of exchange.

Each step in the development of the bourgeoisie was accompanied by a corresponding political advance of that class. An oppressed class under the sway of the feudal nobility, an armed and self-governing association in the mediaeval commune; here independent urban republic (as in Italy and Germany), there taxable "third estate" of the monarchy (as in France), afterwards, in the period of manufacture proper, serving either the semi-feudal or the absolute monarchy as a counterpoise against the nobility, and, in fact, corner-stone of the great monarchies in general, the bourgeoisie has at last, since the establishment of Modern Industry and of the world-market, conquered for itself, in the modern representative State, exclusive political sway. The executive of the modern State is but a committee for managing the common affairs of the whole bourgeoisie.

The bourgeoisie, historically, has played a most revolutionary part.

The bourgeoisie, wherever it has got the upper hand, has put an end to all feudal, patriarchal, idyllic relations. It has pitilessly torn asunder the motley feudal ties that bound man to his "natural superiors," and has left remaining no other nexus between man and man than naked self-interest, than callous "cash payment." It has drowned the most heavenly ecstasies of religious fervour, of chivalrous enthusiasm, of philistine sentimentalism, in the icy water of egotistical calculation. It has resolved personal worth into exchange value, and in place of the numberless and indefeasible chartered freedoms, has set up that single, unconscionable freedom—Free Trade. In one word, for exploitation, veiled by religious and political illusions, naked, shameless, direct, brutal exploitation.

The bourgeoisie has stripped of its halo every occupation hitherto honoured and looked up to with reverent awe. It has converted the physician, the lawyer, the priest, the poet, the man of science, into its paid wage labourers.

The bourgeoisie has torn away from the family its sentimental veil, and has reduced the family relation to a mere money relation.

The bourgeoisie has disclosed how it came to pass that the brutal display of vigour in the Middle Ages, which Reactionists so much admire, found its fitting complement in the most slothful indolence. It has been the first to show what man's activity can bring about. It has accomplished wonders far surpassing Egyptian pyramids, Roman aqueducts, and Gothic cathedrals; it has conducted expeditions that put in the shade all former Exoduses of nations and crusades.

The bourgeoisie cannot exist without constantly revolutionising the instruments of production, and thereby the relations of production, and with them the whole relations of society. Conservation of the old modes of production in unaltered form, was, on the contrary, the first condition of existence for all earlier industrial classes. Constant revolutionising of production, uninterrupted disturbance of all social conditions, everlasting uncertainty and agitation distinguish the bourgeois epoch from all earlier ones. All fixed, fast-frozen relations, with their train of ancient and venerable prejudices and opinions, are swept away, all new-formed ones become antiquated before they can ossify. All that is solid melts into air, all that is holy is profaned, and man is at last compelled to face with sober senses, his real conditions of life, and his relations with his kind.

The need of a constantly expanding market for its products chases the bourgeoisie over the whole surface of the globe. It must nestle everywhere, settle everywhere, establish connexions everywhere.

The bourgeoisie has through its exploitation of the world-market given a cosmopolitan character to production and consumption in every country. To the great chagrin of Reactionists, it has drawn from under the feet of industry the national ground on which it stood. All old-established national industries have been destroyed or are daily being destroyed. They are dislodged by new industries, whose introduction becomes a life and death question for all civilised nations, by industries that no longer work up indigenous raw material, but raw material drawn from the remotest zones; industries whose products are consumed, not only at home, but in every quarter of the globe. In place of the old wants, satisfied by the productions of the country, we find new wants, requiring for their satisfaction the products of distant lands and climes. In place of the old local and national seclusion and self-sufficiency, we have intercourse in every direction, universal inter-dependence of nations. And as in material, so also in intellectual production. The intellectual creations of individual nations become common property. National one-sidedness and narrow-mindedness become more and more impossible, and from the numerous national and local literatures, there arises a world literature.

The bourgeoisie, by the rapid improvement of all instruments of production, by the immensely facilitated means of communication, draws all, even the most barbarian, nations into civilisation. The cheap prices of its commodities are the heavy artillery with which it batters down all Chinese walls, with which it forces the barbarians' intensely obstinate hatred of foreigners to capitulate. It compels all nations, on pain of extinction, to adopt the bourgeois mode of production; it compels them to introduce what it calls civilisation into their midst, i.e., to become bourgeois themselves. In one word, it creates a world after its own image.

The bourgeoisie has subjected the country to the rule of the towns. It has created enormous cities, has greatly increased the urban population as compared with the rural, and has thus rescued a considerable part of the population from the idiocy of rural life. Just as it has made the country dependent on the towns, so it has made barbarian and semi-barbarian countries dependent on the civilised ones, nations of peasants on nations of bourgeois, the East on the West.

The bourgeoisie keeps more and more doing away with the scattered state of the population, of the means of production, and of property. It has agglomerated production, and has concentrated property in a few hands. The necessary consequence of this was political centralisation. Independent, or but loosely connected provinces, with separate interests, laws, governments and systems of taxation, became lumped together into one nation, with one government, one code of laws, one national class-interest, one frontier and one customs-tariff. The bourgeoisie, during its rule of scarce one hundred years, has created more massive and more colossal productive forces than have all preceding generations together. Subjection of Nature's forces to man, machinery, application of chemistry to industry and agriculture, steam-navigation, railways, electric telegraphs, clearing of whole continents for cultivation, canalisation of rivers, whole populations conjured out of the ground—what earlier century had even a presentiment that such productive forces slumbered in the lap of social labour?

We see then: the means of production and of exchange, on whose foundation the bourgeoisie built itself up, were generated in feudal society. At a certain stage in the development of these means of production and of exchange, the conditions under which feudal society produced and exchanged, the feudal organisation of agriculture and manufacturing industry, in one word, the feudal relations of property became no longer compatible with the already developed productive forces; they became so many fetters. They had to be burst asunder; they were burst asunder.

Into their place stepped free competition, accompanied by a social and political constitution adapted to it, and by the economical and political sway of the bourgeois class.

A similar movement is going on before our own eyes. Modern bourgeois society with its relations of production, of exchange and of property, a society that has conjured up such gigantic means of production and of exchange, is like the sorcerer, who is no longer able to control the powers of the nether world whom he has called up by his spells. For many a decade past the history of industry and commerce is but the history of the revolt of modern productive forces against modern conditions of production, against the property relations that are the conditions for the existence of the bourgeoisie and of its rule. It is enough to mention the commercial crises that by their periodical return put on its trial, each time more threateningly, the existence of the entire bourgeois society. In these crises a great part not only of the existing products, but also of the previously created productive forces, are periodically destroyed. In these crises there breaks out an epidemic that, in all earlier epochs, would have seemed an absurdity—the epidemic of over-production. Society suddenly finds itself put back into a state of momentary barbarism; it appears as if a famine, a universal war of devastation had cut off the supply of every means of subsistence; industry and commerce seem to be destroyed; and why? Because there is too much civilisation, too much means of subsistence, too much industry, too much commerce. The productive forces at the disposal of society no longer tend to further the development of the conditions of bourgeois property; on the contrary, they have become too powerful for these conditions, by which they are fettered, and so soon as they overcome these fetters, they bring disorder into the whole of bourgeois society, endanger the existence of bourgeois property. The conditions of bourgeois society are too narrow to comprise the wealth created by them. And how does the bourgeoisie get over these crises? On the one hand inforced destruction of a mass of productive forces; on the other, by the conquest of new markets, and by the more thorough exploitation of the old ones. That is to say, by paving the way for more extensive and more destructive crises, and by diminishing the means whereby crises are prevented.

The weapons with which the bourgeoisie felled feudalism to the ground are now turned against the bourgeoisie itself.

But not only has the bourgeoisie forged the weapons that bring death to itself; it has also called into existence the men who are to wield those weapons—the modern working class—the proletarians.

In proportion as the bourgeoisie, i.e., capital, is developed, in the same proportion is the proletariat, the modern working class, developed—a class of labourers, who live only so long as they find work, and who find work only so long as their labour increases capital. These labourers, who must sell themselves piece-meal, are a commodity, like every other article of commerce, and are consequently exposed to all the vicissitudes of competition, to all the fluctuations of the market.

Owing to the extensive use of machinery and to division of labour, the work of the proletarians has lost all individual character, and consequently, all charm for the workman. He becomes an appendage of the machine, and it is only the most simple, most monotonous, and most easily acquired knack, that is required of him. Hence, the cost of production of a workman is restricted, almost entirely, to the means of subsistence that he requires for his maintenance, and for the propagation of his race. But the price of a commodity, and therefore also of labour, is equal to its cost of production. In proportion therefore, as the repulsiveness of the work increases, the wage decreases. Nay more, in proportion as the use of machinery and division of labour increases, in the same proportion the burden of toil also increases, whether by prolongation of the working hours, by increase of the work exacted in a given time or by increased speed of the machinery, etc.

Modern industry has converted the little workshop of the patriarchal master into the great factory of the industrial capitalist. Masses of labourers, crowded into the factory, are organised like soldiers. As privates of the industrial army they are placed under the command of a perfect hierarchy of officers and sergeants. Not only are they slaves of the bourgeois class, and of the bourgeois State; they are daily and hourly enslaved by the machine, by the over-looker, and, above all, by the individual bourgeois manufacturer himself. The more openly this despotism proclaims gain to be its end and aim, the more petty, the more hateful and the more embittering it is.

The less the skill and exertion of strength implied in manual labour, in other words, the more modern industry becomes developed, the more is the labour of men superseded by that of women. Differences of age and sex have no longer any distinctive social validity for the working class. All are instruments of labour, more or less expensive to use, according to their age and sex.

No sooner is the exploitation of the labourer by the manufacturer, so far at an end, that he receives his wages in cash, than he is set upon by the other portions of the bourgeoisie, the landlord, the shopkeeper, the pawnbroker, etc.

The lower strata of the middle class—the small tradespeople, shopkeepers, retired tradesmen generally, the handicraftsmen and peasants—all these sink gradually into the proletariat, partly because their diminutive capital does not suffice for the scale on which Modern Industry is carried on, and is swamped in the competition with the large capitalists, partly because their specialized skill is rendered worthless by the new methods of production. Thus the proletariat is recruited from all classes of the population.

The proletariat goes through various stages of development. With its birth begins its struggle with the bourgeoisie. At first the contest is carried on by individual labourers, then by the workpeople of a factory, then by the operatives of one trade, in one locality, against the individual bourgeois who directly exploits them. They direct their attacks not against the bourgeois conditions of production, but against the instruments of production themselves; they destroy imported wares that compete with their labour, they smash to pieces machinery, they set factories ablaze, they seek to restore by force the vanished status of the workman of the Middle Ages.

At this stage the labourers still form an incoherent mass scattered over the whole country, and broken up by their mutual competition. If anywhere they unite to form more compact bodies, this is not yet the consequence of their own active union, but of the union of the bourgeoisie, which class, in order to attain its own political ends, is compelled to set the whole proletariat in motion, and is moreover yet, for a time, able to do so. At this stage, therefore, the proletarians do not fight their enemies, but the enemies of their enemies, the remnants of absolute monarchy, the landowners, the non-industrial bourgeois, the petty bourgeoisie. Thus the whole historical movement is concentrated in the hands of the bourgeoisie; every victory so obtained is a victory for the bourgeoisie.

But with the development of industry the proletariat not only increases in number; it becomes concentrated in greater masses, its strength grows, and it feels that strength more. The various interests and conditions of life within the ranks of the proletariat are more and more equalised, in proportion as machinery obliterates all distinctions of labour, and nearly everywhere reduces wages to the same low level. The growing competition among the bourgeois, and the resulting commercial crises, make the wages of the workers ever more fluctuating. The unceasing improvement of machinery, ever more rapidly developing, makes their livelihood more and more precarious; the collisions between individual workmen and individual bourgeois take more and more the character of collisions between two classes. Thereupon the workers begin to form combinations (Trades Unions) against the bourgeois; they club together in order to keep up the rate of wages; they found permanent associations in order to make provision beforehand for these occasional revolts. Here and there the contest breaks out into riots.

Now and then the workers are victorious, but only for a time. The real fruit of their battles lies, not in the immediate result, but in the ever-expanding union of the workers. This union is helped on by the improved means of communication that are created by modern industry and that place the workers of different localities in contact with one another. It was just this contact that was needed to centralise the numerous local struggles, all of the same character, into one national struggle between classes. But every class struggle is a political struggle. And that union, to attain which the burghers of the Middle Ages, with their miserable highways, required centuries, the modern proletarians, thanks to railways, achieve in a few years.

This organisation of the proletarians into a class, and consequently into a political party, is continually being upset again by the competition between the workers themselves. But it ever rises up again, stronger, firmer, mightier. It compels legislative recognition of particular interests of the workers, by taking advantage of the divisions among the bourgeoisie itself. Thus the ten-hours' bill in England was carried.

Altogether collisions between the classes of the old society further, in many ways, the course of development of the proletariat. The bourgeoisie finds itself involved in a constant battle. At first with the aristocracy; later on, with those portions of the bourgeoisie itself, whose interests have become antagonistic to the progress of industry; at all times, with the bourgeoisie of foreign countries. In all these battles it sees itself compelled to appeal to the proletariat, to ask for its help, and thus, to drag it into the political arena. The bourgeoisie itself, therefore, supplies the proletariat with its own instruments of political and general education, in other words, it furnishes the proletariat with weapons for fighting the bourgeoisie.

Further, as we have already seen, entire sections of the ruling classes are, by the advance of industry, precipitated into the proletariat, or are at least threatened in their conditions of existence. These also supply the proletariat with fresh elements of enlightenment and progress.

Finally, in times when the class struggle nears the decisive hour, the process of dissolution going on within the ruling class, in fact within the whole range of society, assumes such a violent, glaring character, that a small section of the ruling class cuts itself adrift, and joins the revolutionary class, the class that holds the future in its hands. Just as, therefore, at an earlier period, a section of the nobility went over to the bourgeoisie, so now a portion of the bourgeoisie goes over to the proletariat, and in particular, a portion of the bourgeois ideologists, who have raised themselves to the level of comprehending theoretically the historical movement as a whole.

Of all the classes that stand face to face with the bourgeoisie today, the proletariat alone is a really revolutionary class. The other classes decay and finally disappear in the face of Modern Industry; the proletariat is its special and essential product. The lower middle class, the small manufacturer, the shopkeeper, the artisan, the peasant, all these fight against the bourgeoisie, to save from extinction their existence as fractions of the middle class. They are therefore not revolutionary, but conservative. Nay more, they are reactionary, for they try to roll back the wheel of history. If by chance they are revolutionary, they are so only in view of their impending transfer into the proletariat, they thus defend not their present, but their future interests, they desert their own standpoint to place themselves at that of the proletariat.

The "dangerous class," the social scum, that passively rotting mass thrown off by the lowest layers of old society, may, here and there, be swept into the movement by a proletarian revolution; its conditions of life, however, prepare it far more for the part of a bribed tool of reactionary intrigue.

In the conditions of the proletariat, those of old society at large are already virtually swamped. The proletarian is without property; his relation to his wife and children has no longer anything in common with the bourgeois family-relations; modern industrial labour, modern subjection to capital, the same in England as in France, in America as in Germany, has stripped him of every trace of national character. Law, morality, religion, are to him so many bourgeois prejudices, behind which lurk in ambush just as many bourgeois interests.

All the preceding classes that got the upper hand, sought to fortify their already acquired status by subjecting society at large to their conditions of appropriation. The proletarians cannot become masters of the productive forces of society, except by abolishing their own previous mode of appropriation, and thereby also every other previous mode of appropriation. They have nothing of their own to secure and to fortify; their mission is to destroy all previous securities for, and insurances of, individual property.

All previous historical movements were movements of minorities, or in the interests of minorities. The proletarian movement is the self-conscious, independent movement of the immense majority, in the interests of the immense majority. The proletariat, the lowest stratum of our present society, cannot stir, cannot raise itself up, without the whole superincumbent strata of official society being sprung into the air.

Though not in substance, yet in form, the struggle of the proletariat with the bourgeoisie is at first a national struggle. The proletariat of each country must, of course, first of all settle matters with its own bourgeoisie.

In depicting the most general phases of the development of the proletariat, we traced the more or less veiled civil war, raging within existing society, up to the point where that war breaks out into open revolution, and where the violent overthrow of the bourgeoisie lays the foundation for the sway of the proletariat.

Hitherto, every form of society has been based, as we have already seen, on the antagonism of oppressing and oppressed classes. But in order to oppress a class, certain conditions must be assured to it under which it can, at least, continue its slavish existence. The serf, in the period of serfdom, raised himself to membership in the commune, just as the petty bourgeois, under the yoke of feudal absolutism, managed to develop into a bourgeois. The modern laborer, on the contrary, instead of rising with the progress of industry, sinks deeper and deeper below the conditions of existence of his own class. He becomes a pauper, and pauperism develops more rapidly than population and wealth. And here it becomes evident, that the bourgeoisie is unfit any longer to be the ruling class in society, and to impose its conditions of existence upon society as an over-riding law. It is unfit to rule because it is incompetent to assure an existence to its slave within his slavery, because it cannot help letting him sink into such a state, that it has to feed him, instead of being fed by him. Society can no longer live under this bourgeoisie, in other words, its existence is no longer compatible with society.

The essential condition for the existence, and for the sway of the bourgeois class, is the formation and augmentation of capital; the condition for capital is wage-labour. Wage-labour rests exclusively on competition between the laborers. The advance of industry, whose involuntary promoter is the bourgeoisie, replaces the isolation of the labourers, due to competition, by their revolutionary combination, due to association. The development of Modern Industry, therefore, cuts from under its feet the very foundation on which the bourgeoisie produces and appropriates products. What the bourgeoisie, therefore, produces, above all, is its own grave-diggers. Its fall and the victory of the proletariat are equally inevitable.

II. PROLETARIANS AND COMMUNISTS

[...]

All property relations in the past have continually been subject to historical change consequent upon the change in historical conditions.

The French Revolution, for example, abolished feudal property in favour of bourgeois property.

The distinguishing feature of Communism is not the abolition of property generally, but the abolition of bourgeois property. But modern bourgeois private property is the final and most complete expression of the system of producing and appropriating products, that is based on class antagonisms, on the exploitation of the many by the few.

In this sense, the theory of the Communists may be summed up in the single sentence: Abolition of private property.

We Communists have been reproached with the desire of abolishing the right of personally acquiring property as the fruit of a man's own labour, which property is alleged to be the groundwork of all personal freedom, activity and independence.

Hard-won, self-acquired, self-earned property! Do you mean the property of the petty artisan and of the small peasant, a form of property that preceded the bourgeois form? There is no need to abolish that; the development of industry has to a great extent already destroyed it, and is still destroying it daily.

Or do you mean modern bourgeois private property?

But does wage-labour create any property for the labourer? Not a bit. It creates capital, i.e., that kind of property which exploits wage-labour, and which cannot increase except upon condition of begetting a new supply of wage-labour for fresh exploitation. Property, in its present form, is based on the antagonism of capital and wage-labour. Let us examine both sides of this antagonism.

To be a capitalist, is to have not only a purely personal, but a social status in production. Capital is a collective product, and only by the united action of many members, nay, in the last resort, only by the united action of all members of society, can it be set in motion.

Capital is, therefore, not a personal, it is a social power.

When, therefore, capital is converted into common property, into the property of all members of society, personal property is not thereby transformed into social property. It is only the social character of the property that is changed. It loses its class-character.

Let us now take wage-labour.

The average price of wage-labour is the minimum wage, i.e., that quantum of the means of subsistence, which is absolutely requisite in bare existence as a labourer. What, therefore, the wage-labourer appropriates by means of his labour, merely suffices to prolong and reproduce a bare existence. We by no means intend to abolish this personal appropriation of the products of labour, an appropriation that is made for the maintenance and reproduction of human life, and that leaves no surplus wherewith to command the labour of others. All that we want to do away with, is the miserable character of this appropriation, under which the labourer lives merely to increase capital, and is allowed to live only in so far as the interest of the ruling class requires it.

In bourgeois society, living labour is but a means to increase accumulated labour. In Communist society, accumulated labour is but a means to widen, to enrich, to promote the existence of the labourer.

In bourgeois society, therefore, the past dominates the present; in Communist society, the present dominates the past. In bourgeois society capital is independent and has individuality, while the living person is dependent and has no individuality.

And the abolition of this state of things is called by the bourgeois, abolition of individuality and freedom! And rightly so. The abolition of bourgeois individuality, bourgeois independence, and bourgeois freedom is undoubtedly aimed at.

By freedom is meant, under the present bourgeois conditions of production, free trade, free selling and buying.

But if selling and buying disappears, free selling and buying disappears also. This talk about free selling and buying, and all the other "brave words" of our bourgeoisie about freedom in general, have a meaning, if any, only in contrast with restricted selling and buying, with the fettered traders of the Middle Ages, but have no meaning when opposed to the Communistic abolition of buying and selling, of the bourgeois conditions of production, and of the bourgeoisie itself.

You are horrified at our intending to do away with private property. But in your existing society, private property is already done away with for nine-tenths of the population; its existence for the few is solely due to its non-existence in the hands of those nine-tenths. You reproach us, therefore, with intending to do away with a form of property, the necessary condition for whose existence is the non-existence of any property for the immense majority of society.

In one word, you reproach us with intending to do away with your property. Precisely so; that is just what we intend.

From the moment when labour can no longer be converted into capital, money, or rent, into a social power capable of being monopolised, i.e., from the moment when individual property can no longer be transformed into bourgeois property, into capital, from that moment, you say individuality vanishes.

You must, therefore, confess that by "individual" you mean no other person than the bourgeois, than the middle-class owner of property. This person must, indeed, be swept out of the way, and made impossible.

Communism deprives no man of the power to appropriate the products of society; all that it does is to deprive him of the power to subjugate the labour of others by means of such appropriation.

It has been objected that upon the abolition of private property all work will cease, and universal laziness will overtake us.

According to this, bourgeois society ought long ago to have gone to the dogs through sheer idleness; for those of its members who work, acquire nothing, and those who acquire anything, do not work. The whole of this objection is but another expression of the tautology: that there can no longer be any wage-labour when there is no longer any capital.

All objections urged against the Communistic mode of producing and appropriating material products, have, in the same way, been urged against the Communistic modes of producing and appropriating intellectual products. Just as, to the bourgeois, the disappearance of class property is the disappearance of production itself, so the disappearance of class culture is to him identical with the disappearance of all culture.

That culture, the loss of which he laments, is, for the enormous majority, a mere training to act as a machine.

But don't wrangle with us so long as you apply, to our intended abolition of bourgeois property, the standard of your bourgeois notions of freedom, culture, law, etc. Your very ideas are but the outgrowth of the conditions of your bourgeois production and bourgeois property, just as your jurisprudence is but the will of your class made into a law for all, a will, whose essential character and direction are determined by the economical conditions of existence of your class.

The selfish misconception that induces you to transform into eternal laws of nature and of reason, the social forms springing from your present mode of production and form of property—historical relations that rise and disappear in the progress of production—this misconception you share with every ruling class that has preceded you. What you see clearly in the case of ancient property, what you admit in the case of feudal property, you are of course forbidden to admit in the case of your own bourgeois form of property.

Abolition of the family! Even the most radical flare up at this infamous proposal of the Communists.

On what foundation is the present family, the bourgeois family, based? On capital, on private gain. In its completely developed form this family exists only among the bourgeoisie. But this state of things finds its complement in the practical absence of the family among the proletarians, and in public prostitution.

The bourgeois family will vanish as a matter of course when its complement vanishes, and both will vanish with the vanishing of capital.

Do you charge us with wanting to stop the exploitation of children by their parents? To this crime we plead guilty.

But, you will say, we destroy the most hallowed of relations, when we replace home education by social.

And your education! Is not that also social, and determined by the social conditions under which you educate, by the intervention, direct or indirect, of society, by means of schools, etc.? The Communists have not invented the intervention of society in education; they do but seek to alter the character of that intervention, and to rescue education from the influence of the ruling class.

The bourgeois clap-trap about the family and education, about the hallowed co-relation of parent and child, becomes all the more disgusting, the more, by the action of Modern Industry, all family ties among the proletarians are torn asunder, and their children transformed into simple articles of commerce and instruments of labour.

But you Communists would introduce community of women, screams the whole bourgeoisie in chorus.

The bourgeois sees in his wife a mere instrument of production. He hears that the instruments of production are to be exploited in common, and, naturally, can come to no other conclusion than that the lot of being common to all will likewise fall to the women.

He has not even a suspicion that the real point is to do away with the status of women as mere instruments of production.

For the rest, nothing is more ridiculous than the virtuous indignation of our bourgeois at the community of women which, they pretend, is to be openly and officially established by the Communists. The Communists have no need to introduce community of women; it has existed almost from time immemorial.

Our bourgeois, not content with having the wives and daughters of their proletarians at their disposal, not to speak of common prostitutes, take the greatest pleasure in seducing each other's wives.

Bourgeois marriage is in reality a system of wives in common and thus, at the most, what the Communists might possibly be reproached with, is that they desire to introduce, in substitution for a hypocritically concealed, an openly legalised community of women. For the rest, it is self-evident that the abolition of the present system of production must bring with it the abolition of the community of women springing from that system, i.e., of prostitution both public and private.

The Communists are further reproached with desiring to abolish countries and nationality.

The working men have no country. We cannot take from them what they have not got. Since the proletariat must first of all acquire political supremacy, must rise to be the leading class of the nation, must constitute itself the nation, it is, so far, itself national, though not in the bourgeois sense of the word.

National differences and antagonisms between peoples are daily more and more vanishing, owing to the development of the bourgeoisie, to freedom of commerce, to the world-market, to uniformity in the mode of production and in the conditions of life corresponding thereto.

The supremacy of the proletariat will cause them to vanish still faster. United action, of the leading civilised countries at least, is one of the first conditions for the emancipation of the proletariat.

In proportion as the exploitation of one individual by another is put an end to, the exploitation of one nation by another will also be put an end to. In proportion as the antagonism between classes within the nation vanishes, the hostility of one nation to another will come to an end.

The charges against Communism made from a religious, a philosophical, and, generally, from an ideological standpoint, are not deserving of serious examination.

Does it require deep intuition to comprehend that man's ideas, views and conceptions, in one word, man's consciousness, changes with every change in the conditions of his material existence, in his social relations and in his social life?

What else does the history of ideas prove, than that intellectual production changes its character in proportion as material production is changed? The ruling ideas of each age have ever been the ideas of its ruling class.

When people speak of ideas that revolutionise society, they do but express the fact, that within the old society, the elements of a new one have been created, and that the dissolution of the old ideas keeps even pace with the dissolution of the old conditions of existence.

When the ancient world was in its last throes, the ancient religions were overcome by Christianity. When Christian ideas succumbed in the 18th century to rationalist ideas, feudal society fought its death battle with the then revolutionary bourgeoisie. The ideas of religious liberty and freedom of conscience merely gave expression to the sway of free competition within the domain of knowledge.

"Undoubtedly," it will be said, "religious, moral, philosophical and juridical ideas have been modified in the course of historical development. But religion, morality philosophy, political science, and law, constantly survived this change."

"There are, besides, eternal truths, such as Freedom, Justice, etc. that are common to all states of society. But Communism abolishes eternal truths, it abolishes all religion, and all morality, instead of constituting them on a new basis; it therefore acts in contradiction to all past historical experience."

What does this accusation reduce itself to? The history of all past society has consisted in the development of class antagonisms, antagonisms that assumed different forms at different epochs.

But whatever form they may have taken, one fact is common to all past ages, viz., the exploitation of one part of society by the other. No wonder, then, that the social consciousness of past ages, despite all the multiplicity and variety it displays, moves within certain common forms, or general ideas, which cannot completely vanish except with the total disappearance of class antagonisms.

The Communist revolution is the most radical rupture with traditional property relations; no wonder that its development involves the most radical rupture with traditional ideas.

[...]

Workers of the World, Unite. You have nothing to lose but your chains!

DISCUSSION QUESTIONS

- What are some of the key traits of capitalism? Socialism?
- How do we move from one economic system to another?
- How do Marx and Engels's claims relate to gender?

Three Essays on the Theory of Sexuality

SELECTIONS

By SIGMUND FREUD

NEGLECT OF THE INFANTILE FACTOR

One feature of the popular view of the sexual instinct is that it is absent in childhood and only awakens in the period of life described as puberty. This, however, is not simple error but one that has had grave consequences, for it is mainly to this idea that we owe our present ignorance of the fundamental conditions of sexual life. A thorough study of the sexual manifestations of childhood would probably reveal the essential characters of the sexual instinct and would show us the course of its development and the way in which it is put together from various sources.

It is noticeable that writers who concern themselves with explaining the characteristics and reactions of the adult have devoted much more attention to the primaeval period which is comprised in the life of the individual's ancestors—have, that is, ascribed much more influence to heredity—than to the other primaeval period, which falls within the lifetime of the individual himself—that is, to childhood. One would surely have supposed that the influence of this latter period would be easier to understand and could claim to be considered before that of heredity.[1] It is true that in the literature of the subject one occasionally comes across remarks upon precocious sexual activity in small children—upon erections, masturbation and even activities resembling coitus. But these are always quoted only as exceptional events, as oddities or as horrifying instances of precocious depravity. So far as I know, not a single author has clearly recognized the regular existence of a sexual instinct in childhood; and in the writings that have become so numerous on the development of children, the chapter on 'Sexual Development' is as a rule omitted.[2]

Infantile Amnesia

The reason for this strange neglect is to be sought, I think, partly in considerations of propriety, which the authors obey as a result of their own upbringing, and partly in a psychological phenomenon which has itself hitherto eluded explanation. What I have in mind is the peculiar amnesia which, in the case of most people, though by no means all, hides the earliest beginnings of their childhood up to their sixth or eighth year. Hitherto it has not occurred to us to feel any astonishment at the fact of this amnesia, though we might have had good grounds for doing so. For we learn from other people that during these years, of which at a later date we retain nothing in our memory but a few unintelligible and fragmentary recollections, we reacted in a lively manner to impressions, that we were capable of expressing pain and joy in a human fashion, that we gave evidence of love, jealousy and other passionate feelings by which we were strongly moved at the time, and even that we gave utterance to remarks which were regarded by adults as good evidence of our possessing insight and the beginnings of a capacity for judgement. And of all this we, when we are grown up, have no knowledge of our own! Why should our memory lag so far behind the other activities of our minds? We have, on the contrary, good reason to believe that there is no period at which the capacity for receiving and reproducing impressions is greater than precisely during the years of childhood.[3]

On the other hand we must assume, or we can convince ourselves by a psychological examination of other people, that the very same impressions that we have forgotten have none the less left the deepest traces on our minds and have had a determining effect upon the whole of our later development. There can, therefore, be no question of any real abolition of the impressions of childhood, but rather of an amnesia similar to that which neurotics exhibit for later events, and of which the essence consists in a simple witholding of these impressions from consciousness, viz., in their repression. But what are the forces which bring about this repression of the impressions of childhood? Whoever could solve this riddle would, I think, have explained *hysterical* amnesia as well.

Meanwhile we must not fail to observe that the existence of infantile amnesia provides a new point of comparison between the mental states of children and psychoneurotics. We have already [p. 38] come across another such point in the formula to which we were led, to the effect that the sexuality of psychoneurotics has remained at, or been carried back to, an infantile stage. Can it be, after all, that infantile amnesia, too, is to be brought into relation with the sexual impulses of childhood?

Moreover, the connection between infantile and hysterical amnesia is more than a mere play upon words. Hysterical amnesia, which occurs at the bidding of repression, is only explicable by the fact that the subject is already in possession of a store of memory-traces which have been withdrawn from conscious disposal, and which are now, by an associative link, attracting to themselves the material which the forces of repression are engaged in repelling from consciousness.[4] It may be said that without infantile amnesia there would be no hysterical amnesia. [Sec Addenda, p. 112.]

I believe, then, that infantile amnesia, which turns everyone's childhood into something like a prehistoric epoch and conceals from him the beginnings of his own sexual life, is responsible for the fact that in general no importance is attached to childhood in the development of sexual life. The gaps in our knowledge which have arisen in this way cannot be bridged by a single observer. As long ago as in the year 1896[5] I insisted on the significance of the years of childhood in the origin of certain important phenomena connected with sexual life, and since then I have never ceased to emphasize the part played in sexuality by the infantile factor.

◆ ◆ ◆ ◆

Thumb-Sucking

For reasons which will appear later, I shall take thumb-sucking (or sensual sucking) as a sample of the sexual manifestations of childhood. (An excellent study of this subject has been made by the Hungarian paediatrician, Lindner, 1879.)[6]

Thumb-sucking appears already in early infancy and may continue into maturity, or even persist all through life. It consists in the rhythmic repetition of a sucking contact by the mouth (or lips). There is no question of the purpose of this procedure being the taking of nourishment. A portion of the lip itself, the tongue, or any other part of the skin within reach—even the big toe—may be taken as the object upon which this sucking is carried out. In this connection a grasping-instinct may appear and may manifest itself as a simultaneous rhythmic tugging at the lobes of the ears or a catching hold of some part of another person (as a rule the ear) for the same purpose. Sensual sucking involves a complete absorption of the attention and leads either to sleep or even to a motor reaction in the nature of an orgasm.[7] It is not infrequently combined with rubbing some sensitive part of the body such as the breast or the external genitalia. Many children proceed by this path from sucking to masturbation.

Lindner himself[8] clearly recognized the sexual nature of this activity and emphasized it without qualification. In the nursery, sucking is often classed along with the other kinds of sexual 'naughtiness' of children. This view has been most energetically repudiated by numbers of paediatricians and nerve-specialists, though this is no doubt partly due to a confusion between 'sexual' and 'genital'. Their objection raises a difficult question and one which cannot be evaded: what is the general characteristic which enables us to recognize the sexual manifestations of children? The concatenation of phenomena into which we have been given an insight by psycho-analytic investigation justifies us, in my opinion, in regarding thumb-sucking as a sexual manifestation and in choosing it for our study of the essential features of infantile sexual activity.[9]

Auto-Erotism

We are in duty bound to make a thorough examination of this example. It must be insisted that the most striking feature of this sexual activity is that the instinct is not directed towards other people, but obtains satisfaction from the subject's own body. It is 'auto-erotic', to call it by a happily chosen term introduced by Havelock Ellis (1910).[10]

Furthermore, it is clear that the behaviour of a child who indulges in thumb-sucking is determined by a search for some pleasure which has already been experienced and is now remembered. In the simplest case he proceeds to find this satisfaction by sucking rhythmically at some part of the skin or mucous membrane. It is also easy to guess the occasions on which the child had his first experiences of the pleasure which he is now striving to renew. It was the child's first and most vital activity, his sucking at his mother's breast, or at substitutes for it, that must have familiarized him with this pleasure. The child's lips, in our view, behave like an erotogenic zone, and no doubt stimulation by the warm flow of milk is the cause of the pleasurable sensation. The satisfaction of the erotogenic zone is associated, in the first instance, with the satisfaction of the need for nourishment. To begin with, sexual activity attaches itself to functions serving the purpose of self-preservation and does not become independent of them until later.[11] No one who has seen a baby sinking back satiated from the breast and falling asleep with flushed cheeks and a blissful smile can escape the reflection that this picture persists as a prototype of the expression of sexual satisfaction in later life. The need for repeating the sexual satisfaction now becomes detached from the need for taking nourishment—a separation which becomes inevitable when the teeth appear and food is no longer taken in only by sucking, but is also chewed up. The child does not make use of an extraneous body for his sucking, but prefers a part of his own skin because it is more convenient, because it makes him independent of the external world, which he is not yet able to control, and because in that way he provides himself, as it were, with a second erotogenic zone, though one of an inferior kind. The inferiority of this second region is among the reasons why at a later date he seeks the corresponding part—the lips—of another person. ('It's a pity I can't kiss myself', he seems to be saying.)

It is not every child who sucks in this way. It may be assumed that those children do so in whom there is a constitutional intensification of the erotogenic significance of the labial region. If that significance persists, these same children when they are grown up will become epicures in kissing, will be inclined to perverse kissing, or, if males, will have a powerful motive for drinking and smoking. If, however, repression ensues, they will feel disgust at food and will produce hysterical vomiting. The repression extends to the nutritional instinct owing to the dual purpose served by the labial zone. Many[13] of my women patients who suffer from disturbances of eating, *globus hystericus,* constriction of the throat and vomiting, have indulged energetically in sucking during their childhood.

Our study of thumb-sucking or sensual sucking has already given us the three essential characterisitics of an infantile sexual manifestation. At its origin it attaches itself to one of the vital somatic functions;[14] it has as yet no sexual object, and is thus auto-erotic; and its sexual aim is dominated by an erotogenic zone. It is to be anticipated that these characteristics will be found to apply equally to most of the other activities of the infantile sexual instincts.

♦ ♦ ♦ ♦

The Instinct For Knowledge

At about the same time as the sexual life of children reaches its first peak, between the ages of three and five, they also begin to show signs of the activity which may be ascribed to the instinct for knowledge or research. This instinct cannot be counted among the elementary instinctual components, nor can it be classed as exclusively belonging to sexuality. Its activity corresponds on the one hand to a sublimated manner of obtaining mastery, while on the other hand it makes use of the energy of scopophilia. Its relations to sexual life, however, are of particular importance, since we have learnt from psycho-analysis that the instinct for knowledge in children is attracted unexpectedly early and intensively to sexual problems and is in fact possibly first aroused by them.

The Riddle Of The Sphinx

It is not by theoretical interests but by practical ones that activities of research are set going in children. The threat to the bases of a child's existence offered by the discovery or the suspicion of the arrival of a new baby and the fear that he may, as a result of it, cease to be cared for and loved, make him thoughtful and clear-sighted. And this history of the instinct's origin is in line with the fact that the first problem with which it deals is not the question of the distinction between the sexes but the riddle of where babies come from.[15] (This, in a distorted form which can easily be rectified, is the same riddle that was propounded by the Theban Sphinx.) On the contrary, the existence of two sexes does not to begin with arouse any difficulties or doubts in children. It is self-evident to a male child that a genital like his own is to be attributed to everyone he knows, and he cannot make its absence tally with his picture of these other people.

Castration Complex and Penis Envy

This conviction is energetically maintained by boys, is obstinately defended against the contradictions which soon result from observation, and is only abandoned after severe internal struggles (the castration complex). The substitutes for this penis which they feel is missing in women play a great part in determining the form taken by many perversions.[16]

The assumption that all human beings have the same (male) form of genital is the first of the many remarkable and momentous sexual theories of children. It is of little use to a child that the science of biology justifies his prejudice and has been obliged to recognize the female clitoris as a true substitute for the penis.

Little girls do not resort to denial of this kind when they see that boys' genitals are formed differently from their own. They are ready to recognize them immediately and are overcome by envy for the penis—an envy culminating in the wish, which is so important in its consequences, to be boys themselves.

Theories of Birth

Many people can remember clearly what an intense interest they took during the prepubertal period in the question of where babies come from. The anatomical answers to the question were at the time very various: babies come out of the breast, or are cut out of the body, or the navel opens to let them through.[17] Outside analysis, there are very seldom memories of any similar researches having been carried out in the *early* years of childhood. These earlier researches fell a victim to repression long since, but all their findings were of a uniform nature: people get babies by eating some particular thing (as they do in fairy tales) and babies are born through the bowel like a discharge of faeces. These infantile theories remind us of conditions that exist in the animal kingdom—and especially of the cloaca in types of animals lower than mammals.

Sadistic View of Sexual Intercourse

If children at this early age witness sexual intercourse between adults—for which an opportunity is provided by the conviction of grown-up people that small children cannot understand anything sexual—they inevitably regard the sexual act as a sort of ill-treatment or act of subjugation: they view it, that is, in a sadistic sense. Psycho-analysis also shows us that an impression of this kind in early childhood contributes a great deal towards a pre-disposition to a subsequent sadistic displacement of the sexual aim. Furthermore, children are much concerned with the problem of what sexual intercourse—or, as they put it, being married—consists in: and they usually seek a solution of the mystery in some common activity concerned with the function of micturition or defaecation.

♦ ♦ ♦ ♦

THE LIBIDO THEORY[18]

The conceptual scaffolding which we have set up to help us in dealing with the psychical manifestations of sexual life tallies well with these hypotheses as to the chemical basis of sexual excitation. We have defined the concept of libido as a quantitatively variable force which could serve as a measure of processes and transformations occurring in the field of sexual excitation. We distinguish this libido in respect of its special origin from the energy which must be supposed to underlie mental processes in general, and we thus also attribute a *qualitative* character to it. In thus distinguishing between libidinal and other forms of psychical energy we are giving expression to the presumption that the sexual processes occurring in the organism are distinguished from the nutritive processes by a special chemistry. The analysis of the perversions and psychoneuroses has shown us that this sexual excitation is derived not from the so-called sexual parts alone, but from all the bodily organs. We thus reach the idea of a quantity of libido, to the mental representation of which we give the name of 'ego-libido', and whose production, increase or diminution, distribution and displacement should afford us possibilities for explaining the psychosexual phenomena observed.

This ego-libido is, however, only conveniently accessible to analytic study when it has been put to the use of cathecting sexual objects, that is, when it has become object-libido. We can then perceive it concentrating upon objects,[19] becoming fixed upon them or abandoning them, moving from one object to another and, from these situations, directing the subject's sexual activity, which leads to the satisfaction, that is, to the partial and temporary extinction, of the libido. The psycho-analysis of what are termed transference neuroses (hysteria and obsessional neurosis) affords us a clear insight at this point.

We can follow the object-libido through still further vicissitudes. When it is withdrawn from objects, it is held in suspense in peculiar conditions of tension and is finally drawn back into the ego, so that it becomes ego-libido once again. In contrast to object-libido, we also describe ego-libido as 'narcissistic' libido. From the vantage-point of psycho-analysis we can look across a frontier, which we may not pass, at the activities of narcissistic libido, and may form some idea of the relation between it and object-libido.[20] Narcissistic or ego-libido seems to be the great reservoir from which the object-cathexes are sent out and into which they are withdrawn once more; the narcissistic libidinal cathexis of the ego is the original state of things, realized in earliest childhood, and is merely covered by the later extrusions of libido, but in essentials persists behind them.

It should be the task of a libido theory of neurotic and psychotic disorders to express all the observed phenomena and inferred processes in terms of the economics of the libido. It is easy to guess that the vicissitudes of the ego-libido will have the major part to play in this connection, especially when it is a question of explaining the deeper psychotic disturbances. We are then faced by the difficulty that our method of research, psycho-analysis, for the moment affords us assured information only on the transformations that take place in the object-libido,[21] but is unable to make any immediate distinction between the ego-libido and the other forms of energy operating in the ego.[22]

For the present, therefore,[23] no further development of the libido theory is possible, except upon speculative lines. It would, however, be sacrificing all that we have gained hitherto from psycho-analytic observation, if we were to follow the example of G. G. Jung and water down the meaning of the concept of libido itself by equating it with psychical instinctual force in general. The distinguishing of the sexual instinctual impulses from the rest and the consequent restriction of the concept of libido to the former receives strong support from the assumption which I have already discussed that there is a special chemistry of' the sexual function.

THE DIFFERENTIATION BETWEEN MEN AND WOMEN

As we all know, it is not until puberty that the sharp distinction is established between the masculine and feminine characters. From that time on, this contrast has a more decisive influence than any other upon the shaping of human life. It is true that the masculine and feminine dispositions are already easily recognizable in childhood. The development of the inhibitions of sexuality (shame, disgust, pity, etc.) takes place in little girls earlier and in the face of less resistance than in boys; the tendency to sexual repression seems in general to be greater; and, where the component instincts of sexuality appear, they prefer the passive form. The auto-erotic activity of the erotogenic zones is, however, the same in both sexes, and owing to this uniformity there is no possibility of a distinction between the two sexes such as arises after puberty. So far as the autoerotic and masturbatory manifestations of sexuality are concerned, we might lay it down that the sexuality of little girls is of a wholly masculine character. Indeed, if we were able to give a more definite connotation to the concepts of 'masculine' and 'feminine', it would even be possible to maintain that libido is invariably and necessarily of a masculine nature, whether it occurs in men or in women and irrespectively of whether its object is a man or a woman.[24]

Since I have become acquainted[25] with the notion of bisexuality I have regarded it as the decisive factor, and without taking bisexuality into account I think it would scarcely be possible to arrive at an understanding of the sexual manifestations that are actually to be observed in men and women.

◆ ◆ ◆ ◆

NOTES

1. [*Footnote added* 1915:] Nor is it possible to estimate correctly the part played by heredity until the part played by childhood has been assessed.

2. The assertion made in the text has since struck me myself as being so bold that I have undertaken the task of testing its validity by looking through the literature once more. The outcome of this is that I have allowed my statement to stand unaltered. The scientific examination of both the physical and mental phenomena of sexuality in childhood is still in its earliest beginnings. One writer, Bell (1902, 327), remarks: 'I know of no scientist who has given a careful analysis of the emotion as it is seen in the adolescent.' Somatic sexual manifestations from the period before puberty have only attracted attention in connection with phenomena of degeneracy and as indications of degeneracy. In none of the accounts which I have read of the psychology of this period of life is a chapter to be found on the erotic life of children; and this applies to the well-known works of Preyer [1882], Baldwin (1898), Pérez (1886), Strümpell (1899), Groos (1904), Heller (1904), Sully (1895) and others. We can obtain the clearest impression of the state of things in this field to-day from the periodical *Die Kinderfehler* from 1896 onwards. Nevertheless the conviction is borne in upon us that the existence of love in childhood stands in no need of discovery. Pérez (1886, 272 ff.) argues in favour of its existence. Groos (1899, 326) mentions as a generally recognized fact that 'some children are already accessible to sexual impulses at a very early age and feel an urge to have contact with the opposite sex'. The earliest instance of the appearance of 'sex-love' recorded by Bell (1902, 330) concerns a child in the middle of his third year. On this point compare further Havelock Ellis (1913, Appendix B).
   [*Added* 1910:] This judgement upon the literature of infantile sexuality need no longer be maintained since the appearance of Stanley Hall's exhaustive work (1904). No such modification is necessitated by Moll's recent book (1909). See, on the other hand, Bleuler (1908). [*Added* 1915:] Since this was written, a book by Hug-Hellmuth (1913) has taken the neglected sexual factor fully into account.

3. I have attempted to solve one of the problems connected with the earliest memories of childhood in a paper on 'Screen Memories' (1899a). [*Added* 1924:] See also Chapter IV of my *Psychopathology of Everyday Life* (1901 b).

4. [*Footnote added* 1915:] The mechanism of repression cannot be understood unless account is taken of *both* of these two concurrent processes. They may be compared with the manner in

which tourists are conducted to the top of the Great Pyramid of Giza by being pushed from one direction and pulled from the other. [Cf. Freud's paper on 'Repression' (1915*d*).]

5. [E.g. in the last paragraph of Section I of his paper on the aetiology of hysteria (1896*c*).]

6. We are able to make use of the second of these two sources of material since we are justified in expecting that the early years of children who are later to become neurotic are not likely in this respect to differ *essentially* from those of children who are to grow up into normal adults, [*added* 1915:] but only in the intensity and clarity of the phenomena involved.

7. [There seems to be no nursery word in English equivalent to the German '*lutschen*' and *iludelh*', used by Freud alongside '*wonnesaugen*' ('sensual sucking'). Conrad in *Struwwelpeter* was a '*Lutscher*'; but, as will be seen from the context, 'suck-a-thumbs' and 'thumb-sucking' have in fact too narrow a connotation for the present purpose.]

8. Thus we find at this early stage, what holds good all through life, that sexual satisfaction is the best soporific. Most cases of nervous insomnia can be traced back to lack of sexual satisfaction. It is well known that unscrupulous nurses put crying children to sleep by stroking their genitals. [Cf. Freud, 1905*e*, Section III, *S.E.*, 7, 98, *n*. 1.]

9. [This paragraph was added in 1915. In its place the following paragraph appears in the editions of 1905 and 1910 only: 'No observer has felt any doubt as to the sexual nature of this activity. Nevertheless, the best theories formed by adults in regard to this example of the sexual behaviour of children leave us in the lurch. Consider Moll's [1898] analysis of the sexual instinct into an instinct of detumescence and an instinct of contrectation. [See above p. 35, *n*. 2.] The first of these factors cannot be concerned in our present instance, and the second one can only be recognized with difficulty, since, according to Moll, it emerges later than the instinct of detumescence and is directed towards other people.'—In 1910 the following footnote was attached to the first sentence of this cancelled paragraph: 'With the exception of Moll (1909).']

10. [*Footnote added* 1920:] In 1919, a Dr. Galant published, under the title of 'Das Lutscherli', the confession of a grown-up girl who had never given up this infantile sexual activity and who represents the satisfaction to be gained from sucking as something completely analogous to sexual satisfaction, particularly when this is obtained from a lover's kiss: 'Not every kiss is equal to a "*Lutscherli*"—no, no, not by any means! It is impossible to describe what a lovely feeling goes through your whole body when you suck; you are right away from this world. You are absolutely satisfied, and happy beyond desire. It is a wonderful feeling; you long for nothing but peace—uninterrupted peace. It is just unspeakably lovely: you feel no pain and no sorrow, and ah! you are carried into another world.'

11. [*Footnote added* 1920:] Havelock Ellis, it is true, uses the word 'auto-erotic' in a somewhat different sense, to describe an excitation which is not provoked from outside but arises internally. What psycho-analysis regards as the essential point is not the genesis of the excitation, but the question of its relation to an object.—[In all editions before 1920 this footnote read as follows: 'Havelock Ellis, however, has spoilt the meaning of the term he invented by including the whole of hysteria and all the manifestations of masturbation among the phenomena of auto-erotism.']

12. [This sentence was added in 1915. Cf. Section II of Freud's paper on narcissism (1914c).]

13. [In the first edition only this reads 'all'.]

14. [This clause was added in 1915; and in the earlier editions the word 'three' in the last sentence is replaced by 'two'.]

15. [In a later work, Freud (1925:) corrected this statement, saying that it is not true of girls, and not always true of boys.]

16. [*Footnote added* 1920:] We are justified in speaking of a castration complex in women as well. Both male and female children form a theory that women no less than men originally had a penis, but that they have lost it by castration. The conviction which is finally reached by males that women have no penis often leads them to an enduringly low opinion of the other sex.

17. [*Footnote added* 1924:] In these later years of childhood there is a great wealth of sexual theories, of which only a few examples are given in the text.

18. [This whole section, except for its last paragraph, dates from 1915. It is largely based on Freud's paper on narcissism (1914c).]

19. [It is scarcely necessary to explain that here as elsewhere, in speaking of the libido concentrating on 'objects', withdrawing from 'objects', etc., Freud has in mind the mental presentations (*Vorstellungen*) of objects and not, of course, objects in the external world.]

20. [*Footnote added* 1924:] Since neuroses other than the transference neuroses have become to a greater extent accessible to psycho-analysis, this limitation has lost its earlier validity.

21. [*Footnote added* 1924:] See the previous footnote.

22. [*Footnote added* 1915:] Cf. my paper on narcissism (1914c). [*Added* 1920:] The term 'narcissism' was not introduced, as I erroneously stated in that paper, by Nacke, but by Havclock Ellis. [Ellis himself subsequently (1928) discussed this point in detail and considered that the honours should be divided.]

23. [This paragraph was added in 1920.]

24. It is essential to understand clearly that the concepts of 'masculine' and 'feminine', whose meaning seems so unambiguous to ordinary people, are among the most confused that occur in science. It is possible to distinguish at least three uses. 'Masculine' and 'feminine' are used sometimes in the sense of activity and passivity, sometimes in a biological, and sometimes, again, in a sociological sense. The first of these three meanings is the essential one and the most serviceable in psycho-analysis. When, for instance, libido was described in the text above as being 'masculine', the word was being used in this sense, for an instinct is always active even when it has a passive aim in view. The second, or biological, meaning of 'masculine' and 'feminine' is the one whose applicability can be determined most easily. Here 'masculine' and 'feminine' are characterized by the presence of spermatozoa or ova respectively and by the functions proceeding from them. Activity and its concomitant phenomena (more powerful muscular development, aggressiveness, greater intensity of libido) are as a rule linked with biological masculinity; but they are not necessarily so, for there are animal species in which these qualities are on the contrary assigned to the female. The third, or sociological, meaning receives its connotation from the observation of actually existing masculine and feminine

individuals. Such observation shows that in human beings pure masculinity or femininity is not to be found either in a psychological or a biological sense. Every individual on the contrary displays a mixture of the charactcr-traits belonging to his own and to the opposite sex; and he shows a combination of activity and passivity whether or not these last character-traits tally with his biological ones. [A later discussion of this point will be found in a footnote at the end of Chapter IV *of Civilization and its Discontents* (1930*a*).]

25. [In 1905 only: 'through Wilhelm Fliess'. Cf. end of footnote, p. 9.]

DISCUSSION QUESTIONS

- Can you describe the Oedipus complex? How is gender identity established within it?
- How do Freud's claims relate to fights against gender inequity?

SECTION 2

(STEREO-)TYPES AND TROPES

From Reverence to Rape

The Treatment of Women in the Movies

SELECTIONS

By MOLLY HASKELL

When the time came to transfer my allegiance to romantic heroines, I chose Audrey Hepburn and Grace Kelly whose aristocratic cool seemed an extension of the tomboy freedom of Margaret O'Brien, and who were above the sexual profligacy and vulnerability of Marilyn Monroe, Elizabeth Taylor, and Jennifer Jones. The whore-virgin dichotomy took hold with a vengeance in the uptight fifties, in the dialectical caricatures of the "sexpot" and the "nice girl." On the one hand, the tarts and tootsies played by Monroe, Taylor, Russell—even the demonesses played by Ava Gardner—were incapable of an intelligent thought or a lapse of sexual appetite; on the other, the gamines, golightlys, and virgins played by Hepburn, Kelly, Doris Day, and Debbie Reynolds were equally incapable of a base instinct or the hint of sexual appetite. And the split was internalized in the moral code we adopted out of fear as well as out of an instinct for self-preservation The taboos against sex, encoded in the paralyzing edict that no man would marry a woman who was not a virgin (with the unexpressed corollary that untasted sex was a woman's prime attraction for a man) held fearful sway in the southern community where I grew up It was a morality handed down by our parents, but eagerly embraced by my peer group American morals, which had increasingly rigidified

Molly Haskell, *Reverence to Rape: The Treatment of Women in the Movies*, pp. vii-viii, 277-278, 49-50, 119-120, 102-106, 254-256. Copyright © 1987 by Molly Haskell. Reprinted with permission.

after the Jazz Age and the Depression—a tendency that was reflected in Hollywood films and reinforced by the Production Code—could retrench no farther. With smiles frozen on our faces, we had turned into blocks of ice. We were as terrified of being labeled "fast" as girls today are of being labeled "square" by *not* making love or taking grass. What the peer-group pressures of both decades—fifties' repression and sixties' license—have in common is an undue emphasis on sex; sex becomes not simply an appetite or a matter of individual taste, but the supreme, defining quality of the self. She "puts out" or she doesn't. She balls or she doesn't. Will she or won't she becomes the unspoken question when boys discuss girls, will you or won't you the underlying question of heterosexual dialogue. So my generation fell into the trap, internalizing the either/or as we thought of ourselves as "hot" or "cold" and falling victim, once again, to the terms by which our sex had been conveniently divided for so many years.

To the degree that sex was the equivalent of the self, surrender to sex was to lose oneself, whereas abstinence would insure its safeguarding, if not its salvation. Our instincts were substantiated by the movies. The "virgin" was a primal, positive figure, honored and exalted beyond any merits she possessed as a woman (and eventually made to pay for her "superiority" in the professional virgins and teases of the fifties), while the "whore," Americanized into the good-bad girl, was publicly castigated and cautioned against—and privately sought by men.

◆ ◆ ◆ ◆

THE EUROPEANS

Because woman did not fight back, man quickly took the advantage and made her the scapegoat for all his vices and fears.

He was abashed that his penis moved, unbidden, when he looked at Eve, and so he invented penis envy.

He was terrified by the prospect of his own demise, and so he invented God and His Son to resurrect and redeem him.

He was resentful that another man had preceded him and made love to his mother, so he invented the Virgin Birth and vasectomized his father.

He was intimidated by woman's sexual desire, and so he invented the mutually exclusive virgin and the whore.

He was worried lest woman, resenting his freedom, should want to live and work as he did, and so he invented and ordained the mother in honored vassalage to him.

He was ashamed of growing old and ugly, and even more ashamed of being ashamed, and so he invented female vanity to exorcise and account for these fears.

Woman's image of herself is so entwined in the tangle of myths and inventions made by man that it is hard to look at it straight. It is even harder in Europe, where centuries of tradition and all the forces of culture have reinforced these myths. In Europe, a woman is chained to her throne. Sensitive artists, sons, and lovers come to worship at her feet. If she breaks free, their pilgrimage fails; if her light goes out, so does theirs. In America, men and women are not so closely and inextricably, emotionally and ideologically, bound. A woman can more easily invent herself—not easily, but more easily. And she is proportionately less venerated.

◆ ◆ ◆ ◆

From the twenties' frizzy-haired flapper to the seventies' long-haired model, we are never quite as unique as we think we are. If the stars of the twenties look, to our unfamiliar eyes, like an old group photograph in which the distinguishing traits have disappeared and only the physical similarities remain, we too—and the stars who represent us—may look astonishingly alike to our grandchildren. It is one of the properties of perspective that from a distance of time or space everyone, like the Chinese, looks alike.

If the women stars of the twenties were more defined by type than the men—as women always are—they were also more colorful and more central to the myths of the period. The action heroes and the male comedians had a world to themselves, but most of the films of the twenties (a larger proportion than in other decades) were romances and melodramas dominated by a single star, billed above the title, and the women stars outnumbered their male counterparts. Different types coexisted. These were genuinely wild, experimental days in Hollywood, before sound, before the Crash, and before the social crusaders came in, in the form of the Legion of Decency in the early thirties, to legislate morals and arbitrate between good and evil in films. Stars were demoted by box-office failure rather than by social pressure. The falling star of Theda Bara, who reached the peak of her vampire's powers (and largely publicity-induced popularity) in 1915, met Mary Pickford's star going the other way the same year that Griffith's *Birth of a Nation* introduced Lillian Gish. Gish, in turn, would be succeeded by a long line of replica mirror-image virgins.

At this juncture of the Victorian moral world and the allegorical tendency of silent film, the virgin emerges in her purest form, fair-haired, delicate, and above all, tiny, in the time-honored tradition of the "weaker sex." (The symbolic importance of size suggests that women's increased height over the years has influenced their changing self-image.) But it is a true innocence—as if she, like the industry, like the country, had not yet been deflowered—an innocence that belongs not just to her, but to the way she is seen, to the eye of her beholder. For, in the nineteenth-century imagination of such directors as Griffith and Borzage, the vision of woman idealized and debased, above and below, was, as George Eliot suggested in *The Mill on the Floss*, metaphysically the same By the romantic code, woman's chastity was a correlative of male honor, her Fall, of his concupiscence and guilt The notion of the virgin ideal unfortunately out-lived the romantic code which gave it plausibility In film, subsequent virgins, like the medium itself, would be tainted by self-consciousness at best, at worst, depicted in venom, the underside of a chivalry gone sour and of sexual uncertainty in a world of fluctuating values.

But throughout the twenties, the virgin-heroine was still rooted in the romantic spirit of mutual reverence. As late as 1927 and 1928, in Janet Gaynor's sublimely sentimental heroines of *Seventh Heaven* and *Street Angel,* she is alive and well, her chastity imperiled but her purity intact.

Such glistening icons of femininity as Gaynor and Gish were often steely underneath but they belonged to the "women-rule-the-world-but-don't-tell-anybody" school and they made a point of concealing their strength. (We can be sure that when Gish directed her own film she gave orders—or made requests—like a lady, never raising her voice above a genteel chirp.)

◆ ◆ ◆ ◆

Dietrich goes West and becomes virginized, or revirginized. Or she will, paradoxically, once she bears a child, for then, obliterating herself as "woman" or even "wife" (in the curious one-dimensional process of mythic regeneration), she will become "mother" and as such will qualify for the mantle of purity—chaste, an "ex-virgin" (with the emphasis on virgin rather than on "ex") from which all trace of the sin of copulation with the father has been erased by the son, as he recasts his mother in the image of the Virgin Mary. Mother's purity, the most sacred and crucial image of our culture, is entirely a wish fulfillment invented by man, an Oedipal attempt by the son to banish the hated image of sex with the father. In so doing he deprives the woman who is his mother of part of her nature, and all of her past. It is the son, far more than the daughter, who forces the exclusive mother role on the woman who has conceived him. And it is man as son, rather than man as husband or lover, who is most responsible for keeping mother locked in her chastity belt and most responsible for keeping her imprisoned in her biological role. As for woman herself, it is not in catering to men's needs as his secretary, mistress, wife that she is most subservient; it is in fulfilling her Oedipal role as son-worshipper that she most dangerously denies herself, her daughter, and her sex and perpetuates the notion of their inferiority.

The fusion of wife and mother into a character whose chief attributes, even with regard to her husband, are maternal is a reduction through sanctification, a delimiting of the woman's role by placing her on a pedestal. But this process does not always end in apotheosis. While the values the "mother" represents as a domestic, civilizing force are honored by some males and certain (European or Europeanized) societies, they are feared, and fought bitterly, by others, by the adolescent male, for example, and by large segments of American culture, for whom woman, the antimale, becomes the pushy and constricting voice of responsibility.

◆ ◆ ◆ ◆

Although for convenience' sake we think of American and European attitudes toward women as dialectically opposed, the range of feelings expressed by directors would be more accurately reflected in a spectrum (Lubitsch would be in the middle), itself composed of smaller spectrums. Taken in isolation and in extremis, the traditional European conception of women is no healthier or broader than our own and in many ways it is more binding. For if American directors at their most American (Hawks and Walsh) see women, on their individual spectrum, as analogous to men—enterprising, strong, smart, courageous, unmotherly—the Europeans see women as men's complements—Nature's handmaidens, exponents of the "eternal feminine," immanent rather than transcendent; to use another of Simone de Beauvoir's terms, the "other."

The "vamp" was an early example of an Americanization of the "enemy," a European archetype (the "other" as *femme fatale),* literalized and exaggerated into a freak by the puritanical impulse. Even the gravitation to sharply delineated iconography in the early silents can hardly account for the outrageously broad malevolence of such comical carnivores as Theda Bara and Nita Naldi. They are meant to represent demonic natural forces that, like a cyclone, threaten to uproot man from himself, but they are more like storm warnings than the storm itself. Sagging under the excess weight of makeup and jewels—the emblems of their wickedness—they are not likely to seduce anyone unawares, but, with *Caveat Emptor* written on their brow, are self-contained cautionary fables, like a De Mille orgy sequence. But as a crude prototype, Bara presented in the most stylized form certain traits that were modified in her more "normal" successors, the sex goddesses: the hypnotic glare of the bird of prey, eyes smoldering under half-closed lids, like shades partly lowered in a whorehouse. In one "fell swoop" of these lids she reveals the association of images, elaborated by de Beauvoir, by which woman became, for man, the personification of nature as the "other," whether in the benevolent guise of the nutrient-mother or her destructive, inverted counterpart, malefic natural force. In either case, woman, progenitor and life-giver or angel of death, is man's mysterious opposite and potential enemy, a force he must circumvent, dominate, or propitiate with his lifework. This is the (biological) view of woman, always framed from a male viewpoint, that Simone de Beauvoir takes as the starting point and principal opposition of *The Second Sex.* It is fundamentally a classical, European view, characterizing the work of directors as diverse as Bergman, Godard, Pabst, and Fellini, although, to the degree that they are related, by background or religion, to Europe, it has permeated the consciousness of American artists.

In European art and mythology, woman's alliance with nature, hence her "earthiness," is an absolute; her contingent form is dependent upon the artist or mythmaker, that is, whether she is enjoyed as the "whore," feared as the *femme fatale,* or revered as the "muse" or "earth mother." To the American male, whose popular mythology is constructed to forestall an acceptance of death, the very association of women and the life-death cycle is one of terror. With the term "sex goddess" he takes worship of the "mother"/"Madonna" one step farther by redeeming not just woman, but sex itself. Sex, like dirt, disease, and death, is anathema to a country that treasures cleanliness above godliness and innocence above experience. To the number one producer of antiseptics it becomes a matter of both religious and professional honor to sanitize what it cannot dispense with. The terms "vamp" and "sex goddess," like the names of hurricanes or classical deities, are magical words, incantations invented by men to explain the inexplicable and, as in the custom of naming hurricanes after women, to locate the source of destruction within the "mysterious" sex. The Greeks and Romans, notorious chauvinists in real life, at least gave their goddesses such prestigious offices as "wisdom" and "the hunt" (it was, as Freud has pointed out, the tendency of monotheism, as a patriarchal, revolutionary religion, to drive out polytheistic matriarchy); but the Americans, in sanctifying sex, confine woman to a sexual role while simultaneously raising her above nature, above mortal life. While the European male artist or experiencer of life may want to bury himself in woman in order to brush shoulders with death and conquer his own fear, the American wishes to remove woman from the cycle of nature and its reminder of mortality, wishes to keep her young forever.

In this bizarre canonization, the "sex goddess" redeems sex from itself, from both the awkward, fumbling initiatory rites and the odor of death that the French glory in, and turns it into something separate, self-contained, ideal. Not always divine, however, for the title "sex goddess" has been held by many different kinds of women and some have won it for attributes less spiritual than Garbo's face. Amazonian might be a better word to describe the degree to which these stars, by virtue of some specialty or other (Hayworth's lips, Grable's legs, Jane Russell's and Marilyn Monroe's breasts) become overpowering. The inflated value of one feature over the others is an index to the collective male libido at any given time (Dietrich's extraordinary legs were nevertheless but one part of a total picture of her, while Grable's were a substitute for a deficient whole. The mammary fixation is the most infantile—and most American—of the sex fetishes, and indeed the fifties, in which bosom power was supreme, was the least adult decade in movie, and national, history.)

Neither did the sex goddesses serve identical functions, nor were they the straight-faced, monolithic symbols of fan hagiography More often than not, they were consciously playing a role, or "playing up" to a role. Like department store Santa Clauses, they wore a familiar costume, paraded themselves, played a game with the kids, catered to their fantasies, but not always with a straight face. The humor in Pola Negri's vamping, the mincing speech and wide-eyed wonder of Marilyn Monroe, have an element of self-parody. Like the nigger antics of Stepin Fetchit, like the schizophrenic's self-protective mask, they form a subtle, skin-fitting camouflage by which not the slave but the master, not the patient but the doctor, is slyly ridiculed. But it is a strategy that is played out on a tightrope: the tightrope of the "weaker" sex and the disempowered psyche. However much the schizophrenic may elude institutional manipulation, he is hardly in control of his mind. And the sex goddess treads a thin line of self-possession. If she becomes too masculine, she is dismissed as a woman; if she carries her parody too far, she mimics her own sex and falls into the hands of her "camp" followers who play up to the impersonation until it usurps the person underneath.[1]

At its best, the sex goddess's alienation is Brechtian, preserving a dramatic unity while suggesting a certain consciousness of effect: Beyond the pantomime of the regal presence—the seduction, the surrender, the posture of helplessness—we occasionally hear the actress chuckle, or see her peeking out from behind her lines. To attribute high seriousness to these performances is like seeing a silent movie projected at sound speed and mistaking the accelerated motion for the way people actually ran. In *The Princess Comes Across*, Carole Lombard played the entire film as a heavily accented Garbo-like impostor of a princess. And Garbo herself was not without traces of self-mockery. The raised eyebrow indicated infinite knowledge of the world including a playful regard for her own image. But unlike Dietrich, whose irony was a permanent fixture and a defense against disappointment, Garbo subordinated hers to the final certainty that love is more serious and more important, which meant that she herself, as love's embodiment, was beyond disappointment.

♦ ♦ ♦ ♦

Our feelings about Marilyn Monroe have been so colored by her death and not simply, as the uncharitable would have us think, because she is no longer an irritation or a threat, but because her suicide, as suicides do, casts a retrospective light on her life. Her "ending" gives her a beginning and middle, turns her into a work of art with a message and a meaning.

Women, particularly, have become contrite over their previous hostility to Monroe, canonizing her as a martyr to male chauvinism, which in most ways she was. But at the time, women couldn't identify with her and didn't support her. They allowed her to be turned into a figure of ridicule, as they allowed Ingrid Bergman to be crucified by the press. They blamed these stars for acting disadvantageously, whereas they sympathized with Rita Hayworth and Elizabeth Taylor for moving (in the words applied to *That Hamilton Woman*) "lower and lower but always up and up." At the same time, in their defense, women hated Marilyn for catering so shamelessly to a false, regressive, childish, and detached idea of sexuality.

What was she, this breathless, blonde, supplicating symbol of sexuality, the lips anxiously offering themselves as the surrogate orifice, the whisper unconsciouly expressing trepidation? And who made her what she was? She was partly a hypothesis, a pinup fantasy of the other woman as she might be drawn in the marital cartoon fantasies of Maggie and Jiggs, or Blondie

---

[1] The camp reincarnations of forties' and fifties' glamour goddesses by the transvestite stars (Candy Darling, Jackie Curtis, and Holly Woodlawn) of the Warhol-Morissey studio are merely the latest and most extreme example of the appropriation of sex goddesses by their gay devotees. Irony and stylization create the margin for transsexual innuendoes Dietrich was certified by some of her followers to be a female impersonator, by others to have undergone an operation. And gays insist the tag line, "There never was a woman like Gilda," should be taken at face, rather than figurative, value.

and Dagwood, and thus an outgrowth, once again, of misogamy. She was the woman that every wife fears seeing with her husband in a convertible (Hawks' *Monkey Business*) or even in conversation, and that every emasculated or superfluous husband would like to think his wife lives in constant fear of. She was the masturbatory fantasy that gave satisfaction and demanded nothing in return; the wolfbait, the eye-stopper that men exchanged glances over, the erotic sex-and-glamour symbol to Easterners like Arthur Miller turned on by the Hollywood vulgarity the way Nabokov was by that temple of philistinism, the American motel.

The times being what they were, if she hadn't existed we would have had to invent her, and we did, in a way. She was the fifties' fiction, the lie that a woman has no sexual needs, that she is there to cater to, or enhance, a man's needs. She was the living embodiment of half of one of the more grotesque and familiar pseudo-couples—the old man and the "showgirl," immortalized in *Esquire* and *Playboy* cartoons.

The difference between Monroe and the archetypal brassy blonde is the difference between Monroe and Jayne Mansfield, the real cartoon of overblown sex appeal, the fifties' synecdoche (with the part, or rather pair, standing for the whole) whose comic grotesqueness was exploited, with complementary male absurdities, by Frank Tashlin in *Will Success Spoil Rock Hunter?* and *The Girl Can't Help It*. Unlike Mansfield, Monroe's heart wasn't in it; they—the cartoon blondes—are hard but she was soft.

She catered to these fantasies and played these roles because she was afraid that if she stopped—which she did once and for all with sleeping pills—there would turn out to be nothing there, and therefore nothing to love. She was never permitted to mature into a warm, vibrant woman, or fully use her gifts for comedy, despite the signals and flares she kept sending up. Instead, she was turned into a figure of mockery in the parts she played and to the men she played with. In *The Asphalt Jungle* and *All About Eve,* she was a sex object and nincompoop. In *How to Marry a Millionaire, We're Not Married, The Seven Year Itch,* and *Niagara,* she was paired with sexless leading men (David Wayne, David Wayne, Tom Ewell, Joseph Cotten) while the other women (Bacall and Grable in *How to Marry,* for example) were given reasonable partners. In *Bus Stop,* with its covertly homosexual patterns, she played a parody earth mother to Don Murray's innocent stud. In Hawks' *Monkey Business* and *Gentlemen Prefer Blondes* she played a tootsie who is most comfortable with older men (Charles Coburn in both) and little boys (Cary Grant as a regressed scientist and George Winslow as a real youngster). In *Some Like It Hot,* her leading man—Tony Curtis—did a Cary Grant imitation, and was thus a "bogus" romantic lead. In her "serious" roles, in *Don't Bother to Knock* and *Niagara,* she was a psychopath, while Anne Bancroft and Jean Peters played the normal women. When she finally played an ex-saloon singer with brains and feelings who *evolves* emotionally (Preminger's *River of No Return,* opposite Robert Mitchum), the film was a flop: Audiences wouldn't accept her as a real woman. In *Let's Make Love,* she played a silly Cinderella to Yves Montand's millionaire. And in *The Prince and the Showgirl* and *The Misfits,* playing opposite Olivier and Gable, her image as sexpot and/or psychopath, as it had already evolved from her Fox films, was treated almost in the abstract, that is, was accepted, unquestioned, as her identity.

And yet, throughout her career, she was giving more to idiotic parts than they called for—more feeling, more warmth, more anguish, and, as a result, her films have a richer tone than they deserve. The best ones, which is to say, the best she could get under the circumstances, are the films that suggest the discrepancy between the woman (and young girl) and the sexpot, even as their directors (Wilder and Hawks) exploit the image, through exaggeration, more than they have to—though still more gently than other directors.

DISCUSSION QUESTIONS

- What characteristics define female characters?
- What is the virgin-whore dichotomy?
- Can you define the "sex goddess"?
- How does Haskell suggest we overturn these ideals?

EXAMPLES TO THINK ABOUT

- Marilyn Monroe
- The female characters on *Modern Family*
- Female-identified child stars when they have reached maturity

Masculinities

THE SOCIAL ORGANIZATION OF MASCULINITY

By R. W. CONNELL

C hapter 1 traced the main currents of twentieth-century research and showed that they had failed to produce a coherent science of masculinity. This does not reveal the failure of the scientists so much as the impossibility of the task. 'Masculinity' is not a coherent object about which a generalizing science can be produced. Yet we can have coherent knowledge about the issues raised in these attempts. If we broaden the angle of vision, we can see masculinity, not as an isolated object, but as an aspect of a larger structure.

This demands an account of the larger structure and how masculinities are located in it. The task of this chapter is to set out a framework based on contemporary analyses of gender relations. This framework will provide a way of distinguishing types of masculinity, and of understanding the dynamics of change.

First, however, there is some ground to clear. The definition of the basic term in the discussion has never been wonderfully clear.

Defining Masculinity

All societies have cultural accounts of gender, but not all have the concept 'masculinity'. In its modern usage the term assumes that one's behaviour results from the type of person one is. That is to say, an unmasculine person would behave differently: being peaceable rather than violent, conciliatory rather than dominating, hardly able to kick a football, uninterested in sexual conquest, and so forth.

This conception presupposes a belief in individual difference and personal agency. In that sense it is built on the conception of individuality that developed in early-modern Europe with the growth of colonial empires and capitalist economic relations [...] .

But the concept is also inherently relational. 'Masculinity' *does* not exist except in contrast with 'femininity'. A culture which does not treat women and men as bearers of polarized character types, at least in principle, does not have a concept of masculinity in the sense of modern European/American culture.

Historical research suggests that this was true of European culture itself before the eighteenth century. Women were certainly regarded as different from men, but different in the sense of being incomplete or inferior examples of the same character (for instance, having less of the faculty of reason). Women and men were not seen as bearers of qualitatively different characters; this conception accompanied the bourgeois ideology of 'separate spheres' in the nineteenth century.[1]

In both respects our concept of masculinity seems to be a fairly recent historical product, a few hundred years old at most. In speaking of masculinity at all, then, we are 'doing gender' in a culturally specific way. This should be borne in mind with any claim to have discovered transhistorical truths about manhood and the masculine.

Definitions of masculinity have mostly taken our cultural standpoint for granted, but have followed different strategies to characterize the type of person who is masculine. Four main strategies have been followed; they are easily distinguished in terms of their logic, though often combined in practice.

Essentialist definitions usually pick a feature that defines the core of the masculine, and hang an account of men's lives on that. Freud flirted with an essentialist definition when he equated masculinity with activity in contrast to feminine passivity—though he came to see that equation as oversimplified. Later authors' attempts to capture an essence of masculinity have been colourfully varied: risk-taking, responsibility, irresponsibility, aggression, Zeus energy ... Perhaps the finest is the sociobiologist Lionel Tiger's idea that true maleness, underlying male bonding and war, is elicited by 'hard and heavy phenomena'.[2] Many heavymetal rock fans would agree.

The weakness in the essentialist approach is obvious: the choice of the essence is quite arbitrary. Nothing obliges different essentialists to agree, and in fact they often do not.

Claims about a universal basis of masculinity tell us more about the ethos of the claimant than about anything else.

Positivist social science, whose ethos emphasizes finding the facts, yields a simple definition of masculinity: what men actually are. This definition is the logical basis of masculinity/ femininity (M/F) scales in psychology, whose items are validated by showing that they discriminate statistically between groups of men and women. It is also the basis of those ethnographic discussions of masculinity which describe the pattern of men's lives in a given culture and, whatever it is, call the pattern masculinity.[3]

There are three difficulties here. First, as modern epistemology recognizes, there is no description without a standpoint. The apparently neutral descriptions on which these definitions rest are themselves underpinned by assumptions about gender. Obviously enough, to start compiling an M/F scale one must have some idea of what to count or list when making up the items.

Second, to list what men and women do requires that people be already sorted into the categories 'men' and 'women'. This, as Suzanne Kessler and Wendy McKenna showed in their classic ethnomthodological study of gender research, is unavoidably a process of social attribution using common-sense typologies of gender. Positivist procedure thus rests on the very typifications that are supposedly under investigation in gender research.

Third, to define masculinity as what-men-empirically-are is to rule out the usage in which we call some women 'masculine' and some men 'feminine', or some actions or attitudes 'masculine' or 'feminine' regardless of who displays them. This is not a trivial use of the terms. It is crucial, for instance, to psychoanalytic thinking about contradictions within personality.

Indeed, this usage is fundamental to gender analysis. If we spoke only of differences between men as a bloc and women as a bloc, we would not need the terms 'masculine' and 'feminine' at all. We could just speak of 'men's' and 'women's', or 'male' and 'female'. The terms 'masculine' and 'feminine' point beyond categorical sex difference to the ways men differ among themselves, and women differ among themselves, in matters of gender.[4]

Normative definitions recognize these differences and offer a standard: masculinity is what men ought to be. This definition is often found in media studies, in discussions of exemplars such as John Wayne or of genres such as the thriller. Strict sex role theory treats masculinity precisely as a social norm for the behaviour of men. In practice, male sex role texts often blend normative with essentialist definitions, as in Robert Brannon's widely quoted account of 'our culture's blueprint of manhood': No Sissy Stuff, The Big Wheel, The Sturdy Oak and Give 'em Hell.[5]

Normative definitions allow that different men approach the standards to different degrees. But this soon produces paradoxes, some of which were recognized in the early Men's Liberation writings. Few men actually match the 'blueprint' or display the toughness and independence acted by Wayne, Bogart or Eastwood. (This point is picked up by film itself, in spoofs such as *Blazing Saddles* and *Play it Again, Sam.*) What is 'normative' about a norm hardly anyone meets? Are we to say the majority of men are unmasculine? How do we assay the toughness needed to resist the norm of toughness, or the heroism needed to come out as gay?

A more subtle difficulty is that a purely normative definition gives no grip on masculinity at the level of personality. Joseph Pleck correctly identified the unwarranted assumption that role and identity correspond. This assumption is, I think, why sex role theorists often drift towards essentialism.

Semiotic approaches abandon the level of personality and define masculinity through a system of symbolic difference in which masculine and feminine places are contrasted. Masculinity is, in effect, defined as not-femininity.

This follows the formulae of structural linguistics, where elements of speech are defined by their differences from each other. The approach has been widely used in feminist and poststructuralist cultural analyses of gender and in Lacanian psychoanalysis and studies of symbolism. It yields more than an abstract contrast of masculinity and femininity, of the kind found in M/F scales. In the semiotic opposition of masculinity and femininity, masculinity is the unmarked term, the place of symbolic authority. The phallus is master-signifier, and femininity is symbolically defined by lack.

This definition of masculinity has been very effective in cultural analysis. It escapes the arbitrariness of essentialism and the paradoxes of positivist and normative definitions. It is, however, limited in its scope—unless one assumes, as some postmodern theorists do, that discourse is all we can talk about in social analysis. To grapple with the full range of issues about masculinity we need ways of talking about relationships of other kinds too: about gendered places in production and consumption, places in institutions and in natural environments, places in social and military struggles.[6]

What can be generalized is the principle of connection. The idea that one symbol can only be understood within a connected system of symbols applies equally well in other spheres. No masculinity arises except in a system of gender relations.

Rather than attempting to define masculinity as an object (a natural character type, a behavioural average, a norm), we need to focus on the processes and relationships through which men and women conduct gendered lives. 'Masculinity', to the extent the term can be briefly defined at all, is simultaneously a place in gender relations, the practices through which men and women engage that place in gender, and the effects of these practices in bodily experience, personality and culture.

◆ ◆ ◆ ◆

[...] Social science had come to recognize a third site of gender configuration, institutions such as the state, the workplace and the school. Many find it difficult to accept that institutions are substantively, not just metaphorically, gendered. This is, nevertheless, a key point.

The state, for instance, is a masculine institution. To say this is not to imply that the personalities of top male office-holders somehow seep through and stain the institution. It is to say something much stronger: that state organizational practices are structured in relation to the reproductive arena. The overwhelming majority of top office-holders are men because there is a gender configuring of recruitment and promotion, a gender configuring of the internal division of labour and systems of control, a gender configuring of policymaking, practical routines, and ways of mobilizing pleasure and consent.[9]

The gender structuring of practice need have nothing biologially to do with reproduction. The link with the reproductive arena is social. This becomes clear when it is challenged. An example is the recent struggle within the state over 'gays in the military', i.e., the rules excluding soldiers and sailors because of the gender of their sexual object-choice. In the United States, where this struggle was most severe, critics made the case for change in terms of civil liberties and military efficiency, arguing in effect that object-choice has little to do with the capacity to kill. The admirals and generals defended the status quo on a variety of spurious grounds. The unadmitted reason was the cultural importance of a particular definition of masculinity in maintaining the fragile cohesion of modern armed forces.

It has been clear since the work of Juliet Mitchell and Gayle Rubin in the 1970s that gender is an internally complex structure, where a number of different logics are superimposed. This is a fact of great importance for the analysis of masculinities. Any one masculinity, as a configuration of practice, is simultaneously positioned in a number of structures of relationship, which may be following different historical trajectories. Accordingly masculinity, like femininity, is always liable to internal contradiction and historical disruption.

We need at least a three-fold model of the structure of gender, distinguishing relations of (a) power, (b) production and (c) cathexis (emotional attachment). This is a provisional model, but it gives some purchase on issues about masculinity.[10]

(a) *Power relations*   The main axis of power in the contemporary European/American gender order is the overall subordination of women and dominance of men—the structure Women's Liberation named 'patriarchy': This general structure exists despite many local reversals (e.g., woman-headed households, female teachers with male students). It persists despite resistance of many kinds, now articulated in feminism. These reversals and resistances mean continuing difficulties for patriarchal power. They define a problem of legitimacy which has great importance for the politics of masculinity.

(b) *Production relations*   Gender divisions of labour are familiar in the form of the allocation of tasks, sometimes reaching extra ordinarily fine detail. (In the English village studied by the sociologist Pauline Hunt, for instance, it was customary for women to wash the inside of windows, men to wash the outside.) Equal attention should be paid to the economic consequences of gender divisions of labour, the dividend accruing to men from unequal shares of the products of social labour. This is most often discussed in terms of unequal wage rates, but the gendered character of capital should also be noted. A capitalist economy working through a gender division of labour is, necessarily, a gendered accumulation process So it is not a statistical accident, but a part of the social construction of masculinity, that men and not women control the major corporations and the great private fortunes. Implausible as it sounds, the accumulation of wealth has become firmly linked to the reproductive arena, through the social relations of gender.[11]

(c) *Cathexis* [...] Sexual desire is so often seen as natural that it is commonly excluded from social theory. Yet when we consider desire in Freudian terms, as emotional energy being attached to an object, its gendered character is clear. This is true both for heterosexual and homosexual desire. (It is striking that in our culture the non-gendered object choice, 'bisexual' desire, is ill-defined and unstable.) The practices that shape and realize desire are thus an aspect of the gender order. Accordingly we can ask political questions about the relationships involved: whether they are consensual or coercive, whether pleasure is equally given and received. In feminist analyses of sexuality these have become sharp questions about the connection of heterosexuality with men's position of social dominance.

◆ ◆ ◆ ◆

Relations among Masculinities: Hegemony, Subordination, Complicity, Marginalization

With growing recognition of the interplay between gender, race and class it has become common to recognize multiple masculinities: black as well as white, working-class as well as middle-class. This is welcome, but it risks another kind of oversimplification. It is easy in this framework to think that there is *a* black masculinity or *a* working-class masculinity.

To recognize more than one kind of masculinity is only a first step. We have to examine the relations between them. Further, we have to unpack the milieux of class and race and scrutinize the gender relations operating within them. There are, after all, gay black men and effeminate factory hands, not to mention middleclass rapists and cross-dressing bourgeois.

A focus on the gender relations among men is necessary to keep the analysis dynamic, to prevent the acknowledgement of multiple masculinities collapsing into a character typology' as happened with Fromm and the *Authoritarian Personality* research. 'Hegemonic masculinity' is not a fixed character type, always and everywhere the same. It is, rather, the masculinity that occupies the hegemonic position in a given pattern of gender relations, a position always contestable.

A focus on relations also offers a gain in realism. Recognizing multiple masculinities, especially in an individualist culture such as the United States, risks taking them for alternative lifestyles, a matter of consumer choice. A relational approach makes it easier to recognize the hard compulsions under which gender configuration are formed, the bitterness as well as the pleasure in gendered experience.

With these guidelines, let us consider the practices and relations that construct the main patterns of masculinity in the current Western gender order.

Hegemony

The concept of 'hegemony', deriving from Antonio Gramsci's analysis of class relations, refers to the cultural dynamic by which a group claims and sustains a leading position in social life. At any given time, one form of masculinity rather than others is culturally exalted. Hegemonic masculinity can be defined as the configuration of gender practice which embodies the currently accepted answer to the problem of the legitimacy of patriarchy, which guarantees (or is taken to guarantee) the dominant position of men and the subordination of women.[15]

This is not to say that the most visible bearers of hegemonic masculinity are always the most powerful people. They may be exemplars, such as film actors, or even fantasy figures, such as film characters. Individual holders of institutional power or great wealth may be far from the hegemonic pattern in their personal lives. (Thus a male member of a prominent business dynasty was a key figure in the gay/transvestite social scene in Sydney in the 1950s, because of his wealth and the protection this gave in the cold-war climate of political and police harassment.)[16]

Nevertheless, hegemony is likely to be established only if there is some correspondence between cultural ideal and institutional power, collective if not individual. So the top levels of business, the military and government provide a fairly convincing *corporate* display of masculinity, still very little shaken by feminist women or dissenting men. It is the successful claim to authority, more than direct violence, that is the mark of hegemony (though violence often underpins or supports authority).

I stress that hegemonic masculinity embodies a 'currently accepted' strategy. When conditions for the defence of patriarchy change, the bases for the dominance of a particular masculinity are eroded. New groups may challenge old solutions and construct a new hegemony. The dominance of *any* group of men may be challenged by women. Hegemony, then, is a historically mobile relation. Its ebb and flow is a key element of the picture of masculinity proposed in this book. [...].

Subordination

Hegemony relates to cultural dominance in the society as a whole. Within that overall framework there are specific gender relations of dominance and subordination between groups of men.

The most important case in contemporary European/American society is the dominance of heterosexual men and the subordination of homosexual men. This is much more than a cultural stigmatization of homosexuality or gay identity. Gay men are subordinated to straight men by an array of quite material practices.

These practices were listed in early Gay Liberation texts such as Dennis Altman's *Homosexual: Oppression and Liberation*. They have been documented at length in studies such as the NSW Anti-Discrimination Board's 1982 report *Discrimination and Homosexuality*.

They are still a matter of everyday experience for homosexual men. They include political and cultural exclusion, cultural abuse (in the United States gay men have now become the main symbolic target of the religious right), legal violence (such as imprisonment under sodomy statutes), street violence (ranging from intimidation to murder), economic discrimination and personal boycotts. It is not surprising that an Australian working-class man, reflecting on his experience of coming out in a homophobic culture, would remark:

> You know, I didn't totally realize what it was to be gay. I mean it's a bastard of a life.[17]

Oppression positions homosexual masculinities at the bottom of a gender hierarchy among men. Gayness, in patriarchal ideology, is the repository of whatever is symbolically expelled from hegemonic masculinity, the items ranging from fastidious taste in home decoration to receptive anal pleasure. Hence, from the point of view of hegemonic masculinity, gayness is easily assimilated to femininity. And hence—in the view of some gay theorists—the ferocity of homophobic attacks.

Gay masculinity is the most conspicuous, but it is not the only subordinated masculinity. Some heterosexual men and boys too are expelled from the circle of legitimacy. The process is marked by a rich vocabulary of abuse: wimp, milksop, nerd, turkey, sissy, lily liver, jellyfish, yellowbelly, candy ass, ladyfinger, pushover, cookie pusher, cream puff, motherfucker, pantywaist, mother's boy, four-eyes, ear-'ole, dweeb, geek, Milquetoast, Cedric, and so on. Here to the symbolic blurring with femininity is obvious.

Complicity

Normative definitions of masculinity, as I have noted, face the problem that not many men actually meet the normative standards. This point applies to hegemonic masculinity. The number of men rigorously practising the hegemonic pattern in its entirety may be quite small. Yet the majority of men gain from its hegemony, since they benefit from the patriarchal dividend, the advantage men in general gain from the overall subordination of women.

As Chapter 1 showed, accounts of masculinity have generally concerned themselves with syndromes and types, not with numbers. Yet in thinking about the dynamics of society as a whole, numbers matter. Sexual politics is mass politics, and strategic thinking needs to be concerned with where the masses of people are. If a large number of men have some connection with the hegemonic project but do not embody hegemonic masculinity, we need a way of theorizing their specific situation.

This can be done by recognizing another relationship among groups of men, the relationship of complicity with the hegemonic project. Masculinities constructed in ways that realize the patriarchal dividend, without the tensions or risks of being the frontline troops of patriarchy, are complicit in this sense.

It is tempting to treat them simply as slacker versions of hegemonic masculinity—the difference between the men who cheer football matches on TV and those who run out into the mud and the tackles themselves. But there is often something more definite and carefully crafted than that. Marriage, fatherhood and community life often involve extensive compromises with women rather than naked domination or an uncontested display of authority.[18] A great many men who draw the patriarchal dividend also respect their wives and mothers, are never violent towards women, do their accustomed share of the housework, bring home the family wage, and can easily convince themselves that feminists must be bra-burning extremists.

Marginalization

Hegemony, subordination and complicity, as just defined, are relations internal to the gender order. The interplay of gender with other structures such as class and race creates further relationships between masculinities.

[...] New information technology became a vehicle for redefining middle-class masculinities at a time when the meaning of labour for working-class men was in contention. This is not a question of a fixed middle-class masculinity confronting a fixed working-class masculinity. Both are being reshaped, by a social dynamic in which class and gender relations are simultaneously in play.

Race relations may also become an integral part of the dynamic between masculinities. In a white-supremacist context, black masculinities play symbolic roles for white gender construction. For instance, black sporting stars become exemplars of masculine toughness, while the fantasy figure of the black rapist plays an important role in sexual politics among whites, a role much exploited by right-wing politics in the United States. Conversely, hegemonic masculinity among whites sustains the institutional oppression and physical terror that have framed the making of masculinities in black communities.

Robert Staples's discussion of internal colonialism in *Black Masculinity* shows the effect of class and race relations at the same time. As he argues, the level of violence among black men in the United States can only be understood through the changing place of the black labour force in American capitalism and the violent means used to control it. Massive unemployment and urban poverty now powerfully interact with institutional racism in the shaping of black masculinity.[19]

Though the term is not ideal, I cannot improve on 'marginalization' to refer to the relations between the masculinities in dominant and subordinated classes or ethnic groups. Marginalization is always relative to the *authorization* of the hegemonic masculinity of the dominant group. Thus, in the United States, particular black athletes may be exemplars for hegemonic masculinity. But the fame and wealth of individual stars has no trickle-down effect; it does not yield social authority to black men generally.

The relation of marginalization and authorization may also exist between subordinated masculinities. A striking example is the arrest and conviction of Oscar Wilde, one of the first men caught in the net of modern anti-homosexual legislation. Wilde was trapped because of his connections with homosexual working-class youths, a practice unchallenged until his legal battle with a wealthy aristocrat, the Marquess of Queensberry, made him vulnerable.[20]

These two types of relationship—hegemony, domination/subordination and complicity on the one hand, marginalization/authorization on the other—provide a framework in which we can analyse specific masculinities. (This is a sparse framework, but social theory should be hardworking.) I emphasize that terms such as 'hegemonic masculinity' and 'marginalized masculinities' name not fixed character types but configurations of practice generated in particular situations in a changing structure of relationships. Any theory of masculinity worth having must give an account of this process of change.

NOTES

1. Bloch 1978 outlines the argument for the Protestant middle classes of England and North America. Laqueur 1990 offers a more sweeping argument on similar lines about views of the body.

2. Tiger 1969: 211. Tiger goes on to suggest that war may be part of 'the masculine aesthetic', like driving a racing car at high speed ... The passage is still worth reading; like Bly's *Iron John*, a stunning example of the muddled thinking that the question of masculinity seems to provoke, in this case flavoured by what C. Wright Mills once called 'crackpot realism'.

3. The deeply confused logic of M/F scales was laid bare in a classic paper by Constantinople 1973. Ethnographic positivism on masculinity reaches a nadir in Gilmore 1990, who swings between normative theory and positivist practice.

4. Kessler and McKenna 1978 develop the important argument about the 'primacy of gender attribution'. For an illuminating discussion of masculine women, see Devor 1989.

5. Easthope 1986; Brannon 1976.

6. A strictly semiotic approach in the literature on masculinity is not common; this approach is found mostly in more general treatments of gender. However, Saco 1992 offers a very clear defence of the approach, and its potential is shown by the collection in which her paper appears, Craig 1992.

7. Sartre 1968: 159–60.

8. Hollway 1984.

9. Franzway et al. 1989, Grant and Tancred 1992.

10. Mitchell 1971, Rubin 1975. The three-fold model is spelt out in Connell 1987.

11. Hunt 1980. Feminist political economy is, however, under way, and these notes draw on Mies 1986, Waring 1988, Armstrong and Armstrong 1990.

12. Some of the best writing on the politics of heterosexuality comes from Canada: Valverde 1985, Buchbinder et al. 1987. The conceptual approach here is developed in Connell and Dowsett 1992.

13. Interview with Ice-T in *City on a Hill Press* (Santa Cruz, CA), 21 Jan 1993; Hoch 1979.

14. Rose 1992, ch. 6 especially.

15. I would emphasize the dynamic character of Gramsci's concept of hegemony, which is not the functionalist theory of cultural reproduction often portrayed. Gramsci always had in mind a social struggle for leadership in historical change.

16. Wotherspoon 1991 (chapter 3) describes this climate, and discreetly does not mention individuals.

17. Altman 1972; Anti-Discrimination Board 1982. Quotation from Connell, Davis and Dowsett 1993: 122.

18. See, for instance, the white US families described by Rubin 1976.

19. Staples 1982. The more recent United States literature on black masculinity, e.g., Majors and Gordon 1994, has made a worrying retreat from Staples's structural analysis towards sex role theory; its favoured political strategy, not surprisingly, is counselling programs to resocialize black youth.

20. Ellmann 1987.

DISCUSSION QUESTIONS

- Connell lists "essentialist," "positivist social science," and "semiotic approaches" as important but flawed ways of defining gender. Can you explain and critique each of them?

- What forces are at work in Connell's "three-fold structure of masculinity"?

- What does "hegemonic masculinity" mean?

EXAMPLES TO THINK ABOUT

- Movie superheroes
- American presidents
- Steve Jobs, Mark Zuckerberg
- Eminem, Jay-Z, Tyga, A$AP Rocky

SECTION 3

GENDERING CREATION AND RECEPTION

The Feminine Mystique

THE HAPPY HOUSEWIFE HEROINE

By BETTY FRIEDAN

W hy have so many American wives suffered this nameless aching dissatisfaction for so many years, each one thinking she was alone? "I've got tears in my eyes with sheer relief that my own inner turmoil is shared with other women," a young Connecticut mother wrote me when I first began to put this problem into words.[1] A woman from a town in Ohio wrote: "The times when I felt that the only answer was to consult a psychiatrist, times of anger, bitterness and general frustration too numerous to even mention, I had no idea that hundreds of other women were feeling the same way. I felt so completely alone." A Houston, Texas, housewife wrote: "It has been the feeling of being almost alone with my problem that has made it so hard. I thank God for my family, home and the chance to care for them, but my life couldn't stop there. It is an awakening to know that I'm not an oddity and can stop being ashamed of wanting something more."

That painful guilty silence, and that tremendous relief when a feeling is finally out in the open, are familiar psychological signs. What need, what part of themselves, could so many women today be repressing? In this age after Freud, sex is immediately suspect. But this new stirring in women does not seem to be sex; it is, in fact, much harder for women

Betty Friedan, Selections from "The Happy Housewife Heroine," *The Feminine Mystique*, pp. 23-66, 518. Copyright © 1984 by W. W. Norton & Company, Inc. Reprinted with permission.

to talk about than sex. Could there be another need, a part of themselves they have buried as deeply as the Victorian women buried sex?

If there is, a woman might not know what it was, any more than the Victorian woman knew she had sexual needs. The image of a good woman by which Victorian ladies lived simply left out sex. Does the image by which modern American women live also leave something out, the proud and public image of the high-school girl going steady, the college girl in love, the suburban housewife with an up-and-coming husband and a station wagon full of children? This image—created by the women's magazines, by advertisements, television, movies, novels, columns and books by experts on marriage and the family, child psychology, sexual adjustment and by the popularizers of sociology and psychoanalysis—shapes women's lives today and mirrors their dreams. It may give a clue to the problem that has no name, as a dream gives a clue to a wish unnamed by the dreamer. In the mind's ear, a geiger counter clicks when the image shows too sharp a discrepancy from reality. A geiger counter clicked in my own inner ear when I could not fit the quiet desperation of so many women into the picture of the modern American housewife that I myself was helping to create, writing for the women's magazines. What is missing from the image which shapes the American woman's pursuit of fulfillment as a wife and mother? What is missing from the image that mirrors and creates the identity of women in America today?

In the early 1960's *McCall's* has been the fastest growing of the women's magazines. Its contents are a fairly accurate representation of the image of the American woman presented, and in part created, by the large-circulation magazines. Here are the complete editorial contents of a typical issue of *McCall's* (July, 1960):

1. A lead article on "increasing baldness in women," caused by too much brushing and dyeing.
2. A long poem in primer-size type about a child, called "A Boy Is A Boy."
3. A short story about how a teenager who doesn't go to college gets a man away from a bright college girl.
4. A short story about the minute sensations of a baby throwing his bottle out of the crib.
5. The first of a two-part intimate "up-to-date" account by the Duke of Windsor on "How the Duchess and I now live and spend our time. The influence of clothes on me and vice versa."
6. A short story about a nineteen-year-old girl sent to a charm school to learn how to bat her eyelashes and lose at tennis. ("You're nineteen, and by normal American standards, I now am entitled to have you taken off my hands, legally and financially, by some beardless youth who will spirit you away to a one-and-a-half-room apartment in the Village while he learns the chicanery of selling bonds. And no beardless youth is going to do that as long as you volley to his backhand.")
7. The story of a honeymoon couple commuting between separate bedrooms after an argument over gambling at Las Vegas.

8. An article on "how to overcome an inferiority complex."

9. A story called "Wedding Day."

10. The story of a teenager's mother who learns how to dance rock-and-roll.

11. Six pages of glamorous pictures of models in maternity clothes.

12. Four glamorous pages on "reduce the way the models do."

13. An article on airline delays.

14. Patterns for home sewing.

15. Patterns with which to make "Folding Screens—Bewitching Magic."

16. An article called "An Encyclopedic Approach to Finding a Second Husband."

17. A "barbecue bonanza," dedicated "to the Great American Mister who stands, chef's cap on head, fork in hand, on terrace or back porch, in patio or backyard anywhere in the land, watching his roast turning on the spit. And to his wife, without whom (sometimes) the barbecue could never be the smashing summer success it undoubtedly is …"

There were also the regular front-of-the-book "service" columns on new drug and medicine developments, child-care facts, columns by Clare Luce and by Eleanor Roosevelt, and "Pats and Pans," a column of readers' letters.

The image of woman that emerges from this big, pretty magazine is young and frivolous, almost childlike; fluffy and feminine; passive; gaily content in a world of bedroom and kitchen, sex, babies, and home. The magazine surely does not leave out sex; the only passion, the only pursuit, the only goal a woman is permitted is the pursuit of a man. It is crammed full of food, clothing, cosmetics, furniture, and the physical bodies of young women, but where is the world of thought and ideas, the life of the mind and spirit? In the magazine image, women do no work except housework and work to keep their bodies beautiful and to get and keep a man.

This was the image of the American woman in the year Castro led a revolution in Cuba and men were trained to travel into outer space; the year that the African continent brought forth new nations, and a plane whose speed is greater than the speed of sound broke up a Summit Conference; the year artists picketed a great museum in protest against the hegemony of abstract art; physicists explored the concept of anti-matter; astronomers, because of new radio telescopes, had to alter their concepts of the expanding universe; biologists made a breakthrough in the fundamental chemistry of life; and Negro youth in Southern schools forced the United States, for the first time since the Civil War, to face a moment of democratic truth. But this magazine, published for over 5,000,000 American women, almost all of whom have been through high school and nearly half to college, contained almost no mention of the world beyond the home. In the second half of the twentieth century in America, woman's world was confined to her own body and beauty, the charming of man, the bearing of babies, and the physical care and serving of husband, children, and home. And this was no anomaly of a single issue of a single women's magazine.

I sat one night at a meeting of magazine writers, mostly men, who work for all kinds of magazines, including women's magazines. The main speaker was a leader of the desegregation battle. Before he spoke, another man outlined the needs of the large women's magazine he edited:

> Our readers are housewives, full time. They're not interested in the broad pub-lic issues of the day. They are not interested in national or international affairs. They are only interested in the family and the home. They aren't interested in politics, unless it's related to an immediate need in the home, like the price of coffee. Humor? Has to be gentle, they don't get satire. Travel? We have almost completely dropped it. Education? That's a problem. Their own education level is going up. They've generally all had a high-school education and many, college. They're tremendously interested in education for their children—fourth-grade arithmetic. You just can't write about ideas or broad issues of the day for women. That's why we're publishing 90 percent service now and 10 percent general interest.

Another editor agreed, adding plaintively: "Can't you give us something else besides 'there's death in your medicine cabinet'? Can't any of you dream up a new crisis for women? We're always interested in sex, of course."

At this point, the writers and editors spent an hour listening to Thurgood Marshall on the inside story of the desegregation battle, and its possible effect on the presidential election. "Too bad I can't run that story," one editor said. "But you just can't link it to woman's world."

As I listened to them, a German phrase echoed in my mind—*"Kinder, Küche, Kirche,"* the slogan by which the Nazis decreed that women must once again be confined to their biological role. But this was not Nazi Germany. This was America. The whole world lies open to American women. Why, then, does the image deny the world? Why does it limit women to "one passion, one role, one occupation?" Not long ago, women dreamed and fought for equality, their own place in the world. What happened to their dreams; when did women decide to give up the world and go back home?

A geologist brings up a core of mud from the bottom of the ocean and sees layers of sedi-ment as sharp as a razor blade deposited over the years—clues to changes in the geological evolution of the earth so vast that they would go unnoticed during the lifespan of a single man. I sat for many days in the New York Public Library, going back through bound volumes of American women's magazines for the last twenty years. I found a change in the image of the American woman, and in the boundaries of the woman's world, as sharp and puzzling as the changes revealed in cores of ocean sediment.

In 1939, the heroines of women's magazine stories were not always young, but in a certain sense they were younger than their fictional counterparts today. They were young in the same way that the American hero has always been young: they were New Women, creating with a gay determined spirit a new identity for women—a life of their own. There was an aura about them of becoming, of moving into a future that was going to be different from the past.

The majority of heroines in the four major women's magazines (then *Ladies' Home Journal, McCall's, Good Housekeeping, Woman's Home Companion*) were career women—happily, proudly, adventurously, attractively career women—who loved and were loved by men. And the spirit, courage, independence, determination—the strength of character they showed in their work as nurses, teachers, artists, actresses, copywriters, saleswomen—were part of their charm. There was a definite aura that their individuality was something to be admired, not unattractive to men, that men were drawn to them as much for their spirit and character as for their looks.

These were the mass women's magazines—in their heyday. The stories were conventional: girl-meets-boy or girl-gets-boy. But very often this was not the major theme of the story. These heroines were usually marching toward some goal or vision of their own, struggling with some problem of work or the world, when they found their man. And this New Woman, less fuffily feminine, so independent and determined to find a new life of her own, was the heroine of a different kind of love story. She was less aggressive in pursuit of a man. Her passionate involvement with the world, her own sense of herself as an individual, her self-reliance, gave a different flavor to her relationship with the man.

The heroine and hero of one of these stories meet and fall in love at an ad agency where they both work. "I don't want to put you in a garden behind a wall," the hero says. "I want you to walk with me hand in hand, and together we could accomplish whatever we wanted to" ("A Dream to Share," *Redbook*, January, 1939).

These New Women were almost never housewives; in fact, the stories usually ended before they had children. They were young because the future was open. But they seemed, in another sense, much older, more mature than the childlike, kittenish young housewife heroines today. One, for example, is a nurse ("Mother-in-Law," *Ladies' Home Journal*, June, 1939). "She was, he thought, very lovely. She hadn't an ounce of picture book prettiness, but there was strength in her hands, pride in her carriage and nobility in the lift of her chin, in her blue eyes. She had been on her own ever since she left training, nine years ago. She had earned her way, she need consider nothing but her heart."

One heroine runs away from home when her mother insists she must make her debut instead of going on an expedition as a geologist. Her passionate determination to live her own life does not keep this New Woman from loving a man, but it makes her rebel from her parents; just as the young hero often must leave home to grow up. "You've got more courage than any girl I ever saw. You have what it takes," says the boy who helps her get away ("Have a Good Time, Dear," *Ladies' Home Journal*, May, 1939).

Often, there was a conflict between some commitment to her work and the man. But the moral, in 1939, was that if she kept her commitment to herself, she did not lose the man, if he was the right man. A young widow ("Between the Dark and the Daylight," *Ladies' Home Journal*, February, 1939) sits in her office, debating whether to stay and correct the important mistake she has made on the job, or keep her date with a man. She thinks back on her marriage, her baby, her husband's death … "the time afterward which held the struggle for clear judgment, not being afraid of new and better jobs, of having confidence in one's decisions." How can the boss expect her to give up her date! But she stays on the job. "They'd put their life's blood into this campaign. She couldn't let him down." She finds her man, too—the boss!

These stories may not have been great literature. But the identity of their heroines seemed to say something about the housewives who, then as now, read the women's magazines. These magazines were not written for career women. The New Woman heroines were the ideal of yesterday's housewives; they reflected the dreams, mirrored the yearning for identity and the sense of possibility that existed for women then. And if women could not have these dreams for themselves, they wanted their daughters to have them. They wanted their daughters to be more than housewives, to go out in the world that had been denied them.

It is like remembering a long-forgotten dream, to recapture the memory of what a career meant to women before "career woman" became a dirty word in America. Jobs meant money, of course, at the end of the depression. But the readers of these magazines were not the women who got the jobs; career meant more than job. It seemed to mean doing something, being somebody yourself, not just existing in and through others.

I found the last clear note of the passionate search for individual identity that a career seems to have symbolized in the pre-1950 decades in a story called "Sarah and the Seaplane" (*Ladies' Home Journal*, February, 1949). Sarah, who for nineteen years has played the part of docile daughter, is secretly learning to fly. She misses her flying lesson to accompany her mother on a round of social calls. An elderly doctor houseguest says: "My dear Sarah, every day, all the time, you are committing suicide. It's a greater crime than not pleasing others, not doing justice to yourself." Sensing some secret, he asks if she is in love. "She found it difficult to answer. In love? In love with the good-natured, the beautiful Henry [the flying teacher]? In love with the flashing water and the lift of wings at the instant of freedom, and the vision of the smiling, limitless world? 'Yes,' she answered, 'I think I am.'"

The next morning, Sarah solos. Henry "stepped away, slamming the cabin door shut, and swung the ship about for her. She was alone. There was a heady moment when everything she had learned left her, when she had to adjust herself to be alone, entirely alone in the familiar cabin. Then she drew a deep breath and suddenly a wonderful sense of competence made her sit erect and smiling. She was alone! She was answerable to herself alone, and she was sufficient.

"'I can do it!' she told herself aloud. … The wind flew back from the floats in glittering streaks, and then effortlessly the ship lifted itself free and soared." Even her mother can't stop her now from getting her flying license. She is not "afraid of discovering my own way of life." In bed that night she smiles sleepily, remembering how Henry had said, "You're my girl."

"Henry's girl! She smiled. No, she was not Henry's girl. She was Sarah. And that was sufficient. And with such a late start it would be some time before she got to know herself. Half in a dream now, she wondered if at the end of that time she would need someone else and who it would be."

And then suddenly the image blurs. The New Woman, soaring free, hesitates in midflight, shivers in all that blue sunlight and rushes back to the cozy walls of home. In the same year that Sarah soloed, the *Ladies' Home Journal* printed the prototype of the innumerable paeans to "Occupation: housewife" that started to appear in the women's magazines, paeans that resounded throughout the fifties. They usually begin with a woman complaining that when she has to write "housewife" on the census blank, she gets an inferiority complex. ("When I write it I realize that here I am, a middle-aged woman, with a university education, and I've never made anything out of my life. I'm just a housewife.") Then the author of the paean, who somehow never is a housewife (in this case, Dorothy Thompson, newspaper woman, foreign correspondent, famous columnist, in *Ladies' Home Journal,* March, 1949), roars with laughter. The trouble with you, she scolds, is you don't realize you are expert in a dozen careers, simultaneously. "You might write: business manager, cook, nurse, chauffeur, dress-maker, interior decorator, accountant, caterer, teacher, private secretary—or just put down philanthropist. ... All your life you have been giving away your energies, your skills, your talents, your services, for love." But still, the housewife complains, I'm nearly fifty and I've never done what I hoped to do in my youth—music—I've wasted my college education.

Ho-ho, laughs Miss Thompson, aren't your children musical because of you, and all those struggling years while your husband was finishing his great work, didn't you keep a charming home on $3,000 a year, and make all your children's clothes and your own, and paper the living room yourself, and watch the markets like a hawk for bargains? And in time off, didn't you type and proofread your husband's manuscripts, plan festivals to make up the church deficit, play piano duets with the children to make practicing more fun, read their books in high school to follow their study? "But all this vicarious living—through others," the housewife sighs. "As vicarious as Napoleon Bonaparte," Miss Thompson scoffs, "or a Queen. I simply refuse to share your self-pity. You are one of the most successful women I know."

As for not earning any money, the argument goes, let the housewife compute the cost of her services. Women can save more money by their managerial talents inside the home than they can bring into it by outside work. As for woman's spirit being broken by the boredom of household tasks, maybe the genius of some women has been thwarted, but "a world full of feminine genius, but poor in children, would come rapidly to an end. ... Great men have great mothers."

And the American housewife is reminded that Catholic countries in the Middle Ages "elevated the gentle and inconspicuous Mary into the Queen of Heaven, and built their loveliest cathedrals to 'Notre Dame—Our Lady.' ... The homemaker, the nurturer, the creator of children's environment is the constant recreator of culture, civilization, and virtue. Assuming that she is doing well that great managerial task and creative activity, let her write her occupation proudly: 'housewife.'"

In 1949, the *Ladies' Home Journal* also ran Margaret Mead's *Male and Female.* All the magazines were echoing Farnham and Lundberg's *Modern Woman: The Lost Sex,* which came out in 1942, with its warning that careers and higher education were leading to the "masculinization of women with enormously dangerous consequences to the home, the children dependent on it and to the ability of the woman, as well as her husband, to obtain sexual gratification."

And so the feminine mystique began to spread through the land, grafted onto old prejudices and comfortable conventions which so easily give the past a stranglehold on the future. Behind the new mystique were concepts and theories deceptive in their sophistication and their assumption of accepted truth. These theories were supposedly so complex that they were inaccessible to all but a few initiates, and therefore irrefutable. It will be necessary to break through this wall of mystery and look more closely at these complex concepts, these accepted truths, to understand fully what has happened to American women.

The feminine mystique says that the highest value and the only commitment for women is the fulfillment of their own femininity. It says that the great mistake of Western culture, through most of its history, has been the undervaluation of this femininity. It says this femininity is so mysterious and intuitive and close to the creation and origin of life that man-made science may never be able to understand it. But however special and different, it is in no way inferior to the nature of man; it may even in certain respects be superior. The mistake, says the mystique, the root of women's troubles in the past is that women envied men, women tried to be like men, instead of accepting their own nature, which can find fulfillment only in sexual passivity, male domination, and nurturing maternal love.

But the new image this mystique gives to American women is the old image: "Occupation: housewife." The new mystique makes the housewife-mothers, who never had a chance to be anything else, the model for all women; it presupposes that history has reached a final and glorious end in the here and now, as far as women are concerned. Beneath the sophisticated trappings, it simply makes certain concrete, finite, domestic aspects of feminine existence—as it was lived by women whose lives were confined, by necessity, to cooking, cleaning, washing, bearing children—into a religion, a pattern by which all women must now live or deny their femininity.

Fulfillment as a woman had only one definition for American women after 1949—the housewife-mother. As swiftly as in a dream, the image of the American woman as a changing, growing individual in a changing world was shattered. Her solo flight to find her own identity was forgotten in the rush for the security of togetherness. Her limitless world shrunk to the cozy walls of home.

The transformation, reflected in the pages of the women's magazines, was sharply visible in 1949 and progressive through the fifties. "Femininity Begins at Home," "It's a Man's World Maybe," "Have Babies While You're Young," "How to Snare a Male," "Should I Stop Work When We Marry?" "Are You Training Your Daughter to Be a Wife?" "Careers at Home," "Do Women Have to Talk So Much?" "Why GI's Prefer Those German Girls," "What Women Can Learn from Mother Eve," "Really a Man's World, Politics," "How to Hold On to a Happy Marriage," "Don't Be Afraid to Marry Young," "The Doctor Talks about Breast-Feeding," "Our Baby was Born at Home," "Cooking to Me Is Poetry," "The Business of Running a Home."

By the end of 1949, only one out of three heroines in the women's magazines was a career woman—and she was shown in the act of renouncing her career and discovering that what she really wanted to be was a housewife. In 1958, and again in 1959, I went through issue after issue of the three major women's magazines (the fourth, *Woman's Home Companion*, had died) without finding a single heroine who had a career, a commitment to any work, art, profession, or mission in the world, other than "Occupation: housewife." Only one in a hundred heroines had a job; even the young unmarried heroines no longer worked except at snaring a husband.[2]

These new happy housewife heroines seem strangely younger than the spirited career girls of the thirties and forties. They seem to get younger all the time—in looks, and a childlike kind of dependence. They have no vision of the future, except to have a baby. The only active growing figure in their world is the child. The housewife heroines are forever young, because their own image *ends* in childbirth. Like Peter Pan, they must remain young while their children grow up with the world. They must keep on having babies, because the feminine mystique says there is no other way for a woman to be a heroine. Here is a typical specimen from a story called "The Sandwich Maker" (*Ladies' Home Journal,* April, 1959). She took home economics in college, learned how to cook, never held a job, and still plays the child bride, though she now has three children of her own. Her problem is money. "Oh, nothing boring, like taxes or reciprocal trade agreements, or foreign aid programs. I leave all that economic jazz to my constitutionally elected representative in Washington, heaven help him."

The problem is her $42.10 allowance. She hates having to ask her husband for money every time she needs a pair of shoes, but he won't trust her with a charge account. "Oh, how I yearned for a little money of my own! Not much, really. A few hundred a year would have done it. Just enough to meet a friend for lunch occasionally, to indulge in extravagantly colored stockings, a few small items, without having to appeal to Charley. But, alas, Charley was right. I had never earned a dollar in my life, and had no idea of how money was made. So all I did for a long time was brood, as I continued with my cooking, cleaning, cooking, washing, ironing, cooking."

At last the solution comes—she will take orders for sandwiches from other men at her husband's plant. She earns $52.50 a week, except that she forgets to count costs, and she doesn't remember what a gross is so she has to hide 8,640 sandwich bags behind the furnace. Charley says she's making the sandwiches too fancy. She explains: "If it's only ham on rye, then I'm just a sandwich maker, and I'm not interested. But the extras, the special touches— well, they make it sort of creative." So she chops, wraps, peels, seals, spreads bread, starting at dawn and never finished, for $9.00 net, until she is disgusted by the smell of food, and finally staggers downstairs after a sleepless night to slice a salami for the eight gaping lunch boxes. "It was too much. Charley came down just then, and after one quick look at me, ran for a glass of water." She realizes that she is going to have another baby.

"Charley's first coherent words were 'I'll cancel your lunch orders. You're a mother. That's your job. You don't have to earn money, too.' It was all so beautifully simple! 'Yes, boss,' I murmured obediently, frankly relieved." That night he brings her home a checkbook; he will trust her with a joint account. So she decides just to keep quiet about the 8,640 sandwich bags. Anyhow, she'll have used them up, making sandwiches for four children to take to school, by the time the youngest is ready for college.

The road from Sarah and the seaplane to the sandwich maker was traveled in only ten years. In those ten years, the image of American woman seems to have suffered a schizophrenic split. And the split in the image goes much further than the savage obliteration of career from women's dreams.

In an earlier time, the image of woman was also split in two—the good, pure woman on the pedestal, and the whore of the desires of the flesh. The split in the new image opens a different fissure—the feminine woman, whose goodness includes the desires of the flesh, and the career woman, whose evil includes every desire of the separate self. The new feminine morality story is the exorcising of the forbidden career dream, the heroine's victory over Mephistopheles: the devil, first in the form of a career woman, who threatens to take away the heroine's husband or child, and finally, the devil inside the heroine herself, the dream of independence, the discontent of spirit, and even the feeling of a separate identity that must be exorcised to win or keep the love of husband and child.

In a story in *Redbook* ("A Man Who Acted Like a Husband," November, 1957) the child-bride heroine, "a little freckle-faced brunette" whose nickname is "Junior," is visited by her old college roommate. The roommate Kay is "a man's girl, really, with a good head for business ... she wore her polished mahogany hair in a high chignon, speared with two chopstick affairs." Kay is not only divorced, but she has also left her child with his grandmother while she works in television. This career-woman-devil tempts Junior with the lure of a job to keep her from breast-feeding her baby. She even restrains the young mother from going to her baby when he cries at 2 A.M. But she gets her comeuppance when George, the husband, discovers the crying baby uncovered, in a freezing wind from an open window, with blood running down its cheek. Kay, reformed and repentant, plays hookey from her job to go get her own child and start life anew. And Junior, gloating at the 2 A.M. feeding—"I'm glad, glad, glad I'm just a housewife"—starts to dream about the baby, growing up to be a housewife, too.

With the career woman out of the way, the housewife with interests in the community becomes the devil to be exorcised. Even PTA takes on a suspect connotation, not to mention interest in some international cause (see "Almost a Love Affair," *McCall's*, November, 1955). The housewife who simply has a mind of her own is the next to go. The heroine of "I Didn't Want to Tell You" (*McCall's*, January, 1958) is shown balancing the checkbook by herself and arguing with her husband about a small domestic detail. It develops that she is losing her husband to a "helpless little widow" whose main appeal is that she can't "think straight" about an insurance policy or mortgage. The betrayed wife says: "She must have sex appeal and what weapon has a wife against that?" But her best friend tells her: "You're making this too simple. You're forgetting how helpless Tania can be, and how grateful to the man who helps her ..."

"I couldn't be a clinging vine if I tried," the wife says. "I had a better than average job after I left college and I was always a pretty independent person. I'm not a helpless little woman and I can't pretend to be." But she learns, that night. She hears a noise that might be a burglar; even though she knows it's only a mouse, she calls helplessly to her husband, and wins him back. As he comforts her pretended panic, she murmurs that, of course, he was right in their argument that morning. "She lay still in the soft bed, smiling in sweet, secret satisfaction, scarcely touched with guilt."

The end of the road, in an almost literal sense, is the disappearance of the heroine altogether, as a separate self and the subject of her own story. The end of the road is togetherness, where the woman has no independent self to hide even in guilt; she exists only for and through her husband and children.

Coined by the publishers of *McCall's* in 1954, the concept "togetherness" was seized upon avidly as a movement of spiritual significance by advertisers, ministers, newspaper editors. For a time, it was elevated into virtually a national purpose. But very quickly there was sharp social criticism, and bitter jokes about "togetherness" as a substitute for larger human goals—for men. Women were taken to task for making their husbands do housework, instead of letting them pioneer in the nation and the world. Why, it was asked, should men with the capacities of statesmen, anthropologists, physicists, poets, have to wash dishes and diaper babies on weekday evenings or Saturday mornings when they might use those extra hours to fulfill larger commitments to their society?

Significantly, critics resented only that men were being asked to share "woman's world." Few questioned the boundaries of this world for women. No one seemed to remember that women were once thought to have the capacity and vision of statesmen, poets, and physicists. Few saw the big lie of togetherness for women.

Consider the Easter 1954 issue of *McCall's* which announced the new era of togetherness, sounding the requiem for the days when women fought for and won political equality, and the women's magazines "helped you to carve out large areas of living formerly forbidden to your sex." The new way of life in which "men and women in ever-increasing numbers are marrying at an earlier age, having children at an earlier age, rearing larger families and gaining their deepest satisfaction" from their own homes, is one which "men, women and children are achieving together ... not as women alone, or men alone, isolated from one another, but as a family, sharing a common experience."

The picture essay detailing that way of life is called "a man's place is in the home." It describes, as the new image and ideal, a New Jersey couple with three children in a gray-shingle split-level house. Ed and Carol have "centered their lives almost completely around their children and their home." They are shown shopping at the supermarket, carpentering, dressing the children, making breakfast together. "Then Ed joins the members of his car pool and heads for the office."

Ed, the husband, chooses the color scheme for the house and makes the major decorating decisions. The chores Ed likes are listed: putter around the house, make things, paint, select furniture, rugs and draperies, dry dishes, read to the children and put them to bed, work in the garden, feed and dress and bathe the children, attend PTA meetings, cook, buy clothes for his wife, buy groceries.

Ed doesn't like these chores: dusting, vacuuming, finishing jobs he's started, hanging draperies, washing pots and pans and dishes, picking up after the children, shoveling snow or mowing the lawn, changing diapers, taking the baby-sitter home, doing the laundry, ironing. Ed, of course, does not do these chores.

> For the sake of every member of the family, the family needs a head. This means Father, not Mother. … Children of both sexes need to learn, recognize and respect the abilities and functions of each sex. … He is not just a substitute mother, even though he's ready and willing to do his share of bathing, feeding, comforting, playing. He is a link with the outside world he works in. If in that world he is interested, courageous, tolerant, constructive, he will pass on these values to his children.

There were many agonized editorial sessions, in those days at *McCall's*. "Suddenly, everybody was looking for this spiritual significance in togetherness, expecting us to make some mysterious religious movement out of the life everyone had been leading for the last five years—crawling into the home, turning their backs on the world—but we never could find a way of showing it that wasn't a monstrosity of dullness," a former *McCall's* editor reminisces. "It always boiled down to, goody, goody, goody, Daddy is out there in the garden barbecuing. We put men in the fashion pictures and the food pictures, and even the perfume pictures. But we were stifled by it editorially.

"We had articles by psychiatrists that we couldn't use because they would have blown it wide open: all those couples propping their whole weight on their kids. But what else could you do with togetherness but child care? We were pathetically grateful to find anything else where we could show father photographed with mother. Sometimes, we used to wonder what would happen to women, with men taking over the decorating, child care, cooking, all the things that used to be hers alone. But we couldn't show women getting out of the home and having a career. The irony is, what we meant to do was to stop editing for women as women, and edit for the men and women together. We wanted to edit for people, not women."

But forbidden to join man in the world, can women be people? Forbidden independence, they finally are swallowed in an image of such passive dependence that they want men to make the decisions, even in the home. The frantic illusion that togetherness can impart a spiritual content to the dullness of domestic routine, the need for a religious movement to make up for the lack of identity, betrays the measure of women's loss and the emptiness of the image. Could making men share the housework compensate women for their loss of the world? Could vacuuming the living-room floor together give the housewife some mysterious new purpose in life?

In 1956, at the peak of togetherness, the bored editors of *McCall's* ran a little article called "The Mother Who Ran Away." To their amazement, it brought the highest readership of any article they had ever run. "It was our moment of truth," said a former editor. "We suddenly realized that all those women at home with their three and a half children were miserably unhappy."

But by then the new image of American woman, "Occupation: housewife," had hardened into a mystique, unquestioned and permitting no questions, shaping the very reality it distorted.

By the time I started writing for women's magazines, in the fifties, it was simply taken for granted by editors, and accepted as an immutable fact of life by writers, that women were not interested in politics, life outside the United States, national issues, art, science, ideas, adventure, education, or even their own communities, except where they could be sold through their emotions as wives and mothers.

Politics, for women, became Mamie's clothes and the Nixons' home life. Out of conscience, a sense of duty, the *Ladies' Home Journal* might run a series like "Political Pilgrim's Progress," showing women trying to improve their children's schools and playgrounds. But even approaching politics through mother love did not really interest women, it was thought in the trade. Everyone knew those readership percentages. An editor of *Redbook* ingeniously tried to bring the bomb down to the feminine level by showing the emotions of a wife whose husband sailed into a contaminated area.

"Women can't take an idea, an issue, pure," men who edited the mass women's magazines agreed. "It has to be translated in terms they can understand as women." This was so well understood by those who wrote for women's magazines that a natural childbirth expert submitted an article to a leading woman's magazine called "How to Have a Baby in an Atom Bomb Shelter." "The article was not well written," an editor told me, "or we might have bought it." According to the mystique, women, in their mysterious femininity, might be interested in the concrete biological details of having a baby in a bomb shelter, but never in the abstract idea of the bomb's power to destroy the human race.

Such a belief, of course, becomes a self-fulfilling prophecy. In 1960, a perceptive social psychologist showed me some sad statistics which seemed to prove unmistakably that American women under thirty-five are not interested in politics. "They may have the vote, but they don't dream about running for office," he told me. "If you write a political piece, they won't read it. You have to translate it into issues they can understand—romance, pregnancy, nursing, home furnishings, clothes. Run an article on the economy, or the race question, civil rights, and you'd think that women had never heard of them."

Maybe they hadn't heard of them. Ideas are not like instincts of the blood that spring into the mind intact. They are communicated by education, by the printed word. The new young housewives, who leave high school or college to marry, do not read books, the psychological surveys say. They only read magazines. Magazines today assume women are not interested in ideas. But going back to the bound volumes in the library, I found in the thirties and forties that the mass-circulation magazines like *Ladies' Home Journal* carried hundreds of articles about the world outside the home. "The first inside story of American diplomatic relations preceding declared war"; "Can the U. S. Have Peace After This War?" by Walter Lippman; "Stalin at Midnight," by Harold Stassen; "General Stilwell Reports on China"; articles about the last days of Czechoslovakia by Vincent Sheean; the persecution of Jews in Germany; the New Deal; Carl Sandburg's account of Lincoln's assassination; Faulkner's stories of Mississippi, and Margaret Sanger's battle for birth control.

In the 1950's they printed virtually no articles except those that serviced women as housewives, or described women as housewives, or permitted a purely feminine identification like the Duchess of Windsor or Princess Margaret. "If we get an article about a woman who does anything adventurous, out of the way, something by herself, you know, we figure she must be terribly aggressive, neurotic," a *Ladies' Home Journal* editor told me. Margaret Sanger would never get in today.

In 1960, I saw statistics that showed that women under thirty-five could not identify with a spirited heroine of a story who worked in an ad agency and persuaded the boy to stay and fight for his principles in the big city instead of running home to the security of a family business. Nor could these new young housewives identify with a young minister, acting on his belief in defiance of convention. But they had no trouble at all identifying with a young man paralyzed at eighteen. ("I regained consciousness to discover that I could not move or even speak. I could wiggle only one finger of one hand." With help from faith and a psychiatrist, "I am now finding reasons to live as fully as possible.")

Does it say something about the new housewife readers that, as any editor can testify, they can identify completely with the victims of blindness, deafness, physical maiming, cerebral palsy, paralysis, cancer, or approaching death? Such articles about people who cannot see or speak or move have been an enduring staple of the women's magazines in the era of "Occupation: housewife." They are told with infinitely realistic detail over and over again, replacing the articles about the nation, the world, ideas, issues, art and science; replacing the stories about adventurous spirited women. And whether the victim is man, woman or child, whether the living death is incurable cancer or creeping paralysis, the housewife reader can identify.

Writing for these magazines, I was continually reminded by editors "that women *have* to identify." Once I wanted to write an article about an artist. So I wrote about her cooking and marketing and falling in love with her husband, and painting a crib for her baby. I had to leave out the hours she spent painting pictures, her serious work—and the way she felt about it. You could sometimes get away with writing about a woman who was not really a housewife, if you made her *sound* like a housewife, if you left out her commitment to the world outside the home, or the private vision of mind or spirit that she pursued. In February, 1949, the *Ladies' Home Journal* ran a feature, "Poet's Kitchen," showing Edna St. Vincent Millay cooking. "Now I expect to hear no more about housework's being beneath anyone, for if one of the greatest poets of our day, and any day, can find beauty in simple household tasks, this is the end of the old controversy."

The one "career woman" who was always welcome in the pages of the women's magazines was the actress. But her image also underwent a remarkable change: from a complex individual of fiery temper, inner depth, and a mysterious blend of spirit and sexuality, to a sexual object, a babyface bride, or a housewife. Think of Greta Garbo, for instance, and Marlene Dietrich, Bette Davis, Rosalind Russell, Katherine Hepburn. Then think of Marilyn Monroe, Debbie Reynolds, Brigitte Bardot, and "I Love Lucy."

When you wrote about an actress for a women's magazine, you wrote about her as a housewife. You never showed her doing or enjoying her work as an actress, unless she eventually paid for it by losing her husband or her child, or otherwise admitting failure as a woman. A *Redbook* profile of Judy Holliday (June, 1957) described how "a brilliant woman begins to find in her work the joy she never found in life." On the screen, we are told, she plays "with warmth and conviction the part of a mature, intelligent wife and expectant mother, a role unlike anything she had previously attempted." She must find fulfillment in her career because she is divorced from her husband, has "strong feelings of inadequacy as a woman. ... It is a frustrating irony of Judy's life, that as an actress she has succeeded almost without trying, although, as a woman, she has failed ..."

Strangely enough, as the feminine mystique spread, denying women careers or any commitment outside the home, the proportion of American women working outside the home increased to one out of three. True, two out of three were still housewives, but why, at the moment when the doors of the world were finally open to all women, should the mystique deny the very dreams that had stirred women for a century?

I found a clue one morning, sitting in the office of a women's magazine editor—a woman who, older than I, remembers the days when the old image was being created, and who had watched it being displaced. The old image of the spirited career girl was largely created by writers and editors who were women, she told me. The new image of woman as housewife-mother has been largely created by writers and editors who are men.

"Most of the material used to come from women writers," she said, almost nostalgically. "As the young men returned from the war, a great many women writers dropped out of the field. The young women started having a lot of children, and stopped writing. The new writers were all men, back, from the war, who had been dreaming about home, and a cozy domestic life." One by one, the creators of the gay "career girl" heroines of the thirties began to retire. By the end of the forties, the writers who couldn't get the knack of writing in the new housewife image had left the women's magazine field. The new magazine pros were men, and a few women who could write comfortably according to the housewife formula. Other people began to assemble backstage at the women's magazines: there was a new kind of woman writer who lived in the housewife image, or pretended to; and there was a new kind of woman's editor or publisher, less interested in ideas to reach women's minds and hearts, than in selling them the things that interest advertisers—appliances, detergents, lipstick. Today, the deciding voice on most of these magazines is cast by men. Women often carry out the formulas, women edit the housewife "service" departments, but the formulas themselves, which have dictated the new housewife image, are the product of men's minds.

Also during the forties and fifties, serious fiction writers of either sex disappeared from the mass-circulation women's magazines. In fact, fiction of any quality was almost completely replaced by a different kind of article. No longer the old article about issues or ideas, but the new "service" feature. Sometimes these articles lavished the artistry of a poet and the honesty of a crusading reporter on baking chiffon pies, or buying washing machines, or the miracles paint can do for a living room, or diets, drugs, clothes, and cosmetics to make the body into a vision of physical beauty. Sometimes they dealt with very sophisticated ideas: new developments in psychiatry, child psychology, sex and marriage, medicine. It was assumed that women readers could take these ideas, which appealed to their needs as wives and mothers, but only if they were boiled down to concrete physical details, spelled out in terms of the daily life of an average housewife with concrete do's and don'ts. How to keep your husband happy; how to solve your child's bedwetting; how to keep death out of your medicine cabinet ...

But here is a curious thing. Within their narrow range, these women's magazine articles, whether straight service to the housewife or a documentary report about the housewife, were almost always superior in quality to women's magazine fiction. They were better written, more honest, more sophisticated. This observation was made over and over again by intelligent readers and puzzled editors, and by writers themselves. "The serious fiction writers have become too internal. They're inaccessible to our readers, so we're left with the formula writers," an editor of *Redbook* said. And yet, in the old days, serious writers like Nancy Hale, even William Faulkner, wrote for the women's magazines and were not considered inaccessible. Perhaps the new image of woman did not permit the internal honesty, the depth of perception, and the human truth essential to good fiction.

At the very least, fiction requires a hero or, understandably for women's magazines, a heroine, who is an "I" in pursuit of some human goal or dream. There is a limit to the number of stories that can be written about a girl in pursuit of a boy, or a housewife in pursuit of a ball of dust under the sofa. Thus the service article takes over, replacing the internal honesty and truth needed in fiction with a richness of honest, objective, concrete, realistic domestic detail—the color of walls or lipstick, the exact temperature of the oven.

Judging from the women's magazines today, it would seem that the concrete details of women's lives are more interesting than their thoughts, their ideas, their dreams. Or does the richness and realism of the detail, the careful description of small events, mask the lack of dreams, the vacuum of ideas, the terrible boredom that has settled over the American housewife?

I sat in the office of another old-timer, one of the few women editors left in the women's magazine world, now so largely dominated by men. She explained her share in creating the feminine mystique. "Many of us were psychoanalyzed," she recalled. "And we began to feel embarrassed about being career women ourselves. There was this terrible fear that we were losing our femininity. We kept looking for ways to help women accept their feminine role."

If the real women editors were not, somehow, able to give up their own careers, all the more reason to "help" other women fulfill themselves as wives and mothers. The few women who still sit in editorial conferences do not bow to the feminine mystique in their own lives. But such is the power of the image they have helped create that many of them feel guilty. And if they have missed out somewhere on love or children, they wonder if their careers were to blame.

Behind her cluttered desk, a *Mademoiselle* editor said uneasily, "The girls we bring in now as college guest editors seem almost to pity us. Because we are career women, I suppose. At a luncheon session with the last bunch, we asked them to go round the table, telling us their own career plans. Not one of the twenty raised her hand. When I remember how I worked to learn this job and loved it—were we all crazy then?"

Coupled with the women editors who sold themselves their own bill of goods, a new breed of women writers began to write about themselves as if they were "just housewives," reveling in a comic world of children's pranks and eccentric washing machines and Parents' Night at the PTA. "After making the bed of a twelve-year-old boy week after week, climbing Mount Everest would seem a laughable anticlimax," writes Shirley Jackson (*McCall's*, April, 1956). When Shirley Jackson, who all her adult life has been an extremely capable writer, pursuing a craft far more demanding than bedmaking, and Jean Kerr, who is a playwright, and Phyllis McGinley, who is a poet, picture themselves as housewives, they may or may not overlook the housekeeper or maid who really makes the beds. But they implicitly deny the vision, and the satisfying hard work involved in their stories, poems, and plays. They deny the lives they lead, not as housewives, but as individuals.

They are good craftsmen, the best of these Housewife Writers. And some of their work is funny. The things that happen with children, a twelve-year-old boy's first cigarette, the Little League and the kindergarten rhythm band are often funny; they happen in real life to women who are writers as well as women who are just housewives. But there is something about Housewife Writers that isn't funny—like Uncle Tom, or Amos and Andy. "Laugh," the Housewife Writers tell the real housewife, "if you are feeling desperate, empty, bored, trapped in the bedmaking, chauffeuring and dishwashing details. Isn't it funny? We're all in the same trap." Do real housewives then dissipate in laughter their dreams and their sense of desperation? Do they think their frustrated abilities and their limited lives are a joke? Shirley Jackson makes the beds, loves and laughs at her son—and writes another book. Jean Kerr's plays are produced on Broadway. The joke is not on *them*.

Some of the new Housewife Writers *live* the image; *Redbook* tells us that the author of an article on "Breast-Feeding," a woman named Betty Ann Countrywoman, "had planned to be a doctor. But just before her graduation from Radcliffe *cum laude,* she shrank from the thought that such a dedication might shut her off from what she really wanted, which was to marry and have a large family. She enrolled in the Yale University School of Nursing and then became engaged to a young psychiatrist on their first date. Now they have six children, ranging in age from 2 to 13, and Mrs. Countrywoman is instructor in breast-feeding at the Maternity League of Indianapolis" (*Redbook*, June, 1960). She says:

> For the mother, breast-feeding becomes a complement to the act of creation. It gives her a heightened sense of fulfillment and allows her to participate in a relationship as close to perfection as any that a woman can hope to achieve. ... The simple fact of giving birth, however, does not of itself fulfill this need and longing. ... Motherliness is a way of life. It enables a woman to express her total self with the tender feelings, the protective attitudes, the encompassing love of the motherly woman.

When motherhood, a fulfillment held sacred down the ages, is defined as a total way of life, must women themselves deny the world and the future open to them? Or does the denial of that world *force* them to make motherhood a total way of life? The line between mystique and reality dissolves; real women embody the split in the image. In the spectacular Christmas 1956 issue of *Life*, devoted in full to the "new" American woman, we see, not as women's-magazine villain, but as documentary fact, the typical "career woman—that fatal error that feminism propagated"—seeking "help" from a pyschiatrist. She is bright, well-educated, ambitious, attractive; she makes about the same money as her husband; but she is pictured here as "frustrated," so "masculinized" by her career that her castrated, impotent, passive husband is indifferent to her sexually. He refuses to take responsibility and drowns his destroyed masculinity in alcoholism.

Then there is the discontented suburban wife who raises hell at the PTA; morbidly depressed, she destroys her children and dominates her husband whom she envies for going out into the business world. "The wife, having worked before marriage, or at least having been educated for some kind of intellectual work, finds herself in the lamentable position of being 'just a housewife.' ... In her disgruntlement she can work as much damage on the lives of her husband and children (and her own life) as if she were a career woman, and indeed, sometimes more."

And finally, in bright and smiling contrast, are the new housewife-mothers, who cherish their "differentness," their "unique femininity," the "receptivity and passivity implicit in their sexual nature." Devoted to their own beauty and their ability to bear and nurture children, they are "feminine women, with truly feminine attitudes, admired by men for their miraculous, God-given, sensationally unique ability to wear skirts, with all the implications of that fact." Rejoicing in "the reappearance of the old-fashioned three-to-five-child family in an astonishing quarter, the upper- and upper-middle class suburbs," *Life* says:

> Here, among women who might be best qualified for "careers," there is an increasing emphasis on the nurturing and homemaking values. One might guess ... that because these women are better informed and more mature than the average, they

have been the first to comprehend the penalties of "feminism" and to react against them. ... Styles in ideas as well as in dress and decoration tend to seep down from such places to the broader population. ... This is the countertrend which may eventually demolish the dominant and disruptive trend and make marriage what it should be: a true partnership in which ... men are men, women are women, and both are quietly, pleasantly, securely confident of which they are—and absolutely delighted to find themselves married to someone of the opposite sex.

Look glowed at about the same time (October 16, 1956):

> The American woman is winning the battle of the sexes. Like a teenager, she is growing up and confounding her critics. ... No longer a psychological immigrant to man's world, she works, rather casually, as a third of the U. S. labor force, less towards a "big career" than as a way of filling a hope chest or buying a new home freezer. She gracefully concedes the top jobs to men. This wondrous creature also marries younger than ever, bears more babies and looks and acts far more feminine than the "emancipated" girl of the 1920's or even '30's. Steelworker's wife and Junior Leaguer alike do their own housework. ... Today, if she makes an old-fashioned choice and lovingly tends a garden and a bumper crop of children, she rates louder hosannas than ever before.

In the new America, fact is more important than fiction. The documentary *Life* and *Look* images of real women who devote their lives to children and home are played back as the ideal, the way women should be: this is powerful stuff, not to be shrugged off like the heroines of women's magazine fiction. When a mystique is strong, it makes its own fiction of fact. It feeds on the very facts which might contradict it, and seeps into every corner of the culture, bemusing even the social critics.

Adlai Stevenson, in a commencement address at Smith College in 1955, reprinted in *Woman's Home Companion* (September, 1955), dismissed the desire of educated women to play their own political part in "the crises of the age." Modern woman's participation in politics is through her role as wife and mother, said the spokesman of democratic liberalism: "Women, especially educated women, have a unique opportunity to influence us, man and boy." The only problem is woman's failure to appreciate that her true part in the political crisis is as wife and mother.

> Once immersed in the very pressing and particular problems of domesticity, many women feel frustrated and far apart from the great issues and stirring debate for which their education has given them understanding and relish. Once they wrote poetry. Now it's the laundry list. Once they discussed art and philosophy until late in the night. Now they are so tired they fall asleep as

soon as the dishes are finished. There is, often, a sense of contraction, of closing horizons and lost opportunities. They had hoped to play their part in the crises of the age. But what they do is wash the diapers.

The point is that whether we talk of Africa, Islam or Asia, women "never had it so good" as you. In short, far from the vocation of marriage and mother-hood leading you away from the great issues of our day, it brings you back to their very center and places upon you an infinitely deeper and more intimate responsibility than that borne by the majority of those who hit the headlines and make the news and live in such a turmoil of great issues that they end by being totally unable to distinguish which issues are really great.

Woman's political job is to "inspire in her home a vision of the meaning of life and freedom ... to help her husband find values that will give purpose to his specialized daily chores ... to teach her children the uniqueness of each individual human being."

This assignment for you, as wives and mothers, you can do in the living room with a baby in your lap or in the kitchen with a can opener in your hand. If you're clever, maybe you can even practice your saving arts on that unsuspecting man while he's watching television. I think there is much you can do about our crisis in the humble role of housewife. I could wish you no better vocation than that.

Thus the logic of the feminine mystique redefined the very nature of woman's problem. When woman was seen as a human being of limitless human potential, equal to man, any-thing that kept her from realizing her full potential was a problem to be solved: barriers to higher education and political participation, discrimination or prejudice in law or morality. But now that woman is seen only in terms of her sexual role, the barriers to the realization of her full potential, the prejudices which deny her full participation in the world, are no longer problems. The only problems now are those that might disturb her adjustment as a housewife. So career is a problem, education is a problem, political interest, even the very admission of women's intelligence and individuality is a problem. And finally there is the problem that has no name, a vague undefined wish for "something more" than washing dishes, ironing, punishing and praising the children. In the women's magazines, it is solved either by dyeing one's hair blonde or by having another baby. "Remember, when we were all children, how we all planned to 'be something'?" says a young housewife in the *Ladies' Home Journal* (February, 1960). Boasting that she has worn out six copies of Dr. Spock's baby-care book in seven years, she cries, "I'm lucky! Lucky! I'M SO GLAD TO BE A WOMAN!"

In one of these stories ("Holiday," *Mademoiselle*, August, 1949) a desperate young wife is ordered by her doctor to get out of the house one day a week. She goes shopping, tries on dresses, looks in the mirror wondering which one her husband, Sam, will like.

Always Sam, like a Greek chorus in the back of her head. As if she herself hadn't a definiteness of her own, a clarity that was indisputably hers. … Suddenly she couldn't make the difference between pleated and gored skirts of sufficient importance to fix her decision. She looked at herself in the full-length glass, tall, getting thicker around the hips, the lines of her face beginning to slip. She was twenty-nine, but she felt middle-aged, as if a great many years had passed and there wasn't very much yet to come … which was ridiculous, for Ellen was only three. There was her whole future to plan for, and perhaps another child. It was not a thing to be put off too long.

When the young housewife in "The Man Next to Me" (*Redbook*, November, 1948) discovers that her elaborate dinner party didn't help her husband get a raise after all, she is in despair. ("You should say I helped. You should say I'm good for something … Life was like a puzzle with a piece missing, and the piece was me, and I couldn't figure my place in it at all.") So she dyes her hair blonde, and when her husband reacts satisfactorily in bed to the new "blonde me," she "felt a new sense of peace, as if I'd answered the question within myself."

Over and over again, stories in women's magazines insist that woman can know fulfillment only at the moment of giving birth to a child. They deny the years when she can no longer look forward to giving birth, even if she repeats that act over and over again. In the feminine mystique, there is no other way for a woman to dream of creation or of the future. There is no way she can even dream about herself, except as her children's mother, her husband's wife. And the documentary articles play back new young housewives, grown up under the mystique, who do not have even that "question within myself." Says one, described in "How America Lives" (*Ladies' Home Journal*, June, 1959): "If he doesn't want me to wear a certain color or a certain kind of dress, then I truly don't want to, either. The thing is, whatever he has wanted is what I also want. … I don't believe in fifty-fifty marriages." Giving up college and job to marry at eighteen, with no regrets, she "never tried to enter into the discussion when the men were talking. She never disputed her husband in anything. … She spent a great deal of time looking out the window at the snow, the rain, and the gradual emergence of the first crocuses. One great time-passer and consolation was … embroidery: tiny stitches in gold-metal or silken thread which require infinite concentration."

There is no problem, in the logic of the feminine mystique, for such a woman who has no wishes of her own, who defines herself only as wife and mother. The problem, if there is one, can only be her children's, or her husband's. It is the husband who complains to the marriage counselor (*Redbook*, June, 1955): "The way I see it, marriage takes two people, each living his own life and then putting them together. Mary seems to think we both ought to live one life: mine." Mary insists on going with him to buy shirts and socks, tells the clerk his size and color. When he comes home at night, she asks with whom he ate lunch, where, what did he talk about? When he protests, she says, "But darling, I want to share your life, be part of all you do, that's all. … I want us to be one, the way it says in the marriage service …" It doesn't seem reasonable to the husband that "two people can ever be one the way Mary means it. It's just plain ridiculous on the face of it. Besides, I wouldn't like it. I don't want to be so bound to another person that I can't have a thought or an action that's strictly my own."

The answer to "Pete's problem," says Dr. Emily Mudd, the famous marriage counsellor, is to make Mary *feel* she is living his life: invite her to town to lunch with the people in his office once in a while, order his favorite veal dish for her and maybe find her some "healthy physical activity," like swimming, to drain off her excess energy. It is not Mary's problem that she has no life of her own.

The ultimate, in housewife happiness, is finally achieved by the Texas housewife, described in "How America Lives" (*Ladies' Home Journal,* October, 1960), who "sits on a pale aqua satin sofa gazing out her picture window at the street. Even at this hour of the morning (it is barely nine-o'clock), she is wearing rouge, powder and lipstick, and her cotton dress is immaculately fresh." She says proudly: "By 8:30 A.M., when my youngest goes to school, my whole house is clean and neat and I am dressed for the day. I am free to play bridge, attend club meetings, or stay home and read, listen to Beethoven, and just plain loaf.

"Sometimes, she washes and dries her hair before sitting down at a bridge table at 1:30. Mornings she is having bridge at her house are the busiest, for then she must get out the tables, cards, tallies, prepare fresh coffee and organize lunch. ... During the winter months, she may play as often as four days a week from 9:30 to 3 P.M. ... Janice is careful to be home, before her sons return from school at 4 P.M."

She is not frustrated, this new young housewife. An honor student at high school, married at eighteen, remarried and pregnant at twenty, she has the house she spent seven years dreaming and planning in detail. She is proud of her efficiency as a housewife, getting it all done by 8:30. She does the major housecleaning on Saturday, when her husband fishes and her sons are busy with Boy Scouts. ("There's nothing else to do. No bridge games. It's a long day for me.")

"'I love my home,' she says. ... The pale gray paint in her L-shaped living and dining room is five years old, but still in perfect condition. ... The pale peach and yellow and aqua damask upholstery looks spotless after eight years' wear. 'Sometimes, I feel I'm too passive, too content,' remarks Janice, fondly, regarding the wristband of large family diamonds she wears even when the watch itself is being repaired. ... Her favorite possession is her four-poster spool bed with a pink taffeta canopy. 'I feel just like Queen Elizabeth sleeping in that bed,' she says happily. (Her husband sleeps in another room, since he snores.)

"'I'm so grateful for my blessings,' she says. 'Wonderful husband, handsome sons with dispositions to match, big comfortable house. ... I'm thankful for my good health and faith in God and such material possessions as two cars, two TV's and two fireplaces.'"

Staring uneasily at this image, I wonder if a few problems are not somehow better than this smiling empty passivity. If they are happy, these young women who live the feminine mystique, then is this the end of the road? Or are the seeds of something worse than frustration inherent in this image? Is there a growing divergence between this image of woman and human reality?

Consider, as a symptom, the increasing emphasis on glamour in the women's magazines: the housewife wearing eye makeup as she vacuums the floor—"The Honor of Being a Woman." Why does "Occupation: housewife" require such insistent glamorizing year after year? The strained glamour is in itself a question mark: the lady doth protest too much.

The image of woman in another era required increasing prudishness to keep denying sex. This new image seems to require increasing mindlessness, increasing emphasis on things: two cars, two TV's, two fireplaces. Whole pages of women's magazines are filled with gargantuan vegetables: beets, cucumbers, green peppers, potatoes, described like a love affair. The very size of their print is raised until it looks like a first-grade primer. The new *McCall's* frankly assumes women are brainless, fluffy kittens, the *Ladies' Home Journal,* feverishly competing, procures rock-and-roller Pat Boone as a counselor to teenagers; *Redbook* and the others enlarge their own type size. Does the size of the print mean that the new young women, whom all the magazines are courting, have only first-grade minds? Or does it try to hide the triviality of the content? Within the confines of what is now accepted as woman's world, an editor may no longer be able to think of anything big to do except blow up a baked potato, or describe a kitchen as if it were the Hall of Mirrors; he is, after all, forbidden by the mystique to deal with a big idea. But does it not occur to any of the men who run the women's magazines that their troubles may stem from the smallness of the image with which they are truncating women's minds?

They are all in trouble today, the mass-circulation magazines, vying fiercely with each other and television to deliver more and more millions of women who will buy the things their advertisers sell. Does this frantic race force the men who make the images to see women only as thing-buyers? Does it force them to compete finally in emptying women's minds of human thought? The fact is, the troubles of the image-makers seem to be increasing in direct proportion to the increasing mindlessness of their image. During the years in which that image has narrowed woman's world down to the home, cut her role back to housewife, five of the mass-circulation magazines geared to women have ceased publication; others are on the brink.

The growing boredom of women with the empty, narrow image of the women's magazines may be the most hopeful sign of the image's divorce from reality. But there are more violent symptoms on the part of women who are committed to that image. In 1960, the editors of a magazine specifically geared to the happy young housewife—or rather to the new young couples (the wives are not considered separate from their husbands and children)—ran an article asking, "Why Young Mothers Feel Trapped" (*Redbook,* September, 1960). As a promotion stunt, they invited young mothers with such a problem to write in the details, for $500. The editors were shocked to receive 24,000 replies. Can an image of woman be cut down to the point where it becomes itself a trap?

At one of the major women's magazines, a woman editor, sensing that American house-wives might be desperately in need of something to enlarge their world, tried for some months to convince her male colleagues to introduce a few ideas outside the home into the magazine. "We decided against it," the man who makes the final decisions said. "Women are so completely divorced from the world of ideas in their lives now, they couldn't take it." Perhaps it is irrelevant to ask, who divorced them? Perhaps these Frankensteins no longer have the power to stop the feminine monster they have created.

I helped create this image. I have watched American women for fifteen years try to conform to it. But I can no longer deny my own knowledge of its terrible implications. It is not a harmless image. There may be no psychological terms for the harm it is doing. But what happens when women try to live according to an image that makes them deny their minds? What happens when women grow up in an image that makes them deny the reality of the changing world?

The material details of life, the daily burden of cooking and cleaning, of taking care of the physical needs of husband and children—these did indeed define a woman's world a century ago when Americans were pioneers, and the American frontier lay in conquering the land. But the women who went west with the wagon trains also shared the pioneering purpose. Now the American frontiers are of the mind, and of the spirit. Love and children and home are good, but they are not the whole world, even if most of the words now written for women pretend they are. Why should women accept this picture of a half-life, instead of a share in the whole of human destiny? Why should women try to make housework "something more," instead of moving on the frontiers of their own time, as American women moved beside their husbands on the old frontiers?

A baked potato is not as big as the world, and vacuuming the living room floor—with or without makeup—is not work that takes enough thought or energy to challenge any woman's full capacity. Women are human beings, not stuffed dolls, not animals. Down through the ages man has known that he was set apart from other animals by his mind's power to have an idea, a vision, and shape the future to it. He shares a need for food and sex with other animals, but when he loves, he loves as a man, and when he discovers and creates and shapes a future different from his past, he is a man, a human being.

This is the real mystery: why did so many American women, with the ability and education to discover and create, go back home again, to look for "something more" in housework and rearing children? For, paradoxically, in the same fifteen years in which the spirited New Woman was replaced by the Happy Housewife, the boundaries of the human world have widened, the pace of world change has quickened, and the very nature of human reality has become increasingly free from biological and material necessity. Does the mystique keep American woman from growing with the world? Does it force her to deny reality, as a woman in a mental hospital must deny reality to believe she is a queen? Does it doom women to be displaced persons, if not virtual schizophrenics, in our complex, changing world?

It is more than a strange paradox that as all professions are finally open to women in America, "career woman" has become a dirty word; that as higher education becomes available to any woman with the capacity for it, education for women has become so suspect that more and more drop out of high school and college to marry and have babies; that as so many roles in modern society become theirs for the taking, women so insistently confine themselves to one role. Why, with the removal of all the legal, political, economic, and educational barriers that once kept woman from being man's equal, a person in her own right, an individual free to develop her own potential, should she accept this new image which insists she is not a person but a "woman," by definition barred from the freedom of human existence and a voice in human destiny?

The feminine mystique is so powerful that women grow up no longer knowing that they have the desires and capacities the mystique forbids. But such a mystique does not fasten itself on a whole nation in a few short years, reversing the trends of a century, without cause. What gives the mystique its power? Why did women go home again?

NOTES

1. Betty Friedan, "Women Are People Too!" *Good Housekeeping*, September, 1960. The letters received from women all over the United States in response to this article were of such emotional intensity that I was convinced that "the problem that has no name" is by no means confined to the graduates of the women's Ivy League colleges.

2. In the 1960's, an occasional heroine who was not a "happy housewife" began to appear in the women's magazines. An editor of *McCall's* explained it: "Sometimes we run an offbeat story for pure entertainment value." One such novelette, which was written to order by Noel Clad for *Good Housekeeping* (January, 1960), is called "Men Against Women." The heroine—a happy career woman—nearly loses child as well as husband.

DISCUSSION QUESTIONS

- Can you define the "feminine mystique"?
- According to women's magazines, what is the ideal woman like?
- Do you find these kinds of media problematic?

EXAMPLES TO THINK ABOUT

- Women's magazines
- Mommy blogs and Instagram accounts

Ways of Seeing

SELECTIONS

By JOHN BERGER

RECLINING BACCHANTE BY TRUTAT 1824–1848

According to usage and conventions which are at last being questioned but have by no means been overcome, the social presence of a woman is different in kind from that of a man. A man's presence is dependent upon the promise of power which he embodies. If the promise is large and credible his presence is striking. If it is small or incredible, he is found to have little presence. The promised power may be moral, physical, temperamental, economic, social, sexual—but its object is always exterior to the man. A man's presence suggests what he is capable of doing to you or for you. His presence may be fabricated, in the sense that he pretends to be capable of what he is not. But the pretence is always towards a power which he exercises on others.

By contrast, a woman's presence expresses her own attitude to herself, and defines what can and cannot be done to her. Her presence is manifest in her gestures, voice, opinions, expressions, clothes, chosen surroundings, taste—indeed there is nothing she can do which does not contribute to her presence. Presence for a woman is so intrinsic to her person that men tend to think of it as an almost physical emanation, a kind of heat or smell or aura.

To be born a woman has been to be born, within an allotted and confined space, into the keeping of men. The social presence of women has developed as a result of their ingenuity in living under such tutelage within such a limited space. But this has been at the cost of a woman's self being split into two. A woman must continually watch herself. She is almost continually accompanied by her own image of herself. Whilst she is walking across a room or whilst she is weeping at the death of her father, she can scarcely avoid envisaging herself walking or weeping. From earliest childhood she has been taught and persuaded to survey herself continually.

And so she comes to consider the *surveyor* and the *surveyed* within her as the two constituent yet always distinct elements of her identity as a woman.

She has to survey everything she is and everything she does because how she appears to others, and ultimately how she appears to men, is of crucial importance for what is normally thought of as the success of her life. Her own sense of being in herself is supplanted by a sense of being appreciated as herself by another.

Men survey women before treating them. Consequently how a woman appears to a man can determine how she will be treated. To acquire some control over this process, women must contain it and interiorize it. That part of a woman's self which is the surveyor treats the part which is the surveyed so as to demonstrate to others how her whole self would like to be treated. And this exemplary treatment of herself by herself constitutes her presence. Every woman's presence regulates what is and is not 'permissible' within her presence. Every one of her actions— whatever its direct purpose or motivation—is also read as an indication of how she would like to be treated. If a woman throws a glass on the floor, this is an example of how she treats her own emotion of anger and so of how she would wish it to be treated by others. If a man does the same, his action is only read as an expression of his anger. If a woman makes a good joke this is an example of how she treats the joker in herself and accordingly of how she as a joker-woman would like to be treated by others. Only a man can make a good joke for its own sake.

One might simplify this by saying: *men act* and *women appear*. Men look at women. Women watch themselves being looked at. This determines not only most relations between men and women but also the relation of women to themselves. The surveyor of woman in herself is male: the surveyed female. Thus she turns herself into an object—and most particularly an object of vision: a sight.

DISCUSSION QUESTIONS

- What is objectification?
- How does objectification affect the way women behave?
- Can men be objectified? If so, does it have the same implications?

EXAMPLES TO THINK ABOUT

- Bathing suit or going out photos on social media
- Perfume and cosmetics advertisements
- Men's underwear ads (especially Calvin Klein)

Addressing the Body

EXCERPTS FROM: *THE FASHIONED BODY: FASHION, DRESS AND MODERN SOCIAL THEORY*

By JOANNE ENTWISTLE

DRESS AND THE BODY

'There is an obvious and prominent fact about human beings', notes Turner (1985: 1) at the start of *The Body and Society*, 'they have bodies and they are bodies'. In other words, the body constitutes the environment of the self, to be inseparable from the self. However, what Turner omits in his analysis is another obvious and prominent fact: that human bodies are *dressed* bodies. The social world is a world of dressed bodies. Nakedness is wholly inappropriate in almost all social situations and, even in situations where much naked flesh is exposed (on the beach, at the swimming-pool, even in the bedroom), the bodies that meet there are likely to be adorned, if only by jewellery, or indeed, even perfume: when asked what she wore to bed, Marilyn Monroe claimed that she wore only Chanel No. 5, illustrating how the body, even without garments, can still be adorned or embellished in some way. Dress is a basic fact of social life and this, according to anthropologists, is true of all known human cultures: all people 'dress' the body in some way, be it through clothing, tattooing, cosmetics or other forms of body painting. To put it another way, no culture leaves the body unadorned but adds to, embellishes, enhances or decorates the body. In almost all social situations we are required to appear dressed, although what constitutes 'dress' varies from culture to culture and also within a culture, since what is considered appropriate dress will depend on the situation or occasion. A bathing-suit, for example, would be inappropriate and shocking if worn to do the shopping, while swimming in one's coat and shoes would be absurd for the purpose of swimming, but perhaps apt as a fund-raising stunt. The cultural significance of dress extends to all situations, even those in which we can go naked: there are strict rules and codes governing when and with whom we can appear undressed. While bodies may go undressed in certain spaces, particularly in the private sphere of the home, the public arena almost always requires that a body be dressed appropriately, to the extent that the flaunting of flesh, or the inadvertent exposure of it in public, is disturbing, disruptive and potentially subversive. Bodies which do not conform, bodies which flout the conventions of their culture and go without the appropriate clothes are subversive of the most basic social codes and risk exclusion, scorn or ridicule. The 'streaker' who strips off and runs across a cricket pitch or soccer stadium draws attention to these conventions in the act of breaking them: indeed, female streaking is defined as a 'public order offence' while the 'flasher', by comparison, can be punished for 'indecent exposure' (Young, 1995: 7).

The ubiquitous nature of dress would seem to point to the fact that dress or adornment is one of the means by which bodies are made social and given meaning and identity. The individual and very personal act of getting dressed is an act of preparing the body for the social world, making it appropriate, acceptable, indeed respectable and possibly even desirable also. Getting dressed is an ongoing practice, requiring knowledge, techniques and skills, from learning how to tie our shoelaces and do up our buttons as children, to understanding about colours, textures and fabrics and how to weave them together to suit our bodies and our lives. Dress is the way in which individuals learn to live in their bodies and feel at home in them. Wearing the right clothes and looking our best, we feel at ease with our bodies, and the opposite is equally true: turning up for a situation inappropriately dressed, we feel awkward, out of place and vulnerable. In this respect, dress is both an intimate experience of the body and a public presentation of it. Operating on the boundary between self and other is the interface between the individual and the social world, the meeting place of the private and the public. This meeting between the intimate experience of the body and the public realm, through the experience of fashion and dress, is the subject of this chapter.

So potent is the naked body that when it is allowed to be seen, as in the case of art, it is governed by social conventions. Berger (1972) argues that within art and media representations there is a distinction between naked and nude, the latter referring to the way in which bodies, even without garments, are 'dressed' by social conventions and systems of representation. Perniola (1990) has also considered the way in which different cultures, in particular the classical Greek and Judaic, articulate and represent nakedness. According to Ann Hollander (1993) dress is crucial to our understanding of the body to the extent that our ways of seeing and representing the naked body are dominated by conventions of dress. As she argues, 'art proves that nakedness is not universally experienced and perceived any more than clothes are. At any time, the unadorned self has more kinship with its own usual *dressed* aspect than it has with any undressed human selves in other times and other places' (1993: xiii). Hollander points to the ways in which depictions of the nude in art and sculpture correspond to the dominant fashions of the day. Thus the nude is never naked but 'clothed' by contemporary conventions of dress.

Naked or semi-naked bodies that break with cultural conventions, especially conventions of gender, are potentially subversive and treated with horror or derision. Competitive female body builders, such as those documented in the semi-documentary film *Pumping Iron II: The Women* (1984), are frequently seen as 'monstrous', as their muscles challenge deeply held cultural assumptions and beg the questions: 'What is a woman's body? Is there a point at which a woman's body becomes something else? What is the relationship between a certain type of body and "femininity"?' (Kuhn 1988: 16; see also Schulze 1990, St. Martin and Gavey 1996). In body building, muscles are like clothes, but unlike clothes they are supposedly 'natural'. However, according to Annette Kuhn,

> 'Muscles are rather like drag, for female body builders especially: while muscles can be assumed, like clothing, women's assumption of muscles implies a transgression of the proper boundaries of sexual difference'. (1988: 17)

It is apparent from these illustrations that bodies are potentially disruptive. Conventions of dress attempt to transform flesh into something recognizable and meaningful to a culture; a body that does not conform, that transgresses such cultural codes, is likely to cause offence and outrage and be met with scorn or incredulity. This is one of the reasons why dress is a matter of morality: dressed inappropriately we are uncomfortable; we feel ourselves open to social condemnation. According to Bell (1976), wearing the right clothes is so very important that even people not interested in their appearance will dress well enough to avoid social censure. In this sense, he argues, we enter into the realm of feelings 'prudential, ethical and aesthetic, and the workings of what one might call sartorial conscience' (1976: 18–19). He gives the example of a five-day-old beard which could not be worn to the theatre without censure and disapproval 'exactly comparable to that occasioned by dishonourable conduct'. Indeed, clothes are often spoken of in moral terms, using words like 'faultless', 'good', 'correct' (1976: 19). Few are immune to this social pressure and most people are embarrassed by certain mistakes of dress, such as finding one's flies undone or discovering a stain on a jacket. Thus, as Quentin Bell puts it, 'our clothes are too much a part of us for most of us to be entirely indifferent to their condition: it is as though the fabric were indeed a natural extension of the body, or even of the soul' (1976: 19).

This basic fact of the body—that it must, in general, appear appropriately dressed—points to an important aspect of dress, namely its relation to social order, albeit micro-social order. This centrality of dress to social order would seem to make it a prime topic of sociological investigation. However, the classical tradition within sociology failed to acknowledge the significance of dress, largely because it neglected the body and the things that bodies do. More recently, sociology has begun to acknowledge dress, but this literature is still on the margins and is relatively small compared with other sociological areas. A sociology of the body has now emerged which would seem germane to a literature on dress and fashion. However, this literature, as with mainstream sociology, has also tended not to examine dress. While sociology has failed to acknowledge the significance of dress, the literature from history, cultural studies, psychology and so on, where it is often examined, does so almost entirely without acknowledging the significance of the body. Studies of fashion and dress tend to separate dress from the body: art history celebrates the garment as an object, analysing the development of clothing over history and considering the construction and detail of dress (Gorsline 1991, Laver 1969); cultural studies tend to understand dress semiotically, as a 'sign system' (Hebdige 1979, Wright 1992); or to analyse texts and not bodies (Barthes 1985, Brooks 1992 Nixon 1992, Triggs 1992); social psychology looks at the meanings and intentions of dress in social interaction (Cash 1985, Ericksen and Joseph 1985, Tseëlon 1992a, 1992b, 1997). All these studies tend to neglect the body and the meanings the body brings to dress. And yet, dress in everyday life cannot be separated from the living, breathing, moving body it adorns. The importance of the body to dress is such that encounters with dress divorced from the body are strangely alienating.

◆ ◆ ◆ ◆

Discourses of Dress

Since Foucault said nothing about fashion or dress, his ideas about power/knowledge initially seem to have little application to the study of the dressed body. However, his approach to thinking about power and its grip on the body can be utilized to discuss the way in which discourses and practices of dress operate to discipline the body. As I argued at the beginning of this chapter, the dressed body is a product of culture, the outcome of social forces pressing upon the body. Foucault's account therefore offers one way of thinking about the structuring influence of social forces on the body as well as offering a way of questioning commonsense understandings about modern dress. It is common to think about dress in the twentieth century as more 'liberated' than previous centuries, particularly the nineteenth. The style of clothes worn in the nineteenth century now seem rigid and constraining of the body. The corset seems a perfect example of nineteenth-century discipline of the body: it was obligatory for women, and an uncorseted woman was considered to be morally deplorable (or 'loose' which metaphorically refers to lax stays). As such it can be seen as something more than a garment of clothing, something linked to morality and the social oppression of women. In contrast, styles of dress today are said to be more relaxed, less rigid and physically constraining:

casual clothes are commonly worn and gender codes seem less rigidly imposed. However, this conventional story of increasing bodily 'liberation can be told differently if we apply a Foucauldian approach to fashion history: such a simple contrast between nineteenth- and twentieth-century styles is shown to be problematic. As Wilson argues (1992) in place of the whalebone corset of the nineteenth century we have the modern corset of muscle required by contemporary standards of beauty. Beauty now requires a new form of discipline rather than no discipline at all: in order to achieve the firm tummy required today, one must exercise and watch what one eats. While the stomach of the nineteenth-century corseted woman was disciplined from the outside, the twentieth-century exercising and dieting woman has a stomach disciplined by exercise and diet imposed by self-discipline (a transformation of discipline regimes something like Foucault's move from the 'fleshy' to the 'mindful' body). What has taken place has been a *qualitative* shift in the discipline rather than a quantitative one, although one could argue that the self-discipline required by the modern body is *more* powerful and more demanding than before, requiring great effort and commitment on the part of the individual which was not required by the corset wearer.

Foucault's notion of power can be applied to the study of dress in order to consider the ways in which the body acquires meaning and is acted upon by social and discursive forces and how these forces are implicated in the operation of power. Feminists such as McNay (1992) and Diamond and Quinby (1988) argue that Foucault ignores the issue of gender, a crucial feature of the social construction of the body. However, while he may have been 'gender blind', his theoretical concepts and his insights into the way the body is acted on by power can be applied to take account of gender. In this respect, one can use his ideas about power and discourse to examine how dress plays a crucial part in marking out the gender boundary which the fashion system constantly redefines each season. Gaines (1990: 1) argues that dress delivers 'gender as self-evident or natural' when in fact gender is a cultural construction that dress helps to reproduce. Dress codes reproduce gender: the association of women with long evening dresses or, in the case of the professional workplace, skirts, and men with dinner jackets and trousers is an arbitrary one but nonetheless comes to be regarded as 'natural' so that femininity is connoted in the gown, masculinity in the black tie and dinner jacket. Butler's work on performativity (1990, 1993), influenced by Foucault, looks at the way in which gender is the product of styles and techniques such as dress rather than any essential qualities of the body. She argues that the arbitrary nature of gender is most obviously revealed by drag when the techniques of one gender are exaggerated and made unnatural. Similarly Haug (1987), drawing heavily on Foucault, denaturalizes the common techniques and strategies employed to make oneself 'feminine': the 'feminine' body is an effect of styles of body posture, demeanour and dress. Despite the fact that Foucault ignores gender in his account of the body, his ideas about the way in which the body is constructed by discursive practices provides a theoretical framework within which to examine the reproduction of gender through particular technologies of the body.

A further illustration of how dress is closely linked to gender and indeed power is the way in which discourses on dress construct it as a 'feminine' thing. Tseëlon (1997) gives a number of examples of how women have historically been associated with the 'trivialities' of dress in contrast to men who have been seen to rise above such mundane concerns having renounced decorative dress (Flügel 1930). As Tseëlon (1997) suggests, women have historically been defined as trivial, superficial, vain, even evil because of their association with the vanities of dress by discourses ranging from theology to fashion. Furthermore, discourses on or about fashion have therefore constructed women as the object of fashion, even its victim (Veblen 1953, Roberts 1977). Dress was not considered a matter of equal male and female concern and, moreover, a woman's supposed 'natural' disposition to decorate and adorn herself served to construct her as 'weak' or 'silly' and open her to moral condemnation. A Foucauldian analysis could provide insight into the ways in which women are constructed as closer to fashion and 'vain', perhaps by examining, as Efrat Tseëlon (1997) does, particular treatises on women and dress such as those found in the Bible or the letters of St. Paul.

These associations of women with dress and appearance continue even today and are demonstrated by the fact that what a woman wears is still a matter of greater moral concern than what a man wears. Evidence of this can be found in cases of sexual harassment at work as well as sexual assault and rape cases. Discourses on female sexuality and feminine appearance within institutions such as the law associate women more closely with the body and dress than men. Wolf (1991) notes that lawyers in rape cases in all American states except Florida can legally cite what a woman wore at the time of attack and whether or not the clothing was 'sexually provocative'. This is true in other countries as well. Lees (1999) demonstrates how judges in the UK often base their judgements in rape cases on what a woman was wearing at the time of her attack. A woman can be cross-examined and her dress shown in court as evidence of her culpability in the attack or as evidence of her consent to sex. In one case a woman's shoes (not leather but 'from the cheaper end of the market') were used to imply that she too was 'cheap' (1999: 6). In this way, dress is used discursively to construct the woman as 'asking for it'. Although neither Wolf nor Lees draws on Foucault, it is possible to imagine a discourse analysis of legal cases such as these which construct a notion of a culpable female 'victim' through a discourse on sexuality, morality and dress. In addition, greater demands are made upon a woman's appearance than a man's and the emphasis on women's appearance serves to add what Wolf (1991) calls a 'third shift' to the work and housework women do. Hence, the female body is a potential liability for women in the workplace. Women are more closely identified with the body, as Ortner (1974) and others have suggested; anthropological evidence would seem to confirm this (Moore 1994). Cultural association with the body results in women having to monitor their bodies and appearance more closely than men. Finally, codes of dress in particular situations impose more strenuous regimes upon the bodies of women than they do upon men. In these ways, discourses and regimes of dress are linked to power in various and complex ways and subject the bodies of the women to greater scrutiny than men.

Returning to the issue of dress at work, we can apply Foucault's insights to show how institutional and discursive practices of dress act upon the body and are employed in the workplace as part of institutional and corporate strategies of management. Carla Freeman (1993) draws on Foucault's notion of power, particularly his idea about the Panopticon, to consider how dress is used in one data-processing corporation, *Data Air*, as a strategy of corporate discipline and control over the female workforce. In this corporation a strict dress code insisted that the predominantly female workers dress 'smartly' in order to project a 'modern' and 'professional' image of the corporation. If their dress did not meet this standard they were subject to disciplinary techniques by their managers and could even be sent home to change their clothes. The enforcement of this dress code was facilitated by the open-plan office, which subjects the women to constant surveillance from the gaze of managers. Such practices are familiar to many offices, although the mechanisms for enforcing dress codes vary enormously. Particular discourses of dress, categorizing 'smart' or 'professional' dress, for example, and particular strategies of dress, such as the imposition of uniforms and dress codes at work, are utilized by corporations to exercise control over the bodies of the workers within.

As I have demonstrated, Foucault's framework is quite useful for analysing the situated practice of dress. In particular, his notion of discourse is a good starting-point for analysing the relations between ideas on dress and gender and forms of discipline of the body. However, there are problems with Foucault's notion of discourse as well as problems stemming from his conceptualization of the body and of power, in particular his failure to acknowledge embodiment and agency. These problems stem from Foucault's post-structuralist philosophy and these I now want to summarize in order to suggest how his theoretical perspective, while useful in many respects, is also problematic for a study of dress as situated practice.

◆ ◆ ◆ ◆

This chapter has set out the theoretical framework for a sociology of dress as situated bodily practice. Such an approach requires acknowledging the body as a social entity and dress as the outcome both of social factors and individual actions. Foucault's work may contribute to a sociology of the body but is limited by its inattention to the lived body and its practices, and to the body as the site of the 'self'. Understanding dress in everyday life requires understanding not just how the body is represented within the fashion system and its discourses on dress, but also how the body is experienced and lived and the role dress plays in the presentation of the body/self. Abandoning Foucault's discursive model of the body does not, however, mean abandoning his entire thesis. This framework, as shown above, is useful for understanding the structuring influences on the body and the way in which bodies acquire meaning in particular contexts.

Dress involves practical actions directed by the body upon the body, resulting in ways of being and ways of dressing, for example ways of walking to accommodate high heels, ways of breathing to accommodate a corset, ways of bending in a short skirt and so on. In this way, the analysis of dress as embodied and situated practice enables us to see the operations of power in social spaces (and in particular how this power is gendered) and how power impacts upon the lived body and results in particular strategies on the part of individuals. I have attempted to provide such an account in my own research (Entwistle 1997a, 1997b, 2000), which examines the way in which power-dressing operates as a discourse on how the career woman should dress for the professional workplace and how such a discourse, with its array of 'rules', becomes translated into actual dress practice in the everyday life of a number of career women. In sum, the study of dress as situated practice requires moving between, on the one hand, the discursive and representational aspects of dress and the way the body/dress is caught up in relations of power, and on the other, the embodied experience of dress and the use of dress as a means by which individuals orientate themselves to the social world.

BIBLIOGRAPHY

Barthes, R. (1985) *The Fashion System*. London: Cape.

Bell, Q. (1876) *On Human Finery*. London: Hogarth Press

Berger, J. (1872) *Ways of Seeing*. Harmondsworth: Penguin.

Brooks, R. (1992) 'Fashion Photography, the Double-Page Spread: Helmut Newton, Guy Bourdin and Deborah Turberville', in J. Ash and E. Wilson (eds), *Chic Thrills: A Fashion Reader*. London: Pandora Press.

Butler, J. (1990) Gender Trouble: Feminism and the Subversion of Identity. London: Routledge.

Cash, T. F. (11985) 'The Impact of Grooming Style on the Evaluation of Women in Management', in M. R. Soloman (ed.), *The Psychology of Fashion*. New York: Lexington Books.

Diamond, I. and Quinby, L. (eds) (1988) *Feminism and Foucault: Reflections on Resistance*. Boston: Northeastern University Press.

Entwistle, J. (1997a) *Fashioning the Self: Women, Dress, Power and Situated Bodily Practice in the Workplace*. Ph.D., Goldsmiths' College, University of London.

Entwistle, J. (1997b) 'Power Dressing and the Fashioning of the Career Woman', in M. Nava, I. MacRury, A. Blake, and B. Richards (eds), *Buy this Book: Studies in Advertising and Consumption*. London: Routledge.

Entwistle, J. (200) "Fashioning the Career Woman: Power Dressing as a Strategy of Consumption', in M. Talbot and M. Andrews (eds), *All the World and her Husband: Women and Consumption on the Twentieth Century*. London: Cassell.

Erickson, M. K. and Joseph, S. M. (1985) 'Achievement Motivation and Clothing Preferences of White Collar Working Women', in M. R. Soloman (ed.), *The Psychology of Fashion*. New York: Lexington Books.

Flügel, J. C. (1930) *The Psychology of Clothes*. London: Hogarth Press.

Freeman, C. (1993) 'Designing Women: Corporate Discipline and Barbados's Off-shore Pink Collar Sector'. Cultural Anthropology 9 (20).

Gaines, J. (1990) 'Introduction: Fabricating the Female Body', in J. Gaines and C. Herzong (eds), *Fabrications: Costume and the Female Body*. London: Routledge.

Gorsline, D. (1953/1991) *A History of Fashion: A Visual Survey of Costume from Ancient Times*. London: Fitzhouse Books.

Haug (eds) (1987) *Female Sexualization*. London. Verso.

Hebdige, D. (1979) *Subculture: The Meaning of Style*. London: Methuen.

Hollander, A. (1993) *Seeing through Clothes*. Berkeley: University of California Press.

Kuhn, A. (1988) 'The Body and Cinema: Some Problems for Feminism', in S. Sheridan (ed.), *Grafts: Feminist Cultural Criticism*. London. Verso.

Laver, J. (1969) *Modesty in Dress*. Boston: Houghton Miffliln Co.

Lees, S. (1999) 'When in Rome'. *The Guardian,* 16 February, 6–7.

McNay, L. (1992) *Foucault and Feminism: Power, Gender and the Self*. Cambridge: Polity Press.

Moore, H. L. (1994) *A Passion for Difference. Cambridge*: Polity Press.

Nixon, S. (1992) 'Have you got the Look? Masculinities and Shopping Spectacle', in R. Shields (ed.), *Lifestyle Shopping: The Subject of Consumption*. London: Routledge.

Ortner, S. (1974) 'Is Female to Male as Nature is to Culture?', in M. Rosaldo and L. Lamphere (eds), *Women, Culture and Society*. Stanford: Stanford University Press.

Perniola, M. (1990) 'Between Clothing and Nudity', in M. Feher (eds), *Fragments of a History of the Human Body*. New York: MIT Press.

Roberts, H. (1977) 'The Exquisite Slave: The Role of Clothes in the Making of the Victorian Woman'. *Signs* 2(3): 554-69.

Schulze, L. (1990) 'On the Muscle', in J. Gaines and C. Herzong (eds), *Fabrications: Costume and the Female Body*. London: Routledge.

St. Martin, L. and Gavey, N. (1996) 'Women Body Building: Feminist Resistance and/or Femininity's Recuperation'. *Body and Society* 2(4): 45-57.

Triggs, T. (1992) 'Framing Masculinity: Herb Ritts, Bruce Weber and the Body Perfect', in J. Ash and E. Wilson (eds), *Chic Thrills: A Fashion Reader*. London: Pandora.

Tseëlon, E. (1992a) 'Fashion and the Signification of Social Order'. *Semiotica* 91 (1/2): 1-14

Tseëlon E. (1992b) 'Is the Presented Self Sincere? Goffman, Impression Management and the Postmodern Self'. *Theory, Culture and Society* 9 (2).

Tseëlon, E. (1997) *The Masque of Femininity*. London: Sage.

Turner, B. (1985) The Body and Society: Exploration in Soial Theory. Oxford: Basil Blackwell.

Veblen, T. (1899/1953). *The Theory of the Leisure Class: An Economic Study of Institutions*. New York: Mentor)

Wilson E. (1992) "The Postmodern Body', in J. Ash and E. Wilson (eds), *Chic Thrills: A Fashion Reader*. London: Pandora.

Wolf, N. (1991) *The Beauty Myth*. London: Vintage.

Wright, L. (1992) 'Out-grown Clothes for Grown-up People: Constructing a Theory of Fashion', in J. Ash and E. Wilson (eds), *Chic Thrills: A Fashion Reader*. London: Pandora.

Young, I. M. (1995) 'Women Recovering our Clothes', in S. Bentstock and S. Feriss (eds), *On Fashion*. New Bruswick: Rutgers University Press.

READING 9: ADDRESSING THE BODY

DISCUSSION QUESTIONS

- Why do we speak about clothing in "moral terms"?
- How do clothes control us?
- How do they inform our sense of self?

EXAMPLES TO THINK ABOUT

- Leggings
- Spanx and other compression clothing
- Men's suits

Visual Pleasure and Narrative Cinema

SCREEN, VOL. 16, ISSUE 3

BY LAURA MULVEY

I. INTRODUCTION

A. A Political Use of Psychoanalysis

This paper intends to use psychoanalysis to discover where and how the fascination of film is reinforced by pre-existing patterns of fascination already at work within the individual subject and the social formations that have moulded him. It takes as starting point the way film reflects, reveals and even plays on the straight, socially established interpretation of sexual difference which controls images, erotic ways of looking and spectacle. It is helpful to under stand what the cinema has been, how its magic has worked in the past, while attempting a theory and a practice which will challenge this cinema of the past. Psychoanalytic theory is thus appropriated here as a political weapon, demonstrating the way the unconscious of patriarchal society has structured film form.

The paradox of phallocentrism in all its manifestations is that it depends on the image of the castrated woman to give order and meaning to its world. An idea of woman stands as lynch pin to the system: it is her lack that produces the phallus as a symbolic presence, it is her desire to make good the lack that the phallus signifies. Recent wrting in *Screen* about psychoanalysis and the cinema has not sufficiently brought out the importance of the representation of the female form in a symbolic order in which, in the last resort, it speaks castration and nothing else. To summarise briefly: the function of woman in forming the patriarchal unconscious is two-fold, she first symbolises the castration threat by her real absence of a penis and second thereby raises her child into the symbolic. Once this has been achieved, her meaning in the process is at an end, it does not last into the world of law and language except as a memory which oscillates between memory of maternal plenitude and memory of lack. Both are posited on nature (or on anatomy in Freud's famoas phrase). Woman's desire is subjected to her image as bearer of the bleeding wound, she can exist only in relation to castration and cannot transcend it. She turns her child into the signifier of her own desire to possess a penis (the condition, she imagines, of entry into the symbolic). Either she must gracefully give way to the word, the Name of the Father and the Law, or else struggle to keep her child down with her in the half-light of the imaginary. Woman then stands in patriarchal culture as signifier for the male other, bound by a symbolic order in which man can live out his phantasies and obsessions through linguistic command by imposing them on the silent image of woman still tied to her place as bearer of meaning, not maker of meaning.

There is an obvious interest in this analysis for feminists, a beauty in its exact rendering of the frustration experienced under the phallocentric order. It gets us nearer to the roots of our oppression, it brings an articulation of the problem closer, it faces us with the ultimate challenge: how to fight the unconscious structured like a language (formed critically at the moment of arrival of language) while still caught within the language of the patriarchy. There is no way in which we can produce an alternative out of the blue, but we can begin to make a break by examining patriarchy with the tools it provides, of which psychoanalysis is not the only but an important one. We are still separated by a great gap from important issues for the female unconscious which are scarcely relevant to phallocentric theory: the sexing of the female infant and her relationship to the symbolic, the sexually mature woman as non-mother, maternity outside the signification of the phallus, the vagina. ... But, at this point, psychoanalytic theory as it now stands can at least advance our understanding of the status quo, of the patriarchal order in which we are caught.

B. Destruction of Pleasure as a Radical Weapon

As an advanced representation system, the cinema poses questions of the ways the unconscious (formed by the dominant order) structures ways of seeing and pleasure in looking. Cinema has changed over the last few decades. It is no longer the monolithic system based on large capital investment exemplified at its best by Hollywood in the 1930's, 1940's and 1950's. Technological advances (16mm, etc.) have changed the economic conditions of cinematic production, which can now be artisanal as well as capitalist. Thus it has been possible for an alternative cinema to develop. However self-conscious and ironic Hollywood managed to be, it always restricted itself to a formal mise-en-scène reflecting the dominant ideological concept of the cinema. The alternative cinema provides a space for a cinema to be born which is radical in both a political and an aesthetic sense and challenges the basic assumptions of the mainstream film. This is not to reject the latter moralistically, but to highlight the ways in which its formal preoccupations reflect the psychical obsessions of the society which produced it, and, further, to stress that the alternative cinema must start specifically by reacting against these obsessions and assumptions. A politically and aesthetically avant-garde cinema is now possible, but it can still only exist as a counterpoint.

The magic of the Hollywood style at its best (and of all the cinema which fell within its sphere of influence) arose, not exclusively, but in one important aspect, from its skilled and satisfying manipulation of visual pleasure. Unchallenged, mainstream film coded the erotic into the language of the dominant patriarchal order. In the highly developed Hollywood cinema it was only through these codes that the alienated subject, torn in his imaginary memory by a sense of loss, by the terror of potential lack in phantasy, came near to finding a glimpse of satisfaction: through its formal beauty and its play on his own formative obsessions. This article will discuss the interweaving of that erotic pleasure in film, its meaning, and in particular the central place of the image of woman. It is said that analysing pleasure, or beauty, destroys it. That is the intention of this article. The satisfaction and reinforcement of the ego that represent the high point of film history hitherto must be attacked. Not in favour of a reconstructed new pleasure, which cannot exist in the abstract, nor of intellectualised unpleasure, but to make way for a total negation of the ease and plenitude of the narrative fiction film. The alternative is the thrill that comes from leaving the past behind without rejecting it, transcending outworn or oppressive forms, or daring to break with normal pleasurable expectations in order to conceive a new language of desire.

II. PLEASURE IN LOOKING/FASCINATION WITH THE HUMAN FORM

A. The cinema offers a number of possible pleasures. One is scopophilia. There are circumstances in which looking itself is a source of pleasure, just as, in the reverse formation, there is pleasure in being looked at. Originally, in his *Three Essays on Sexuality,* Freud isolated scopophilia as one of the component instincts of sexuality which exist as drives quite independently of the erotogenic zones. At this point he associated scopophilia with taking other people as objects, subjecting them to a controlling and curious gaze. His particular examples center around the voyeuristic activities of children, their desire to see and make sure of the private and the forbidden (curiosity about other people's genital and bodily functions, about the presence or absence of the penis and, retrospectively, about the primal scene). In this analysis scopophilia is essentially active. (Later, in *Instincts and their Vicissitudes,* Freud developed his theory of scopophilia further, attaching it initially to pre-genital auto-eroticism, after which the pleasure of the look is transferred to others by analogy. There is a close working here of the relationship between the active instinct and its further development in a narcissistic form.) Although the instinct is modified by other factors, in particular the constitution of the ego, it continues to exist as the erotic basis for pleasure in looking at another person as object. At the extreme, it can become fixated into a perversion, producing obsessive voyeurs and Peeping Toms, whose only sexual satisfaction can come from watching, in an active controlling sense, an objectified other.

At first glance, the cinema would seem to be remote from the undercover world of the surreptitious observation of an unknowing and unwilling victim. What is seen of the screen is so manifestly shown. But the mass of mainstream film, and the conventions within which it has consciously evolved, portray a hermetically sealed world which unwinds magically, indifferent to the presence of the audience, producing for them a sense of separation and playing on their voyeuristic phantasy. Moreover, the extreme contrast between the darkness in the auditorium (which also isolates the spectators from one another) and the brilliance of the shifting patterns of light and shade on the screen helps to promote the illusion of voyeuristic separation. Although the film is really being shown, is there to be seen, conditions of screening and narrative conventions give the spectator an illusion of looking in on a private world. Among other things, the position of the spectators in the cinema is blatantly one of repression of their exhibitionism and projection of the repressed desire on to the performer.

B. The cinema satisfies a primordial wish for pleasurable looking, but it also goes further, developing scopophilia in its narcissistic aspect. The conventions of mainstream film focus attention on the human form. Scale, space, stories are all anthropomorphic. Here, curiosity and the wish to look intermingle with a fascination with likeness and recognition: the human face, the human body, the relationship between the human form and its surroundings, the visible presence of the person in the world. Jacques Lacan has described how the moment when a child recognises its own image in the mirror is crucial for the constitution of the ego. Several aspects of this analysis are relevant here. The mirror phase occurs at a time when the child's physical ambitions outstrip his motor capacity, with the result that his recognition of himself is joyous in that he imagines his mirror image to be more complete, more perfect than he experiences his own body. Recognition is thus overlaid with mis-recognition: the image recognised is conceived as the reflected body of the self, but its misrecognition as superior projects this body outside itself as an ideal ego, the alienated subject, which, re-introjected as an ego ideal, gives rise to the future generation of identification with others. This mirror-moment predates language for the child.

Important for this article is the fact that it is an image that constitutes the matrix of the imaginary, of recognition/misrecognition and identification, and hence of the first articulation of the ' I ', of subjectivity. This is a moment when an older fascination with looking (at the mother's face, for an obvious example) collides with the initial inklings of self-awareness. Hence it is the birth of the long love affair/despair between image and self-image which has found such intensity of expression in film and such joyous recognition in the cinema audience. Quite apart from the extraneous similarities between screen and mirror (the framing of the human form in its surroundings, for instance), the cinema has structures of fascination strong enough to allow temporary loss of ego while simultaneously reinforcing the ego. The sense of forgetting the world as the ego has subsequently come to perceive it (I forgot who I am and where I was) is nostalgically reminiscent of that pre-subjective moment of image recognition. At the same time the cinema has distinguished itself in the production of ego ideals as expressed in particular in the star system, the stars centring both screen presence and screen story as they act out a complex process of likeness and difference (the glamorous impersonates the ordinary).

C. Sections II. A and B have set out two contradictory aspects of the pleasurable structures of looking in the conventional cinematic situation. The first, scopophilic, arises from pleasure in using another person as an object of sexual stimulation through sight. The second, developed through narcissism and the constitution of the ego, comes from identification with the image seen. Thus, in film terms, one implies a separation of the erotic identity of the subject from the object on the screen (active scopophilia), the other demands identification of the ego with the object on the screen through the spectator's fascination with and recognition of his like. The first is a function of the sexual instincts, the second of ego libido. This dichotomy was crucial for Freud. Although he saw the two as interacting and overlaying each other, the tension between instinctual drives and self-preservation continues to be a dramatic polarisation in terms of pleasure. Both are formative structures, mechanisms not meaning. In themselves they have no signification, they have to be attached to an idealisation. Both pursue aims in indifference to perceptual reality, creating the imagised, erotidsed concept of the world that forms the perception of the subject and makes a mockery of empirical objectivity.

During its history, the cinema seems to have evolved a particular illusion of reality in which this contradiction between libido and ego has found a beautifully complementary phantasy world. In *reality* the phantasy world of the screen is subject to the law which produces it. Sexual instincts and identification processes have a meaning within the symbolic order which articulates desire. Desire, bom with language, allows the possibility of transcending the instinctual and the imaginary, but its point of reference continually returns to the traumatic moment of its birth: the castration complex. Hence the look, pleasurable in form, can be threatening in content, and it is woman as representation/image that crystallises this paradox.

III. WOMAN AS IMAGE, MAN AS BEARER OF THE LOOK

A. In a world ordered by sexual imbalance, pleasure in looking has been split between active/male and passive/female. The determining male gaze projects its phantasy on to the female figure which is styled accordingly. In their traditional exhibitionist role women are simultaneously looked at and displayed, with their appearance coded for strong visual and erotic impact so that they can be said to connote *to-be-looked-at-ness*. Woman displayed as sexual object is the leit-motif of erotic spectacle: from pin-ups to strip-tease, from Ziegfeld to Busby Berkeley, she holds the look, plays to and signifies male desire. Mainstream film neatly combined spectacle and narrative. (Note, however, how in the musical song- and-dance numbers break the flow of the diegesis.) The presence of woman is an indispensable element of spectacle in normal narrative film, yet her visual presence tends to work against the development of a story line, to freeze the flow of action in moments of erotic contemplation. This alien presence then has to be integrated into cohesion with the narrative. As Budd Boetticher has put it:

> 'What counts is what the heroine provokes, or rather what she represents. She is the one, or rather the love or fear she inspires in the hero, or else the concern he feels for her, who makes him act the way he does. In herself the woman has not the slightest importance.'

(A recent tendency in narrative film has been to dispense with this problem altogether: hence the development of what Molly Haskell has called the 'buddy movie', in which the active homosexual eroticism of the central male figures can carry the story without distraction.) Traditionally, the woman displayed has functioned on two levels: as erotic object for the characters within the screen story, and as erotic object for the spectator within the auditorium, with a shifting tension between the looks on either side of the screen. For instance, the device of the show-girl allows the two looks to be unified technically without any apparent break in the diegesis. A woman performs within the narrative, the gaze of the spectator and that of the male characters in the film are neatly combined without breaking narrative verisimilitude. For a moment the sexual impact of the performing woman takes the film into a no-man's-land outside its own time and space. Thus Marilyn Monroe's first appearance in *The River of No Return* and Lauren Bacall's songs in *To Have or Have Not*. Similarly, conventional close-ups of legs (Dietrich, for instance) or a face (Garbo) integrate into the narrative a different mode of eroticism. One part of a fragmented body destroys the Renaissance space, the illusion of depth demanded by the narrative, it gives flatness, the quality of a cut-out or icon rather than verisimilitude to the screen.

B. An active/passive heterosexual division of labour has similarly controlled narrative structure. According to the principles of the ruling ideology and the psychical structures that back it up, the male figure cannot bear the burden of sexual objectification. Man is reluctant to gaze at his exhibitionist like. Hence the split between spectacle and narrative supports the man's role as the active one of forwarding the story, making things happen. The man controls the film phantasy and also emerges as the representative of power in a further sense: as the bearer of the look of the spectator, transferring it behind the screen to neutralise the extra- diegetic tendencies represented by woman as spectacle. This is made possible through the processes set in motion by structuring the film around a main controlling figure with whom the specta- tor can identify. As the spectator identifies with the main male[1] protagonist, he projects his look on to that of his like, his screen surrogate, so that the power of the male protagonist as he controls events coincides with the active power of the erotic look, both giving a satisfying sense of omnipotence. A male movie star's glamorous characteristics are thus not those of the erotic object of the gaze, but those of the more perfect, more complete, more powerful ideal ego conceived in the original moment of recognition in front of the mirror. The character in the story can make things happen and control events better than the subject/spectator, just as the image in the mirror was more in control of motor coordination. In contrast to woman as icon, the active male figure (the ego ideal of the identification process) demands a three-dimensional space corresponding to that of the mirror-recognition in which the alienated subject internalised his own representation of this imaginary existence. He is a figure in a landscape. Here the function of film is to reproduce as accurately as possible the so-called natural conditions of human perception. Camera technology (as exemplified by deep focus in particular) and camera movements (determined by the action of the protagonist), combined with invisible editing (demanded by realism) all tend to blur the limits of screen space. The male protagonist is free to command the stage, a stage of spatial illusion in which he articu-lates the look and creates the action.

C.1 Sections III. A and B have set out a tension between a mode of representation of woman in film and conventions surrounding the diegesis. Each is associated with a look: that of the spectator in direct scopophilic contact with the female form displayed for his enjoyment (connoting male phantasy) and that of the spectator fascinated with the image of his like set in an illusion of natural space, and through him gaining control and possession of the woman within the diegesis. (This tension and the shift from one pole to the other can structure a single text. Thus both in *Only Angels Have Wings* and in *To Have and Have* Not, the film opens with the woman as object of the combined gaze of spectator and all the male protagonists in the film. She is isolated, glamorous, on display, sexualised. But as the narrative progresses she falls in love with the main male protagonist and becomes his property, losing her out-ward glamorous characteristics, her generalised sexuality, her show-girl connotations; her eroticism is subjected to the male star alone. By means of identification with him, through participation in his power, the spectator can indirectly possess her too.)

But in psychoanalytic terms, the female figure poses a deeper problem. She also connotes something that the look continually circles around but disavows: her lack of a penis, implying a threat of castration and hence unpleasure. Ultimately, the meaning of woman is sexual difference, the absence of the penis as visually ascertainable, the material evidence on which is based the castration complex essential for the organisation of entrance to the symbolic order and the law of the father. Thus the woman as icon, displayed for the gaze and enjoyment of men, the active controllers of the look, always threatens to evoke the anxiety it originally signified. The male unconscious has two avenues of escape from this castration anxiety: preoccupation with the re-enactment of the original trauma (investigating the woman, demystifying her mystery), counterbalanced by the devaluation, punishment or saving of the guilty object (an avenue typified by the concerns of the *film noir*); or else complete disavowal of castration by the substitution of a fetish object or turning the represented figure itself into a fetish so that it becomes reassuring rather than dangerous (hence over-valuation, the cult of the female star). This second avenue, fetishistic scopophilia, builds up the physical beauty of the object, transforming it into something satisfying in itself. The first avenue, voyeurism, on the contrary, has associations with sadism: pleasure lies in ascertaining guilt (immediately associated with castration), asserting control and subjecting the guilty person through punishment or forgiveness. This sadistic side fits in well with narrative. Sadism demands a story, depends on making something happen, forcing a change in another person, a battle of will and strength, victory/defeat, all occuring in a linear time with a beginning and an end. Fetishistic scopophilia, on the other hand, can exist outside linear time as the erotic instinct is focussed on the look alone. These contradictions and ambiguities can be illustrated more simply by using works by Hitchcock and Sternberg. both of whom take the look almost as the content or subject matter of many of their films. Hitchcock is the more complex, as he uses both mechanisms. Sternberg's work, on the other hand, provides many pure examples of fetishistic scopophilia.

◆ ◆ ◆

IV. SUMMARY

The psychoanalytic background that has been discussed in this article is relevant to the pleasure and unpleasure offered. by traditional narrative film. The scopophilic instinct (pleasure in looking at another person as an erotic object), and, in contradistinction, ego libido (forming identification processes) act as formations, mechanisms, which this cinema has played on. The image of woman as (passive) raw material for the (active) gaze of man takes the argument a step further into the structure of representation, adding a further layer demanded by the ideology of the patriarcnal order as it is worked out in its favourite cinematic form—illusionistic narrative film. The argument returns again to the psychoanalytic background in that woman as representation signifies castration, inducing voyeuristic or fetishistic mechanisms to circumvent her threat. None of these interacting layers is intrinsic to film, but it is only in the film form that they can reach a perfect and beautiful contradiction thanks to the possibility in the cinema of shifting the emphasis of the look. It is the place of the look that defines cinema, the possibility of varying it and exposing it. This is what makes cinema quite different in its voyeuristic potential from, say, strip-tease, theatre, shows, etc. Going far beyond highlighting a woman's *to-be-looked-at-ness*, cinema builds the way she is to be looked at into the spectacle itself. Playing on the tension between film as controlling the dimension of time (editing, narrative) and film as controlling the dimension of space (changes in distance, editing), cinematic codes create a gaze, a world, and an object, thereby producing an illusion cut to the measure of desire. It is these cinematic codes and their relationship to formative external structures that must be broken down before mainstream film and the pleasure it provides can be challenged.

To begin with (as an ending), the voyeuristic-scopophilic look that is a crucial part of traditional filmic pleasure can itself be broken down. There are three different looks associated with cinema: that of the camera as it records the profilmic event, that of the audience as it watches the final product, and that of the characters at each other within the screen illusion. The conventions of narrative film deny the first two and subordinate them to the third, the conscious aim being always to eliminate intrusive camera presence and prevent a distancing awareness in the audience. Without these two absences (the material existence of the recording process, the critical reading of the spectator), fictional drama cannot achieve reality, obviousness and truth. Nevertheless, as this article has argued, the structure of looking in narrative fiction film contains a contradiction in its own premises: the female image as a castration threat constantly endangers the unity of the diegesis and bursts through the world of illusion as an intrusive, static, one-dimensional fetish. Thus the two looks materially present in time and space are obsessively subordinated to the neurotic needs of the male ego. The camera becomes the mechanism for producing an illusion of Renaissance space, flowing movements compatible with the human eye, an ideology of representation that revolves around the perception of the subject: the camera's look is disavowed in order to create a convincing world in which the spectator's surrogate can perform with verisimilitude. Simultaneously, the look of the audience is denied an intrinsic force: as soon as fetishistic representation of the female image threatens to break the spell of illusion, and the erotic image on the screen appears directly (without mediation) to the spectator, the fact of fetishisation, concealing as it does castration fear, freezes the look, fixates the spectator and prevents him from achieving any distance from the image in front of him.

This complex interaction of looks is specific to film. The first blow against the monolithic accumulation of traditional film conventions (already undertaken by radical film-makers) is to free the look of the camera into its materiality in time and space and the look of the audience into dialectics, passionate detachment. There is no doubt that this destroys the satisfaction, pleasure and privilege of the 'invisible guest', and highlights how film has depended on voyeuristic active/passive mechanisms. Women, whose image has continually been stolen and used for this end, cannot view the decline of the traditional film form with anything much more than sentimental regret.[2]

NOTES

1. There are films with a woman as main protagonist, of course. To analyse this phenomenon seriously here would take me too far afield. Pam Cook and Claire Johnston's study of *The Revolt of Mamie Stover* in Phil Hardy, ed: *Raoul Walsh,* Edinburgh 1974, shows in a striking case how the strength of this female protagonist is more apparent than real.

2. This article is a reworked version of a paper given in the French Department of the University of Wisconsin, Madison, in the Spring of 1973.

READING 10: VISUAL PLEASURE AND NARRATIVE CINEMA

DISCUSSION QUESTIONS

- Mulvey says that the Oedipus complex can be mapped onto the structure of film. Try to outline how Freud's ideas relate to the protagonist, the female supporting characters, and the narrative.

- How is castration anxiety allayed by conventional Hollywood cinema?

- What are the differences between the male gaze and objectification?

EXAMPLES TO THINK ABOUT

- Alfred Hitchcock's *Rear Window*
- The *John Wick* series

Film and the Masquerade

Theorising the Female Spectator

SCREEN, VOL. 23, ISSUE 3–4

By MARY ANN DOANE

I. A LASS BUT NOT A LACK

Theories of female spectatorship are thus rare, and when they are produced, seem inevitably to confront certain blockages in conceptualisation. The difficulties in thinking female spectatorship demand consideration. After all, even if it is admitted that the woman is frequently the object of the voyeuristic or fetishistic gaze in the cinema, what is there to prevent her from reversing the relation and appropriating the gaze for her own pleasure? Precisely the fact that the reversal itself remains locked within the same logic. The male striptease, the gigolo—both inevitably signify the mechanism of reversal itself, constituting themselves as aberrations whose acknowledgment simply reinforces the dominant system of aligning sexual difference with a subject/object dichotomy. And an essential attribute of that dominant system is the matching of male subjectivity with the agency of the look.

The supportive binary opposition at work here is not only that utilised by Laura Mulvey—an opposition between passivity and activity, but perhaps more importantly, an opposition between proximity and distance in relation to the image.[1] It is in this sense that the very logic behind the structure of the gaze demands a sexual division. While the distance between image and signified (or even referent) is theorised as minimal, if not non-existent, that between the film and the spectator must be maintained, even measured. One need only think of Noël Burch's mapping of spectatorship as a perfect distance from the screen (two times the width of the image)—a point in space from which the filmic discourse is most accessible.[2]

But the most explicit representation of this opposition between proximity and distance is contained in Christian Metz's analysis of voyeuristic desire in terms of a kind of social hierarchy of the senses: 'It is no accident that the main socially acceptable arts are based on the senses at a distance, and that those which depend on the senses of contact are often regarded as "minor" arts (=culinary arts, art of perfumes, etc.).'[3] The voyeur, according to Metz, must maintain a distance between himself and the image—the cinéphile *needs* the gap which represents for him the very distance between desire and its object. In this sense, voyeurism is theorised as a type of meta-desire:

> If it is true of all desire that it depends on the infinité pursuit of its absent object, voyeuristic desire, along with certain forms of sadism, is the only desire whose principle of distance symbolically and spatially evokes this fundamental rent.[4]

Yet even this status as meta-desire does not fully characterise the cinema for it is a feature shared by other arts as well (painting, theatre, opera, etc.). Metz thus adds another reinscription of this necessary distance. What specifies the cinema is a further re-duplication of the lack which prompts desire. The cinema is characterised by an illusory sensory plenitude (there is 'so much to see') and yet haunted by the absence of those very objects which are there to be seen. Absence is an absolute and irrecoverable distance. In other words, Noël Burch is quite right in aligning spectatorial desire with a certain spatial configuration. The viewer must not sit either too close or too far from the screen. The result of both would be the same—he would lose the image of his desire.

It is precisely this opposition between proximity and distance, control of the image and its loss, which locates the possibilities of spectatorship within the problematic of sexual difference. For the female spectator there is a certain over-presence of the image—she *is* the image. Given the closeness of this relationship, the female spectator's desire can be described only in terms of a kind of narcissism—the female look demands a becoming. It thus appears to negate the very distance or gap specified by Metz and Burch as the essential precondition for voyeurism. From this perspective, it is important to note the constant recurrence of the motif of proximity in feminist theories (especially those labelled 'new French feminisms') which purport to describe a feminine specificity. For Luce Irigaray, female anatomy is readable as a constant relation of the self to itself, as an autoeroticism based on the embrace of the two lips which allow the woman to touch herself without mediation. Furthermore, the very notion of property, and hence possession of something which can be constituted as other, is antithetical to the woman: '*Nearness* however, is not foreign to woman, a nearness so close that any identification of one or the other, and therefore any form of property, is impossible. Woman enjoys a closeness with the other that is *so near she cannot possess it any more than she can possess herself.*'[5] Or, in the case of female madness or delirium, '… women do not manage to articulate their madness: they suffer it directly in their body…'.[6] The distance necessary to detach the signifiers of madness from the body in the construction of even a discourse which exceeds the boundaries of sense is lacking. In the words of Hélène Cixous, 'More so than men who are coaxed toward social success, toward sublimation, women are body.'[7]

This theme of the overwhelming presence-to-itself of the female body is elaborated by Sarah Kofman and Michèle Montrelay as well. Kofman describes how Freudian psycho-analysis outlines a scenario whereby the subject's passage from the mother to the father is simultaneous with a passage from the senses to reason, nostalgia for the mother henceforth signifying a longing for a different positioning in relation to the sensory or the somatic, and the degree of civilization measured by the very distance from the body.[8] Similarly, Montrelay argues that while the male has the possibility of displacing the first object of desire (the mother), the female must become that object of desire:

Recovering herself as maternal body (and also as phallus), the woman can no longer repress, 'lose, the first stake of representation. … From now on, anxiety, tied to the presence of this body, can only be insistent, continuous. This body, so close, which she has to occupy, is an object in excess which must be 'lost,' that is to say, repressed, in order to be symbolised.[9]

This body so close, so excessive, prevents the woman from assuming a position similar to the man's in relation to signifying systems. For she is haunted by the loss of a loss, the lack of that lack so essential for the realisation of the ideals of semiotic systems.

Female specificity is thus theorised in terms of spatial proximity. In opposition to this 'closeness' to the body, a spatial distance in the male's relation to his body rapidly becomes a temporal distance in the service of knowledge. This is presented quite explicitly in Freud's analysis of the construction of the 'subject supposed to know'. The knowledge involved here is a knowledge of sexual difference as it is organised in relation to the structure of the look, turning on the visibility of the penis. For the little girl in Freud's description seeing and knowing are simultaneous—there is no temporal gap between them. In 'Some Psychological Consequences of the Anatomical Distinction Between the Sexes', Freud claims that the girl, upon seeing the penis for the first time, 'makes her judgement and her decision in a flash. She has seen it and knows that she is without it and wants to have it.'[10] In the lecture on 'Femininity' Freud repeats this gesture, merging perception and intellection: 'They [girls] at once notice the difference and, it must be admitted, its significance too.'[11]

The little boy, on the other hand, does not share this immediacy of understanding. When he first sees the woman's genitals he 'begins by showing irresolution and lack of interest; he sees nothing or disowns what he has seen, he softens it down or looks about for expedients for bringing it into line with his expectations'.[12] A second event, the threat of castration, is necessary to prompt a rereading of the image, endowing it with a meaning in relation to the boy's own subjectivity. It is in the distance between the look and the threat that the boy's relation to knowledge of sexual difference is formulated. The boy, unlike the girl in Freud's description, is capable of a re-vision of earlier events, a retrospective understanding which invests the events with a significance which is in no way linked to an immediacy of sight. This gap between the visible and the knowable, the very possibility of disowning what is seen, prepares the ground for fetishism. In a sense, the male spectator is destined to be a fetishist, balancing knowledge and belief.

The female, on the other hand, must find it extremely difficult, if not impossible, to assume the position of fetishist. That body which is so close continually reminds her of the castration which cannot be 'fetishised away'. The lack of a distance between seeing and understanding, the mode of judging 'in a flash', is conducive to what might be termed as 'over-identification' with the image. The association of tears and 'wet wasted afternoons' (in Molly Haskell's words)[13] with genres specified as feminine (the soap opera, the 'woman's picture') points very precisely to this type of over-identification, this abolition of a distance, in short, this inability to fetishise. The woman is constructed differently in relation to processes of looking. For Irigaray, this dichotomy between distance and proximity is described as the fact that:

The masculine can partly look at itself, speculate about itself represent itself and describe itself for what it is, whilst the feminine can try to speak to itself through a new language, but cannot describe itself from outside or in formal terms, except by identifying itself with the masculine, thus by losing itself.[14]

Irigaray goes even further: the woman always has a problematic relation to the visible, to form, to structures of seeing. She is much more comfortable with, closer to, the sense of touch.

The pervasiveness, in theories of the feminine, of descriptions of such a claustrophobic closeness, a deficiency in relation to structures of seeing and the visible, must clearly have consequences for attempts to theorise female spectatorship. And, in fact, the result is a tendency to view the female spectator as the site of an oscillation between a feminine position and a masculine position, invoking the metaphor of the transvestite. Given the structures of cinematic narrative, the woman who identifies with a female character must adopt a passive or masochistic position, while identification with the active hero necessarily entails an acceptance of what Laura Mulvey refers to as a certain 'masculinisation' of spectatorship.

*... as desire is given cultural materiality in a text, for women (from childhood onwards) trans-sex identification is a **habit** that very easily becomes **second Nature**. However, this Nature does not sit easily and shifts restlessly in its borrowed transvestite clothes.*[15]

The transvestite wears clothes which signify a different sexuality, a sexuality which, for the woman, allows a mastery over the image and the very possibility of attaching the gaze to desire. Clothes make the man, as they say. Perhaps this explains the ease with which women can slip into male clothing. As both Freud and Cixous point out, the woman seems to be *more* bisexual than the man. A scene from Cukor's *Adam's Rib* graphically demonstrates this ease of female transvestism. As Katherine Hepburn asks the jury to imagine the sex role reversal of the three major characters involved in the case, there are three dissolves linking each of the characters successively to shots in which they are dressed in the clothes of the opposite sex. What characterises the sequence is the marked facility of the transformation of the two women into men in contradistinction to a certain resistance in the case of the man. The acceptability of the female reversal is quite distinctly opposed to the male reversal which seems capable of representation only in terms of farce. Male transvestism is an occasion for laughter; female transvestism only another occasion for desire.

Thus, while the male is locked into sexual identity, the female can at least pretend that she is other—in fact, sexual mobility would seem to be a distinguishing feature of femininity in its cultural construction. Hence, transvestism would be fully recuperable. The idea seems to be this: it is understandable that women would want to be men, for everyone wants to be elsewhere than in the feminine position. What is not understandable within the given terms is why a woman might flaunt her femininity, produce herself as an excess of femininity, in other words, foreground the masquerade. Masquerade is not as recuperable as transvestism precisely because it constitutes an acknowledgement that it is femininity itself which is constructed as mask—as the decorative layer which conceals a non-identity. For Joan Riviere, the first to theorise the concept, the masquerade of femininity is a kind of reaction-formation against the woman's trans-sex identification, her transvestism. After assuming the position of the subject of discourse rather than its object, the intellectual woman whom Riviere analyses felt compelled to compensate for this theft of masculinity by over-doing the gestures of feminine flirtation.

Womanliness therefore could be assumed and worn as a mask, both to hide the possession of masculinity and to avert the reprisals expected if she was found to possess it—much as a thief will turn out his pockets and ask to be searched to prove that he has not the stolen goods. The reader may now ask how I define womanliness or where I draw the line between genuine womanliness and the masquerade. My suggestion is not, however, that there is any such difference; whether radical or superficial, they are the same thing.[16]

The masquerade, in flaunting femininity, holds it at a distance. Womanliness is a mask which can be worn or removed. The masquerade's resistance to patriarchal positioning would therefore lie in its denial of the production of femininity as closeness, as presence-to-itself, as, precisely, imagistic. The transvestite adopts the sexuality of the other—the woman becomes a man in order to attain the necessary distance from the image. Masquerade, on the

other hand, involves a realignment of femininity, the recovery, or more accurately, simula-
tion, of the missing gap or distance. To masquerade is to manufacture a lack in the form of a
certain distance between oneself and one's image. If, as Moustafa Safouan points out, '… to
wish to include in oneself as an object the cause of the desire of the Other is a formula for the
structure of hysteria',[17] then masquerade is anti-hysterical for it works to effect a separation
between the cause of desire and oneself. In Montrelay's words, 'the woman uses her own
body as a disguise.'[18]

The very fact that we can speak of a woman 'using' her sex or 'using' her body for
particular gains is highly significant—it is not that a man cannot use his body in this way
but that he doesn't have to. The masquerade doubles representation; it is constituted by a
hyperbolisation of the accoutrements of femininity. *A propos* of a recent performance by
Marlene Dietrich, Sylvia Bovenschen claims, '… we are watching a woman demonstrate the
representation of a woman's body.'[19] This type of masquerade, an excess of femininity, is
aligned with the *femme fatale* and, as Montrelay explains, is necessarily regarded by men
as evil incarnate: 'It is this evil which scandalises whenever woman plays out her sex in
order to evade the word and the law. Each time she subverts a law or a word which relies
on the predominantly masculine structure of the look.'[20] By destabilising the image, the
masquerade confounds this masculine structure of the look. It effects a defamiliarisation of
female iconography. Nevertheless, the preceding account simply specifies masquerade as a
type of representation which carries a threat, disarticulating male systems of viewing. Yet, it
specifies nothing with respect to female spectatorship. What might it mean to masquerade
as spectator? To assume the mask in order to see in a different way?

◆ ◆ ◆

II. OUT OF THE CINEMA AND INTO THE STREETS:
THE CENSORSHIP OF THE FEMALE GAZE

This process of narrativising the negation of the female gaze in the classical Hollywood cinema finds its perfect encapsulation in a still photograph taken in 1948 by Robert Doisneau,
'Un Regard Oblique'. Just as the Hollywood narratives discussed above purport to centre a
female protagonist, the photograph appears to give a certain prominence to a woman's look.
Yet, both the title of the photograph and its organisation of space indicate that the real site
of scopophiliac power is on the margins of the frame. The man is not centred; in fact, he
occupies a very narrow space on the extreme right of the picture. Nevertheless, it is his gaze
which defines the problematic of the photograph; it is his gaze which effectively erases that
of the woman. Indeed, as subject of the gaze, the woman looks intently. But not only is the
object of her look concealed from the spectator, her gaze is encased by the two poles defining

FIGURE 10-1 *'Un Regard Oblique'*: a dirty joke at the expense of the woman's look.

the masculine axis of vision. Fascinated by nothing visible—a blankness or void for the spectator—unanchored by a 'sight' (there is nothing 'proper' to her vision—save, perhaps, the mirror), the female gaze is left freefloating, vulnerable to subjection. The faint reflection in the shop window of only the frame of the picture at which she is looking serves merely to rearticulate, *en abŷme*, the emptiness of her gaze, the absence of her desire in representation.

On the other hand, the object of the male gaze is fully present, *there* for the spectator. The fetishistic representation of the nude female body, fully in view, insures a masculinisation of the spectatorial position. The woman's look is literally outside the triangle which traces a complicity between the man, the nude, and the spectator. The feminine presence in the photograph, despite a diegetic centring of the female subject of the gaze, is taken over by the picture as object. And, as if to doubly 'frame' her in the act of looking, the painting situates its female figure as a spectator (although it is not clear whether she is looking at herself in a mirror or peering through a door, or window). While this drama of seeing is played out at the surface of the photograph, its deep space is activated by several young boys, out-of-focus, in front of a belt shop. The opposition out-of-focus/in-focus reinforces the supposed clarity accorded to the representation of the woman's 'non-vision'. Furthermore, since this out-of-focus area constitutes the precise literal centre of the image, it also demonstrates how the photograph makes figurative the operation of centring—draining the actual centre point of significance in order to deposit meaning on the margins. The male gaze is centred, in control—although it is exercised from the periphery.

The spectator's pleasure is thus produced through the framing/negation of the female gaze. The woman is there as the butt of a joke—a 'dirty joke' which, as Freud has demonstrated, is always constructed at the expense of a woman. In order for a dirty joke to emerge in its specificity in Freud's description, the object of desire—the woman—must be absent and a third person (another man) must be present as witness to the joke—'so that gradually, in place of the woman, the onlooker, now the listener, becomes the person to whom the smut is addressed...'.[21] The terms of the photograph's address as joke once again insure a masculinisation of the place of the spectator. The operation of the dirty joke is also inextricably linked by Freud to scopophilia and the exposure of the female body:

Smut is like an exposure of the sexually different person to whom it is directed. By the utterance of the obscene words it compels the person who is assailed to imagine the part of the body or the procedure in question and shows her that the assailant is himself imagining it. It cannot be doubted that the desire to see what is sexual exposed is the original motive of smut.[22]

From this perspective, the photograph lays bare the very mechanics of the joke through its depiction of sexual exposure and a surreptitious act of seeing (and desiring). Freud's description of the joke-work appears to constitute a perfect analysis of the photograph's orchestration of the gaze. There is a 'voice-off' of the photographic discourse, however—a component of the image which is beyond the frame of this little scenario of voyeurism. On the far left-hand side of the photograph, behind the wall holding the painting of the nude, is the barely detectable painting of a woman imaged differently, in darkness—*out of sight* for the male, blocked by his fetish. Yet, to point to this almost invisible alternative in imaging is also only to reveal once again the analyst's own perpetual desire to find a not-seen that might break the hold of representation. Or to laugh last.

There is a sense in which the photograph's delineation of a sexual politics of looking is almost uncanny. But, to counteract the very possibility of such a perception, the language of the art critic effects a naturalisation of this joke on the woman. The art-critical reception of the picture emphasizes a natural but at the same time 'imaginative' relation between photography and life, ultimately subordinating any formal relations to a referential ground: 'Doisneau's lines move from right to left, directed by the man's glance; the woman's gaze creates a line of energy like a hole in space. ... The creation of these relationships from life itself is imagination in photography.'[23] 'Life itself', then, presents the material for an 'artistic' organisation of vision along the lines of sexual difference. Furthermore, the critic would have us believe that chance events and arbitrary clicks of the shutter cannot be the agents of a generalised sexism because they are particular, unique—'Keitesz and Doisneau depend entirely upon our recognition that they were present at the instant of the unique intersection of events.'[24] Realism seems always to reside in the streets and, indeed, the out-of-focus boy across the street, at the centre of the photograph, appears to act as a guarantee of the 'chance' nature of the event, its arbitrariness, in short—its realism. Thus, in the discourse of the art critic the photograph, in capturing a moment, does not construct it; the camera finds a naturally given series of subject and object positions. What the critic does not consider are the conditions of reception of photography as an art form, its situation within a much larger network of representation. What is it that makes the photograph not only readable but pleasurable—at the expense of the woman? The critic does not ask what makes the photograph a negotiable item in a market of signification.

◆ ◆ ◆ ◆

NOTES

1. This argument focuses on the image to the excusion of any consideration of the soundtrack primarily because it is the process of imaging which seems to constitute the major difficulty in theorising female spectatorship. The image is also popularly understood as metonymic signifier for the cinema as a whole and for good reason: historically, sound has been subordinate to the image within the dominant classical system. For more on the image/sound distinction in relation to sexual difference see my article, 'The Voice in the Cinema: The Articulation of Body and Space', *Yale French Studies*, no. 60, pp. 33–50.

2. Noël Burch, *Theory of Film Practice*, trans Helen R. Lane, New York and Washington, Praeger Publishers, 1973, p. 35.

3. Christian Metz, 'The Imaginary Signifier', *Screen*, Summer 1975, vol. 16 no. 2, p. 60.

4. ibid, p. 61.

5. Luce Irigaray, 'This Sex Which Is Not One', *New French Feminisms*, ed Elaine Marks and Isabelle de Courtivron, Amherst, The University of Massachusetts Press, 1980, pp. 104–105.

6. Irigaray, 'Women's Exile', *Ideology and Consciousness*, no. 1 (May 1977), p. 74.

7. Hélène Cixous, 'The Laugh of the Medusa', *New French Feminisms*, p. 257.

8. Sarah Kofman, 'Ex: The Woman's Enigma', *Enclitic*, vol. IV no. 2 (Fall 1980), p. 20.

9. Michèle Montrelay, 'Inquiry into Femininity', *m/f*, no. 1 (1978), pp. 91–92.

10. Freud, 'Some Psychological Consequences of the Anatomical Distinction Between the Sexes', *Sexuality and the Psychology of Love*, ed Philip Rieff, New York, Collier Books, 1963, pp. 187–188.

11. Freud, 'Femininity', op. cit., p. 125.

12. Freud, 'Some Psychological Consequences ...', op. cit., p. 187.

13. Molly Haskell, *From Reverence to Rape*, Baltimore, Penguin Books, 1974, p. 154.

14. Irigaray, 'Women's Exile', op. cit., p. 65.

15. Mulvey, 'Afterthoughts ... inspired by Duel in the Sun', *Framework*, (Summer 1981), p. 13.

16. Joan Riviere, 'Womanliness as a Masquerade', *Psychoanalysis and Female Sexuality*, ed. Hendrik M Ruitenbeek, New Haven, College and University Press, 1966, p. 213. My analysis of the concept of masquerade differs markedly from that of Luce Irigaray. See *Ce sexe qui n'en est pas*

un (Paris: Les Éditions de Minuit, 1977), pp. 131–132. It also diverges to a great extent from the very important analysis of masquerade presented by Claire Johnston in 'Femininity and the Masquerade: Anne of the Indies', *Jacques Tourneur* London, British Film Institute, 1975, pp. 36–44. I am indebted to her for the reference to Riviere's article.

17. Moustafa Safouan, 'Is the Oedipus Complex Universal?', *m/f*, nos. 5–6 (1981), pp. 84–85.

18. Montrelay, op. cit., p. 93.

19. Silvia Bovenschen, 'Is There a Feminine Aesthetic?', *New German Critique*, no. 10 (Winter 1977), p. 129.

20. Montrelay, op. cit., p. 93.

21. Freud, *Jokes and Their Relation to the Unconscious*, trans James Strachey, New York, W W Norton & Company, Inc, 1960, p. 99.

22. ibid, p. 98.

23. Weston J Naef, *Counterparts: Form and Emotion in Photographs*, New York, E P Dutton and the Metropolitan Museum of Art, 1982, pp. 48–49.

24. ibid.

DISCUSSION QUESTIONS

- According to Doane, is the female gaze possible? Do you agree?
- Can you explain what masquerade and transvestitism have to do with viewing?

EXAMPLES TO THINK ABOUT

- Alfred Hitchcock's *Rear Window*
- The *John Wick* series

The Search for Tomorrow in Today's Soap Operas

FILM QUARTERLY, VOL. 33, NO.1

By TANIA MODLESKI

If, as Mulvey claims, the identification of the spectator with "a main male protagonist" results in the spectator's becoming "the representative of power,"[1] the multiple identification which occurs in soap opera results in the spectator's being divested of power. For the spectator is never permitted to identify with a character completing an entire action. Instead of giving us one "powerful ideal ego ... who can make things happen and control events better than the subject/spectator can,"[2] soaps present us with numerous limited egos, each in conflict with one another and continually thwarted in its attempts to "control events" because of inadequate knowledge of other peoples' plans, motivations, and schemes. Sometimes, indeed, the spectator, frustrated by the sense of powerlessness induced by soaps, will, like an interfering mother, try to control events directly:

> Thousands and thousands of letters [from soap fans to actors] give advice, warn the heroine of impending doom, caution the innocent to beware of the nasties ("Can't you see that your brother-in-law is up to no good?"), inform

one character of another's doings, or reprimand a character for unseemly behavior.[3]

Presumably this intervention is ineffectual, and feminine powerlessness is reinforced on yet another level.

The subject/spectator of soaps, it could be said, is constituted as a sort of ideal mother: a person who possesses greater wisdom than all her children, whose sympathy is large enough to encompass the conflicting claims of her family (she identifies with them all), and who has no demands or claims of her own (she identifies with no one character exclusively). The connection between melodrama and mothers is an old one. Harriet Beecher Stowe, of course, made it explicit in *Uncle Tom's Cabin*, believing that if her book could bring its female readers to see the world as one extended family, the world would be vastly improved. But in Stowe's novel, the frequent shifting of perspective identifies the reader with a variety of characters in order ultimately to ally her with the mother/author and with God who, in their higher wisdom and understanding, can make all the hurts of the world go away, thus insuring the "essential 'rightness' of the world order." Soap opera, however, denies the "mother" this extremely flattering illusion of her power. On the one hand, it plays upon the spectator's expectations of the melodramatic form, continually stimulating (by means of the hermeneutic code) the desire for a just conclusion to the story, and, on the other hand, it constantly presents the desire as unrealizable, by showing that conclusions only lead to further tension and suffering. Thus soaps convince women that their highest goal is to see their families united and happy, while consoling them for their inability to bring about familial harmony.

This is reinforced by the image of the good mother on soap operas. In contrast to the manipulating mother who tries to interfere with her children's lives, the good mother must sit helplessly by as her children's lives disintegrate; her advice, which she gives only when asked, is temporarily soothing, but usually ineffectual. Her primary function is to be sympathetic, to tolerate the foibles and errors of others.

It is important to recognize that soap operas serve to affirm the primacy of the family not by presenting an ideal family, but by portraying a family in constant turmoil and appealing to the spectator to be understanding and tolerant of the many evils which go on within that family. The spectator/mother, identifying with each character in turn, is made to see "the larger picture" and extend her sympathy to both the sinner and the victim. She is thus in a position to forgive most of the crimes against the family: to know all is to forgive all. As a rule, only those issues which can be tolerated and ultimately pardoned are introduced on soaps. The list includes careers for women, abortions, premarital and extramarital sex, alcoholism, divorce, mental and even physical cruelty. An issue like homosexuality which, perhaps, threatens to explode the family structure rather than temporarily disrupt it, is simply ignored. Soaps, contrary to many people's conception of them, are not conservative but liberal, and the mother is the liberal *par excellence*. By constantly presenting her with the many-sidedness of any question, by never reaching a permanent conclusion, soaps undermine her capacity to form unambiguous judgments.

These remarks must be qualified. If soaps refuse to allow us to condemn most characters and actions until all the evidence is in (and of course it never is), there is one character whom we are allowed to hate unreservedly: the villainess,[4] the negative image of the spectator's ideal self. Although much of the suffering on soap operas is presented as unavoidable, the surplus suffering is often the fault of the villainess who tries to "make things happen and control events better than the subject/spectator can." The villainess might very possibly be a mother, trying to manipulate her children's lives or ruin their marriages. Or perhaps she is avenging herself on her husband's family because it has never fully accepted her.

This character cannot be dismissed as easily as many critics seem to think.[5] The extreme delight viewers apparently take in despising the villainess[6] testifies to the enormous amount of energy involved in the spectator's repression and to her (albeit unconscious) resentment at being constituted as an egoless receptacle for the suffering of others. This aspect of melodrama can be traced back to the middle of the nineteenth century when *Lady Audley's Secret*, a drama about a governess turned bigamist and murderess, became one of the most popular stage melodramas of all time.[7] Discussing the novel upon which the stage drama was based, Elaine Showalter shows how the author, while playing lipservice to conventional notions about the feminine role, managed to appeal to "thwarted female energy":

> The brilliance of *Lady Audley's Secret* is that Braddon makes her would-be murderess the fragile blond angel of domestic realism. … The dangerous woman is not the rebel or the blue-stocking, but the "pretty little girl" whose indoctrination in the female role has taught her secrecy and deceitfulness, almost as secondary sex characteristics.[8]

Thus the villainess is able to transform traditional feminine weaknesses into the sources of her strength.

Similarly, on soap operas, the villainess seizes those aspects of a woman's life which normally render her most helpless and tries to turn them into weapons for manipulating other characters. She is, for instance, especially good at manipulating pregnancy, unlike most women, who, as Mary Ellmann wittily points out, tend to feel manipulated by it:

> At the same time, women cannot help observing that conception (their highest virtue, by all reports) simply happens or doesn't. It lacks the style of enterprise. It can be prevented by foresight and device (though success here, as abortion rates show, is exaggerated), but it is accomplished by luck (good or bad). Purpose often seems, if anything, a deterrent. A devious business benefitting by indirection, by pretending not to care, as though the self must trick the body.

In the regrettable conception, the body instead tricks the self—much as it does in illness or death.[9]

In contrast to the numerous women on soap operas who are either trying unsuccessfully to become pregnant or have become pregnant as a consequence of a single unguarded moment in their lives, the villainess manages, for a time at least, to make pregnancy work for her. She gives it "the style of enterprise." If she decides she wants to marry a man, she will take advantage of him one night when he is feeling especially vulnerable and seduce him. And if she doesn't achieve the hoped-for pregnancy, undaunted, she simply lies about being pregnant. The villainess thus reverses male/female roles: anxiety about conception is transferred to the male. He is the one who had better watch his step and curb any promiscuous desires or he will find himself saddled with an unwanted child.

Moreover, the villainess, far from allowing her children to rule her life, often uses them in order to further her own selfish ambitions. One of her typical ploys is to threaten the father or the woman possessing custody of the child with the deprivation of that child. She is the opposite of the woman at home, who at first is forced to have her children constantly with her, and later is forced to let them go—for a time on a daily recurring basis and then permanently. The villainess enacts for the spectator a kind of reverse *fort-da* game,[10] in which the mother is the one who attempts to send the child away and bring it back at will, striving to overcome feminine passivity in the process of the child's appearance and loss. Into the bargain, she also tries to manipulate the man's disappearance and return by keeping the fate of his child always hanging in the balance. And again, male and female roles tend to get reversed: the male suffers the typically feminine anxiety over the threatened absence of his children.

The villainess thus continually works to make the most out of events which render other characters totally helpless. Literal paralysis turns out, for one villainess, to be an active blessing, since it prevents her husband from carrying out his plans to leave her; when she gets back the use of her legs, therefore, she doesn't tell anyone. And even death doesn't stop another villainess from wreaking havoc; she returns to haunt her husband and convince him to try to kill his new wife.

The popularity of the villainess would seem to be explained in part by the theory of repetition compulsion, which Freud saw as resulting from the individual's attempt to become an active manipulator of her/his own powerlessness.[11] The spectator, it might be thought, continually tunes in to soap operas to watch the villainess as she tries to gain control over her feminine passivity, thereby acting out the spectator's fantasies of power. Of course, most formula stories (like the Western) appeal to the spectator/reader's compulsion to repeat: the spectator constantly returns to the same story in order to identify with the main character and achieve, temporarily, the illusion of mastery denied him in real life. But soap operas refuse the spectator even this temporary illusion of mastery. The villainess's painstaking attempts to turn her powerlessness to her own advantage are always thwarted just when victory seems most assured, and she must begin her machinations all over again. Moreover, the spectator does not comfortably identify with the villainess. Since the spectator despises the villainess as the negative image of her ideal self, she not only watches the villainess act out her own hidden wishes, but simultaneously sides with the forces conspiring against fulfillment of those wishes. As a result of this "internal contestation," the spectator comes to enjoy repetition for its own sake and takes her adequate pleasure in the building up and tearing down of the plot. In this way, perhaps, soaps help reconcile her to the meaningless, repetitive nature of much of her life and work within the home.

Soap operas, then, while constituting the spectator as a "good mother" provide in the person of the villainess an outlet for feminine anger: in particular, as we have seen, the spectator has the satisfaction of seeing men suffer the same anxieties and guilt that women usually experience and seeing them receive similar kinds of punishment for their transgressions. But that anger is neutralized at every moment in that it is the special object of the spectator's hatred. The spectator, encouraged to sympathize with almost everyone, can vent her frustration on the one character who refuses to accept her own powerlessness, who is unashamedly self-seeking. Woman's anger is directed at woman's anger, and an eternal cycle is created.

And yet … if the villainess never succeeds, if, in accordance with the spectator's conflicting desires, she is doomed to eternal repetition, then she obviously never permanently fails either. When, as occasionally happens, a villainess reforms, a new one immediately supplants her. Generally, however, a popular villainess will remain true to her character for most or all of the soap opera's duration. And if the villainess constantly suffers because she is always foiled, we should remember that she suffers no more than the good characters, who don't even try to interfere with their fates. Again, this may be contrasted to the usual imperatives of melodrama, which demands an ending to justify the suffering of the good and punish the wicked. While soap operas thrive, they present a continual reminder that woman's anger is alive, if not exactly well.

We must therefore view with ambivalence the fact that soap operas never come to a full conclusion. One critic, Dennis Porter, who is interested in narrative structures and ideology, completely condemns soap operas for their failure to resolve all problems:

> Unlike all traditionally end-oriented fiction and drama, soap opera offers process without progression, not a climax and a resolution, but mini-climaxes and provisional denouements that must never be presented in such a way as to eclipse the suspense experienced for associated plot lines. Thus soap opera is the drama of perepetia without anagnorisis. It deals forever in reversals but never portrays the irreversible change which traditionally marks the passage out of ignorance into true knowledge. For actors and audience alike, no action ever stands revealed in the terrible light of its consequences.[12]

These are strange words indeed, coming from one who purports to be analyzing the ideology of narrative form! They are a perfect illustration of how a high-art bias, an eagerness to demonstrate the utter worthlessness of "low" art, can lead us to make claims for high art which we would ordinarily be wary of professing. Terms like "progression," "climax," "resolution," "irreversible change," "true knowledge," and "consequences" are certainly tied to an ideology; they are "linked to classical metaphysics," as Barthes observes. "The hermeneutic narrative, in which truth predicates an incomplete subject, based on expectation and desire for its imminent closure, is … linked to the kerygmatic civilization of meaning and truth, appeal and fulfillment."[13] To criticize classical narrative because, for example, it is based on a suspect notion of progress and then criticize soap opera because it *isn't* will never get us anywhere—certainly not "out of ignorance into true knowledge." A different approach is needed.

This approach might also help us to formulate strategies for developing a feminist art. Claire Johnston has suggested that such a strategy should embrace "both the notion of films as a political tool and film as entertainment":

> For too long these have been regarded as two opposing poles with little common ground. In order to counter our objectification in the cinema, our collective fantasies must be released: women's cinema must embody the working through of desire: such an objective demands the use of the entertainment film. Ideas derived from the entertainment film, then, should inform the political film, and political ideas should inform the entertainment cinema: a two-way process.[14]

Clearly, women find soap operas eminently entertaining, and an analysis of the pleasure that soaps afford can provide clues not only about how feminists can challenge this pleasure, but also how they can incorporate it. For, outrageous as this assertion may at first appear, I would suggest that soap operas are not altogether at odds with a possible feminist aesthetics.

"Deep in the very nature of soaps is the implied promise that they will last forever."[15] This being the case, a great deal of interest necessarily becomes focused upon those events which retard or impede the flow of the narrative. The importance of interruptions on soap operas cannot be overemphasized. A single five-minute sequence on a soap opera will contain numerous interruptions both from within and without the diegesis. To give an example from a recent soap opera: a woman tries to reach her lover by telephone one last time before she elopes with someone else. The call is intercepted by the man's current wife. Meanwhile, he prepares to leave the house to prevent the elopement, but his ex-wife chooses that moment to say she has something crucial to tell him about their son. Immediately there is a cut to another couple embroiled in an entirely different set of problems. The man speaks in an ominous tone: "Don't you think it's time you told me what's going on?" Cut to a commercial. When we return, the woman responds to the man's question in an evasive manner. And so it goes.

If, on the one hand, these constant interruptions and deflections provide consolation for the housewife's sense of missed opportunities, by illustrating for her the enormous difficulty of geting from desire to fulfillment, on the other hand, the notion of what Porter contemptuously calls "process without progression" is one endorsed by many innovative women artists. In praising Nathalie Sarraute, for example, Mary Ellmann observes that she is not

> interested in the explicit speed of which the novel is capable, only in the nuances which must tend to delay it. In her own discussions of the novel, Nathalie Sarraute is entirely antiprogressive. In criticizing ordinary dialogue, she dislikes its haste: there not being "time" for the person to consider a remark's ramifications, his having to speak and to listen frugally, his having to rush ahead toward his object—which is of course "to order his own conduct."[16]

Soap opera is similarly antiprogressive. Just as Sarraute's work is opposed to the traditional novel form, soap opera is opposed to the classic (male) film narrative, which, with maximum action and minimum, always pertinent dialogue, speeds its way to the restoration of order.

In soaps, the important thing is that there always be time for a person to consider a remark's ramifications, time for people to speak and listen lavishly. Actions and climaxes are only of secondary importance. I may be accused of wilfully misrepresenting soaps. Certainly they appear to contain a ludicrous number of climaxes and actions: people are always getting blackmailed, having major operations, dying, conducting extra marital affairs, being kidnapped, going mad, and losing their memories. The list goes on and on. But just as in real life (one constantly hears it said) it takes a wedding or a funeral to reunite scattered families, so soap opera catastrophes provide convenient occasions for people to come together, confront one another, and explore intense emotions. Thus in direct contrast to the male narrative film, in which the climax functions to resolve difficulties, the "mini-climaxes" of soap opera function to introduce difficulties and to complicate rather than simplify characters' lives.*

Furthermore, as with much women's narrative (such as the fiction of Ivy Compton-Burnett, who strongly influenced Sarraute), dialogue in soap operas is an enormously tricky business. Again, I must take issue with Porter, who says, "Language here is of a kind that takes itself for granted and assumes it is always possible to mean no more and no less than what one intends."[17] More accurately, in soaps the gap between what is intended and what is actually spoken is often very wide. Secrets better left buried may be blurted out in moments of intensity, or they are withheld just when a character most desires to tell all. This is very different from nighttime television programs and classic Hollywood films with their particularly naive belief in the beneficence of communication. The full revelation of a secret on these shows usually begins or proclaims the restoration of order. Marcus Welby can then get his patient to agree to treatment; Perry Mason can exonerate the innocent and punish the guilty. The necessity of confession, the means through which, according to Michel Foucault, we gladly submit to power,[18] is whole heartedly endorsed. In soap operas, on the other hand, the effects of confession are often ambiguous, providing relief for some of the characters and dreadful complications for others. Moreover, it is remarkable how seldom in soaps a character can talk another into changing his/her ways. Ordinarily, it takes a major disaster to bring about self-awareness—whereas all Marcus Welby has to do is give his stop-feeling-sorry-for-yourself speech and the character undergoes a drastic personality change. Perhaps more than men, women in our society are aware of the pleasures of language—though less sanguine about its potential as an instrument of power.

An analysis of soap operas reveals that "narrative pleasure" can mean very different things to men and women. This is an important point. Too often feminist criticism implies that there is only one kind of pleasure to be derived from narrative and that it is essentially a masculine one. Hence, it is further implied, feminist artists must first of all challenge this pleasure and then out of nothing begin to construct a feminist aesthetics and a feminist form. This is a mistaken position, in my view, for it keeps us constantly in an adversary role, always on the defensive, always, as it were, complaining about the family but never leaving home. Feminist artists *don 't* have to start from nothing; rather, they can look for ways to rechannel and make explicit the criticisms of masculine power and masculine pleasure implied in the narrative form of soap operas.

One further point: feminists must also seek ways, as Johnston puts it, of releasing "our collective fantasies." To the dismay of many feminist critics, the most powerful fantasy

FIGURE 11-1   Gerald Anthony and Judith Light face another unresolvable issue in ONE LIFE TO LIVE. [Photo courtesy ABC.]

embodied in soap operas appears to be the fantasy of a fully self-sufficient family. Carol Lopate complains:

> Daytime television … promises that the family can be everything, if only one is willing to stay inside it. For the woman confined to her house, daytime television fills out the empty spaces of the long day when she is home alone, channels her fantasies toward love and family dramas, and promises her that the life she is in can fulfill her needs. But it does not call to her attention her aloneness and isolation, and it does not suggest to her that it is precisely in her solitude that she has a possibility for gaining a self.[19]

This statement merits close consideration. It implies that the family in soap operas is a mirror-image of the viewer's own family. But for most viewers, this is definitely not the case. What the spectator is looking at and perhaps longing for is a kind of *extended* family, the direct opposite of her own isolated nuclear family. Most soap operas follow the lives of several generations of a large family, all living in the same town and all intimately involved in one another's lives. The fantasy here is truly a "collective fantasy"—a fantasy of community, but put in terms with which the viewer can be comfortable. Lopate is wrong, I believe, to end her peroration with a call for feminine solitude. For too long women have had too much solitude and, quite rightly, they resent it. In a thought-provoking essay on the family, Barbara Easton persuasively argues the insufficiency of feminist attacks on the family:

> With the geographical mobility and breakdown of communities of the twentieth century, women's support networks outside the family have weakened, and they are likely to turn to their husbands for intimacy that earlier generations would have found elsewhere.[20]

If women are abandoned to solitude by feminists eager to undermine this last support network, they are apt to turn to the right. People like Anita Bryant and Mirabel Morgan, says Easton, "feed on fears of social isolation that have a basis in reality."[21] So do soap operas.

For it is crucial to recognize that soap opera allays *real* anxieties, satisfies *real* needs and desires, even while it may distort them.[22] The fantasy of community is not only a real desire (as opposed to the "false" ones mass culture is always accused of trumping up), it is a salutary one. As feminists, we have a responsibility to devise ways of meeting these needs that are more creative, honest, and interesting than the ones mass culture has come up with. Otherwise, the search for tomorrow threatens to go on, endlessly.

FIGURE 11-2 In DAYS OF OUR LIVES, Marlena and Don (Deidre Hall and Jed Allan—at right) marry only after several postponements. Many complications will ensue, since the bridal party includes the bride's twin sister ... [Photo courtesy NBC]

NOTES

1. Roland Barthes, *S/Z*, Richard Miller, trans. (New York: Hill and Wang, 1974), p. 76.

2. Dennis Porter, "Soap Time: Thoughts on a Commodity Art Form," *College English* (April 1977), p. 783.

3. Madeleine Edmondson and David Rounds, *From Mary Noble to Mary Hartman: The Complete Soap Opera Book* (New York: Stein And Day, 1976), pps. 104–110.

4. Barthes, p. 135.

5. John Cawelti, *Adventure, Mystery, and Romance* (Chicago: The University of Chicago Press, 1976), pps. 45–46.

6. Laura Mulvey, "Visual Pleasure and Narrative Cinema" in *Women and the Cinema,* Karyn Kay and Gerald Peary, eds. (New York: E. P. Dutton, 1977), p. 420.

7. Mulvey, p. 420.

8. Mulvey, p. 420.

9. Edmondson and Rounds, p. 193.

10. There are still villains in soap operas, but their numbers have declined considerably since radio days—to the point where they are no longer indispensable to the formula. *The Young and the Restless,* for example, does without them.

11. See, for example, Kathryn Weibel, *Mirror Mirror: Images of Women Reflected in Popular Culture* (New York: Anchor Books, 1977), p. 62. According to Weibel, we quite simply "deplore" the victimizers and totally identify with the victims.

12. "A soap opera without a bitch is a soap opera that doesn't get watched. The more hateful the bitch the better. Erica of 'All My Children' is a classic. If you want to hear some hairy rap, just listen to a bunch of women discussing Erica.

'Girl, that Erica needs her tail whipped.'

'I wish she'd try to steal my man and plant some marijuana in my purse. I'd be mopping up the street with her new hairdo.'" Bebe Moore Campbell, "Hooked on Soaps," *Essence* (November 1978), p. 103.

13. "The author, Mary Elizabeth Braddon, belonged to the class of writers called by Charles Reade 'obstacles to domestic industry.'" Frank Rahill, *The World of Melodrama* (University Park: The Pennsylvania University Press, 1967), p. 204.

14. Elaine Showalter, *A Literature of Their Own* (Princeton, New Jersey: Princeton University Press, 1977), p. 165.

15. Mary Ellmann, *Thinking About Women* (New York: Harvest Books, 1968), p. 181.

16. The game, observed by Freud, in which the child plays "disappearance and return" with a wooden reel tied to a string. "What he did was to hold the reel by the string and very skilfully throw it over the edge of his curtained cot, so that it disappeared into it, at the same time uttering his expressive 'o-o-o-o.' [Freud speculates that this represents the German word *fort*' or 'gone.'] He then pulled the reel out of the cot again by the string and hailed its reappearing with a joyful '*da*' ['there']." According to Freud, "Throwing away the object so that it was 'gone' might satisfy an impulse of the child's, which was suppressed in his actual life, to revenge himself on his mother for going away from him. In that case it would have a defiant meaning: 'All right, then go away! I don't need you. I'm sending you away myself.'" Sigmund Freud, *Beyond the Pleasure Principle,* James Strachey, trans. (New York: W. W. Norton, 1961), pps. 10–11.

17. Speaking of the child's *fort-da* game, Freud notes, "At the outset he was in a *passive* situation—he was overpowered by experience; but by repeating it, unpleasurable though it was, as a game, he took on an *active* part. These efforts might be put down to an instinct for mastery that was acting independently of whether the memory was in itself pleasurable or not." Freud, p. 10.

18. Porter, pps. 783–784.

19. Barthes, p. 76.

20. Claire Johnston, "Women's Cinema as Counter-Cinema" in *Movies and Methods,* Bill Nichols, ed. (Berkeley: University of California Press, 1976), p. 217.

21. Edmondson and Rounds, p. 112.

22. Ellmann, pps. 222–223.

* In a provocative review of *Scenes from a Marriage,* Marsha Kinder points out the parallels between Bergman's work and soap operas. She speculates that the "open-ended, slow paced, multi-climaxed structure" of soap operas is "in tune with patterns of female sexuality" and thus perhaps lends itself more readily than other forms to the portrayal of feminine growth and developing self-awareness (*Film Quarterly,* [Winter 1974–75], p. 51). It would be

interesting to consider Kinder's observation in the light of other works utilizing the soap opera format. Many segments of *Upstairs Downstairs,* for instance, were written by extremely creative and interesting women (Fay Weldon, for one). The only disagreement I have with Kinder is over her contention that "The primary distinction between *Scenes from a Marriage* and soap opera is the way it affects us emotionally. ... Instead of leading us to forget about our own lives and to get caught up vicariously in the intrigues of others, it throws us back on our own experience" (p. 53). But soap opera viewers constantly claim that their favorite shows lead them to reflect upon their own problems and relationships. Psychologists, recognizing the tendency of viewers to make comparisons between screen life and real life, have begun to use soap operas in therapy sessions (see Dan Wakefield, *All Her Children* [Garden City, New York: Doubleday & Company, 1976], pp. 140–43). We may not like what soap operas have to teach us about our lives, but that they *do* teach and encourage self-reflection appears indisputable.

READING 12: THE SEARCH FOR
TOMORROW IN TODAY'S SOAP OPERAS

DISCUSSION QUESTIONS

- Does Modleski agree or disagree with Doane?
- How do soap operas connect to female viewers?

EXAMPLES TO THINK ABOUT

- *This is Us*

Why Have There Been No Great Women Artists?

ART NEWS [ETC.]

By LINDA NOCHLIN

While the recent upsurge of feminist activity in this country has indeed been a liberating one, its force has been chiefly emotional—personal, psychological and subjective—centered, like the other radical movements to which it is related, on the present and its immediate needs, rather than on historical analysis of the basic intellectual issues which the feminist attack on the status quo automatically raises.[1] Like any revolution, however, the feminist one ultimately must come to grips with the intellectual and ideological basis of the various intellectual or scholarly disciplines—history, philosophy, sociology, psychology, etc.—in the same way that it questions the ideologies of present social institutions. If, as John Stuart Mill suggested, we tend to accept whatever *is* as natural, this is just as true in the realm of academic investigation as it is in our social arrangements. In the former, too, "natural" assumptions must be questioned and the mythic basis of much so-called "fact" brought to light. And it is here that the very position of woman as an acknowledged outsider, the maverick "she" instead of the presumably neutral "one"—in reality the white-male-position-accepted-as-natural, or the hidden "he" as the subject of all scholarly predicates—is a decided advantage, rather than merely a hindrance of a subjective distortion.

FIGURE 12-1 A banner for Women's Lib could be Artemisia Gentileschi's *Judith Beheading Holofernes*, one of this Roman painter's favorite subject. This version dates ca. 1614–20, shortly after the scandal of her alleged promiscuous relations with her teacher.

VIA WIKIMEDIA COMMONS

In the field of art history, the white Western male viewpoint, unconsciously accepted as *the* viewpoint of the art historian, may—and does—prove to be inadequate not merely on moral and ethical grounds, or because it is elitist, but on purely intellectual ones. In revealing the failure of much academic art history, and a great deal of history in general, to take account of the unacknowledged value system, the very *presence* of an intruding subject in historical investigation, the feminist critique at the same time lays bare its conceptual smugness, its meta-historical naïveté. At a moment when all disciplines are becoming more self-conscious, more aware of the nature of their presuppositions as exhibited in the very languages and structures of the various fields of scholarship, such uncritical acceptance of "what is" as "natural" may be intellectually fatal. Just as Mill saw male domination as one of a long series of social injustices that had to be overcome if a truly just social order were to be created, so we may see the unstated domination of white male subjectivity as one in a series of intellectual distortions which must be corrected in order to achieve a more adequate and accurate view of historical situations.

It is the engaged feminist intellect (like John Stuart Mill's) that can pierce through the cultural-ideological limitations of the time and its specific "professionalism" to reveal biases and inadequacies not merely in the dealing with the question of women, but in the very way of formulating the crucial questions of the discipline as a whole. Thus, the so-called woman question, far from being a minor, peripheral and laughably provincial sub-issue grafted on to a serious, established discipline, can become a catalyst, an intellectual instrument, probing basic and "natural" assumptions, providing a paradigm for other kinds of internal questioning, and in turn providing links with paradigms established by radical approaches in other fields. Even a simple question like "Why have there been no great women artists?" can, if answered adequately, create a sort of chain reaction, expanding not merely to encompass the accepted assumptions of adequacy, create a sort of chain reaction, expanding not merely to encompass the accepted assumptions of the single field, but outward to embrace history and the social sciences, or even psychology and literature, and thereby, from the outset, to challenge the assumption that the traditional divisions of intellectual inquiry are still adequate to deal with the meaningful questions of our time, rather than the merely convenient or self-generated ones.

Let us, for example, examine the implications of that perennial question (one can, of course, substitute almost any field of human endeavor, with appropriate changes in phrasing): "Well, if women really *are* equal to men, why have there never been any great women artists (or composers, or mathematicians, or philosophers, or so few of the same)?"

"Why have there been no great women artists?" The question tolls reproachfully in the background of most discussions of the so-called woman problem. But like so many other so-called questions involved in the feminist "controversy," it falsifies the nature of the issue at the same time that it insidiously supplies its own answer: "There are no great women artists because women are incapable of greatness."

The assumptions behind such a question are varied in range and sophistication, running anywhere from "scientifically proven" demonstrations of the inability of human beings with wombs rather than penises to create anything significant, to relatively open-minded wonderment that women, despite so many years of near-equality—and after all, a lot of men have had their disadvantages too—have still not achieved anything of exceptional significance in the visual arts.

The feminist's first reaction is to swallow the bait, hook, line and sinker, and to attempt to answer the question as it is put: i.e., to dig up examples of worthy or insufficiently appreciated women artists throughout history; to rehabilitate rather modest, if interesting and productive careers; to "re-discover" forgotten flower-painters or David-followers and make out a case for them; to demonstrate that Berthe Morisot was really less dependent upon Manet than one had been led to think—in other words, to engage in the normal activity of the specialist

FIGURE 12-2 The Swiss-born Angelica Kauffman, most of whose prolific career was spent in Italy, combines allegory with portraiture in *Angelica Hesitating between Music and Painting*, 1791.

VIA WIKIMEDIA COMMONS

scholar who makes a case for the importance of his very own neglected or minor master. Such attempts, whether undertaken from a feminist point of view, like the ambitious article on women artists which appeared in the 1858 *Westminster Review*,[2] or more recent scholarly studies on such artists as Angelica Kauffmann and Artemisia Gentileschi,[3] are certainly worth the effort, both in adding to our knowledge of women's achievement and of art history generally. But they do nothing to question the assumptions lying behind the question "Why have there been no great women artists?" On the contrary, by attempting to answer it, they tacitly reinforce its negative implications.

Another attempt to answer the question involves shifting the ground slightly and asserting, as some contemporary feminists do, that there is a different kind of "greatness" for women's art than for men's, thereby postulating the existence of a distinctive and recognizable feminine style, different both in its formal and its expressive qualities and based on the special character of women's situation and experience.

This, on the surface of it, seems reasonable enough: in general, women's experience and situation in society, and hence as artists, is different from men's, and certainly the art produced by a group of consciously united and purposefully articulate women intent on bodying forth a group consciousness of feminine experience might indeed be stylistically identifiable as feminist, if not feminine, art. Unfortunately, though this remains within the realm of possibility it has so far not occurred. While the members of the Danube School, the followers of Caravaggio, the painters gathered around Gauguin at Pont-Aven, the Blue Rider, or the Cubists may be recognized by certain clearly defined stylistic or expressive qualities, no such common qualities of "femininity" would seem to link the styles of women artists generally, any more than such qualities can be said to link women writers, a case brilliantly argued, against the most devastating, and mutually contradictory, masculine critical clichés, by Mary Ellmann in her *Thinking about Women*.[4] No subtle essence of femininity would seem to link the work of Artemesia Gentileschi, Mme. Vigée-Lebrun, Angelica Kauffmann, Rosa Bonheur, Berthe Morisot, Suzanne Valadon, Kaethe Kollwitz, Barbara Hepworth, Georgia O'Keeffe, Sophie Taeuber-Arp, Helen Frankenthaler, Bridget Riley, Lee Bontecou or Louise Nevelson, any more than that of Sappho, Marie de France, Jane Austen, Emily Brontë, George Sand, George Eliot, Virginia Woolf, Gertrude Stein, Anaïs Nin, Emily Dickinson, Sylvia Plath and Susan Sontag. In every instance, women artists and writers would seem to be closer to other artists and writers of their own period and outlook than they are to each other.

◆ ◆ ◆ ◆

W omen artists are more inward-looking, more delicate and nuanced in their treatment of their medium, it may be asserted. But which of the women artists cited above is more inward-turning than Redon, more subtle and nuanced in the handling of pigment than Corot? Is Fragonard more or less feminine than Mme. Vigée-Lebrun? Or is it not more a question of the whole Rococo style of 18th-century France being "feminine," if judged in terms of a two-valued scale of "masculinity" vs. "femininity"? Certainly though, if daintiness, delicacy and preciousness are to be counted as earmarks of a feminine style, there is nothing fragile about Rosa Bonheur's *Horse Fair*, nor dainty and introverted about Helen Frankenthaler's giant canvases. If women have turned to scenes of domestic life, or of children, so did Jan Steen, Chardin and the Impressionists—Renoir and Monet as well as Morisot and Cassatt. In any case, the mere choice of a certain realm of subject matter, or the restriction to certain subjects, is not to be equated with a style, much less with some sort of quintessentially feminine style.

The problem lies not so much with the feminists' concept of what femininity is, but rather with their misconception—shared with the public at large—of what art is: with the naïve idea that art is the direct, personal expression of individual emotional experience, a translation of personal life into visual terms. Art is almost never that, great art never is. The making of art involves a self-consistent language of form, more or less dependent upon, or free from, given temporally-defined conventions, schemata or systems of notation, which have to be learned or worked out, either through teaching, apprenticeship or a long period of individual experimentation. The language of art is, more materially, embodied in paint and line on canvas or paper, in stone or clay or plastic or metal—it is neither a sob-story nor a confidential whisper.

The fact of the matter is that there have been no supremely great women artists, as far as we know, although there have been many interesting and very good ones who remain insufficiently investigated or appreciated; nor have there been any great Lithuanian jazz pianists,

FIGURE 12-3 Judith Leyster's *The Jolly Toper* was called a Frans Hal until the discovery of her typical signature, "J," and the date 1629, in upper right center.

nor Eskimo tennis players, no matter how much we might wish there had been. That this should be the case is regrettable, but no amount of manipulating the historical or critical evidence will alter the situation; nor will accusations of male-chauvinist distortion of history. The fact, dear sisters, is that there *are* no women equivalents for Michelangelo or Rembrandt, Delacroix or Cézanne, Picasso or Matisse, or even, in very recent times, for de Kooning or Warhol, any more than there are Black American equivalents for the same. If there actually were large numbers of "hidden" great women artists, or if there really should be different standards for women's art as opposed to men's—and one can't have it both ways—then what are the feminists fighting for? If women have in fact achieved the same status as men in the arts, then the status quo is fine as it is.

But in actuality, as we all know, things as they are and as they have been, in the arts as in a hundred other areas, are stultifying, oppressive and discouraging to all those, women among them, who did not have the good fortune to be born white, preferably middle class and, above all, male. The fault, dear brothers, lies not in our stars, our hormones, our menstrual cycles or our empty internal spaces, but in our institutions and our education—education understood to include everything that happens to us from the moment we enter this world of meaningful symbols, signs and signals. The miracle is, in fact, that given the overwhelming odds against women, or blacks, that so many of both have managed to achieve so much sheer excellence, in those bailiwicks of white masculine prerogative like science, politics or the arts.

It is when one really starts thinking about the implications of "Why have there been no great women artists?" that one begins to realize to what extent our consciousness of how things are in the world has been conditioned—and often falsified—by the way the most important questions are posed. We tend to take it for granted that there really is an East Asian Problem, a Poverty Problem, a Black Problem—and a Woman Problem. But first we must ask ourselves who is formulating these "questions," and then, what purposes such formulations may serve. (We may, of course, refresh our memories with the connotations of the Nazi's "Jewish Problem.") Indeed, in our time of instant communication, "problems" are rapidly formulated to rationalize the bad conscience of those with power: thus the problem posed by Americans in Vietnam and Cambodia is referred to by Americans as "the East Asian Problem," whereas East Asians may view it, more realistically, as "the American Problem"; the so-called Poverty Problem might more directly be viewed as the "Wealth Problem" by denizens of urban ghettos or rural wastelands; the same irony twists the White Problem into its opposite: a Black Problem; and the same inverse logic turns up in the formulation of our own present state of affairs as the "Woman Problem."

Now the "Woman Problem," like all human problems, so-called (and the very idea of calling anything to do with human beings a "problem" is, of course, a fairly recent one) is not amenable to "solution" at all, since what human problems involve is re-interpretation of the nature of the situation, or a radical alteration of stance or program *on the part of the "problems" themselves.* Thus women and their situation in the arts, as in other realms of endeavor, are not a "problem" to be viewed through the eyes of the dominant male power elite. Instead, *women* must conceive of themselves as potentially, if not actually, equal subjects, and must be willing to look the facts of their situation full in the face, without self-pity, or cop-outs; at the same time they must view their situation with that high degree of emotional and intellectual commitment necessary to create a world in which equal achievement will be not only made possible but actively encouraged by social institutions.

It is certainly not realistic to hope that a majority of men, in the arts, or in any other field, will soon see the light and find that it is in their own self-interest to grant complete equality to women, as some feminists optimistically assert, or to maintain that men themselves will soon realize that they are diminished by denying themselves access to traditionally "feminine" realms and emotional reactions. After all, there are few areas that are really "denied" to men, if the level of operations demanded be transcendent, responsible or rewarding enough: men who have a need for "feminine" involvement with babies or children gain status as pediatricians or child psychologists, with a nurse (female) to do the more routine work; those who feel the urge for kitchen creativity may gain fame as master chefs; and, of course, men who yearn to fulfill themselves through what are often termed "feminine" artistic interests can find

FIGURE 12-4 At Thomas Eakins' life-class at the Pennsylvania Academy around 1855, a cow, instead of a nude man, served as a model for the women students.

themselves as painters or sculptors, rather than as volunteer museum aides or part time ceramists, as their female counterparts so often end up doing; as far as scholarship is concerned, how many men would be willing to change their jobs as teachers and researchers for those of unpaid, part-time research assistants and typists as well as full-time nannies and domestic workers?

Those who have privileges inevitably hold on to them, and hold tight, no matter how marginal the advantage involved, until compelled to bow to superior power of one sort or another.

Thus the question of women's equality—in art as in any other realm—devolves not upon the relative benevolence or ill-will of individual men, nor the self-confidence or abjectness of individual women, but rather on the very nature of our institutional structures themselves and the view of reality which they impose on the human beings who are part of them. As John Stuart Mill pointed out more than a century ago: "Everything which is usual appears natural. The subjection of women to men being a universal custom, any departure from it quite naturally appears unnatural."[5] Most men, despite lip-service to equality, are reluctant to give up this "natural" order of things in which their advantages are so great; for women, the case is further complicated by the fact that, as Mill astutely pointed out, unlike other oppressed groups or castes, men demand of her not only submission but unqualified affection as well; thus women are often weakened by the internalized demands of the male-dominated society itself, as well as by a plethora of material goods and comforts: the middle-class woman has a great deal more to lose than her chains.

The question "Why have there been no great women artists?" is simply the top tenth of an iceberg of misinterpretation and misconception; beneath lies a vast dark bulk of shaky *idées reçues* about the nature of art and its situational concomitants, about the nature of human abilities in general and of human excellence in particular, and the role that the social order plays in all of this. While the "woman problem" as such may be a pseudo-issue, the misconceptions involved in the question "Why have there been no great women artists?" points to major areas of intellectual obfuscation beyond the specific political and ideological issues involved in the subjection of women. Basic to the question are many naïve, distorted, uncritical assumptions about the making of art in general, as well as the making of great art. These assumptions, conscious or unconscious, link together such unlikely superstars as Michelangelo and van Gogh, Raphael and Jackson Pollock under the rubric of "Great"—an honorific attested to by the number of scholarly monographs devoted to the artist in question—and the Great Artist is, of course, conceived of as one who has "Genius"; Genius, in turn, is thought of as an atemporal and mysterious power somehow embedded in the person of the Great Artist.[6] Such ideas are related to unquestioned, often unconscious, meta-historical premises that make Hippolyte Taine's race-milieu-moment formulation of the dimensions of historical thought seem a model of sophistication. But these assumptions are intrinsic to a great deal of art-historical writing. It is no accident that the crucial question of the conditions *generally* productive of great art has so rarely been investigated, or that attempts to investigate such general problems have, until fairly recently, been dismissed as unscholarly, too broad, or the province of some other discipline, like sociology. To encourage a dispassionate, impersonal, sociological and institutionally-oriented approach would reveal the entire romantic, elitist, individual-glorifying and monograph-producing substructure upon which the profession of art history is based, and which has only recently been called in to question by a group of younger dissidents.

Underlying the question about woman as artist, then, we find the myth of the Great Artist—subject of a hundred monographs, unique, godlike—bearing within his person since birth a mysterious essence, rather like the golden nugget in Mrs. Grass's chicken soup, called Genius or Talent, which, like murder, must always out, no matter how unlikely or unpromising the circumstances.

The magical aura surrounding the representational arts and their creators has, of course, given birth to myths since the earliest times. Interestingly enough, the same magical abilities attributed by Pliny to the Greek sculptor Lysippos in antiquity—the mysterious inner call in early youth, the lack of any teacher but Nature herself—is repeated as late as the 19th century by Max Buchon in his biography of Courbet. The supernatural powers of the artist as imitator, his control of strong, possibly dangerous powers, have functioned historically to set him off from others as a godlike creator, one who creates Being out of nothing. The fairy tale of the Boy Wonder, discovered by an older artist or discerning patron, usually in the guise of a lowly shepherd boy, has been a stock-in-trade of artistic mythology ever since Vasari immortalized the young Giotto, discovered by the great Cimabue while the lad was guarding his flocks, drawing sheep on a stone; Cimabue, overcome with admiration by the realism of the drawing, immediately invited the humble youth to be his pupil.[7] Through some mysterious coincidence, later artists including Beccafumi, Andrea Sansovino, Andrea del Castagno, Mantegna, Zurbaran and Goya were all discovered in similar pastoral circumstances. Even when the young Great Artist was not fortunate enough to come equipped with a flock of sheep, his talent always seems to have manifested itself very early, and independent of any external encouragement: Filippo Lippi and Poussin, Courbet and Monet are all reported to have drawn caricatures in the margins of their schoolbooks instead of studying the required subjects—we never, of course, hear about the youths who neglected their studies and scribbled in the margins of their notebooks without ever becoming anything more elevated than department-store clerks or shoe salesmen. The great Michelangelo himself, according to his biographer and pupil, Vasari, did more drawing than studying as a child. So pronounced was his talent, reports Vasari, that when his master, Ghirlandaio, absented himself momentarily from his work in Santa Maria Novella, and the young art student took the opportunity to draw "the scaffolding, trestles, pots of paint, brushes and the apprentices at their tasks" in this brief absence, he did it so skillfully that upon his return the master exclaimed: "This boy knows more than I do."

As is so often the case, such stories, which probably have some truth in them, tend both to reflect and perpetuate the attitudes they subsume. Despite any basis in fact of these myths about the early manifestations of Genius, the tenor of the tales is misleading. It is no doubt true, for example, that the young Picasso passed all the examinations for entrance to the Barcelona, and later to the Madrid, Academy of Art at the age of 15 in but a single day, a feat of such difficulty that most candidates required a month of preparation. But one would like to find out more about similar precocious qualifiers for art academies who then went on to achieve nothing but mediocrity or failure—in whom, of course, art historians are uninterested—or to study in greater detail the role played by Picasso's art-professor father in the pictorial precocity of his son. What if Picasso had been born a girl? Would Señor Ruiz have paid as much attention or stimulated as much ambition for achievement in a little Pablita?

What is stressed in all these stories is the apparently miraculous, non-determined and asocial nature of artistic achievement; this semi-religious conception of the artist's role is elevated to hagiography in the 19th-century, when both art historians, critics and, not least, some of the artists themselves tended to elevate the making of art into a substitute religion, the last bulwark of Higher Values in a materialistic world. The artist, in the 19th-century Saints' Legend, struggles against the most determined parental and social opposition, suffering the slings and arrows of social opprobrium like any Christian martyr, and ultimately succeeds against all odds—generally, alas, after his death—because from deep within himself radiates

FIGURE 12-5 Elisabeth Vigée-Lebrun's immense following at the French court was largely due to the patronage of Marie-Antoinette, whom she has been credited with making sympathetic to posterity through her portraits of the queen. *Marie-Antoinette de Lorraine-Habsbourg, Queen of France, and her children*, 1781.

that mysterious, holy effulgence: Genius. Here we have the mad van Gogh, spinning out sunflowers despite epileptic seizures and near-starvation; Cézanne, braving paternal rejection and public scorn in order to revolutionize painting; Gauguin throwing away respectability and financial security with a single existential gesture to pursue his Calling in the tropics, or Toulouse-Lautrec, dwarfed, crippled and alchoholic [*sic*], sacrificing his aristocratic birth-right in favor of the squalid surroundings that provided him with inspiration, etc.

Now no serious contemporary art historian takes such obvious fairy tales at their face value. Yet it is this sort of mythology about artistic achievement and its concomitants which forms the unconscious or unquestioned assumptions of scholars, no matter how many crumbs are thrown

FIGURE 12-6   Berthe Morisot was a close friend of Manet and later married his brother. *Eugene Manet on the Isle of Wight*, 1875.

VIA WIKIMEDIA COMMONS

to social influences, ideas of the times, economic crises and so on. Behind the most sophisticated investigations of great artists— more specifically, the art-historical monograph, which accepts the notion of the Great Artist as primary, and the social and institutional structures within which he lived and worked as mere secondary "influences" or "background"—lurks the golden-nugget theory of genius and the free-enterprise conception of individual achievement. On this basis, women's lack of major achievement in art may be formulated as a syllogism: If women had the golden nugget of artistic genius then it would reveal itself. But it has never revealed itself. Q.E.D. Women do not have the golden nugget of artistic genius. If Giotto, the obscure shepherd boy, and van Gogh with his fits could make it, why not women?

Yet as soon as one leaves behind the world of fairy-tale and self-fulfilling prophecy and, instead, casts a dispassionate eye on the actual situations in which important art production has existed, in the total range of its social and institutional structures throughout history, one finds that the very questions which are fruitful or relevant for the historian to ask shape up rather differently. One would like to ask, for instance, from what social classes artists were most likely to come at different periods of art history, from what castes and sub-group. What proportion of painters and sculptors, or more specifically, of major painters and sculptors, came from families in which their fathers or other close relatives were painters and sculptors or engaged in related professions? As Nikolaus Pevsner points out in his discussion of the French Academy in the 17th and 18th centuries, the transmission of the artistic profession from father to son was considered a matter of course (as it was with the Coypels, the Coustous, the Van Loos, etc); indeed, sons of academicians were exempted from the customary fees for lessons.[8] Despite the noteworthy and dramatically satisfying cases of the great father-rejecting *révoltés* of the 19th century, one might be forced to admit that a large proportion of artists, great and not-so-great, in the days when it was normal for sons to follow in their fathers' footsteps, had artist fathers. In the rank of major artists, the names of Holbein and Dürer, Raphael and Bernini, immediately spring to mind; even in our own times, one can cite the names of Picasso, Calder, Giacometti and Wyeth as members of artist-families.

As far as the relationship of artistic occupation and social class is concerned, an interesting paradigm for the question "Why have there been no great women artists?" might well be provided by trying to answer the question: "Why have there been no great artists from the aristocracy?" One can scarcely think, before the anti-traditional 19th century at least, of any artist who sprang from the ranks of any more elevated class than the upper bourgeoisie; even in the 19th century, Degas came from the lower nobility—more like the haute bourgeoisie, in fact—and only Toulouse-Lautrec, metamorphosed into the ranks of the marginal by accidental deformity, could be said to have come from the loftier reaches of the upper classes. While the aristocracy has always provided the lion's share of the patronage and the audience for art—as, indeed, the aristocracy of wealth does even in our more democratic days—it has contributed little beyond amateurish efforts to the creation of art itself, despite the fact that aristocrats (like many women) have had more than their share of educational advantages, plenty of leisure and, indeed, like women, were often encouraged to dabble in the arts and even develop into respectable amateurs, like Napoleon III's cousin, the Princess Mathilde, who exhibited at the official Salons, or Queen Victoria, who, with Prince Albert, studied art with no less a figure than Landseer himself. Could, it be that the little golden nugget—Genius—is missing from the aristocratic make-up in the same way that it is from the feminine psyche? Or rather, is it not, that the kinds of demands and expectations placed before both aristocrats and women—the amount of time necessarily devoted to social functions, the very kinds of activities demanded—simply made total devotion to professional art production out of the question, indeed unthinkable, both for upper-class males and for women generally, rather than its being a question of genius and talent?

When the right questions are asked about the conditions for producing art, of which the production of great art is a sub-topic, there will no doubt have to be some discussion of the situational concomitants of intelligence and talent generally, not merely of artistic genius. Piaget and others have stressed in their genetic epistemology that in the development of reason and in the unfolding of imagination in young children, intelligence—or, by implication, what we choose to call genius—is a dynamic activity rather than a static essence, and an activity of a subject *in a situation*. As further investigations in the field of child development imply, these abilities, or this intelligence, are built up minutely, step by step, from infancy onward, and the patterns of adaptation-accommodation may be established so early within the subject-in-an-environment that they may indeed *appear* to be innate to the unsophisticated observer. Such investigations imply that, even aside from meta-historical reasons, scholars will have to abandon the notion, consciously articulated or not, of individual genius as innate, and as primary to the creation of art.[9]

The question "Why have there been no great women artists?" has led us to the conclusion, so far, that art is not a free, autonomous activity of a super-endowed individual, "influenced" by previous artists, and, more vaguely and superficially, by "social forces," but rather, that the total situation of art making, both in terms of the development of the art maker and in the nature and quality of the work of art itself, occur in a social situation, are integral elements of this social structure, and are mediated and determined by specific and definable social institutions, be they art academies, systems of patronage, mythologies of the divine creator, artist as he-man or social outcast.

◆ ◆ ◆

CONCLUSION

We have tried to deal with one of the perennial questions used to challenge women's demand for true, rather than token, equality, by examining the whole erroneous intellectual substructure upon which the question "Why have there been no great women artists?" is based; by questioning the validity of the formulation of so-called "problems" in general and the "problem" of women specifically; and then, by probing some of the limitations of the discipline of art history itself. Hopefully, by stressing the *institutional*—i.e. the public—rather than the *individual*, or private, pre-conditions for achievement or the lack of it in the arts, we have provided a paradigm for the investigation of other areas in the field. By examining in some detail a single instance of deprivation or disadvantage—the unavailability of nude models to women art students—we have suggested that it was indeed institutionally made impossible for women to achieve artistic excellence, or success, on the same footing as men, no matter what the potency of their so-called talent, or genius. The existence of a tiny band of successful, if not great, women artists throughout history does nothing to gainsay this fact, any more than does the existence of a few superstars or token achievers among the members of any minority groups. And while great achievement is rare and difficult at best, it is still rarer and more difficult if, while you work, you must at the same time wrestle with inner demons of self-doubt and guilt and outer monsters of ridicule or patronizing encouragement, neither of which have any specific connection with the quality of the art work as such.

What is important is that women face up to the reality of their history and of their present situation, without making excuses or puffing mediocrity. Disadvantage may indeed be an excuse; it is not, however, an intellectual position. Rather, using as a vantage point their situation as underdogs in the realm of grandeur, and outsiders in that of ideology, women can reveal institutional and intellectual weaknesses in general, and, at the same time that they destroy false consciousness, take part in the creation of institutions in which clear thought—and true greatness—are challenges open to anyone, man or woman, courageous enough to take the necessary risk, the leap into the unknown.

NOTES

1. Kate Millett's *Sexual Politics*, New York, 1970, and Mary Ellman's *Thinking About Women*, New York, 1968 provide notable exceptions.

2. "Women Artists." Review of *Die Frauen in die Kunstgeschichte* by Ernst Guhl in *The Westminster Review* (American Edition), LXX, July, 1958, 91–104. I am grateful to Elaine Showalter for having brought this review to my attention.

3. See, for example, Peter S. Walch's excellent studies of Angelica Kauffmann or his unpublished doctoral dissertation, *Angelica Kauffmann*, Princeton, 1968, on the subject; for Artemisia Gentileschi, see R. Ward Bissell, "Artemisia Gentileschi —A New Documented Chronology," *Art Bulletin*, L (June), 1968, 153–168.

4. New York, 1968.

5. John Stuart Mill, *The Subjection of Women* (1869) in *Three Essays* by John Stuart Miff, World's Classics Series, London, 1966, p. 441.

6. For the relatively recent genesis of the emphasis on the artist as the nexus of esthetic experience, see M. H. Abrams, *The Mirror and the Lamp: Romantic Theory and the Critical Tradition*, New York, 1953, and Maurice Z. Shrader, *Icarus: The Image of the Artist in French Romanticism*, Cambridge, Massachusetts, 1961.

7. A comparison with the parallel myth for women, the Cinderella Story, is revealing: Cinderella gains higher status on the basis of a passive, "sex-object" attribute—small feet—whereas the Boy Wonder always proves himself through active accomplishment. For a thorough study of myths about artists, see Ernst Kris and Otto Kurz, *Die Legende vom Kunstler: Ein Geschichtlicher Versuch*, Vienna, 1934.

8. Nikolaus Pevsner, *Academies of Art, Past and Present*, Cambridge, 1940, p. 96f.

9. Contemporary directions—earthworks, conceptual art, art as information, etc.—certainly point *away* from emphasis on the individual genius and his salable products; in art history, Harrison C. and Cynthia A. White's *Canvases and Careers: Institutional Change in the French Painting World*, New York, 1965, opens up a fruitful new direction of investigation, as did Nikolaus Pevsner's pioneering *Academies of Art*. Ernst Gombrich and Pierre Francastel, in their very different ways, always have tended to view art and the artist as part of a total situation rather than in lofty isolation.

10. Female models were introduced in the life-class in Berlin in 1875, in Stockholm in 1839, in Naples in 1870, at the Royal College of Art in London, after 1875. Pevsner, *op. cit.*, p. 231. Female models at the Pennsylvania Academy of the Fine Arts wore masks to hide their identity as late as about 1866—as attested to in a charcoal drawing by Thomas Eakins—if not later.

11. Pevsner, *op. cit.*, p. 231.

12. H. C. and C. A. White, *op. cit.*, p. 51.

13. *Ibid.*, Table 5.

14. Mrs. Ellis, *The Daughters of England: Their Position in Society, Character, and Responsibilities* (1844) in *The Family Monitor*, New York, 1844, p. 35.

15. *Ibid.*, 38–39.

16. Patricia Thomson, *The Victorian Heroine: A Changing Ideal*, London, 1956, p. 77.

17. H. C. and C . A. White, *op. cit.*, p. 91.

18. Anna Klumpke, *Rosa Bonheur: Sa Vie, son oeuvre*, Paris, 1908, p. 311.

19. Betty Friedan, *The Feminine Mystique*, New York, 1963, p. 158.

20. A. Klumpke, *op. cit.*, p. 166.

21. Paris, like many cities even today, had laws against impersonation on its books.

22. A. Klumpke, *op. cit.*, pp. 308–309.

23. *Ibid.*, pp. 310–311.

24. Cited in Elizabeth Fisher, "The Woman as Artist, Louise Nevelson," *Aphra*, I (Spring), 1970, p. 32.

READING 13: WHY HAVE THERE BEEN NO GREAT WOMEN ARTISTS?

DISCUSSION QUESTIONS

• Why haven't there been any great women artists or scientists?

• What does Nochlin see as the problem with looking for historical examples and/or highlighting feminine values?

• What would Nochlin say about genius?

EXAMPLES TO THINK ABOUT

• Popular celebrations of female scientists (Ada Lovelace, *Hidden Figures*)

Living Room Wars

Rethinking Media Audiences for a Postmodern World

EXCERPTS FROM: *GENDER AND/IN MEDIA CONSUMPTION*

BY IEN ANG

Wouldn't it be much better for women and girls to choose identification figures that represent strong, powerful and independent women who are able and determined to change and improve their lives, such as Christine Cagney?

Such concerns are, of course, often heard in feminist accounts of popular fiction, but it is important to note here that they are often based upon a theoretical approach—what could be called a role/image approach, or, more conventionally, 'images of women' approach—which analyses images of women in the media and in fiction by setting them against 'real' women. Fictional female heroines are then seen as images of women functioning as role models for female audiences (Moi 1985; Rakow 1986). From such a perspective, it is only logical to claim that one should strive to offer positive role models by supplying positive images of women. And from this perspective, feminist common-sense would undoubtedly ascribe the Sue Ellen character to the realm of negative images, reflecting a traditional, stereotyped or trivialized model of womanhood.

However, this approach contains both theoretical and political problems. Most importantly here, because it implies a rationalistic view of the relationship between image and viewer (whereby it is assumed that the image is seen by the viewer as a more or less adequate model of reality), it can only account for the popularity of soap operas among women as something irrational. In other words, what the role/image approach tends to overlook is the large *emotional involvement* which is invested in identification with characters of popular fiction.

To counteract this attitude, we first of all need to acknowledge that these characters are products of *fiction,* and that fiction is not a mere set of images to be read referentially, but an ensemble of textual devices for engaging the viewer at the level of fantasy (Walkerdine 1983; see also Cowie 1984; Kaplan 1986). As a result, female fictional characters such as Sue Ellen Ewing or Christine Cagney cannot be conceptualized as 'realistic' images of women, but must be approached as textual constructions of possible *modes of femininity*: as embodying versions of gendered subjectivity endowed with specific forms of psychical and emotional satisfaction and dissatisfaction, and specific ways of dealing with conflicts and dilemmas. In relation to this, they do not function as role models but are symbolic realizations of feminine subject positions with which viewers can identify *in fantasy.*

Fantasy is central here. In line with psychoanalytic theory, fantasy should not be seen as mere illusion, an unreality, but as a reality in itself, a fundamental aspect of human existence: a necessary and unerasable dimension of psychical reality. Fantasy is an imagined scene in which the fantasizing subject is the protagonist, and in which alternative, imaginary scenarios for the subject's real life are evoked. Fantasizing obviously affords the subject pleasure, which, according to the psychoanalysts, has to do with the fulfilment of a conscious or unconscious wish. More generally, I want to suggest that the pleasure of fantasy lies in its offering the subject an opportunity to take up positions which she could not assume in real life: through fantasy she can move beyond the structural constraints of everyday life and explore other, more desirable situations, identities, lives. In this respect, it is unimportant whether these imaginary scenarios are 'realistic' or not: the appeal of fantasy lies precisely in that it can create imagined worlds which can take us beyond what is possible or acceptable in the 'real' world. As Lesley Stern has remarked, 'gratification is to be achieved not through acting out the fantasies, but through the activity of fantasising itself' (1982: 56).

Fantasies, and the act of fantasizing, are usually a private practice in which we can engage at any time and the content of which we generally keep to ourselves. Fictions, on the other hand, are collective and public fantasies; they are textual elaborations, in narrative form, of fantastic scenarios which, being mass-produced, are offered ready-made to audiences. We are not the originators of the public fantasies offered to us in fiction. This explains, of course, why we are not attracted to all the fictions available to us: most of them are irrelevant to our personal concerns and therefore not appealing. Despite this, the pleasure of consuming fictions that do attract us may still relate to that of fantasy: that is, it still involves the imaginary occupation of other subject positions which are outside the scope of our everyday social and cultural identities.

Implicit in the theoretical perspective I have outlined so far is a post-structuralist theory on subjectivity (see Weedon 1987). Central to this is the idea that subjectivity is not the essence or the source from which the individual acts and thinks and feels; on the contrary, subjectivity should be seen as a product of the society and culture in which we live: it is through the meaning systems or discourses circulating in society and culture that subjectivity is constituted and individual identities are formed. Each individual is the site of a multiplicity of subject positions proposed to her by the discourses with which she is confronted; her identity is the precarious and contradictory result of the specific set of subject positions she inhabits at any moment in history.

Just as the fictional character is not a unitary image of womanhood, then, so is the individual viewer not a person whose identity is something static and coherent. If a woman is a social subject whose identity is at least partially marked out by her being a person of a certain sex, it is by no means certain that she will always inhabit the same mode of feminine subjectivity. On the contrary, many different and sometimes contradictory sets of femininities or feminine subject positions (ways of being a woman) are in principle available to her, although it is likely that she will be drawn to adopt some of those more than others.

> My concern about whether I could persuade Dot's customers to elaborate honestly about their motives for reading was unwarranted, for after an initial period of mutually felt awkwardness, we conversed frankly and with enthusiasm.

> (Radway 1984: 47)

From this point on, Radway ceases to reflect on the nature of her own relationship to the 'Smithton women', and offers instead an often fascinating account of what she has learned from them. She quotes them extensively and is at times genuinely 'taken by surprise' by the unexpected turns of her conversations with Dot and the Smithton women. However, precisely because she does not seem to feel any real strain about the way in which she and her informants are positioned towards each other, she represents the encounter as one that is strictly confined to the terms of a relationship between two parties with fixed identities: that of a researcher/feminist and that of interviewees/romance fans. This ontological and epistemological separation between subject and object allows her to present the Smithton readers as a pre-existent 'interpretive community', a sociological entity whose characteristics and peculiarities were already there when the researcher set out to investigate it. It may well be, however, that this group of women only constituted itself as a 'community' in the research process itself—in a very literal sense indeed: at the moment that they were brought together for the collective interviews Radway conducted with them; at the moment that they were invited to think of themselves as a group that shares something, namely their fondness for romance reading, and the fact that they are all Dot's customers. An indication of this is offered by Radway herself:

> In the beginning, timidity seemed to hamper the responses as each reader took turns answering each question. When everyone relaxed, however, the

conversation flowed more naturally as the participants disagreed among themselves, contradicted one another, and *delightedly* discovered that they still agreed about many things

(Radway 1984: 48, emphasis added)

In relying on a realist epistemology, then, Radway tends to overlook the constructivist aspect of her own enterprise. In a sense, doing ethnography is itself a political intervention in that it helps to *construct* the culture it seeks to describe and understand, rather than merely reflect it. The concrete political benefit, in this specific case, could be that Radway's temporary presence in Smithton, and the lengthy conversations she had with the women, had an empowering effect on them, in that they were given the rare opportunity to come to a collective understanding and validation of their own reading experiences. Such an effect might be regarded as utterly limited by feminists with grander aims, and it is certainly not without its contradictions (after all, how can we ever be sure how such temporary, cultural empowerment relates to the larger stakes of the more structural struggles over power in which these women lead their lives?), but it is worth noticing, nevertheless, if we are to consider the value and predicaments of doing feminist research in its most material aspects (see McRobbie 1982).

For Radway, however, other concerns prevail. The separation between her world and that of her informants becomes progressively more absolute towards the end of the book. In the last few chapters the mode of writing becomes almost completely monologic, and the Smithton women are definitively relegated to the position of 'them', a romance reading community towards which Radway is emphatically sympathetic, but from which she remains fundamentally distant. Radway's analysis first recognizes the 'rationality' of romance reading by interpreting it as an act of symbolic resistance, but ends up constructing a deep chasm between the ideological world inhabited by the Smithton women and the convictions of feminism:

[W]hen the act of romance reading is viewed as it is by the readers themselves, from within the belief system that accepts as given the institutions of heterosexuality and monogamous marriage, it can be conceived as an activity of mild protest and longing for reform necessitated by those institutions' failure to satisfy the emotional needs of women. Reading therefore functions for them as an act of recognition and contestation whereby that failure is first admitted and then partially reversed.[...] At the same time, however, when viewed from the vantage point of a feminism that would like to see the women's oppositional impulse lead to real social change, romance reading can also be seen as an activity that could potentially disarm that impulse. It might do so because it supplies vicariously those very needs and requirements that might otherwise be formulated as demands in the real world and lead to the potential restructuring of sexual relations.

(Radway 1984: 213)

These are the theoretical terms in which Radway conceives the troubled relationship between feminism and romance reading. A common ground—the perceived sharing of the experiential pains and costs of patriarchy—is analytically secured, but from a point of view that assumes the mutual exteriority of the two positions. The distribution of identities is clearcut: Radway, the researcher, is a feminist and *not* a romance fan; the Smithton women, the researched, are romance readers and *not* feminists. From such a perspective, the political aim of the project becomes envisaged as one of bridging this profound separation between 'us' and 'them'. Elsewhere, Radway has formulated the task as follows:

> I am troubled by the fact that it is all too easy for us, as academic feminists and Marxists who are preoccupied with the *analysts* of ideological formations that produce consciousness, to forget that our entailed and parallel project is the political one of convincing those very real people to see how their situation intersects with our own and why it will be fruitful for them to see it as we do. Unless we wish to tie this project to some new form of coercion, we must remain committed to the understanding that these individuals are capable of coming to recognize their set of beliefs as an ideology that limits their view of their situation.

(Radway 1986: 105)

Does this mean then that doing feminist research is a matter of pedagogy? The militant ending of *Reading the Romance* leaves no doubt about it:

> I think it absolutely essential that we who are committed to social change learn not to overlook [the] minimal but nonetheless legitimate form of protest [expressed in romance reading]. We should seek it out not only to understand its origins and its utopian longing but also to learn how best to encourage it and bring it to fruition. If we do not, we have already conceded the fight and, in the case of the romance at least, admitted the impossibility of creating a world where the vicarious pleasure supplied by its reading would be unnecessary.

(Radway 1984: 222)

Here, Radway's feminist desire is expressed in its most dramatic form: its aim is directed at raising the consciousness of romance reading women, its mode is that of persuasion, conversion even. 'Real' social change can only be brought about, Radway seems to believe, if romance readers would stop reading romances and become feminist activists instead. In other words, underlying Radway's project is what Angela McRobbie has termed a 'recruitist' conception of the politics of feminist research (1982: 52). What makes me feel so uncomfortable about this move is the unquestioned certainty with which feminism is posed as the superior solution for all women's problems, as if feminism automatically possessed the relevant and effective formulas for all women to change their lives and acquire happiness. In the course of the book Radway has thus inverted the pertinent relations: whereas in the beginning the ethnographer's position entails a vulnerable stance that puts her assumptions at risk, what is achieved in the end is an all but complete restoration of the authority of feminist discourse. This, then, is the therapeutic effect of *Reading the Romance*: it reassures where certainties threaten to dissolve, it comforts where divisions among women, so distressing and irritating to feminism, seem almost despairingly insurmountable—by holding the promise that, with hard work for sure, unity *would* be reached if we could only rechannel the energy that is now put in romance reading in the direction of 'real' political action. In short, what is therapeutic (for feminism) about *Reading the Romance* is its construction of romance readers as embryonic feminists.

I do agree with Radway that the relationship between 'feminism' and 'women' is one of the most troublesome issues for the women's movement. However, it seems untenable to me to maintain a vanguardist view of feminist politics, to see feminist consciousness as the linear culmination of political radically. With McRobbie (1982), I think that we should not underestimate the struggles for self-empowerment engaged in by 'ordinary women' outside the political and ideological frameworks of the self-professed women's movement. I am afraid therefore that Radway's radical intent is drawing dangerously near a form of political moralism, propelled by a desire to make 'them' more like 'us'. Indeed, what Radway's conception of political intervention tends to arrive at is the deromanticization of the romance in favour of a romanticized feminism!

This is not the place to elaborate on the practical implications of this political predicament. What I do want to point out, however, is how the therapeutic upshot of *Reading the Romance* is prepared for in the very analysis Radway has made of the meaning of romance reading for the Smithton women, that is, how the analytical and the therapeutic are inextricably entwined with one another.

Strangely missing in Radway's interpretive framework, I would say, is any careful account of the *pleasurableness* of the pleasure of romance reading. The absence of pleasure *as* pleasure in *Reading the Romance* is made apparent in Radway's frequent, downplaying qualifications of the enjoyment that the Smithton women have claimed to derive from their favourite genre: that it is a form of *vicarious* pleasure, that it is *only temporarily* satisfying because it is *compensatory* literature; that even though it does create 'a kind of female community', through it 'women join forces only symbolically and in a mediated way in the privacy of their homes and in the devalued sphere of leisure activity' (Radway 1984: 212). Revealed in such qualifications is a sense that the pleasure of romance reading is somehow not really real, as though there were other forms of pleasure that could be considered 'more real' because they are more 'authentic', more enduring, more veritable, or whatever.

Radway's explanation of repetitive romance reading is a case in point. She analyses this in terms of romance reading's ultimate inadequacy when it comes to the satisfaction of psychic needs for which the readers cannot find an outlet in their actual social lives. In her view, romance reading is inadequate precisely because it gives these women the *illusion* of pleasure while it leaves their 'real' situation unchanged. In line with the way in which members of the Birmingham Centre for Contemporary Cultural Studies have interpreted youth subcultures (see Hall and Jefferson 1976; Hebdige 1979), then, Radway comes to the conclusion that romance reading is a sort of 'imaginary solution' to real, structural problems and contradictions produced by patriarchy. (The real solution, one could guess, lies in the bounds of feminism.) All this amounts to a quite functionalist explanation of romance reading, one that is preoccupied with its effects rather than its mechanisms. Consequently, pleasure as such cannot possibly be taken seriously in this theoretical framework, because the whole explanatory movement is directed towards the *ideological function* of pleasure.

Are the Smithton women ultimately only fooling themselves then? At times Radway seems to think so. For example, when the Smithton women state that it is impossible to describe the 'typical romantic heroine' because in their view, the heroines 'are all different', Radway is drawn to conclude that 'they refuse to admit that the books they read have a standard plot' (ibid.: 199). In imposing such a hasty interpretation, however, she forgets to take the statement seriously, as if it were only the result of the women's being lured by the realistic illusion of the narrative text.[1] But perhaps the statement that all heroines are different says more about the reading experience than Radway assumes. Perhaps it could be seen as an index of the pleasure that is solicited by what may be termed 'the grain of the story': the subtle, differentiated texture of each book's staging of the romantic tale that makes its reading a 'new' experience even though the plot is standard. In fact, Radway's own findings seem to testify to this when she reports that 'although the women almost never remembered the names of the principal characters, they could recite in surprising detail not only what had happened to them but also how they managed to cope with particularly troublesome situations' (ibid.: 201).

Attention to this pleasure of detail could also give us a fresh perspective on another thing often asserted by many of the Smithton women that puzzled Radway, namely that they always want to ascertain in advance that a book finishes with a happy ending. Radway sees this peculiar behaviour as an indication that these women cannot bear 'the threat of the unknown as it opens out before them and demand continual reassurance that the events they suspect will happen [i.e. the happy ending], in fact, will finally happen' (1984: 205). But isn't it possible to develop a more positive interpretation here? When the reader is sure *that* the heroine and the hero will finally get each other, she can concentrate all the more on *how* they will get each other. Finding out about the happy ending in advance could then be seen as a clever reading strategy aimed at obtaining maximum pleasure: a pleasure that is oriented towards the *scenario* of romance, rather than its outcome. If the outcome is predictable in the romance genre, the variety of the ways in which two lovers can find one another is endless. Cora Kaplan's succinct specification of what in her view is central to the pleasure of romance reading for women is particularly illuminating here, suggesting 'that the reader identifies with both terms in the seduction scenario, but most of all with *the process of seduction*' (1986: 162, emphasis added).

This emphasis on the staging of the romantic encounter, on the details of the moments of seducing and being seduced as the characteristic elements of pleasure in romance reading, suggests another absence in the interpretive framework of *Reading the Romance*: the meaning of fantasy, or, for that matter, of romantic fantasy. In Radway's account, fantasy is too easily equated with the unreal, with the world of illusions, that is, false ideas about how life 'really' is. It is this pitting of reality against fantasy that brings her to the sad conclusion that repetitive romance reading 'would enable a reader to tell herself again and again that a love like the heroine's might indeed occur in a world such as hers. She thus teaches herself to believe that men *are able* to satisfy women's needs fully' (1984: 201). In other words, it is Radway's reductionist conception of phantasmatic scenarios as incorrect models of reality—in Radway's feminist conception of social reality, there is not much room for men's potential capacity to satisfy women—that drives her to a more or less straightforward 'harmful effects' theory.

If, however, as I have already suggested in chapter 5, we were to take fantasy seriously as a reality in itself, as a necessary dimension of our psychical reality, we could conceptualize the world of fantasy as the place of excess, where the unimaginable can be imagined. Fiction could then be seen as the social materialization and elaboration of fantasies, and thus, in the words of Allison Light, 'as the explorations and productions of desires which may be in excess of the socially possible or acceptable' (1984: 7).

This insight may lead to another interpretation of the repetitiveness of romance reading as an activity among women (some critics would speak of 'addiction'), which does not accentuate their ultimate psychic subordination to patriarchal relations, but rather emphasizes the rewarding quality of the fantasizing activity itself. As Radway would have it, romance fans pick up a book again and again because romantic fiction does *not satisfy them enough*, as it is only a poor, illusory and transitory satisfaction of needs unmet in 'real life'. But couldn't the repeated readings be caused by the fact that the romance novel *satisfies them too much*, because it constitutes a secure space in which an imaginary perpetuation of an emphatically utopian state of affairs (something that is an improbability in 'real life' in the first place) is possible?

After all, it is more than striking that romance novels always abruptly *end* at the moment that the two lovers have finally found each other, and thus never go beyond the point of no return: romantic fiction generally is exclusively about the titillating period *before* the wedding! This could well indicate that what repetitive reading of romantic fiction offers is the opportunity to continue to enjoy the excitement of romance and romantic scenes without being interrupted by the dark side of sexual relationships. In the symbolic world of the romance novel, the struggle between the sexes (while being one of the ongoing central themes of melodramatic soap operas; see Ang 1985: esp. chapter 4), will always be overcome in the end, precisely because that is what the romantic imagination self-consciously tries to make representable. Seen this way, the politics of romance reading is a politics of fantasy in which women engage precisely because it does *not* have 'reality value'. Thus, the romance reader can luxuriate in never having to enter the conflictual world that comes after the 'happy ending'. Instead, she leaves the newly formed happy couple behind and joins another heroine, another hero, who are to meet each other in a new book, in a new romantic setting.

What is achieved by this deliberate fictional bracketing of life after the wedding, it seems to me, is the phantasmatic perpetuation of the romantic state of affairs. Whatever the concrete reasons for women taking pleasure in this—here some further ethnographic inquiry could provide us with new answers—it seems clear to me that what is fundamentally involved is a certain determination to maintain the *feeling* of romance, or a refusal to give it up, even though it may be temporarily or permanently absent in 'real life,' against all odds. And it is this enduring emotional quest that, I would suggest, should be taken seriously as a psychical strategy by which women empower themselves in everyday life, leaving apart what its ideological consequences in social reality are.

If this interpretation is at all valid, then I am not sure how feminism should respond to it. Radway's rationalist proposal—that romance readers should be convinced to see that their reading habits are ultimately working against their own 'real' interests—will not do, for it slights the fact that what is above all at stake in the energy invested in romance reading is the actualization of romantic feelings, which are by definition 'unrealistic', excessive, utopian, inclined towards the sensational and the adventurous. That the daring quality of romanticism tends to be tamed by the security of the happy ending in the standard romance novel is not so important in this respect. What is important is the tenacity of the desire to feel romantically.

This is not to say that romantic fiction should be considered above all criticism. The ideological consequences of its mass production and consumption should be a continuing object of reflection and critique for feminism. Questions of sexual politics, definitions of femininity and masculinity, and the cultural meanings of the romance in general will remain important issues. However, all this should not invalidate the significance of the craving for and pleasure in romantic feelings that so many women have in common and share. In fact, I am drawn to conclude that it might be this common experience that could serve as the basis for overcoming the paralysing opposition between 'feminism' and 'romance reading'. While feminists, as Elizabeth Wilson (1986: 17) has noted, have often dismissed romanticism, it has a psychic reality that cannot simply be banished. However, by taking the love for romantic feelings seriously as a starting point for engagement with 'non-feminist' women, the feminist researcher might begin to establish a 'comprehension of self by the detour of the comprehension of the other' (Rabinow 1977: 5), in a confrontation with other women who may have more expertise and experience in the meanings, pleasures and dangers of romanticism than herself.

What could change as a result of such an ethnographic encounter—and to my mind it is this process-oriented, fundamentally dialogic and dialectical character of knowledge acquisition that marks the distinctive critical edge of ethnography—is not only 'their' understanding of what 'we', as self-proclaimed feminists, are struggling for, but, more importantly, the sense of identity that is constructed by feminism itself.

NOTE

1. This is not to say that generalizations as such should at all cost be avoided (indeed, this would make the production of knowledge virtually impossible); it is merely to point to the importance, in understanding social phenomena, of complementing the generalizing tendency with an opposite, *particularizing* one. See Billig (1987) and Abu-Lughold (1991).

READING 14: LIVING ROOM WARS

DISCUSSION QUESTIONS

- What is "investment" and how does it relate to identity?
- How do your viewing patterns changes depending on who is watching with you?

EXAMPLES TO THINK ABOUT

- Social media

SECTION 4

THEORIZING SINGLE GENDER CULTURES

Volume Fluidity

EXCERPT FROM: *SPECULUM OF THE OTHER WOMAN*

BY LUCE IRIGARAY

S o woman has not yet taken (a) place. The "not yet" probably corresponds to a *system of hysterical fantasy* but/and it acknowledges a *historical condition*. Woman is still the place, the whole of the place in which she cannot take possession of herself as such. She is experienced as all-powerful precisely insofar as her indifferentiation makes her radically powerless. She is never here and now because it is she who sets up that eternal elsewhere from which the "subject" continues to draw his reserves, his resources, though without being able to recognize them/her. She is not uprooted from matter, from the earth, but yet, but still, she is already scattered into *x* number of places that are never gathered together into anything she knows of herself, and these remain the basis of reproduction—particularly of discourse—in all its forms.

Woman remains this nothing at all, or this all at nothing, in which each (male) one seeks to find the means to replenish the resemblance to self (as) to same. Thus she moves from place to place, yet, up to the present, it has never been she that was displaced. She must continue to hold the place she constitutes for the subject, a place to which no eternal value can be assigned lest the subject remain paralyzed forever by the irreplaceableness of his cathected investments. Therefore she has to wait for him to move her in accordance with his needs and desires. In accordance with the urgency of the economy in operation. She is patient in her reserve, her modesty, her silence, even when the moment comes to endure violent consummation, to be torn apart, drawn and quartered. Enough of the stitches closing her vagina are taken out, sexuality is permitted her—but as a mother only?—to allow him to penetrate her body again, in the hope of finally losing his "soul" there. Such corruption is too calculated, and he risks ending up more of a child, and thus more enslaved, than ever. Meanwhile, her shining raiment, her gleaming skin conceal the disaster within, hide all that devours and rends her body. *A female one,* thus, at least as far as the eye can see; the striking makeup, the motherly role she plays, cover up the fact that she is torn to pieces. Fragments: of women, of discourse, of silences, of blanks that are still immaculate (?)... Everything thrust aside wherever the "subject" seeks to escape from his emprisonment. But even as he struggles to fracture that specular matrix, that enveloping discursivity, that body of the text in which he has made himself a prisoner, it is Nature he finds, Nature who, unknown to him, has nourished his project, his production. It is Nature who now fuses for him with that glass enclosure, that spangled sepulcher, from which—imaginary and therefore absent—she is unable to articulate her difference. Thus she allows herself to be consumed again for new speculations, or thrown away as unfit for consumption. Without saying a word. Scarcely does she try to promote her usefulness or ensure her exchange value by means of a few gadgets; the latest brilliant novelties put into circulation by men and only a little warped by her faintly baroque frivolity.

Everything has to be (re)invented to avoid the *vacuum.* And if the place is plowed over again in this way, it is always in search of the lost roots of sameness. Because, on the horizon, a hint was appearing of a "world" so inconceivable, so other, that it was preferable to go back underground rather than witness so dizzying an event. Although the mother represents only a mute soil, a mystery beyond metaphor, at least she is still *pregnant.* Obviously, you will find opaqueness and resistance in the mother, even the repulsiveness of matter, the horror of blood, the ambivalence of milk, the threatening traces of the father's phallus, and even that hole that you left behind when you came into the world. But she—at least—is not nothing. She is not this vacuum (of) woman. This void of representation, this negation of all representation, this limit set on all present representations (of self). The mother is pulled apart, indeed, but by the child being born or tearing at the breast. He can believe this at any rate. That gap, break, or fault, then, is well known to him since he has made use of it and closed if off in his systematics. It is not the gap (of) woman, which he defends himself against by changing her into a mother, or which he combats, in his effort to block any "other," by means of the protective veil of a language that has already changed even its evasions into fetishes.

(LI's title is "L'incontournable volume." "Contourner" means to trace an outline or shape, and also to distort, twist, or evade.—Tr.)

Woman is neither open nor closed. She is indefinite, infinite, *form is never complete in her.* She is not infinite but neither is she *a* unit(y), such as letter, number, figure in a series, proper noun, unique object (in a) world of the senses, simple ideality in an intelligible whole, entity of a foundation, etc. This incompleteness in her form, her morphology, allows her continually to become something else, though this is not to say that she is ever univocally nothing. No metaphor completes her. Never is she this, then that, this and that. ... But she is becoming that expansion that she neither is nor will be at any moment as definable universe. Perhaps this is what is meant by her insatiable (hysterical) thirst for satisfaction. No one single thing—no form, act, discourse, subject, masculine, feminine—can complete the development of woman's desire. And for her the risk of maternity is that of limiting (herself and her desire) to the world of *one* child. By closing herself up over the unit of that conception, by curling around that one, her desire hardens. *Perhaps it becomes phallic through this relationship to the one?* And likewise a femininity that conforms and corresponds too exactly to an idea—Idea—of woman, that is too obedient to a sex—to an Idea of sex—or to a fetish sex has already frozen into phallomorphism. Is already metabolized by phallogocratism. Whereas what happens in the jouissance of women exceeds all this. It is indefinite flood in which all manner of developments can be inscribed. The fullness of their coming into being is hinted, is proclaimed as possible, but within an extension swelling outward without discernible limits. Without telos or arche. Provided that it is not already phallic. That it has not already submitted to the prescriptions of a hommosexual imaginary and to its relationship to the origin, to a logos that claims to lead the potency of the maternal back into the same—to Sameness—in itself and for itself.

But woman is not to be resolved like that. Except in her phallosensical capitulations and capitalizations. For (the) woman neither is able to give herself some meaning by speech nor means to be able to speak in such a way that she is assigned to some concept or that some fixed notion is assigned to her. Woman is not to be related to any simple designatable being, subject, or entity. Nor is the whole group (called) women. One woman + one woman + one woman will never add up to some generic entity: woman. (The/a) woman refers to what cannot be defined, enumerated, formulated or *formalized*. Woman is a common noun for which no identity can be defined. (The/a) woman does not obey the principle of self-identity, however the variable x for self is defined. She is identified with every x variable, not in any specific way. Presupposed is an excess of all identification to/of self. But this excess is nothing: it is vacancy of form, gap in form, the return to another edge where she retouches herself with the help of—nothing. Lips of the same form—but of a form that is never simply defined—ripple outwards as they touch and send one another on a course that is never fixed into a single configuration.

This will already have taken place without the consent or assent of any object, or subject. This is an other topo-(logy) of jouissance. Alien to masculine self-affectation that has seen there only its own negative—the death of its logic and not its alter(n)ation in a still undefined copulation. Man's auto-erotism presupposes an individualization of the subject, of the object, and of the instrument appropriate(d) to jouissance. If only for an instant, for the time it takes to switch. (The/a) woman is always already in a state of anamorphosis in which every figure becomes fuzzy. A state of cyclic discontinuity closing in a slit whose lips merge into one another. Thus she cannot *repeat herself* nor produce herself as something *quite other* in pleasure, for the other already within her affects her, touches her without ever becoming either one or the other (male or female). The separation of this unforming contact cannot be formulated in the simplicity of any present. And since she has never raised herself up to that simple present, woman remains (in) her indifference. Remains what he undertakes to rape and rend. What he acts to speak for and touch, here and now. Even if to act is to feel again. For to be (the/a) woman is already to feel oneself before anything else has specifically intervened. She is beyond all pairs of opposites, all distinctions between active and passive or past and future. But this surreptitious self-affection is not overt, cannot be expressed in words. It is *true* that women don't tell all. And even if one begs them to speak, if he begs them to speak, they will or would never express anything but the will and the word of the "subject" who rapes and robs them of their jouissance. Women have already lost something more intimate—something that finds no communion in "soul"—and "gained" only propositions in exchange. They are already dominated by an intent, a meaning, a thought. By the laws of *a* language. Even in their madness, which turns language upside down and inside out. Telling all for the/a woman has no meaning or has no one meaning, since she cannot express this nothing that affects her, in which she is always already touched. This is the "nothing to tell" that history—History—duplicates by removing both it and her from the economy of discourse.

Thus (the/a) woman may, in a pinch, be a signifier—even below the line—in the logical system of representations and representatives-representers, of the "subject." This does not mean that, as this signifier, she may in any way recognize herself. Or even that man, as representer of the power (of the) phallus, corresponds for her to any meaning, except perhaps that of her exclusion from herself. For man is placed in such a way as to re-mark the distance, the separation, in which she finds herself, but the "subject's" imprisonment in the autarchy of his metaphorical system implies that, even when such "re-marking" occurs, it does so only in the context of that contiguousness in which she is contained, retained, in her jouissance, and which steers her away from her own course in order to articulate a phallic whole: her function henceforward will be as *hole*. And for her, metaphor will continue to work as violation and separation, except if, *empty of all meaning that is already appropriate(d)*, she keeps open the indefinite possibilities of her jouissance—that is, God, the design introducing a "figure" that resists using its allegiance to an individual as a firm foundation. A figure that still has extension, but that does not break up into more and more comprehensive forms. God, whose desire is a closed book to mere expertise, left to/in ignorance. Perhaps because He refuses hatred? Yes, if hatred comes from the particular character of knowledge. In which each one, male and female, would try to get the *best bit* of knowledge, and struggle to use his specul(ariz)ation to tear apart the representation of the other, thereby preserving the power (of) truth of the spectacle upon which he/she gazes. Denying the fiction of the mirror that lies beneath. But, for someone who knew everything, rivalry in appropriate (self)knowledge would be meaningless. Woman certainly does not know everything (about herself), she doesn't know (herself to be) anything, in fact. But her relationship to (self)knowledge provides access to a whole of what might be known or of what she might know—that is to God. And here again, by duplicating that speculative condition as a kind of caricature, that is, by excluding it—except as phallic proxies—from all individual science, from the appropriation of all knowledge (of self), "History" has manipulated the desire of woman—who is forced to function as an object, or more rarely as a subject—so as to perpetuate the existence of God as the stake in an omniscience quite alien to its determination. God is adored even as He is abhorred in his power. And because God has been set aside in/by female jouissance, He will bring horror and aversion down upon it, because of its "un-likeness," because its "not yet" defies all comparison. And if in the attention the "subject" now devotes to defining woman's sexuality, he aims to become identical to the being—the Being—of the other—the Other?—and seeks to resorb otherness into Sameness, wanting that, the Id, her, and her … knowledge in order to be more like Self, to act more like Self, woman can only reply: not . yet. And in fact, in one sense, in this sense, never.

For man needs an instrument to touch himself with: a hand, a woman, or some substitute. This mechanism is sublated in and by language. Man produces language for self-arousal. And in the various forms of discourse, the various modes of the "subject's" self-arousal can be analyzed. The most ideal of these would be philosophical discourse, which gives privileged status to "self-representing." This mode of self-arousal reduces the need for an instrument to *virtually* nothing—to the thought (of) the soul: soul defined as a mirror placed inside whereby the "subject," in the most secret as well as most subtle way, ensures the immortality of his auto-erotism.

Sciences and technologies also need instruments for their self-arousal. And to some extent they are thereby freed from the "subject's" control, and risk depriving him of a fraction of his solitary profit, competing with him in a bid for their autonomy. But thought still subsists. At least for a while, for as long as it takes to think (oneself) woman. Is this the last resource available to the self-arousal of the "subject" as such in/by language? Or is it rather a small opening in his vicious circle, in the logos of sameness? If machines, even machines of theory, can be aroused all by themselves, may woman not do likewise? Now a crisis breaks out, an age in which the "subject" no longer knows where to turn, whom or what to turn to, amid all these many foci of "liberation," none rigorously homogeneous with another and all heterogeneous to his conception. And since he had long sought in that conception the instrument, the lever and, in more cases than one, the term of his pleasure, these objects of mastery have perhaps brought the subject to his doom. *So now man struggles to be science, machine, woman, … to prevent any of these from escaping his service and ceasing to be interchangeable.* But he will never quite manage to do this as in none of these things—science, machine, woman—will form ever achieve the same completeness it does in him, in the inner sanctuary of his mind. In them form has always already exploded. Indeed it is in this way that form can take pleasure in herself—in edges touching each other—or sustain that illusion for the other. Whereas the "subject" must always re-exhibit (his) form in front of the self in order to taste its possession once more. The master in his pleasure is enslaved to his power.

When the/a woman touches herself, on the other hand, a whole touches itself because it is in-finite, because it has neither the knowledge nor the power to close up or to swell definitively to the extension of an infinite. This self-touching gives woman a form that is in(de)finitely transformed without closing over her appropriation. Metamorphoses occur in which there is no complete set, where no set theory of the One is established. Transmutations occur, always unexpectedly, since they do not conspire to accomplish any telos. *That*, after all, would rest on the assumption that one figure takes up—sublates—the previous one and dictates the next one, that there is *one* specified form, that becomes *another*. But this happens only in the imaginary of the (male) subject, who projects onto all others the reason for the capture of his desire: his language, which claims to designate him perfectly.

DISCUSSION QUESTIONS

- Irigaray is trying to explain what a feminine mode of thought would be like. Can you list some of its features?
- Is the kind of thought valorized in our culture a masculine mode of thought?
- What do you think of Irigaray's invocation of the female body?

EXAMPLES TO THINK ABOUT

- Categorization, formal logic, analytic thought

Female Imagery

EXCERPT FROM: *WOMANSPACE JOURNAL*

BY JUDY CHICAGO AND MIRIAM SCHAPIRO

O'keeffe began, she painted a haunting mysterious passage through the black portal of an iris, making the first recognized step into the darkness of female identity. That step moved her out of the reference points of art-making as it had been defined by men, throughout history. She painted out of an urgency to understand her own being and to communicate as yet unknown information about being a woman.

What does it feel like to be a woman? To be formed around a central core and have a secret place which can be entered and which is also a passageway from which life emerges? What kind of imagery does this state of feeling engender? There is now evidence that many women artists have defined a central orifice whose formal organization is often a metaphor for a woman's body. The center of the painting is the tunnel; the experience of female sexuality. In the case of O'Keeffe, the metaphor is extended into a world of life and death. In "Black Iris" the forms suggest and then transcend womanliness to metamorphose into an image of death and resurrection. [See Frontispiece.]

There is a contradiction in the experience of a woman who is also an artist. She feels herself to be "subject" in a world which treats her as "object". Her works often become a symbolic arena where she establishes her sense of personal, sexual identity.

She asks: "Who am I? Am I active or passive? How does the vulnerable center inside me affect my perception of reality? How does my own sense of interior space and receptivity differ from the sense of being outside and thrusting inward? Where is the mirror in the world to reveal who I am? If I repeat the shape of my question many times, will that shape be seen?"

In answering these questions she often defines a sculptural or pictorial image which is central and, in doing so, she gives out her own information about who she is, often to a world that doesn't listen, doesn't look, and certainly doesn't care.

When women began to speak about themselves, they were not understood. Men had established a code of regulations for the making and judging of art which derived from their sense of what was or was not significant. Women, thought to be inferior to men, obviously could not occupy center stage unless they concerned themselves with the ideas men deemed appropriate. If they dealt with areas of experience in the female domain, men paid no attention because they were not used to women making their experience visible. In fact those women whose work was built on their own identity in terms of female iconography have been treated by men as if they were dealing with masculine experience. This is a false assumption since the cultural experience of women has differed greatly from that of men. For centuries, women were educated to different tasks and remained outside of the scientific and mechanical culture built by men. Now that women are beginning to recognize their right to display their own symbology, they find themselves met with a mask of non-comprehension on the part of the male art critics.

The best example of this is the case of Georgia O'Keeffe. Here is a woman of major stature who appears in the 20th century.

In 1923, a year before she married Stieglitz, O'Keeffe painted a 48″ × 30″ oil on canvas called "Grey Line with Black, Blue and Yellow". In this painting, which resembles a watercolor more than an oil in its transparent paint quality, we see a central image constructed like the labia of the vagina, opening into a thin, black, membranous cavity. The entire central orifice is surrounded on each side by a white, sheltering form which rises and moves out from the center to embrace another space beyond the flesh of the flower-like orifice, a space which suggests infinity. Describing the central opening are a series of delicately painted folds, which suggest nothing less than orgiastic throbbing or contractions of labor. There is in the uppermost regions of the orifice, a dark movement towards a peak where again the sensuous perception is that of the highly focused feeling of clitoral sensation.

In 1946, the year Stieglitz died, she painted an oil on paper, 30″ × 24″, called "In the Patio 1." The essential motif of this painting as well as others, is the patio of her house in the southwest. Again the central image appears. Here in opposition to the repeated oval and/or circular motions in the last painting discussed, we find the central image in the shape of a rectangle, actually housed within the space of a larger rectangle (perhaps a door frame or a window frame). Seen through the space of the central image are several more rectangular, periscoping spaces. In order to understand the preoccupation with building structure, one has to read it as a metaphor for a housing or casing of the soul or the body. Once we acknowledge this proposition, then the opening in the middle of the picture provides an insight into the mystery of black and white forms intertwining in the Yin/Yang manner; we see a complexity of meaning stemming from O'Keeffe's preoccupation with life and death. There are light motifs in the painting, such as the two darts in the large framework and the curve upwards of the framework itself, as well as the ambivalent floor opening on the left-hand side of the painting. All of this iconography seems to subordinate itself to the larger issue of looking through the window or door into infinity; or discovering the view of the soul; or tunnelling forward into infinity or backwards to the past which now becomes black and white or "clear".

In 1964 she painted an oil on canvas, 24¼″ × 30⅛″, "Road Past the View". Here we see other aspects of O'Keeffe's femininity. The painting is a landscape which conveys the curves of flesh in the quietness of a dream. The color is as soft as has ever been seen in abstract painting, not just pale, but soft like a cloud or a light caress. As a woman, O'Keeffe has no taboo (as in the case with men) about allowing herself to be gentle and tender. Women in our society are allowed to retain this aspect of themselves—the expression of softness inside themselves which has been acculturated into the mothering aspect of the female role. For men, conditioned to the role of toughness, fragility is associated with womanliness and men cannot allow those feelings in themselves lest they risk the fantasy of emasculinization. Because O'Keeffe doesn't have this problem, the range of expression in her work is far greater than one ordinarily sees in the lifetime of a man's work.

O'Keeffe's oeuvre opens up the possibility of human expressiveness heretofore unavailable, particularly to men. Implicit in this is a suggestion that just as women have suffered when measured by male standards, so men might be found lacking when measured by the standards of that work by women which asserts softness, vulnerability and self-exposure.

Better to deny, obscure or mystify the achievements of women than to have to be measured by those achievements. The structure of male personality has led to an artmaking that aggrandizes abstract ideas, formal innovation, and concern with materials and tools. This reflects the conditioning of men towards manipulation of reality and away from exposure of vulnerability and dependency. It is with this conditioning that men approach the work of women, and whatever expressiveness lies outside the possibilities of their own acculturated perception, remains unseen. If the emperor's new clothes are really the vestments of women's feelings, then the men are unprepared to see them, because they have not been perceptually educated to accept the language of female form.

Let us examine the work of a number of women artists from the point of view that we are suggesting, and see what we discover. Remember, we are looking for the ways in which these artists' femaleness shapes both the form and context of their work. The central image is frequently used by these artists, either alone or in repetition, which asserts the identity of the form by repeating it.

1. In Emily Carr's "Forest of British Columbia" an ominous landscape becomes the metaphor for the murky, unknown female interior. The winding and binding forms

sometimes cavern, sometimes womb, sometimes forest, reiterates, as in O'Keeffe, the mysterious and infinite life process.

2. J. de Feo's "White Rose" is composed of layer upon layer upon layer of paint applied, then scraped off, over a period of several years, finally encrusting the canvas with memories of the now hidden manifestations of female sensuality. This voyage conveys an almost frightening process of revealing and obscuring self.

3. Lee Bontecou's drawing "Unknown" is part of a series of work that made a profound contribution to an understanding of female identity through imagery. In Lee Bontecou we find the essential answer to one of the perplexing questions about the nature of female identity. The question is: Is woman passive or active? Society defines women's vaginas and hence women as passive, receptive, responsive and acceptant; yet women know that their vaginas expand in childbirth, contract in orgasm, rip, bleed, want, assert, and in doing so define their nature in defiance of the society's narrow definition. The large, velvet lined cores of Bontecou's work deal exclusively with defining the central cavity of the female and thus the female herself. Bontecou establishes definitely that female identity is both active and passive.

4. In Deborah Remington's painting "Ansonia", the red egg recalls early Mother cult symbology and floats in a landscape of a machine culture. The deification of the egg, respondent in its place of honor, clearly in the center of the painting, speaks for itself.

5. In Barbara Hepworth's "Nesting Stones" of 1937, we see not only a repeat of the pregnant rock form used by O'Keeffe in her "Black Rock with Blue 3" but also an unmistakable mother and child nesting image and a centralized hollow, which reveals Hepworth's stated belief in a female sensibility in art.

6. In "Ox" 1969 by Miriam Schapiro, central imagery and the nature of female identity appear in their clearest forms. Body form which can be penetrated in its soft flesh center becomes an insignia for the assertion of self that all female artists search for, a female counterpart to Vetruvial Man. The image, which seems to be a mechanical, formalized structure, houses a soft and inviting tunnel.

7. Nevelson's boxes become the containers, the voids, the empty spaces of self and of life which must be filled, replenished and satisfied. Again, Nevelson is the artist who reveals a woman's need to fill and be filled, and in so doing attests to the simultaneity of giving and being given to.

8. In "Desert Fan" 1971, by Judy Chicago, the central core image reveals the merging of flesh and landscape. The surrounding forms echo and repeat the assertion of the central core which invites penetrability and implies self-expansion. The softness of the color enhances the delicate vulnerable depth of the interior space, which is shown to be vibrant and beautiful.

The visual symbology that we have been describing must not be seen in a simplistic sense as "vaginal or womb art". Rather, we are suggesting that women artists have used the central cavity which defines them as women as the framework for an imagery which allows for the complete reversal of the way in which women are seen by the culture. That is, to be a woman is to be an object of contempt, and the vagina, stamp of femaleness, is devalued. The woman artist, seeing herself as loathed, takes that very mark of her otherness and by asserting it as the hallmark of her iconography, establishes a vehicle by which to state the truth and beauty of her identity.

One of the reasons that this work by women has been either misunderstood or ignored is that it asserts a set of values that differ from the mainstream of culture. It seems obvious that a woman artist who goes into her studio every day and sees the clear evidence of her abilities will see that the values of the society which define her as passive and inferior, cannot be right. If she challenges those values, she will inevitably challenge others as she discovers in her creative journey that most of what she has been taught to believe about herself is inaccurate and distorted. It is with this differing self perception that the woman artist moves into the world and begins to define all aspects of experience through her own modes of perception which, at their very base, differ from the society's, inasmuch as her self-definition is in direct conflict with the definition of woman held by the society at large.

Perhaps the paradoxes of life which define the human condition have another dimension. If women are not what we have assumed them to be, what about other assumptions we have made? If to be female is, in Bontecou's metaphorical structures, active as well as passive, what is it to be male? Does that alter the definition of the male as well? If vulnerability is asserted as something to accept, as in Chicago's open, exposed imagery, does that suggest that we might question our fear of our own softness? If Nevelson reveals to us the simultaneous, yet seemingly contradictory, essence of self, as giver and as receiver, does that mean that men, as well as women can nurture and be nurtured, fill, and be filled? O'Keeffe's flower houses both life and death, and Remington's egg is both portal and protuberance. In Schapiro's "Ox", femaleness turns out to be the other side of maleness, with a hard outside and a soft inside. The central image assumes universality in these works because it is used to define first, the nature of female identity and then, the nature of human identity and the human dilemma. The sense of double identity, both male and female, has allowed these artists to reveal all of the contradictions of life, unified within the image of female self which becomes the house of life. These women, who have made art in solitude and in anguish, rather than being honoured for their unique vision of reality, have seen their imagery lost in the plethora of culture. It is our hope that female perception of reality, as it is beginning to be described, will enrich our language, expand our perceptions and enlarge our humanity.

DISCUSSION QUESTIONS

- What does "central core" imagery look like?
- Are traditional ways of organizing pictures masculine?

EXAMPLES TO THINK ABOUT

- Georgia O'Keefe
- *The Dinner Party*

Between Men

English Literature and Male Homosocial Desire

SELECTION

By EVE KOSOFSKY SEDGWICK

I. HOMOSOCIAL DESIRE

The subject of this book is a relatively short, recent, and accessible passage of English culture, chiefly as embodied in the mid-eighteenth- to mid-nineteenth-century novel. The attraction of the period to theorists of many disciplines is obvious: condensed, self reflec-tive, and widely influential change in economic, ideological, and gender arrangements. I will be arguing that concomitant changes in the structure of the continuum of male "homosocial desire" were tightly, often causally bound up with the other more visible changes; that the emerging pattern of male friendship, mentorship, entitlement, rivalry, and hetero- and homosexuality was in an intimate and shifting relation to class; and that no element of that pattern can be understood outside of its relation to women and the gender system as a whole.

"Male homosocial desire": the phrase in the title of this study is intended to mark both discriminations and paradoxes. "Homosocial desire," to begin with, is a kind of oxymo-ron. "Homosocial" is a word occasionally used in history and the social sciences, where it describes social bonds between persons of the same sex; it is a neologism, obviously

Eve Kosofsky Sedgwick, *Between Men: English Literature and Male Homosocial Desire*, pp. 1-7, 219-220. Copyright © 1985 by Columbia University Press. Reprinted with permission.

formed by analogy with "homosexual" and just as obviously meant to be distinguished from "homosexual." In fact, it is applied to such activities as "male bonding," which may, as in our society, be characterized by intense homophobia, fear and hatred of homosexuality.[1] To draw the "homosocial" back into the orbit of "desire," of the potentially erotic, then, is to hypothesize the potential unbrokenness of a continuum between homosocial and homosexual—a continuum whose visibility, for men, in our society, is radically disrupted. It will become clear, in the course of my argument, that my hypothesis of the unbrokenness of this continuum is not a *genetic* one—I do not mean to discuss genital homosexual desire as "at the root of" other forms of male homosociality—but rather a strategy for making generalizations about, and marking historical differences in, the *structure* of men's relations with other men. "Male homosocial desire" is the name this book will give to the entire continuum.

I have chosen the word "desire" rather than "love" to mark the erotic emphasis because, in literary critical and related discourse, "love" is more easily used to name a particular emotion, and "desire" to name a structure; in this study, a series of arguments about the structural permutations of social impulses fuels the critical dialectic. For the most part, I will be using "desire" in a way analogous to the psychoanalytic use of "libido"—not for a particular affective state or emotion, but for the affective or social force, the glue, even when its manifestation is hostility or hatred or something less emotively charged, that shapes an important relationship. How far this force is properly sexual (what, historically, it means for something to be "sexual") will be an active question.

The title is specific about *male* homosocial desire partly in order to acknowledge from the beginning (and stress the seriousness of) a limitation of my subject; but there is a more positive and substantial reason, as well. It is one of the main projects of this study to explore the ways in which the shapes of sexuality, and what *counts* as sexuality, both depend on and affect historical power relationships.[2] A corollary is that in a society where men and women differ in their access to power, there will be important gender differences, as well, in the structure and constitution of sexuality.

For instance, the diacritical opposition between the "homosocial" and the "homosexual" seems to be much less thorough and dichotomous for women, in our society, than for men. At this particular historical moment, an intelligible continuum of aims, emotions, and valuations links lesbianism with the other forms of women's attention to women: the bond of mother and daughter, for instance, the bond of sister and sister, women's friendship, "networking," and the active struggles of feminism.[3] The continuum is crisscrossed with deep discontinuities—with much homophobia, with conflicts of race and class—but its intelligibility seems now a matter of simple common sense. However agonistic the politics, however conflicted the feelings, it seems at this moment to make an obvious kind of sense to say that women in our society who love women, women who teach, study, nurture, suckle, write about, march for, vote for, give jobs to, or otherwise promote the interests of other women, are pursuing congruent and closely related activities. Thus the adjective "homosocial" as applied to women's bonds (by, for example, historian Carroll Smith-Rosenberg)[4] need not be pointedly dichotomized as against "homosexual"; it can intelligibly denominate the entire continuum.

The apparent simplicity—the unity—of the continuum between "women loving women" and "women promoting the interests of women," extending over the erotic, social, familial, economic, and political realms, would not be so striking if it were not in strong contrast to the arrangement among males. When Ronald Reagan and Jesse Helms get down to serious logrolling on "family policy," they are men promoting men's interests. (In fact, they embody Heidi Hartmann's definition of patriarchy: "relations between men, which have a material base, and which, though hierarchical, establish or create interdependence and solidarity among men that enable them to dominate women.")[5] Is their bond in any way congruent with the bond of a loving gay male couple? Reagan and Helms would say no—disgustedly. Most gay couples would say no—disgustedly. But why not? Doesn't the continuum between "men-loving-men" and "men-promoting-the-interests-of-men" have the same intuitive force that it has for women?

Quite the contrary: much of the most useful recent writing about patriarchal structures suggests that "obligatory heterosexuality" is built into male-dominated kinship systems, or that homophobia is a *necessary* consequence of such patriarchal institutions as heterosexual marriage.[6] Clearly, however convenient it might be to group together all the bonds that link males to males, and by which males enhance the status of males—usefully symmetrical as it would be, that grouping meets with a prohibitive structural obstacle. From the vantage point of our own society, at any rate, it has apparently been impossible to imagine a form of patriarchy that was not homophobic. Gayle Rubin writes, for instance, "The suppression of the homosexual component of human sexuality, and by corollary, the oppression of homosexual, is ... a product of the same system whose rules and relations oppress women."[7]

The historical manifestations of this patriarchal oppression of homosexuals have been savage and nearly endless. Louis Crompton makes a detailed case for describing the history as genocidal.[8] Our own society is brutally homophobic; and the homophobia directed against both males and females is not arbitrary or gratuitous, but tightly knit into the texture of family, gender, age, class, and race relations. Our society could not cease to be homophobic and have its economic and political structures remain unchanged.

Nevertheless, it has yet to be demonstrated that, because most patriarchies structurally include homophobia, therefore patriarchy structurally *requires* homophobia. K. J. Dover's recent study, *Greek Homosexuality*, seems to give a strong counterexample in classical Greece. Male homosexuality, according to Dover's evidence, was a widespread, licit, and very influential part of the culture. Highly structured along lines of class, and within the citizen class along lines of age, the pursuit of the adolescent boy by the older man was described by stereotypes that we associate with romantic heterosexual love (conquest, surrender, the "cruel fair," the absence of desire in the love object), with the passive part going to the boy. At the same time, however, because the boy was destined in turn to grow into manhood, the assignment of roles was not permanent.[9] Thus the love relationship, while temporarily oppressive to the object, had a strongly educational function; Dover quotes Pausanias in Plato's *Symposium* as saying "that it would be right for him [the boy] to perform any service for one who improves him in mind and character."[10] Along with its erotic component, then, this was a bond of mentorship; the boys were apprentices in the ways and virtues of Athenian citizenship, whose privileges they inherited. These privileges included the power to command the labor of slaves of both sexes, and of women of any class including their own. "Women and slaves belonged and lived together," Hannah Arendt writes. The system of sharp class and gender subordination was a necessary part of what the male culture valued most in itself: "Contempt for laboring originally [arose] out of a passionate striving for freedom from necessity and a no less passionate impatience with every effort that left no trace, no monument, no great work worthy to remembrance";[11] so the contemptible labor was left to women and slaves.

The example of the Greeks demonstrates, I think, that while heterosexuality is necessary for the maintenance of any patriarchy, homophobia, against males at any rate, is not. In fact, for the Greeks, the continuum between "men loving men" and "men promoting the interests of men" appears to have been quite seamless. It is as if, in our terms, there were no perceived discontinuity between the male bonds at the Continental Baths and the male bonds at the Bohemian Grove[12] or in the board room or Senate cloakroom.

It is clear, then, that there is an asymmetry in our present society between, on the one hand, the relatively continuous relation of female homosocial and homosexual bonds, and, on the other hand, the radically discontinuous relation of male homosocial and homosexual bonds. The example of the Greeks (and of other, tribal cultures, such as the New Guinea "Sambia" studied by G. H. Herdt) shows, in addition, that the structure of homosocial continuums is culturally contingent, not an innate feature of either "madness" or "femaleness." Indeed, closely tied though it obviously is to questions of male vs. female power, the explanation will require a more exact mode of historical categorization than "patriarchy," as well, since patriarchal power structures (in Hartmann's sense) characterize both Athenian and American societies. Nevertheless, we may take as an explicit axiom that the historically differential shapes of male and female homosociality—much as they themselves may vary over time—will always be articulations and mechanisms of the enduring inequality of power between women and men.

Why should the different shapes of the homosocial continuum be an interesting question? Why should it be a *literary* question? Its importance for the practical politics of the gay movement as a minority rights movement is already obvious from the recent history of strategic and philosophical differences between lesbians and gay men. In addition, it is theoretically interesting partly as a way of approaching a larger question of "sexual politics": What docs it mean—what difference does it make—when a social or political relationship is sexualized? If the relation of homosocial to homosexual bonds is so shifty, then what theoretical framework do we have for drawing any links between sexual and power relationships?

II. SEXUAL POLITICS AND SEXUAL MEANING

This question, in a variety of forms, is being posed importantly by and for the different gender-politics movements right now. Feminist along with gay male theorists, for instance, are disagreeing actively about how direct the relation is between power domination and sexual sadomasochism. Start with two arresting images: the naked, beefy motorcyclist on the front cover, or the shockingly battered nude male corpse on the back cover, of the recent so-called "Polysexuality" issue of *Semiotext(e)* (4, no. 1 [1981])—which, for all the women in it, ought to have been called the semisexuality issue of *Polytext*. It seemed to be a purpose of that issue to insist, and possibly not only for reasons of radical-chic titillation, that the violence imaged in sadomasochism is not mainly theatrical, but is fully continuous with violence in the real world. Women Against Pornography and the framers of the 1980 NOW Resolution on Lesbian and Gay Rights share the same view, but without the celebratory glamor: to them too it seems intuitively clear that to sexualize violence or an image of violence is simply to extend, unchanged, its reach and force.[13] But, as other feminist writers have reminded us, another view is possible. For example: is a woman's masochistic sexual fantasy really only an internalization and endorsement, if not a cause, of her more general powerlessness and sense of worthlessness? Or may not the sexual drama stand in some more oblique, or even oppositional, relation to her political experience of oppression?[14]

The debate in the gay male community and elsewhere over "man-boy love" asks a cognate question: can an adult's sexual relationship with a child be simply a continuous part of a more general relationship of education and nurturance? Or must the inclusion of sex qualitatively alter the relationship, for instance in the direction of exploitiveness? In this case, the same NOW communiqué that had assumed an unbroken continuity between sexualized violence and real, social violence, came to the opposite conclusion on pedophilia: that the injection of the sexual charge *would* alter (would corrupt) the very substance of the relationship. Thus, in moving from the question of sadomasochism to the question of pedophilia, the "permissive" argument and the "puritanical" argument have essentially exchanged their assumptions about how the sexual relates to the social.

So the answer to the question "what difference does the inclusion of sex make" to a social or political relationship, is—it varies: just as, for different groups in different political circumstances, homosexual activity can be either supportive of or oppositional to homosocial bonding. From this and the other examples I have mentioned, it is clear that there is not some ahistorical *Stoff* of sexuality, some sexual charge that can be simply added to a social relationship to "sexualize" it in a constant and predictable direction, or that splits off from it unchanged. Nor does it make sense to *assume* that the sexualized form epitomizes or simply condenses a broader relationship. (As, for instance, Kathleen Barry, in *Female Sexual Slavery*, places the Marquis de Sade at the very center of all forms of female oppression, including traditional genital mutilation, incest, and the economic as well as the sexual exploitation of prostitutes.)

Instead, an examination of the relation of sexual desire to political power must move along two axes. First, of course, it needs to make use of whatever forms of analysis are most potent for describing historically variable power asymmetries, such as those of class and race, as well as gender. But in conjunction with that, an analysis of representation itself is necessary. Only the model of representation will let us do justice to the (broad but not infinite or random) range of ways in which sexuality functions as a signifier for power relations. The importance of the rhetorical model in this case is not to make the problems of sexuality or of violence or oppression sound less immediate and urgent; it is to help us analyze and use the really very disparate intuitions of political immediacy that come to us from the sexual realm.

For instance, a dazzling recent article by Catherine MacKinnon, attempting to go carefully over and clear out the grounds of disagreement between different streams of feminist thought, arrives at the following summary of the centrality of sexuality per se for every issue of gender:

> Each element of the female *gender* stereotype is revealed as, in fact, *sexual.* Vulnerability means the appearance/reality of easy sexual access; passivity means receptivity and disabled resistance... ; softness means pregnability by something hard. ... Woman's infantilization evokes pedophilia; fixation on dismembered body parts ... evokes fetishism; idolization of vapidity, necrophilia. Narcissism insures that woman identifies with that image of herself that man holds up. ... Masochism means that pleasure in violation becomes her sensuality.

And MacKinnon sums up this part of her argument: "Socially, femaleness means femininity, which means attractiveness to men, which means sexual attractiveness, which means sexual availability on male terms."[15]

There's a whole lot of "mean"-ing going on. MacKinnon manages to make every manifestation of sexuality mean the same thing, by making every instance of "meaning" mean something different. A trait can "mean" as an element in a semiotic system such as fashion ("softness means pregnability"); or anaclitically, it can "mean" its complementary opposite ("Woman's infantilization evokes pedophilia"); or across time, it can "mean" the consequence that it enforces ("Narcissism insures that woman identifies. ... Masochism means that pleasure in violation becomes her sensuality"). MacKinnon concludes, "What defines woman as such is what turns men on." But what defines "defines"? That every node of sexual experience is in *some* signifying relation to the whole fabric of gender oppression, and vice versa, is true and important, but insufficiently exact.

◆ ◆ ◆ ◆

NOTES

1. The notion of "homophobia" is itself fraught with difficulties. To begin with, the word is etymologically nonsensical. A more serious problem is that the linking of fear and hatred in the "phobia" suffix, and in the word's usage, does tend to prejudge the question of the cause of homosexual oppression: it is attributed to fear, as opposed to (for example) a desire for power, privilege, or material goods. An alternative term that is more suggestive of collective, structurally inscribed, perhaps materially based oppression is "heterosexism." This study will, however, continue to use "homophobia," for three reasons. First, it will be an important concern here to question, rather than to reinforce, the presumptively symmetrical opposition between homo- and heterosexuality, which seems to be implicit in the term "heterosexism." Second, the etiology of individual people's attitudes toward male homosexuality will not be a focus of discussion. And third, the ideological and thematic treatments of male homosexuality to be discussed from the late eighteenth century onward do combine fear and hatred in a way that is appropriately called phobic. For a good summary of social science research on the concept of homophobia, see Morin and Garfinkle, "Male Homophobia."

2. For a good survey of the background to this assertion, see Weeks, *Sex,* pp. 1–18.

3. Adrienne Rich describes these bonds as forming a "lesbian continuum," in her essay, "Compulsory Heterosexuality and Lesbian Existence," in Stimpson and Person, *Women,* pp. 62–91, especially pp. 79–82.

4. "The Female World of Love and Ritual," in Cott and Pleck, *Heritage,* pp. 311–42; usage appears on, e.g., pp. 316, 317.

5. "The Unhappy Marriage of Marxism and Feminism: Towards a More Progressive Union," in Sargent, *Women and Revolution,* pp. 1–41; quotation is from p. 14.

6. See, for example, Rubin, "Traffic," pp. 182–83.

7. Rubin, "Traffic," p. 180.

8. Crompton, "Gay Genocide"; but see chapter 5 for a discussion of the limitations of "genocide" as an understanding of the fate of homosexual men.

9. On this, see Miller, *New Psychology,* ch. 1.

10. Dover, *Greek Homosexuality,* p. 91.

11. Arendt, *Human Condition,* p. 83, quoted in Rich, *On Lies,* p. 206.

12. On the Bohemian Grove, an all-male summer camp for American ruling-class men, see Domhoff, *Bohemian Grove;* and a more vivid, although homophobic, account, van der Zee, *Men's Party.*

13. The NOW resolution, for instance, explicitly defines sadomasochism, pornography, and "pederasty" (meaning pedophilia) as issues of "exploitation and violence," *as opposed to* "affectional/sexual preference/orientation." Quoted in *Heresies 12,* vol. 3, no. 4 (1981), p. 92.

14. For explorations of these viewpoints, see *Heresies, ibid.;* Snitow et al., *Powers;* and Samois, *Coming.*

15. MacKinnon, "Feminism," pp. 530–31.

BIBLIOGRAPHY

Arendt, Hannah. *The Human Condition*. Chicago: University of Chicago Press, 1958.

Barry, Kathleen. *Female Sexual Slavery*. New York: Prentice-Hall, 1979.

Cott, Nancy F. and Elizabeth H. Pleck, eds. *A Heritage of Her Own: Toward a New Social History of American Women*. New York: Simon and Schuster. 1979.

Crompton, Louis. "Gay Genocide: From Leviticus to Hitler." In *The Gay Academic*. Ed. Louie Crew. Palm Springs, Claif.: ETC Publications, 1978. pp. 87-91.

Domhomm, F. William. *The Bohemian Grove and Other Retreats: A Study in Ruling-Class Cohesiveness*. New York: Harper & Row, 1974.

Dover, K.J. *Greek Homosexuality*, New York; Random House--Vintage 1980.

Herd, G. H. *Guardians of the Flutes, Idioms of Masculinity: A Study of Ritualized Homosexual Behavior*. New York: McGraw Hill, 1981.

MacKinnon, Catharine A.. "Feminism, Marxism, Method, and the State: An Agenda for Theory." *Signs* 7 no. 3 (Spring 1982), pp. 515–44

Miller, Jean Baker. *Toward a New Psychology of Women*. Boston: Beacon Press, 1976

Morin, Stephen M., and Ellen M. Garfinkle. "Male Homophobia." In *Gayspeak; Gay Male and Lesbian Communication*. Ed. James W. Chesebro. New York: Pilgrim Press, 1981, pp.117-29.

Rich, Adrienne. *On Lies, Secrets, and Silence*: Selected Prose 1977–1978. New York: Norton, 1979.

Rubin, Gayle. "The Traffic in Women: Notes Toward a Political Economy of Sex." In *Toward an Anthropology of Women*. Ed. Rayna Reiter, New York: Monthly REview Press, 1975, pp. 157–210.

Samois, ed. *Coming to Power: Writing and Graphics on Lesbian S/M*. Boston: Alyson. 1982.

Sargent, Lydia, ed. *Women and Revolution: A Discussion of the Unhappy Marriage of Marxism and Feminism*. Boston: South End Press, 1981.

Snitow, Anne, Chritine Stansell, and Sharon Thompson, eds. *Power so Desire: The Politics of Sexuality*. New York: Monthly Review Press--New Feminist Library, 983.

Stimpson, Catharine R., and Ethel Spector Person, eds, *Women: Sex and Sexuality*. Chicago; University of Chicago Press, 1980.

van der Zee, John. *The Greatest Men's Party on Earth: Inside the Bohemian Grove*. New York: Harcourt Brace Jovanovich, 1974.

Weeks, Jeffery. *Sex, Politics, and Society; The Regulation of Sexuality Since 1900*. London: Longman, 1981

DISCUSSION QUESTIONS

- Sedgwick talks about the "homosocial" rather than homosexuality. What's the difference?
- What kinds of activities and relationships are included in the homosocial?
- What do you think of the idea that sexuality historically defined?

EXAMPLES TO THINK ABOUT

- *Sons of Anarchy*
- Fraternities
- Men's sports teams

SECTION 5

IMPORTANT CORRECTIONS

Black Looks

Race and Representation

EXCERPTS FROM: *THE OPPOSITIONAL GAZE*

By bell hooks

When thinking about black female spectators, I remember being punished as a child for staring, for those hard intense direct looks children would give grown-ups, looks that were seen as confrontational, as gestures of resistance, challenges to authority. The "gaze" has always been political in my life. Imagine the terror felt by the child who has come to understand through repeated punishments that one's gaze can be dangerous. The child who has learned so well to look the other way when necessary. Yet, when punished, the child is told by parents, "Look at me when I talk to you." Only, the child is afraid to look. Afraid to look, but fascinated by the gaze. There is power in looking.

Amazed the first time I read in history classes that white slaveowners (men, women, and children) punished enslaved black people for looking, I wondered how this traumatic relationship to the gaze had informed black parenting and black spectatorship. The politics of slavery, of racialized power relations, were such that the slaves were denied their right to gaze. Connecting this strategy of domination to that used by grown folks in southern black rural communities where I grew up, I was pained to think that there was no absolute difference between whites who had oppressed black people and ourselves.

Years later, reading Michel Foucault, I thought again about these connections, about the ways power as domination reproduces itself in different locations employing similar apparatuses, strategies, and mechanisms of control. Since I knew as a child that the dominating power adults exercised over me and over my gaze was never so absolute that I did not dare to look, to sneak a peep, to stare dangerously, I knew that the slaves had looked. That all attempts to repress our/black peoples' right to gaze had produced in us an overwhelming longing to look, a rebellious desire, an oppositional gaze. By courageously looking, we defiantly declared: "Not only will I stare. I want my look to change reality." Even in the worse circumstances of domination, the ability to manipulate one's gaze in the face of structures of domination that would contain it, opens up the possibility of agency. In much of his work, Michel Foucault insists on describing domination in terms of "relations of power" as part of an effort to challenge the assumption that "power is a system of domination which controls everything and which leaves no room for freedom." Emphatically stating that in all relations of power "there is necessarily the possibility of resistance," he invites the critical thinker to search those margins, gaps, and locations on and through the body where agency can be found.

Stuart Hall calls for recognition of our agency as black spectators in his essay "Cultural Identity and Cinematic Representation." Speaking against the construction of white representations of blackness as totalizing, Hall says of white presence: "The error is not to conceptualize this 'presence' in terms of power, but to locate that power as wholly external to us—as extrinsic force, whose influence can be thrown off like the serpent sheds its skin. What Franz Fanon reminds us, in *Black Skin, White Masks*, is how power is inside as well as outside:

> … the movements, the attitudes, the glances of the Other fixed me there, in the sense in which a chemical solution is fixed by a dye. I was indignant; I demanded an explanation. Nothing happened. I burst apart. Now the fragments have been put together again by another self. This "look," from—so to speak—the place of the Other, fixes us, not only in its violence, hostility and aggression, but in the ambivalence of its desire.

Spaces of agency exist for black people, wherein we can both interrogate the gaze of the Other but also look back, and at one another, naming what we see. The "gaze" has been and is a site of resistance for colonized black people globally. Subordinates in relations of power learn experientially that there is a critical gaze, one that "looks" to document, one that is oppositional. In resistance struggle, the power of the dominated to assert agency by claiming and cultivating "awareness" politicizes "looking" relations—one learns to look a certain way in order to resist.

When most black people in the United States first had the opportunity to look at film and television, they did so fully aware that mass media was a system of knowledge and power reproducing and maintaining white supremacy. To stare at the television, or mainstream movies, to engage its images, was to engage its negation of black representation. It was the oppositional black gaze that responded to these looking relations by developing independent black cinema. Black viewers of mainstream cinema and television could chart the progress of political movements for racial equality via the construction of images, and did so. Within my family's southern black working-class home, located in a racially segregated neighborhood, watching television was one way to develop critical spectatorship. Unless you went to work in the white world, across the tracks, you learned to look at white people by staring at them on the screen. Black looks, as they were constituted in the context of social movements for racial uplift, were interrogating gazes. We laughed at television shows like *Our Gang* and *Amos 'n' Andy*, at these white representations of blackness, but we also looked at them critically. Before racial integration, black viewers of movies and television experienced visual pleasure in a context where looking was also about contestation and confrontation.

Writing about black looking relations in "Black British Cinema: Spectatorship and Identity Formation in Territories," Manthia Diawara identifies the power of the spectator: "Every narration places the spectator in a position of agency; and race, class and sexual relations influence the way in which this subjecthood is filled by the spectator." Of particular concern for him are moments of "rupture" when the spectator resists "complete identification with the film's discourse." These ruptures define the relation between black spectators and dominant cinema prior to racial integration. Then, one's enjoyment of a film wherein representations of blackness were stereotypically degrading and dehumanizing co-existed with a critical practice that restored presence where it was negated. Critical discussion of the film while it was in progress or at its conclusion maintained the distance between spectator and the image. Black films were also subject to critical interrogation. Since they came into being in part as a response to the failure of white-dominated cinema to represent blackness in a manner that did not reinforce white supremacy, they too were critiqued to see if images were seen as complicit with dominant cinematic practices.

Critical, interrogating black looks were mainly concerned with issues of race and racism, the way racial domination of blacks by whites overdetermined representation. They were rarely concerned with gender. As spectators, black men could repudiate the reproduction of racism in cinema and television, the negation of black presence, even as they could feel as though they were rebelling against white supremacy by daring to look, by engaging phallocentric politics of spectatorship. Given the real life public circumstances wherein black men were murdered/lynched for looking at white womanhood, where the black male gaze was always subject to control and/or punishment by the powerful white Other, the private realm of television screens or dark theaters could unleash the repressed gaze. There they could "look" at white womanhood without a structure of domination overseeing the gaze, interpreting, and punishing. That white supremacist structure that had murdered Emmet Till after interpreting his look as violation, as "rape" of white womanhood, could not control black male responses to screen images. In their role as spectators, black men could enter an imaginative space of phallocentric power that mediated racial negation. This gendered relation to looking made the experience of the black male spectator radically different from that of the black female spectator. Major early black male independent filmmakers represented black women in their films as objects of male gaze. Whether looking through the camera or as spectators watching films, whether mainstream cinema or "race" movies such as those made by Oscar Micheaux, the black male gaze had a different scope from that of the black female.

Black women have written little about black female spectatorship, about our moviegoing practices. A growing body of film theory and criticism by black women has only begun to emerge. The prolonged silence of black women as spectators and critics was a response to absence, to cinematic negation. In "The Technology of Gender," Teresa de Lauretis, drawing on the work of Monique Wittig, calls attention to "the power of discourses to 'do violence' to people, a violence which is material and physical, although produced by abstract and scientific discourses as well as the discourses of the mass media." With the possible exception of early race movies, black female spectators have had to develop looking relations within a cinematic context that constructs our presence as absence, that denies the "body" of the black female so as to perpetuate white supremacy and with it a phallocentric spectatorship where the woman to be looked at and desired is "white." (Recent movies do not conform to this paradigm but I am turning to the past with the intent to chart the development of black female spectatorship.)

Talking with black women of all ages and classes, in different areas of the United States, about their filmic looking relations, I hear again and again ambivalent responses to cinema. Only a few of the black women I talked with remembered the pleasure of race movies, and even those who did, felt that pleasure interrupted and usurped by Hollywood. Most of the black women I talked with were adamant that they never went to movies expecting to see compelling representations of black femaleness. They were all acutely aware of cinematic racism—its violent erasure of black womanhood. In Anne Friedberg's essay "A Denial of Difference: Theories of Cinematic Identification" she stresses that "identification can only be made through recognition, and all recognition is itself an implicit confirmation of the ideology of the status quo." Even when representations of black women were present in film, our bodies and being were there to serve—to enhance and maintain white womanhood as object of the phallocentric gaze.

Commenting on Hollywood's characterization of black women in *Girls on Film*, Julie Burchill describes this absent presence:

> Black women have been mothers without children (Mammies—who can ever forget the sickening spectacle of Hattie MacDaniels waiting on the simpering Vivien Leigh hand and foot and enquiring like a ninny, "What's ma lamb gonna wear?") ... Lena Home, the first black performer signed to a long term contract with a major (MGM), looked gutless but was actually quite spirited. She seethed when Tallulah Bankhead complimented her on the paleness of her skin and the non-Negroidness of her features.

When black women actresses like Lena Home appeared in mainstream cinema most white viewers were not aware that they were looking at black females unless the film was specifically coded as being about blacks. Burchill is one of the few white women film critics who has dared to examine the intersection of race and gender in relation to the construction of the category "woman" in film as object of the phallocentric gaze. With characteristic wit she asserts: "What does it say about racial purity that the best blondes have all been brunettes (Harlow, Monroe, Bardot)? I think it says that we are not as white as we think." Burchill could easily have said "we are not as white as we want to be," for clearly the obsession to have white women film stars be ultra-white was a cinematic practice that sought to maintain a distance, a separation between that image and the black female Other; it was a way to perpetuate white supremacy. Politics of race and gender were inscribed into mainstream cinematic narrative from *Birth of A Nation* on. As a seminal work, this film identified what the place and function of white womanhood would be in cinema. There was clearly no place for black women.

Remembering my past in relation to screen images of black womanhood, I wrote a short essay, "Do you remember Sapphire?" which explored both the negation of black female representation in cinema and television and our rejection of these images. Identifying the character of "Sapphire" from *Amos 'n' Andy* as that screen representation of black femaleness I first saw in childhood, I wrote:

> She was even then backdrop, foil. She was bitch—nag. She was there to soften images of black men, to make them seem vulnerable, easygoing, funny, and unthreatening to a white audience. She was there as man in drag, as castrating bitch, as someone to be lied to, someone to be tricked, someone the white and black audience could hate. Scapegoated on all sides. *She was not us.* We laughed with the black men, with the white people. We laughed at this black woman who was not us. And we did not even long to be there on the screen. How could we long to be there when our image, visually constructed, was so ugly. We did not long to be there. We did not long for her. We did not want our construction to be this hated black female thing—foil, backdrop. Her black female image was not the body of desire. There was nothing to see. She was not us.

Grown black women had a different response to Sapphire; they identified with her frustrations and her woes. They resented the way she was mocked. They resented the way these screen images could assault black womanhood, could name us bitches, nags. And in opposition they claimed Sapphire as their own, as the symbol of that angry part of themselves white folks and black men could not even begin to understand.

◆ ◆ ◆ ◆

When I returned to films as a young woman, after a long period of silence, I had developed an oppositional gaze. Not only would I not be hurt by the absence of black female presence, or the insertion of violating representation, I interrogated the work, cultivated a way to look past race and gender for aspects of content, form, language. Foreign films and U.S. independent cinema were the primary locations of my filmic looking relations, even though I also watched Hollywood films.

From "jump," black female spectators have gone to films with awareness of the way in which race and racism determined the visual construction of gender. Whether it was *Birth of A Nation* or Shirley Temple shows, we knew that white womanhood was the racialized sexual difference occupying the place of stardom in mainstream narrative film. We assumed white women knew it to. Reading Laura Mulvey's provocative essay, "Visual Pleasure and Narrative Cinema," from a standpoint that acknowledges race, one sees clearly why black women spectators not duped by mainstream cinema would develop an oppositional gaze. Placing ourselves outside that pleasure in looking, Mulvey argues, was determined by a "split between active/male and passive/female." Black female spectators actively chose not to identify with the film's imaginary subject because such identification was disenabling.

Looking at films with an oppositional gaze, black women were able to critically assess the cinema's construction of white womanhood as object of phallocentric gaze and choose not to identify with either the victim or the perpetrator. Black female spectators, who refused to identify with white womanhood, who would not take on the phallocentric gaze of desire and possession, created a critical space where the binary opposition Mulvey posits of "woman as image, man as bearer of the look" was continually deconstructed. As critical spectators, black women looked from a location that disrupted, one akin to that described by Annette Kuhn in *The Power of The Image*:

> ...the acts of analysis, of deconstruction and of reading "against the grain" offer an additional pleasure—the pleasure of resistance, of saying "no": not to "unsophisticated" enjoyment, by ourselves and others, of culturally dominant images, but to the structures of power which ask us to consume them uncritically and in highly circumscribed ways.

Mainstream feminist film criticism in no way acknowledges black female spectatorship. It does not even consider the possibility that women can construct an oppositional gaze via an understanding and awareness of the politics of race and racism. Feminist film theory rooted in an ahistorical psychoanalytic framework that privileges sexual difference actively suppresses recognition of race, reenacting and mirroring the erasure of black womanhood that occurs in films, silencing any discussion of racial difference—of racialized sexual difference. Despite feminist critical interventions aimed at deconstructing the category "woman" which highlight the significance of race, many feminist film critics continue to structure their discourse as though it speaks about "women" when in actuality it speaks only about white women. It seems ironic that the cover of the recent anthology *Feminism and Film Theory* edited by Constance Penley has a graphic that is a reproduction of the photo of white actresses Rosalind Russell and Dorothy Arzner on the 1936 set of the film *Craig's Wife* yet there is no acknowledgment in any essay in this collection that the woman "subject" under discussion is always white. Even though there are photos of black women from films reproduced in the text, there is no acknowledgment of racial difference.

It would be too simplistic to interpret this failure of insight solely as a gesture of racism. Importantly, it also speaks to the problem of structuring feminist film theory around a totalizing narrative of woman as object whose image functions solely to reaffirm and reinscribe patriarchy. Mary Ann Doane addresses this issue in the essay "Remembering Women: Psychical and Historical Construction in Film Theory":

> This attachment to the figure of a degeneralizible Woman as the product of the apparatus indicates why, for many, feminist film theory seems to have reached an impasse, a certain blockage in its theorization...In focusing upon the task of delineating in great detail the attributes of woman as effect of the apparatus, feminist film theory participates in the abstraction of women.

The concept "Woman" effaces the difference between women in specific socio-historical contexts, between women defined precisely as historical subjects rather than as a psychic subject (or non-subject). Though Doane does not focus on race, her comments speak directly to the problem of its erasure. For it is only as one imagines "woman" in the abstract, when woman becomes fiction or fantasy, can race not be seen as significant. Are we really to imagine that feminist theorists writing only about images of white women, who subsume this specific historical subject under the totalizing category "woman," do not "see" the whiteness of the image? It may very well be that they engage in a process of denial that eliminates the necessity of revisioning conventional ways of thinking about psychoanalysis as a paradigm of analysis and the need to rethink a body of feminist film theory that is firmly rooted in a denial of the reality that sex/sexuality may not be the primary and/or exclusive signifier of difference. Doane's essay appears in a very recent anthology, *Psychoanalysis and Cinema* edited by E. Ann Kaplan, where, once again, none of the theory presented acknowledges or discusses racial difference, with the exception of one essay, "Not Speaking with Language, Speaking with No Language," which problematizes notions of orientalism in its examination of Leslie Thornton's film *Adynata*. Yet in most of the essays, the theories espoused are rendered problematic if one includes race as a category of analysis.

Constructing feminist film theory along these lines enables the production of a discursive practice that need never theorize any aspect of black female representation or spectatorship. Yet the existence of black women within white supremacist culture problematizes, and makes complex, the overall issue of female identity, representation, and spectatorship. If, as Friedberg suggests, "identification is a process which commands the subject to be displaced by an other; it is a procedure which breeches the separation between self and other, and, in this way, replicates the very structure of patriarchy." If identification "demands sameness, necessitates similarity, disallows difference"—must we then surmise that many feminist film critics who are "over-identified" with the mainstream cinematic apparatus produce theories that replicate its totalizing agenda? Why is it that feminist film criticism, which has most claimed the terrain of woman's identity, representation, and subjectivity as its field of analysis, remains aggressively silent on the subject of blackness and specifically representations of black womanhood? Just as mainstream cinema has historically forced aware black female spectators not to look, much feminist film criticism disallows the possibility of a theoretical dialogue that might include black women's voices. It is difficult to talk when you feel no one is listening, when you feel as though a special jargon or narrative has been created that only the chosen can understand. No wonder then that black women have for the most part confined our critical commentary on film to conversations. And it must be reiterated that this gesture is a strategy that protects us from the violence perpetuated and advocated by discourses of mass media. A new focus on issues of race and representation in the field of film theory could critically intervene on the historical repression reproduced in some arenas of contemporary critical practice, making a discursive space for discussion of black female spectatorship possible.

When I asked a black woman in her twenties, an obsessive moviegoer, why she thought we had not written about black female spectatorship, she commented: "We are afraid to talk about ourselves as spectators because we have been so abused by 'the gaze.'" An aspect of that abuse was the imposition of the assumption that black female looking relations were not important enough to theorize. Film theory as a critical "turf" in the United States has been and continues to be influenced by and reflective of white racial domination. Since feminist film criticism was initially rooted in a women's liberation movement informed by racist practices, it did not open up the discursive terrain and make it more inclusive. Recently, even those white film theorists who include an analysis of race show no interest in black female spectatorship. In her introduction to the collection of essays *Visual and Other Pleasures*, Laura Mulvey describes her initial romantic absorption in Hollywood cinema, stating:

> Although this great, previously unquestioned and unanalyzed love was put in crisis by the impact of feminism on my thought in the early 1970s, it also had an enormous influence on the development of my critical work and ideas and the debate within film culture with which I became preoccupied over the next fifteen years or so. Watched through eyes that were affected by the changing climate of consciousness, the movies lost their magic.

Watching movies from a feminist perspective, Mulvey arrived at that location of disaffection that is the starting point for many black women approaching cinema within the lived harsh reality of racism.

◆ ◆ ◆ ◆

[...] *Illusions, Daughters of the Dust,* and *A Passion of Remembrance* employ a deconstructive filmic practice to undermine existing grand cinematic narratives even as they retheorize subjectivity in the realm of the visual. Without providing "realistic" positive representations that emerge only as a response to the totalizing nature of existing narratives, they offer points of radical departure. Opening up a space for the assertion of a critical black female spectatorship, they do not simply offer diverse representations, they imagine new transgressive possibilities for the formulation of identity.

In this sense they make explicit a critical practice that provides us with different ways to think about black female subjectivity and black female spectatorship. Cinematically, they provide new points of recognition, embodying Stuart Hall's vision of a critical practice that acknowledges that identity is constituted "not outside but within representation," and invites us to see film "not as a second-order mirror held up to reflect what already exists, but as that form of representation which is able to constitute us as new kinds of subjects, and thereby enable us to discover who we are." It is this critical practice that enables production of feminist film theory that theorizes black female spectatorship. Looking and looking back, black women involve ourselves in a process whereby we see our history as counter-memory, using it as a way to know the present and invent the future.

SELECTED BIBLIOGRAPHY

Burchill, Julie. *Girls on Film*. New York: Pantheon, 1986.

de Lauretis, Teresa. *Technologies of Gender: Essays on Theory, Film, and Fiction*. Bloomington, IN: Indiana University Press, 1987.

Diawara, Manthia. "Black British Cinema: Spectatorship and Identity Formation in Territories." *Public Culture*, Vol. 1, No. 3 (Summer 1989).

Doane, Mary Ann. "Remembering Women: Psychical and Historical Constructions in Film Theory." *In Psychoanalysts and Cinema*, edited by E. Ann Kaplan. London: Routledge, 1990.

Fanon, Franz. *Black Skin, White Masks*. New York: Monthly Review, 1967.

Foucault, Michel. *Language, Counter-memory, Practice: Selected Essays and Interviews*. Edited by Donald F. Bouchard, translated by Bouchard and Sherry Simon. Ithaca, NY: Cornell University Press, 1977.

Foucault, Michel. *Power/Knowledge: Selected Interviews and Other Writings*. Edited by Colin Gordon, translated by Gordon et al. New York: Pantheon, 1980.

Friedberg, Anne. "A Denial of Difference: Theories of Cinematic Identification." In *Psychoanalysts & Cinema*, edited by E. Ann Kaplan. London: Routledge, 1990.

Kaplan, E. Ann, ed., *Psychoanalysts & Cinema: AFI Film Readers*. New York: Routledge, 1989.

Kuhn, Annette. *Power of the Image: Essays on Representation and Sexuality*. New York: Routledge, 1985.

Mulvey, Laura. *Visual and Other Pleasures*. Bloomington, IN: Indiana University Press, 1989.

Penley, Constance. *Feminism and Film Theory*. New York: Routledge, 1988.

DISCUSSION QUESTIONS

- What is hooks's critique of Mulvey's theories?
- What is the "oppositional gaze"?
- Can anyone take up this viewing position?

EXAMPLES TO THINK ABOUT

- *Real Housewives of Atlanta, Basketball Wives, Married to Medicine*
- *Empire*
- *Black Panther*

SECTION 6

EXAMPLES AND ISSUES:
WOMEN'S WORK

Theorizing Patriarchy

SELECTIONS

By SYLVIA WALBY

The variety of definitions of patriarchy has been a problem in some early texts (see Barrett, 1980); however, it would be surprising if developing theories of patriarchy did not use the term in slightly different ways. Patriarchy as a concept has a history of usage among social scientists, such as Weber (1947), who used it to refer to a system of government in which men ruled societies through their position as heads of households (cf., Pateman, 1988). In this usage the domination of younger men who were not household heads was as important as, if not more important than, the element of men's domination over women via the household.

The meaning of the term has evolved since Weber, especially in the writings by radical feminists, who developed the element of the domination of women by men and who paid less attention to the issue of how men dominated each other, and by dual-systems theorists, who have sought to develop a concept and theory of patriarchy as a system which exists alongside capitalism (and sometimes racism too).

[...]

Before developing the details of its forms, I shall define patriarchy as a system of social structures and practices in which men dominate, oppress and exploit women.

The use of the term social structure is important here, since it clearly implies rejection both of biological determinism, and the notion that every individual man is in a dominant position and every woman in a subordinate one.

Patriarchy needs to be conceptualized at different levels of abstraction. At the most abstract level it exists as a system of social relations. In contemporary Britain this is present in articulation with capitalism, and with racism. However, I do not wish to imply that it is homologous in internal structure with capitalism. At a less abstract level patriarchy is composed of six structures: the patriarchal mode of production, patriarchal relations in paid work, patriarchal relations in the state, male violence, patriarchal relations in sexuality, and patriarchal relations in cultural institutions. More concretely, in relation to each of the structures, it is possible to identify sets of patriarchal practices which are less deeply sedimented. Structures are emergent properties of practices. Any specific empirical instance will embody the effects, not only of patriarchal structures, but also of capitalism and racism.

The six structures have causal effects upon each other, both reinforcing and blocking, but are relatively autonomous. The specification of several rather than simply one base is necessary in order to avoid reductionism and essentialism. The presence of only one base, for instance, reproduction for Firestone (1974) and rape for Brownmiller (1976), is the reason for their difficulty with historical change and cultural variation. It is not necessary to go to the other extreme of denying significant social structures to overcome the charge of essentialism, as some of the postmodernist post-structuralists have done. The six identified are real, deep structures and necessary to capture the variation in gender relations in Westernized societies.

Patriarchal production relations in the household are my first structure. It is through these that women's household labour is expropriated by their husbands or cohabitees. The woman may receive her maintenance in exchange for her labour, especially when she is not also engaged in waged labour. Housewives are the producing class, while husbands are the expropriating class.

The second patriarchal structure within the economic level is that of patriarchal relations within paid work. A complex of forms of patriarchal closure within waged labour exclude women from the better forms of work and segregate them into the worse jobs which are deemed to be less skilled.

The state is patriarchal as well as being capitalist and racist. While being a site of struggle and not a monolithic entity, the state has a systematic bias towards patriarchal interests in its policies and actions.

Male violence constitutes a further structure, despite its apparently individualistic and diverse form. It is behaviour routinely experienced by women from men, with standard effects upon the actions of most women. Male violence against women is systematically condoned and legitimated by the state's refusal to intervene against it except in exceptional instances, though the practices of rape, wife beating, sexual harassment, etc., are too decentralized in their practice to be part of the state itself.

Patriarchal relations in sexuality constitute a fifth structure. Compulsory heterosexuality and the sexual double standard are two of the key forms of this structure.

Patriarchal cultural institutions completes the array of structures. These are significant for the generation of a variety of gender-differentiated forms of subjectivity. This structure is composed of a set of institutions which create the representation of women within a patriarchal gaze in a variety of arenas, such as religions, education and the media.

♦ ♦ ♦ ♦

I am distinguishing between two forms of patriarchy: private and public. They differ on a variety of levels: firstly, in terms of the relations between the structures and, secondly, in the institutional form of each structure. Further, they are differentiated by the main form of patriarchal strategy: exclusionary in private patriarchy and segregationist in public patriarchy. Private patriarchy is based upon household production, with a patriach controlling women individually and directly in the relatively private sphere of the home. Public patriarchy is based on structures other than the household, although this may still be a significant patriarchal site. Rather, institutions conventionally regarded as part of the public domain are central in the maintenance of patriarchy.

In private patriarchy it is a man in his position as husband or father who is the direct oppressor and beneficiary, individually and directly, of the subordination of women. This does not mean that household production is the sole patriarchal structure. Indeed it is importantly maintained by the active exclusion of women from public arenas by other structures. The exclusion of women from these other spheres could not be perpetuated without patriarchal activity at these levels.

Public patriarchy is a form in which women have access to both public and private arenas. They are not barred from the public arenas, but are nonetheless subordinated within them. The expropriation of women is performed more collectively than by individual patriarchs. The household may remain a site of patriarchal oppression, but it is no longer the main place where women are present.

In each type of patriarchy the six structures are present, but the relationship between them, and their relative significance, is different. For instance, I am not arguing that in private patriarchy the only significant site is that of the household. In the different forms there are different relations between the structures to maintain the system of patriarchy.

In the private system of patriarchy the exploitation of women in the household is maintained by their non-admission to the public sphere. In a sense the term 'private' for this form of patriarchy might be misleading, in that it is the exclusion from the public which is the central causal mechanism. Patriarchal relations outside the household are crucial in shaping patriarchal relations within it. However, the effect is to make women's experience of patriarchy privatized, and the immediate beneficiaries are also located there.

In the public form of patriarchy the exploitation of women takes place at all levels, but women are not formally excluded from any. In each institution women are disadvantaged.

The second aspect of the difference between private and public patriarchy is in the institutional form of each of the structures. This is a movement from an individual to a more collective form of appropriation of women. There has also been a shift in patriarchal strategy from exclusionary to segregationist and subordinating.

I have traced the movement from private to public patriarchy within each of the six patriarchal structures during the course of this book. Within paid work there was a shift from an exclusionary strategy to a segregationist one, which was a movement from attempting to exclude women from paid work to accepting their presence but confining them to jobs which were segregated from and graded lower than those of men. In the household there was a reduction in the confinement of women to this sphere over a lifetime and a shift in the main locus of control over reproduction. The major cultural institutions ceased to exclude women, while subordinating women within them. Sexual controls over women significantly shifted from the specific control of a husband to that of a broader public arena; women were no longer excluded from sexual relations to the same extent, but subordinated within them. Women's exclusion from the state was replaced by their subordination within it.

REFERENCES

Barrett, Michele (1980), *Women's Oppression Today: problems in Marxist feminist analysis* (London: Verso).

Brownmiller, Susan (1976), *Against Our Will: men, women and rape* (Harmondsworth: Penguin).

Firestone, Shulamith (1974), *The Dialectic of Sex: the case for feminist revolution* (New York: Morrow).

Hartmann, Heidi I. (1979), 'Capitalism, patriarchy and job segregation by sex', in *Capitalist Patriarchy,* ed. Zillah R. Eisenstein (New York: Monthly Review Press).

———— (1981b), 'The unhappy marriage of Marxism and Feminism: towards a more progressive union', in *Women and Revolution,* ed. Lydia Sargent (London: Pluto Press).

Pateman, Carole (1988), *The Sexual Contract* (Cambridge: Polity Press).

Weber, Max (1947), *The Theory of Social and Economic Organisation* (New York: Free Press).

DISCUSSION QUESTIONS

- Why would Walby define patriarchy in terms of how power is taken from women?
- Can you describe each of Walby's six structures of patriarchy?
- How do they differ from "patriarchal practices"?

EXAMPLES TO THINK ABOUT

- Images of American presidents
- Pictures of Hillary Clinton, Cheryl Sandburg, Mary Barra

Women, Race & Class

EXCERPTS FROM: *THE APPROACHING OBSOLESCENCE OF HOUSEWORK: A WORKING-CLASS PERSPECTIVE*

By ANGELA Y. DAVIS

T he countless chores collectively known as "housework"—cooking, washing dishes, doing laundry, making beds, sweeping, shopping, etc.—apparently consume some three to four thousand hours of the average housewife's year.[1] As startling as this statistic may be, it does not even account for the constant and unquantifiable attention mothers must give to their children. Just as a woman's maternal duties are always taken for granted, her neverending toil as a housewife rarely occasions expressions of appreciation within her family. Housework, after all, is virtually invisible: "No one notices it until it isn't done—we notice the unmade bed, not the scrubbed and polished floor."[2] Invisible, repetitive, exhausting, unproductive, uncreative—these are the adjectives which most perfectly capture the nature of housework.

The new consciousness associated with the contemporary women's movement has encouraged increasing numbers of women to demand that their men provide some relief from this drudgery. Already, more men have begun to assist their partners around the house, some of them even devoting equal time to household chores. But how many of these men have liberated themselves from the assumption that housework is "women's work"? How many of them would not characterize their housecleaning activities as "helping" their women partners?

If it were at all possible simultaneously to liquidate the idea that housework is women's work and to redistribute it equally to men and women alike, would this constitute a satisfactory solution? Freed from its exclusive affiliation with the female sex, would housework thereby cease to be oppressive? While most women would joyously hail the advent of the "househusband," the desexualization of domestic labor would not really alter the oppressive nature of the work itself. In the final analysis, neither women nor men should waste precious hours of their lives on work that is neither stimulating, creative nor productive.

One of the most closely guarded secrets of advanced capitalist societies involves the possibility—the real possibility—of radically transforming the nature of housework. A substantial portion of the housewife's domestic tasks can actually be incorporated into the industrial economy. In other words, housework need no longer be considered necessarily and unalterably private in character. Teams of trained and well-paid workers, moving from dwelling to dwelling, engineering technologically advanced cleaning machinery, could swiftly and efficiently accomplish what the present-day housewife does so arduously and primitively. Why the shroud of silence surrounding this potential of radically redefining the nature of domestic labor? Because the capitalist economy is structurally hostile to the industrialization of housework. Socialized housework implies large government subsidies in order to guarantee accessibility to the working-class families whose need for such services is most obvious. Since little in the way of profits would result, industrialized housework—like all unprofitable enterprises—is anathema to the capitalist economy. Nonetheless, the rapid expansion of the female labor force means that more and more women are finding it increasingly difficult to excel as housewives according to the traditional standards. In other words, the industrialization of housework, along with the socialization of housework, is becoming an objective social need. Housework as individual women's private responsibility and as female labor per formed under primitive technical conditions, may finally be approaching historical obsolescence.

Although housework as we know it today may eventually become a bygone relic of history, prevailing social attitudes continue to associate the eternal female condition with images of brooms and dustpans, mops and pails, aprons and stoves, pots and pans. And it is true that women's work, from one historical era to another, has been associated in general with the homestead. Yet female domestic labor has not always been what it is today, for like all social phenomena, housework is a fluid product of human history. As economic systems have arisen and faded away, the scope and quality of housework have undergone radical transformations.

As Frederick Engels argued in his classic work on the *Origin of the Family, Private Property and the State*,[3] sexual inequality as we know it today did not exist before the advent of private property. During early eras of human history the sexual division of labor within the system of economic production was complementary as opposed to hierarchical. In societies where men may have been responsible for hunting wild animals and women, in turn, for gathering wild vegetables and fruits, both sexes performed economic tasks that were equally essential to their community's survival. Because the community, during those eras, was essentially an extended family, women's central role in domestic affairs meant that they were accordingly valued and respected as productive members of the community.

The centrality of women's domestic tasks in pre-capitalist cultures was dramatized by a personal experience during a jeep trip I took in 1973 across the Masai Plains. On an isolated dirt road in Tanzania, I noticed six Masai women enigmatically balancing an enormous board on their heads. As my Tanzanian friends explained, these women were probably transporting a house roof to a new village which they were in the process of constructing. Among the Masai, as I learned, women are responsible for all domestic activities, thus also for the construction of their nomadic people's frequently relocated houses. Housework, as far as Masai women are concerned, entails not only cooking, cleaning, child-rearing, sewing, etc., but house-building as well. As important as their men's cattle-raising duties may be, the women's "housework" is no less productive and no less essential than the economic contributions of Masai men.

Within the pre-capitalist, nomadic economy of the Masai, women's domestic labor is as essential to the economy as the cattle-raising jobs performed by their men. As producers, they enjoy a correspondingly important social status. In advanced capitalist societies, on the other hand, the service-oriented domestic labor of housewives, who can seldom produce tangible evidence of their work, diminishes the social status of women in general. When all is said and done, the housewife, according to bourgeois ideology, is, quite simply, her husband's lifelong servant.

The source of the bourgeois notion of woman as man's eternal servant is itself a revealing story. Within the relatively short history of the United States, the "housewife" as a finished historical product is just a little more than a century old. Housework, during the colonial era, was entirely different from the daily work routine of the housewife in the United States today.

> A woman's work began at sunup and continued by firelight as long as she could hold her eyes open. For two centuries, almost everything that the family used or ate was produced at home under her direction. She spun and dyed the yarn that she wove into cloth and cut and hand-stitched into garments. She grew much of the food her family ate, and preserved enough to last the winter months. She made butter, cheese, bread, candles, and soap and knitted her family's stockings.[4]

In the agrarian economy of pre-industrial North America, a woman performing her household chores was thus a spinner, weaver and seamstress as well as a baker, butter-churner, candle-maker and soap-maker. And et cetera, et cetera, et cetera. As a matter of fact,

> ... the pressures of home production left very little time for the tasks that we would recognize today as housework. By all accounts, pre-industrial revolution women were sloppy housekeepers by today's standards. Instead of the daily

cleaning or the weekly cleaning, there was the *spring* cleaning. Meals were simple and repetitive; clothes were changed infrequently; and the household wash was allowed to accumulate, and the washing done once a month, or in some households once in three months. And, of course, since each wash required the carting and heating of many buckets of water, higher standards of cleanliness were easily discouraged.[5]

Colonial women were not "house-cleaners" or "housekeepers" but rather full-fledged and accomplished workers within the home-based economy. Not only did they manufacture most of the products required by their families, they were also the guardians of their families' and their communities' health.

> It was [the colonial woman's] responsibility to gather and dry wild herbs used ... as medicines; she also served as doctor, nurse, and midwife within her own family and in the community.[6]

Included in the *United States Practical Receipt Book*—a popular colonial recipe book—are recipes for foods as well as for household chemicals and medicines. To cure ringworm, for example, "obtain some blood-root ... slice it in vinegar, and afterwards wash the place affected with the liquid."[7]

The economic importance of women's domestic functions in colonial America was complemented by their visible roles in economic activity outside the home. It was entirely acceptable, for example, for a woman to become a tavern keeper.

> Women also ran sawmills and gristmills, caned chairs and built furniture, operated slaughterhouses, printed cotton and other cloth, made lace, and owned and ran dry goods and clothing stores. They worked in tobacco shops, drug shops (where they sold concoctions they made themselves), and general stores that sold everything from pins to meat scales. Women ground eyeglasses, made netting and rope, cut and stitched leather goods, made cards for wool carding, and even were housepainters. Often they were the town undertakers ... [8]

The postrevolutionary surge of industrialization resulted in a proliferation of factories in the northeastern section of the new country. New England's textile mills were the factory system's successful pioneers. Since spinning and weaving were traditional female domestic occupations, women were the first workers recruited by the mill-owners to operate the new power looms. Considering the subsequent exclusion of women from industrial production in general, it is one of the great ironies of this country's economic history that the first industrial workers were women.

As industrialization advanced, shifting economic production from the home to the factory, the importance of women's domestic work suffered a systematic erosion. Women were the losers in a double sense: as their traditional jobs were usurped by the burgeoning factories, the entire economy moved away from the home, leaving many women largely bereft of significant economic roles. By the middle of the nineteenth century the factory provided textiles, candles and soap. Even butter, bread and other food products began to be mass-produced.

> By the end of the century, hardly anyone made their own starch or boiled their laundry in a kettle. In the cities, women bought their bread and at least their underwear ready-made, sent their children out to school and probaby some clothes out to be laundered, and were debating the merits of canned foods … The flow of industry' had passed on and had left idle the loom in the attic and the soap kettle in the shed."[9]

As industrial capitalism approached consolidation, the cleavage between the new economic sphere and the old home economy became ever more rigorous. The physical relocation of economic production caused by the spread of the factory system was undoubtedly a drastic transformation. But even more radical was the generalized revaluation of production necessitated by the new economic system. While home-manufactured goods were valuable primarily because they fulfilled basic family needs, the importance of factory-produced commodities resided overwhelmingly in their exchange value—in their ability to fulfill employers' demands for profit. This revaluation of economic production revealed—beyond the physical separation of home and factory—a fundamental *structural* separation between the domestic home economy and the profit-oriented economy of capitalism. Since housework does not generate profit, domestic labor was naturally defined as an inferior form of work as compared to capitalist wage labor.

An important ideological by-product of this radical economic transformation was the birth of the "housewife." Women began to be ideologically redefined as the guardians of a devalued domestic life. As ideology, however, this redefinition of women's place was boldly contradicted by the vast numbers of immigrant women flooding the ranks of the working class in the Northeast. These white immigrant women were wage earners first and only secondarily housewives. And there were other women—millions of women—who toiled away from home as the unwilling producers of the slave economy in the South. The reality of women's place in nineteenth-century U.S. society involved white women, whose days were spent operating factory machines for wages that were a pittance, as surely as it involved Black women, who labored under the coercion of slavery. The "housewife" reflected a partial reality, for she was really a symbol of the economic prosperity enjoyed by the emerging middle classes.

Although the "housewife" was rooted in the social conditions of the bourgeoisie and the middle classes, nineteenth-century ideology established the housewife and the mother as universal models of womanhood. Since popular propaganda represented the vocation of *all* women as a function of their roles in the home, women compelled to work for wages came to be treated as alien visitors within the masculine world of the public economy. Having stepped outside their "natural" sphere, women were not to be treated as full-fledged wage workers. The price they paid involved long hours, substandard working conditions and grossly inadequate wages. Their exploitation was even more intense than the exploitation suffered by their male counterparts. Needless to say, sexism emerged as a source of outrageous super profits for the capitalists.

The structural separation of the public economy of capitalism and the private economy of the home has been continually reinforced by the obstinate primitiveness of household labor. Despite the proliferation of gadgets for the home, domestic work has remained qualitatively unaffected by the technological advances brought on by industrial capitalism. Housework still consumes thousands of hours of the average housewife's year. In 1903 Charlotte Perkins Gilman proposed a definition of domestic labor which reflected the upheavals which had changed the structure and content of housework in the United States:

> ... The phrase "domestic work" does not apply to a special kind of work, but to a certain grade of work, a state of development through which all kinds pass. All industries were once "domestic," that is, were performed at home and in the interests of the family. All industries have since that remote period risen to higher stages, except one or two which have never left their primal stage.[10]

"The home," Gilman maintains, "has not developed in proportion to our other institutions." The home economy reveals

> ... the maintenance of primitive industries in a modern industrial community and the confinement of women to these industries and their limited area of expression.[11]

Housework, Gilman insists, vitiates women's humanity:

> She is feminine, more than enough, as man is masculine, more than enough; but she is not human as he is human. The house-life does not bring out our humanness, for all the distinctive lines of human progress lie outside.[12]

The truth of Gilman's statement is corroborated by the historical experience of Black women in the United States. Throughout this country's history, the majority of Black women have worked outside their homes. During slavery, women toiled alongside their men in the cotton and tobacco fields, and when industry moved into the South, they could be seen in tobacco factories, sugar refineries and even in lumber mills and on crews pounding steel for the railroads. In labor, slave women were the equals of their men. Because they suffered a grueling sexual equality at work, they enjoyed a greater sexual equality at home in the slave quarters than did their white sisters who were "housewifes."

As a direct consequence of their outside work—as "free" women no less than as slaves—housework has never been the central focus of Black women's lives. They have largely escaped the psychological damage industrial capitalism inflicted on white middle-class housewives, whose alleged virtues were feminine weakness and wifely submissiveness. Black women could hardly strive for weakness; they had to become strong, for their families and their communities needed their strength to survive. Evidence of the accumulated strengths Black women have forged through work, work and more work can be discovered in the contributions of the many outstanding female leaders who have emerged within the Black community. Harriet Tubman, Sojourner Truth, Ida Wells and Rosa Parks are not exceptional Black women as much as they are epitomes of Black womanhood.

Black women, however, have paid a heavy price for the strengths they have acquired and the relative independence they have enjoyed. While they have seldom been "just housewives," they have always done their housework. They have thus carried the double burden of wage labor and housework—a double burden which always demands that working women possess the persevering powers of Sisyphus. As W. E. B. DuBois observed in 1920:

> ... some few women are born free, and some amid insult and scarlet letters achieve freedom; but our women in black had freedom thrust contemptuously upon them. With that freedom they are buying an untrammeled independence and dear as is the price they pay for it, it will in the end be worth every taunt and groan.[13]

Like their men, Black women have worked until they could work no more. Like their men, they have assumed the responsibilities of family providers. The unorthodox feminine qualities of assertiveness and self-reliance—for which Black women have been frequently praised but more often rebuked—are reflections of their labor and their struggles outside the home. But like their white sisters called "housewives," they have cooked and cleaned and have nurtured and reared untold numbers of children. But unlike the white housewives, who learned to lean on their husbands for economic security, Black wives and mothers, usually workers as well, have rarely been offered the time and energy to become experts at domesticity. Like their white working-class sisters, who also carry the double burden of working for a living and servicing husbands and children, Black women have needed relief from this oppressive predicament for a long, long time.

For Black women today and for all their working-class sisters, the notion that the burden of housework and child care can be shifted from their shoulders to the society contains one of the radical secrets of women's liberation. Child care should be socialized, meal preparation should be socialized, housework should be industrialized—and all these services should be readily accessible to working-class people.

The shortage, if not absence, of public discussion about the feasibility of transforming housework into a social possibility bears witness to the blinding powers of bourgeois ideology. It is not even the case that women's domestic role has received no attention at all. On the contrary, the contemporary women's movement has represented housework as an essential ingredient of women's oppression. There is even a movement in a number of capitalist countries, whose main concern is the plight of the housewife. Having reached the conclusion that housework is degrading and oppressive primarily because it is *unpaid* labor, this movement has raised the demand for wages. A weekly government paycheck, its activists argue, is the key to improving the housewife's status and the social position of women in general.

♦ ♦ ♦

NOTES

1. Oakley, *op. cit.,* p. 6.
2. Barbara Ehrenreich and Deirdre English, "The Manufacture of Housework," *in Socialist Revolution,* No. 26, Vol. 5, No. 4 (October-December 1975), p. 6.
3. Frederick Engels, *Origin of the Family, Private Property and the State,* edited, with an introduction, by Eleanor Burke Leacock (New York: International Publishers, 1973). See Chapter II. Leacock's introduction to this edition contains numerous enlightening observations on Engels' theory of the historical emergence of male supremacy.
4. Wertheimer, *op. cit.,* p. 12.
5. Ehrenreich and English, "The Manufacture of Housework," p. 9.
6. Wertheimer, *op. cit.,* p. 12.
7. Quoted in Baxandall *et al., op. cit.,* p. 17.
8. Wertheimer, *op. cit.,* p. 13.
9. Ehrenreich and English, "The Manufacture of Housework," p. 10.
10. Charlotte Perkins Gilman, *The Home: Its Work and Its Influence* (Urbana, Chicago, London: University of Illinois Press, 1972. Reprint of the 1903 edition), pp. 30–31.
11. *Ibid.,* p. 10.
12. *Ibid.,* p. 217.
13. DuBois, *Darkwater,* p. 185.

DISCUSSION QUESTIONS

- How are capitalism and the idea of the housewife related?
- Who is left out of the category of housewife?
- Davis suggests socializing housework. What do you think of that idea?

EXAMPLES TO THINK ABOUT

- HGTV
- Martha Stewart
- Cooking shows
- Tasty videos

SECTION 7

EXAMPLES AND ISSUES:
SPACE

Panopticism

EXCERPT FROM: *DISCIPLINE & PUNISH:*
THE BIRTH OF THE PRISON

By MICHEL FOUCAULT

Bentham's *Panopticon* is the architectural figure of this composition. We know the principle on which it was based: at the periphery, an annular building; at the centre, a tower; this tower is pierced with wide windows that open onto the inner side of the ring; the peripheric building is divided into cells, each of which extends the whole width of the building; they have two windows, one on the inside, corresponding to the windows of the tower; the other, on the outside, allows the light to cross the cell from one end to the other. All that is needed, then, is to place a supervisor in a central tower and to shut up in each cell a madman, a patient, a condemned man, a worker or a schoolboy. By the effect of backlighting, one can observe from the tower, standing out precisely against the light, the small captive shadows in the cells of the periphery. They are like so many cages, so many small theatres, in which each actor is alone, perfectly individualized and constantly visible. The panoptic mechanism arranges spatial unities that make it possible to see constantly and to recognize immediately. In short, it reverses the principle of the dungeon; or rather of its three functions—to enclose, to deprive of light and to hide—it preserves only the first and eliminates the other two. Full lighting and the eye of a supervisor capture better than darkness, which ultimately protected. Visibility is a trap.

To begin with, this made it possible—as a negative effect—to avoid those compact, swarming, howling masses that were to be found in places of confinement, those painted by Goya or described by Howard. Each individual, in his place, is securely confined to a cell from which he is seen from the front by the supervisor; but the side walls prevent him from coming into contact with his companions. He is seen, but he does not see; he is the object of information, never a subject in communication. The arrangement of his room, opposite the central tower, imposes on him an axial visibility; but the divisions of the ring, those separated cells, imply a lateral invisibility. And this invisibility is a guarantee of order. If the inmates are convicts, there is no danger of a plot, an attempt at collective escape, the planning of new crimes for the future, bad reciprocal influences; if they are patients, there is no danger of contagion; if they are madmen there is no risk of their committing violence upon one another; if they are schoolchildren, there is no copying, no noise, no chatter, no waste of time; if they are workers, there are no disorders, no theft, no coalitions, none of those distractions that slow down the rate of work, make it less perfect or cause accidents. The crowd, a compact mass, a locus of multiple exchanges, individualities merging together, a collective effect, is abolished and replaced by a collection of separated individualities. From the point of view of the guardian, it is replaced by a multiplicity that can be numbered and supervised; from the point of view of the inmates, by a sequestered and observed solitude (Bentham, 60–64).

Hence the major effect of the Panopticon: to induce in the inmate a state of conscious and permanent visibility that assures the automatic functioning of power. So to arrange things that the surveillance is permanent in its effects, even if it is discontinuous in its action; that the perfection of power should tend to render its actual exercise unnecessary; that this architectural apparatus should be a machine for creating and sustaining a power relation independent of the person who exercises it; in short, that the inmates should be caught up in a power situation of which they are themselves the bearers. To achieve this, it is at once too much and too little that the prisoner should be constantly observed by an inspector: too little, for what matters is that he knows himself to be observed; too much, because he has no need in fact of being so. In view of this, Bentham laid down the principle that power should be visible and unverifiable. Visible: the inmate will constantly have before his eyes the tall outline of the central tower from which he is spied upon. Unverifiable: the inmate must never know whether he is being looked at any one moment; but he must be sure that he may always be so. In order to make the presence or absence of the inspector unverifiable, so that the prisoners, in their cells, cannot even see a shadow, Bentham envisaged not only venetian blinds on the windows of the central observation hall, but, on the inside, partitions that intersected the hall at right angles and, in order to pass from one quarter to the other, not doors but zig-zag openings; for the slightest noise, a gleam of light, a brightness in a half-opened door would betray the presence of the guardian.[1] The Panopticon is a machine for dissociating the see/being seen dyad: in the peripheric ring, one is totally seen, without ever seeing; in the central tower, one sees everything without ever being seen.[2]

It is an important mechanism, for it automatizes and disindividualizes power. Power has its principle not so much in a person as in a certain concerted distribution of bodies, surfaces, lights, gazes; in an arrangement whose internal mechanisms produce the relation in which individuals are caught up. The ceremonies, the rituals, the marks by which the sovereign's surplus power was manifested are useless. There is a machinery that assures dissymmetry, disequilibrium, difference. Consequently, it does not matter who exercises power. Any individual, taken almost at random, can operate the machine: in the absence of the director, his family, his friends, his visitors, even his servants (Bentham, 45). Similarly, it does not matter what motive animates him: the curiosity of the indiscreet, the malice of a child, the thirst for knowledge of a philosopher who wishes to visit this museum of human nature, or the perversity of those who take pleasure in spying and punishing. The more numerous those anonymous and temporary observers are, the greater the risk for the inmate of being surprised and the greater his anxious awareness of being observed. The Panopticon is a marvellous machine which, whatever use one may wish to put it to, produces homogeneous effects of power.

A real subjection is born mechanically from a fictitious relation. So it is not necessary to use force to constrain the convict to good behaviour, the madman to calm, the worker to work, the schoolboy to application, the patient to the observation of the regulations. Bentham was surprised that panoptic institutions could be so light: there were no more bars, no more chains, no more heavy locks; all that was needed was that the separations should be clear and the openings well arranged. The heaviness of the old 'houses of security', with their fortress-like architecture, could be replaced by the simple, economic geometry of a 'house of certainty'. The efficiency of power, its constraining force have, in a sense, passed over to the other side—to the side of its surface of application. He who is subjected to a field of visibility, and who knows it, assumes responsibility for the constraints of power; he makes them play spontaneously upon himself; he inscribes in himself the power relation in which he simultaneously plays both roles; he becomes the principle of his own subjection. By this very fact, the external power may throw off its physical weight; it tends to the non-corporal; and, the more it approaches this limit, the more constant, profound and permanent are its effects: it is a perpetual victory that avoids any physical confrontation and which is always decided in advance.

Bentham does not say whether he was inspired, in his project, by Le Vaux's menagerie at Versailles: the first menagerie in which the different elements are not, as they traditionally were, distributed in a park (Loisel, 104–7). At the centre was an octagonal pavilion which, on the first floor, consisted of only a single room, the king's *salon*; on every side large windows looked out onto seven cages (the eighth side was reserved for the entrance), containing different species of animals. By Bentham's time, this menagerie had disappeared. But one finds in the programme of the Panopticon a similar concern with individualizing observation, with characterization and classification, with the analytical arrangement of space. The Panopticon is a royal menagerie; the animal is replaced by man, individual distribution by specific grouping and the king by the machinery of a furtive power. With this exception, the Panopticon also does the work of a naturalist. It makes it possible to draw up differences: among patients, to observe the symptoms of each individual, without the proximity of beds, the circulation of miasmas, the effects of contagion confusing the clinical tables; among school-children, it makes it possible to observe performances (without there being any imitation or copying), to map aptitudes, to assess characters, to draw up rigorous classifications and, in relation to normal development, to distinguish 'laziness and stubbornness' from 'incurable imbecility'; among workers, it makes it possible to note the aptitudes of each worker, compare the time he takes to perform a task, and if they are paid by the day, to calculate their wages (Bentham, 60–64).

So much for the question of observation. But the Panopticon was also a laboratory; it could be used as a machine to carry out experiments, to alter behaviour, to train or correct individuals. To experiment with medicines and monitor their effects. To try out different punishments on prisoners, according to their crimes and character, and to seek the most effective ones. To teach different techniques simultaneously to the workers, to decide which is the best. To try out pedagogical experiments—and in particular to take up once again the well-debated problem of secluded education, by using orphans. One would see what would happen when, in their sixteenth or eighteenth year, they were presented with other boys or girls; one could verify whether, as Helvetius thought, anyone could learn anything; one would follow 'the genealogy of every observable idea'; one could bring up different children according to different systems of thought, making certain children believe that two and two do not make four or that the moon is a cheese, then put them together when they are twenty or twenty-five years old; one would then have discussions that would be worth a great deal more than the sermons or lectures on which so much money is spent; one would have at least an opportunity of making discoveries in the domain of metaphysics. The Panopticon is a privileged place for experiments on men, and for analysing with complete certainty the transformations that may be obtained from them. The Panopticon may even provide an apparatus for supervising its own mechanisms. In this central tower, the director may spy on all the employees that he has under his orders: nurses, doctors, foremen, teachers, warders; he will be able to judge them continuously, alter their behaviour, impose upon them the methods he thinks best; and it will even be possible to observe the director himself. An inspector arriving unexpectedly at the centre of the Panopticon will be able to judge at a glance, without anything being concealed from him, how the entire establishment is functioning. And, in any case, enclosed as he is in the middle of this architectural mechanism, is not the director's own fate entirely bound up with it? The incompetent physician who has allowed contagion to spread, the incompetent prison governor or workshop manager will be the first victims of an epidemic or a revolt. "By every tie I could devise", said the master of the Panopticon, "my own fate had been bound up by me with theirs" (Bentham, 177). The Panopticon functions as a kind of laboratory of power. Thanks to its mechanisms of observation, it gains in efficiency and in the ability to penetrate into men's behaviour; knowledge follows the advances of power, discovering new objects of knowledge over all the surfaces on which power is exercised.

NOTES

1. Cf. what La Métherie wrote after a visit to Le Creusot: 'The buildings for so fine an establishment and so large a quantity of different work should cover a sufficient area, so that there will be no confusion among the workers during working time' (La Métherie, 66).

2. J.-B. de la Salle, *Conduite des écoles chrétiennes*, B.N. Ms. 11759, 248–9. A little earlier Batencour proposed that classrooms should be divided into three parts: 'The most honourable for those who are learning Latin… It should be stressed that there are as many places at the tables as there will be writers, in order to avoid the confusion usually caused by the lazy.' In another, those who are learning to read: a bench for the rich and a bench for the poor 'so that vermin will not be passed on'. A third section for newcomers: 'When their ability has been recognized, they will be given a place' (M.I.D.B., 56–7).

REFERENCES

Bentham, J., *Works*, ed. Bowring, IV, 1843.
La Métherie, C. de, *Journal de physique*, XXX, 1787.
Loisel, G., *Histoire des ménageries*, II, 1912.
M.I.D.B. (Batencourt), *Instruction méthodique pour l'école paroissiale*, 1669.

READING 21: PANOPTICISM

DISCUSSION QUESTIONS

- "Visibility is a trap," writes Foucault. Why and how does it work?
- What is the layout of the panopticon and what affect does it have on those incarcerated there?
- What does prison design have to do with gender?

EXAMPLES TO THINK ABOUT

- Shopping malls
- Lecture halls
- Closed-circuit TV

The Geography of Women's Fear

AREA, VOL. 21, NO. 4

By GILL VALENTINE

I n March 1988 Deborah Linsley was stabbed to death in an empty train compartment on the Orpington to Victoria line.

It is well established in the sociology and criminology literatures of western Europe that women are the gender more fearful of crime and that this is related to women's sense of physical vulnerability to men, particularly to rape and sexual murder, and an awareness of the seriousness and horror of such an experience (Baumer 1978; Riger *et al.* 1978; Balkin 1979; Gordon *et al.* 1980; Toseland 1982; Warr 1985; and Stanko 1987). However little has been written about the geography of this fear (Scheppele and Bart 1983). This article considers issues raised by events such as the murder mentioned above and uses my own research conducted in Reading[1] to explore the relationship between women's fear of male violence and their perception and use of public space.

Concern surrounding Deborah Linsley's death raised as many issues about her use of space as about male violence. Deborah was in an isolated public space away from the protection of others, thus allowing a man the opportunity to kill her. In subsequent comments on the murder both the police and the media implied that Deborah was to a certain degree responsible for her own fate by putting herself in such a situation, and warned other women to avoid putting themselves in similar situations of vulnerability. This assumption about women's lack of freedom to be in certain public spaces, at certain times is reflected in comments made by Reading women[2].

> 'You hear it on the news and things about attacks and you wonder why that girl was out on her own anyway. I'm never going to let myself get into a situation where I'm alone, cos you just don't know who will be there'. (Lower Earley young woman)

Public blame of victims who were in public places, for being in a dangerous or inappropriate place when they were attacked, encourages all women to transfer their threat appraisal from men to certain public spaces where they may encounter attackers. The other side of this fear of being in public space is for women to adopt false assumptions about their security when in places falsely deemed safe for women, such as the home.

THE GEOGRAPHY OF FEAR

The association of male violence with certain environmental contexts has a profound effect on many women's use of space. Every day most women in western societies negotiate public space alone. Many of their apparently 'taken for granted' choices of routes and destinations are in fact the product of 'coping strategies' women adopt to stay safe (Riger and Gordon 1981; Riger *et al.* 1982; Stanko 1987). The predominant strategy adopted by the women I interviewed is the avoidance of perceived 'dangerous places' at 'dangerous times'. By adopting such defensive tactics women are pressurised into a restricted use and occupation of public space. Therefore an understanding of women's use of space necessitates an awareness of their geography of fear. A woman's ability to choose a coping strategy and therefore her consequent use and experience of public space is largely determined by her age, income and lifestyle (Valentine forthcoming).

Women develop individual mental maps of places where they fear assault as a product of their past experience of space and secondary information. In particular girls are socialised into a restricted use of public space through observing both their parents' differential fears for them and the control of the spatial range of their activities in relation to boys (Hart 1979). Consequently most girls have mental images of places where strange men may approach them instilled at an early age. However, despite their fears and possible avoidance of 'dangerous places' my research suggests that most young women do have some form of frightening experience such as being flashed at or followed (see also Hall 1984; Kelly 1987; Wise and Stanley 1987). Such incidents then become associated with the environmental context in which they took place, so reinforcing or developing the young woman's geography of fear. Additionally, these mental maps of feared environments are elaborated by images gained from hearing the frightening experiences and advice of others; and from media reporting, such as that of Deborah Linsley's death.

Women assume that the location of male violence is unevenly distributed through space and time. In particular women learn to perceive danger from strange men in public space despite the fact that statistics on rape and attack emphasise clearly that they are more at risk at home and from men they know. This is because when in public the behaviour of any stranger encountered is potentially unpredictable and uncontrollable. (In this context my research suggests that women perceive only men as strangers). Public space is defined by Waltzer (1986) as 'the space we share with strangers, people who aren't our relatives, friends or work associates'. Unlike men women find that when in public space their personal space is frequently invaded by whistles, comments or actual physical assault from strange men. This inability of women to choose with whom they interact and communicate profoundly affects their sense of security in public (Hanmer and Saunders 1984).

The type of places in which Reading women anticipate themselves to be most at risk are therefore those where they perceive the behaviour of others, specifically men, who may be sharing that space to be unregulated. First, large open spaces which are frequently deserted: parks, woodland, wasteground, canals, rivers and countryside. Frequently local place mythologies develop around such places. The Reading findings reflect an association between wooded parks and 'dirty old men' similar to that noted in Burgess's open space project (1987). Secondly, closed spaces with limited exits where men may be concealed and able to attack women out of the visual range of others: subways, alleyways, multistorey carparks and empty railway carriages. Such opportunities for concealed attack are often exacerbated by bad lighting and ill considered and thoughtless building design and landscaping (Heing and Maxfield 1978).

Reading women say that when they are in places where they perceive themselves to be at risk they are constantly alert to their physical surroundings, listening for every rustle in the bushes or approach of footsteps. As a result, most women, especially at night, have a heightened consciousness of the micro design features of their environment, and adjust their pace and path accordingly: running past or crossing the road to avoid alleyways, indented doorways, over-grown bushes and other perceived shadowy areas.

> 'You've gotta be alert at night. I mean I'm always aware, I'm like a radar at night, the slightest noise and I'll hear it' (Whitley Wood young woman).

> 'When you're alone you suddenly realise how bad the lighting is, or the kind of road you're walking down, whether it's fairly well lit or got lots of trees and things. You're just so aware. But you don't notice it if you're with somebody' (Lower Earley young woman).

As a product of their fear, many women not only perceive, but also experience, their environment differently to men (Mazey and Lee 1983; Tuan 1974).

SOCIAL CONTROL, SPACE AND TIME

Not all public places are perceived as equally threatening all the time because in many places or at some times the behaviour of those occupying the space is externally regulated either formally or informally, so reducing the perceived opportunity for attack. Formal control of public space is exercised not only directly by the police or private security guards, but more indirectly by store managers, bus conductors, park wardens and other authorised personnel in the process of providing a public service. Recent public spending cuts, resulting in fewer staff, particularly in public transport services, have eroded this formal control and contributed to women's sense of vulnerability in public space.

Informal social control in public areas relies upon the potential intervention of others present to act as a deterrent to those contemplating crime. This is more successful in stable neighbourhoods where people have strong social and family ties through long periods of residence. They become familiar with the place ballet (Seamon 1979) and are therefore more easily able to recognise strangers and inappropriate behaviour. As such they are more likely to feel confident to intervene to help others, or to know where or from whom to seek help if they perceive themselves to be threatened (Conklin 1975; Riger and Lavrakas 1981; Riger *et al.* 1981).

> 'I've lived here all my life so I feel more safe in Whitley than what I do anywhere else. Cos I know that if I'm round here even if I didn't know anybody I could just knock on their door, just cos I live round here and so most people I know them, or seen 'em, you know round sometime, or the family knows 'em' (Whitley Wood married mother).

However, in affluent private housing estates where there is a high turnover of population, the emphasis on privacy and individual mobility tends to result in the use of the space solely as a place of residence, rather than as multiuse community space. Consequently the inhabitants are frequently strangers to each other and the place, and therefore informal social control has to be generated artificially through neighbourhood watch schemes.

> 'I mean here it's the commuter belt so people are in and out all the time. I never expect to think people will stay very long here, they just pass through. So there are so many people around who are strangers you just don't know people. I know they call it the Lower Earley community but I don't see any evidence of it' (Lower Earley married mother).

A woman's perception of her safety in her local neighbourhood is therefore strongly related to how well she knows and feels at ease with both her social and physical surroundings.

When a woman is in an area beyond her local environment she makes judgements about her safety in public space on the basis of preconceived images she holds about that area and its occupants, as well as from cues she receives about social behaviour from the actual physical surroundings. For example signs of incivility such as vandalism and graffiti suggest inappropriate or threatening behaviour is possible or permitted, whereas signs of care such as neat, litter-free streets suggest the opposite (Lewis and Maxfield 1980; Brower *et al.* 1983). A woman will therefore not automatically assume safety in a public space occupied by others, if she perceives those present or perceived to be controlling that space as a threatening or alien group. These fears of potential hostility are particularly centred upon the town centre and residential areas identified on the basis of ethnicity or class. In Reading both the middle and working class white women interviewed hold an image of a predominantly Afro-Caribbean residential area as dangerous for white women because of a racist assumption about the violent nature of black males. Similarly, the middle class women also anticipate a large 'rundown' council estate to be rough, whereas the residents of that area perceive themselves to be safer than the middle class women do in their own housing area.

Beyond this general attribution of control to the major residential group, the group which is actually dominant in a public space is time specific, the controlling group fluctuating with time of day. Public space is segregated through time according to gender and age, due to different lifestyles and hence time-space routines. During the daytime in towns and cities such as Reading, public places such as streets, shops, parks, public transport and town centres are numerically dominated by women in part-time paid work, housewives, young children and the elderly[3]. This is because of their limited access to private transport, flexible time budgets and need to fulfil domestic tasks, such as shopping. Those men who are present are usually engaged in work related activity and therefore their behaviour appears both predictable and controllable. As evening draws in, it is younger people, and particularly men who are visible. Freed from the confines of work, and usually without the family responsibilities of most women, they have the time, energy and financial resources to go out in the pursuit of leisure activities and therefore to numerically dominate public space. Consequently, whilst women identify specific isolated places as frightening during the day, they express a fear of all public space alone at night. This is not only because night reduces visibility and therefore increases the opportunity for attackers to strike unobserved, but because the nature of public space changes, being dominated in the evening by the group women have most to fear, men.

> 'I don't feel safe in the evening, I think it's because you think there'll be drunken men coming out of the pub and what have you. And you know you get "dirty old men" around at that time of night that there aren't in the day. Cos you know in the evening they've got an excuse to be out roaming the streets, you know they can go to the shop or pub or whatever' (Whitley Wood young woman).

This domination is achieved not only through numerical appropriation of space, but through assertive and aggressive behaviour which intimidates and embarasses women. Examples referred to during my Reading group discussions include: male use of physical size and comportment to intimidate women, for example when trying to be served at a bar; male mockery of the ability of women engaged in sporting or leisure activities such as running or playing pool; and male verbal harassment or the physical forcing of attentions upon women unaccompanied by other males. Such behaviour by unknown men is particularly unpredictable and threatening when their need to assert their masculinity is heightened by drink and the social pressures of a peer group context. Consequently, women are told and soon learn through experience that it is inappropriate and potentially unsafe to be alone in male dominated space, especially at night.

Women's fear of male violence does not therefore just take place in space but is tied up with the way public space is used, occupied and controlled by different groups at different times. There is a vicious circle in operation. The majority of women still adopt a traditional gender role, and as a consequence are pressurised into a temporally segregated use of space. The subsequent control by men of public space in the evening means that despite the career success and independence gained by some women in the past decade (during which time there has been a significant rise in reported sexual and violent crime) the fear of male violence deters the majority of women from being independent. It robs them of the confidence to live alone, to work in certain occupations, and to socialise without a group or male chaperon.

> 'I've often thought when I was 21, I've often thought about getting a place on my own, I mean even when I was at school I wanted to do that, but now I don't think I could live on my own. I'd feel so unsafe' (Lower Earley young woman).

> 'With my last job which was at Northsea they started opening at ten o'clock at night, and I only did a couple of hours in the evening, but it wasn't that it was the coming home in the evening, you know, I was dead scared of coming home on my own and I couldn't arrange for anyone to meet me cos my Dad he won't, anyway and it used to make me scared and I said I just can't go in like this in the evenings because it's frightening me. I gave that job up' (Whitley Wood young woman).

This inability of women to enjoy independence and freedom to move safely in public space is therefore one of the pressures which encourages them to seek from one man protection from all, initially through having a boyfriend and later through cohabitation. This dependence on a single man commonly limits women's career opportunities and general life world. This in turn results in a restricted use of public space by women, especially at night, allowing men to appropriate it and hence making women feel unsafe to go out, reinforcing their comparative confinement in the home. Consequently this cycle of fear becomes one subsystem by which male dominance, patriarchy[4], is maintained and perpetuated. Women's inhibited use and occupation of public space is therefore a spatial expression of patriarchy.

NOTES

1. This paper is generated from research about the nature and implications of women's feelings of fear when in public space currently being undertaken as part of a PhD thesis at the University of Reading. The results are based on 80 in depth interviews (with accompanying spatial diaries) and six small-group discussions with Reading women of varied age, lifestyle and income. In addition, periodic recorded observation of specific public space is being made.
2. The research is concentrated on two main areas of Reading, a middle class housing estate (Lower Earley) and a council estate (Whitley Wood).
3. This may not be true for the centre of major cities such as London, where the unique character of the transport systems and the more varied use of space for example by groups such as tourists means the presence of more non working men in public space during the day.
4. For a discussion of patriarchy see Sargent 1981; Jagger 1983; Foord and Gregson 1986.

REFERENCES

Balkin, S. (1979) 'Victimisation rates, safety and fear of crime' *Social Problems* 26, 343–58.

Baumer, T. (1978) 'Research on fear of crime in the US' *Victimology* 3, 254–67.

Brower, S., Dockett, K. and Taylor, R. B. (1983) 'Residents perceptions of territorial features and perceived local threat' *Environment and Behaviour* 15, 419–37.

Burgess, J. (1987) Unpublished paper presented at Reading University Seminar, 1 December.

Conklin, J. E. (1975) *The impact of crime.* Macmillan, New York.

Foord, J. and Gregson, N. (1986) 'Patriarchy: towards a reconceptulisation' *Antipode* 18, 186–211.

Gordon, M. T., Riger, S., LeBailly, R. K. and Heath, L. (1980) 'Crime, women and the quality of urban life' *Signs* 5, 144–60.

Hall, R. E. (1984) *Ask any woman: a London inquiry into rape and sexual assault.* Falling Wall Press, Bristol.

Hanmer, J. and Saunders, S. (1984) *Well founded fear: a community study of violence to women.* Hutchinson, London.

Hart, R. (1979) *Childrens experience of place.* Irvington, New York.

Heing, J. and Maxfield, M. (1978) 'Reducing fear of crime: strategies for intervention' *Victimology* 3, 279–313.

Jaggar, A. (1983) *Feminist politics and human nature.* Harvester Press, Sussex.

Kelly, L. (1987) 'The continuum of sexual violence' in Hanmer, J. and Maynard, M. (eds) *Women violence and social control.* Macmillan, Basingstoke, 46–60.

Lewis, D. A. and Maxfield, M. G. (1980) 'Fear in the neighbourhood: an investigation of the impact of crime' *Journal of Research in Crime and Delinquency* 17, 140–59.

Mazey, M. E. and Lee, D. R. (1983) *Her space, her place—a geography of women.* AAG, Washington.

Riger, S. and Gordon, M. T. (1981) 'The fear of rape a study in social control' *Journal of Social Issues* 37, 71–92.

Riger, S. and Lavrakas, P. (1981) 'Community ties: patterns of attachment and social interaction in urban neighbourhoods' *American Journal of Community Psychology* 9, 653–65.

Riger, S., Gordon, M. T. and LeBailly, R. K. (1978) 'Women's fear of crime from blaming to restricting the victim' *Victimology* 3, 274–83.

Riger, S., Gordon, M. T. and LeBailly, R. K. (1982) 'Coping with urban crime: women's use of precautionary behaviour' *American Journal of Community Psychology* 10, 369–86.

Sargent, L. (ed) (1981) *The unhappy marriage of marxism and feminism: a debate on class and patriarchy.* Pluto Press, London.

Scheppele, K. L. and Bart, P. B. (1983) 'Through women's eyes: defining danger in the wake of sexual assault' *Journal of Social Issues* 39, 63–81.

Seamon, D. (1979) *A geography of the lifeworld.* Croom Helm, London.

Stanko, E. A. (1987) 'Typical violence normal precaution: men, women and interpersonal violence in England, Wales, Scotland and USA' Hanmer, J. and Maynard, M. (eds) *Women, violence and social control.* Macmillan, Basingstoke, 122–34.

Toseland, R. W. (1982) 'Fear of crime: who is most vulnerable' *Journal of Criminal Justice* 10, 199–209.

Tuan, Y. F. (1974) *Topophilia.* Prentice Hall, London.

Valentine, G. M. (forthcoming) *Women's fear of violence in public space* PhD thesis, Department of Geography, University of Reading.

Waltzer, M. (1986) 'Public space: a discussion on the shape of our cities' *Dissent* (Fall), 470–94.

Warr, M. (1985) 'Fear of rape among urban women' *Social Problems* 32, 238–50

Wise, S. and Stanley, L. (1987) *Georgie porgie: sexual harassment in everyday life.* Pandora Press, London.

DISCUSSION QUESTIONS

- What types of public spaces do women fear? Why?
- According to Valentine, how does the safety advice given to women reinforce patriarchy?

EXAMPLES TO THINK ABOUT

- Safety tips from institutions, family, and friends
- Areas that you avoid, especially at night

What Would a Non-Sexist City Be Like?

Speculations on Housing, Urban Design, and Human Work

SIGNS, VOL. 5, NO. 3

By DOLORES HAYDEN

A woman's place is in the home" has been one of the most important principles of architectural design and urban planning in the United States for the last century. An implicit rather than explicit principle for the conservative and male-dominated design professions, it will not be found stated in large type in textbooks on land use. It has generated much less debate than the other organizing principles of the contemporary American city in an era of monopoly capitalism, which include the ravaging pressure of private land development, the fetishistic dependence on millions of private automobiles, and the wasteful use of energy.[1] However, women have rejected this dogma and entered the paid labor force in larger and larger numbers. Dwellings, neighborhoods, and cities designed for homebound women constrain women physically, socially, and economically. Acute frustration occurs when women defy these constraints to spend all or part of the work day in the paid labor force. I contend that the only remedy for this situation is to develop a new paradigm of the home, the neighborhood, and the city; to begin to describe the physical, social, and economic design of a human settlement that would support, rather than restrict, the activities of employed women and their families. It is essential to recognize such needs in order to begin both the rehabilitation of the existing housing stock and the construction of new housing to meet the needs of a new and growing majority of Americans—working women and their families.

When speaking of the American city in the last quarter of the twentieth century, a false distinction between "city" and "suburb" must be avoided. The urban region, organized to separate homes and workplaces, must be seen as a whole. In such urban regions, more than half of the population resides in the sprawling suburban areas, or "bedroom communities." The greatest part of the built environment in the United States consists of "suburban sprawl": single-family homes grouped in class-segregated areas, crisscrossed by freeways and served by shopping malls and commercial strip developments. Over 50 million small homes are on the ground. About two-thirds of American families "own" their homes on long mortgages; this includes over 77 percent of all AFL-CIO members.[2] White, male skilled workers are far more likely to be homeowners than members of minority groups and women, long denied equal credit or equal access to housing. Workers commute to jobs either in the center or elsewhere in the suburban ring. In metropolitan areas studied in 1975 and 1976, the journey to work, by public transit or private car, averaged about nine miles each way. Over 100 million privately owned cars filled two- and three-car garages (which would be considered magnificent housing by themselves in many developing countries). The United States, with 13 percent of the world's population, uses 41 percent of the world's passenger cars in support of the housing and transportation patterns described.[3]

The roots of this American settlement form lie in the environmental and economic policies of the past. In the late nineteenth century, millions of immigrant families lived in the crowded, filthy slums of American industrial cities and despaired of achieving reasonable living conditions. However, many militant strikes and demonstrations between the 1890s and 1920s made some employers reconsider plant locations and housing issues in their search for industrial order.[4] "Good homes make contented workers" was the slogan of the Industrial Housing Associates in 1919. These consultants and many others helped major corporations plan better housing for white male skilled workers and their families, in order to eliminate industrial conflict. "Happy workers invariably mean bigger profits, while unhappy workers are never a good investment," they chirruped.[5] Men were to receive "family wages," and become home "owners" responsible for regular mortgage payments, while their wives became home "managers" taking care of spouse and children. The male worker would return from his day in the factory or office to a private domestic environment, secluded from the tense world of work in an industrial city characterized by environmental pollution, social degradation, and personal alienation. He would enter a serene dwelling whose physical and emotional maintenance would be the duty of his wife. Thus the private suburban house was the stage set for the effective sexual division of labor. It was the commodity par excellence, a spur for male paid labor and a container for female unpaid labor. It made gender appear a more important self-definition than class, and consumption more involving than production. In a brilliant discussion of the "patriarch as wage slave," Stuart Ewen has shown how capitalism and antifeminism fused in campaigns for homeownership and mass consumption: the patriarch whose home was his "castle" was to work year in and year out to provide the wages to support this private environment.[6]

• • • •

More and more married women joined the paid labor force, as the suggestible housewife needed to be both a frantic consumer and a paid worker to keep up with the family's bills. Just as the mass of white male workers had achieved the "dream houses" in suburbia where fantasies of patriarchal authority and consumption could be acted out, their spouses entered the world of paid employment. By 1975, the two-worker family accounted for 39 percent of American households. Another 13 percent were single-parent families, usually headed by women. Seven out of ten employed women were in the work force because of financial need. Over 50 percent of all children between one and seventeen had employed mothers.[7]

How does a conventional home serve the employed woman and her family? Badly. Whether it is in a suburban, exurban, or inner-city neighborhood, whether it is a split-level ranch house, a modern masterpiece of concrete and glass, or an old brick tenement, the house or apartment is almost invariably organized around the same set of spaces: kitchen, dining room, living room, bedrooms, garage or parking area. These spaces require someone to undertake private cooking, cleaning, child care, and usually private transportation if adults and children are to exist within it. Because of residential zoning practices, the typical dwelling will usually be physically removed from any shared community space—no commercial or communal day-care facilities, or laundry facilities, for example, are likely to be part of the dwelling's spatial domain. In many cases these facilities would be illegal if placed across property lines. They could also be illegal if located on residentially zoned sites. In some cases sharing such a private dwelling with other individuals (either relatives or those unrelated by blood) is also against the law.[8]

Within the private spaces of the dwelling, material culture works against the needs of the employed woman as much as zoning does, because the home is a box to be filled with commodities. Appliances are usually single-purpose, and often inefficient, energy-consuming machines, lined up in a room where the domestic work is done in isolation from the rest of the family. Rugs and carpets which need vacuuming, curtains which need laundering, and miscellaneous goods which need maintenance fill up the domestic spaces, often decorated in "colonial," "Mediterranean," "French Provincial," or other eclectic styles purveyed by discount and department stores to cheer up that bare box of an isolated house. Employed mothers usually are expected to, and almost invariably do, spend more time in private housework and child care than employed men; often they are expected to, and usually do, spend more time on commuting per mile traveled than men, because of their reliance on public transportation. One study found that 70 percent of adults without access to cars are female.[9] Their residential neighborhoods are not likely to provide much support for their work activities. A "good" neighborhood is usually defined in terms of conventional shopping, schools, and perhaps public transit, rather than additional social services for the working parent, such as day care or evening clinics.

While two-worker families with both parents energetically cooperating can overcome some of the problems of existing housing patterns, households in crisis, such as subjects of wife and child battering, for example, are particularly vulnerable to its inadequacies. According to Colleen McGrath, every thirty seconds a woman is being battered somewhere in the United States. Most of these batterings occur in kitchens and bedrooms. The relationship between household isolation and battering, or between unpaid domestic labor and battering, can only be guessed, at this time, but there is no doubt that America's houses and households are literally shaking with domestic violence.[10] In addition, millions of angry and upset women are treated with tranquilizers in the private home—one drug company advertises to doctors: "You can't change her environment but you can change her mood."[11]

The woman who does leave the isolated, single-family house or apartment finds very few real housing alternatives available to her.[12] The typical divorced or battered woman currently seeks housing, employment, and child care simultaneously. She finds that matching her complex family requirements with the various available offerings by landlords, employers, and social services is impossible. One environment that unites housing, services, and jobs could resolve many difficulties, but the existing system of government services, intended to stabilize households and neighborhoods by ensuring the minimum conditions for a decent home life to all Americans, almost always assumes that the traditional household with a male worker and an unpaid homemaker is the goal to be achieved or simulated. In the face of massive demographic changes, programs such as public housing, AFDC, and food stamps still attempt to support an ideal family living in an isolated house or apartment, with a full-time homemaker cooking meals and minding children many hours of the day.

By recognizing the need for a different kind of environment, far more efficient use can be made of funds now used for subsidies to individual households. Even for women with greater financial resources the need for better housing and services is obvious. Currently, more affluent women's problems as workers have been considered "private" problems—the lack of good day care, their lack of time. The aids to overcome an environment without child care, public transportation, or food service have been "private," commercially profitable solutions: maids and baby-sitters by the hour; franchise day care or extended television viewing; fast food service; easier credit for purchasing an automobile, a washer, or a microwave oven. Not only do these commercial solutions obscure the failure of American housing policies, they also generate bad conditions for other working women. Commercial day-care and fast-food franchises are the source of low-paying nonunion jobs without security. In this respect they resemble the use of private household workers by bourgeois women, who may never ask how their private maid or child-care worker arranges care for her own children. They also resemble the insidious effects of the use of television in the home as a substitute for developmental child care in the neighborhood. The logistical problems which all employed women face are not private problems, and they do not succumb to market solutions.

The problem is paradoxical: women cannot improve their status in the home unless their overall economic position in society is altered; women cannot improve their status in the paid labor force unless their domestic responsibilities are altered. Therefore, a program to achieve economic and environmental justice for women requires, by definition, a solution which overcomes the traditional divisions between the household and the market economy, the private dwelling and the workplace. One must transform the economic situation of the traditional homemaker whose skilled labor has been unpaid, but economically and socially necessary to society; one must also transform the domestic situation of the employed woman. If architects and urban designers were to recognize all employed women and their families as a constituency for new approaches to planning and design and were to reject all previous assumptions about "woman's place" in the home, what could we do? Is it possible to build non-sexist neighborhoods and design non-sexist cities? What would they be like?

NOTES

This paper comprised part of the text of a talk for the conference "Planning and Designing a Non-Sexist Society," University of California, Los Angeles, April 21, 1979. I would like to thank Catharine Stimpson, Peter Marris, S. M. Miller, Kevin Lynch, Jeremy Brecher, and David Thompson for extensive written comments on drafts of this paper.

1. There is an extensive Marxist literature on the importance of spatial design to the economic development of the capitalist city, including Henri Lefebre, *La Production de l'espace* (Paris: Editions Anthropos, 1974); Manuel Castells, *The Urban Question* (Cambridge, Mass.: M.I.T. Press, 1977); David Harvey, *Social Justice and the City* (London: Edward Arnold, 1974); and David Gordon, "Capitalist Development and the History of American Cities," in *Marxism and the Metropolis*, ed. William K. Tabb and Larry Sawyers (New York: Oxford University Press, 1978). None of this work deals adequately with the situation of women as workers and homemakers, nor with the unique spatial inequalities they experience. Nevertheless, it is important to combine the economic and historical analysis of these scholars with the empirical research of non-Marxist feminist urban critics and sociologists who have examined women's experience of conventional housing, such as Gerda Wekerle, "A Woman's Place Is in the City" (paper for the Lincoln Institute of Land Policy, Cambridge, Mass., 1978); and Suzanne Keller, "Women in a Planned Community" (paper for the Lincoln Institute of Land Policy, Cambridge, Mass., 1978). Only then can one begin to provide a socialist-feminist critique of the spatial design of the American city. It is also essential to develop research on housing similar to Sheila B. Kamerman, "Work and Family in Industrialized Societies," *Signs: Journal of Women in Culture and Society* 4, no. 4 (Summer 1979): 632–50, which reviews patterns of women's employment, maternity provisions, and child-care policies in Hungary, East Germany, West Germany, France, Sweden, and the United States. A comparable study of housing and related services for employed women could be the basis for more elaborate proposals for change. Many

attempts to refine socialist and feminist economic theory concerning housework are discussed in an excellent article by Ellen Malos, "Housework and the Politics of Women's Liberation," *Socialist Review* 37 (January-February 1978): 41–47. A most significant theoretical piece is Movimento di Lotta Femminile, "Programmatic Manifesto for the Struggle of Housewives in the Neighborhood," *Socialist Revolution* 9 (May-June 1972):85–90.

2. *Survey of AFL-CIO Members Housing 1975* (Washington, D.C.: AFL-CIO, 1975), p. 16. I am indebted to Allan Heskin for this reference.

3. *Transit Fact Book,* 1977–78 ed. (Washington, D.C.: American Public Transit Association, 1978), p. 29; *Motor Vehicle Facts and Figures* (Detroit, Mich.: Motor Vehicle Manufacturers Association, 1977), pp. 29, 31, 53.

4. Gordon, pp. 48–50, discusses suburban relocation of plants and housing.

5. Industrial Housing Associates, "Good Homes Make Contented Workers," 1919, Edith Elmer Wood Papers, Avery Library, Columbia University. Also see Barbara Ehrenreich and Deirdre English, "The Manufacture of Housework," *Socialist Revolution* 5 (1975):16. They quote an unidentified corporate official (ca. 1920): "Get them to invest their savings in homes and own them. Then they won't leave and they won't strike. It ties them down so they have a stake in our prosperity."

6. Stuart Ewen, *Captains of Consciousness: Advertising and the Social Roots of the Consumer Culture* (New York: McGraw-Hill Book Co., 1976).

7. Rosalyn Baxandall, Linda Gordon, and Susan Reverby, eds., *America's Working Women: A Documentary History, 1600 to the Present* (New York: Vintage Books, 1976). For more detail, see Louise Kapp Howe, *Pink Collar Workers: Inside the World of Woman's Work* (New York: Avon Books, 1977).

8. Recent zoning fights on the commune issue have occurred in Santa Monica, Calif.; Wendy Schuman, "The Return of Togetherness," *New York Times* (March 20, 1977), reports frequent illegal down zoning by two-family groups in one-family residences in the New York area.

9. Study by D. Foley cited in Wekerle (see n. 1 above).

10. Colleen McGrath, "The Crisis of Domestic Order," *Socialist Review* 9 (January–February 1979):12, 23.

11. Research by Malcolm MacEwen, cited in *Associate Collegiate Schools of Architecture Newsletter* (March 1973), p. 6.

12. See, for example, Carol A. Brown, "Spatial Inequalities and Divorced Mothers" (paper delivered at the annual meeting of the American Sociological Association, San Francisco, 1978); Susan Anderson-Khleif, research report for HUD on single-parent families and their housing, summarized in "Housing for Single Parents," *Research Report, MIT-Harvard Joint Center for Urban Studies* (April 1979), pp. 3–4.

DISCUSSION QUESTIONS

- Hayden suggests that domestic architecture is implicitly designed to keep women in the home. What features of suburban homes support that idea?
- Are there alternatives to suburban living?

EXAMPLES TO THINK ABOUT

- Suburban planning and building codes
- Co-ops and alternative communities

Bourgeois Utopias

The Rise and Fall of Suburbia

EXCERPTS FROM: INTRODUCTION

By ROBERT FISHMAN

Our suburban architecture ... reveals the spirit and character of modern civlization, just as the temples of Egypt and Greece, the baths and amphi-theaters of Rome, and the cathedrals and castles of the Middle Ages help us to comprehend and penetrate the spirit of previous civilizations.

—*Cesar Daly, 1864*

However modest each suburban house might be, suburbia represents a collective assertion of class wealth and privilege as impressive as any medieval castle. Most importantly, suburbia embodies a new ideal of family life, an ideal so emotionally charged that it made the home more sacred to the bourgeoisie than any place of worship. The hundred years of massive suburban development that have passed since Daly wrote can only confirm his judgment that the true center of any bourgeois society is the middle-class house. If you seek the monuments of the bourgeoisie, go to the suburbs and look around.

Suburbia is more than a collection of residential buildings; it expresses values so deeply embedded in bourgeois culture that it might also be called the bourgeois utopia. Yet this "utopia" was always at most a partial paradise, a refuge not only from threatening elements in the city but also from discordant elements in bourgeois society itself. From its origins, the suburban world of leisure, family life, and union with nature was based on the principle of exclusion. Work was excluded from the family residence; middle-class villas were segregated from working-class housing; the greenery of suburbia stood in contrast to a gray, polluted urban environment. Middle-class women were especially affected by the new suburban dichotomy of work and family life. The new environment supposedly exalted their role in the family, but it also segregated them from the world of power and productivity. This self-segregation soon enveloped all aspects of bourgeois culture. Suburbia, therefore, represents more than the bourgeois utopia, the triumphant assertion of middle-class values. It also reflects the alienation of the middle classes from the urban-industrial world they themselves were creating.

◆ ◆ ◆ ◆

Suburbia can thus be defined first by what it includes—middle-class residences—and second (perhaps more importantly) by what it excludes: all industry, most commerce except for enterprises that specifically serve a residential area, and all lower-class residents (except for servants). These social and economic characteristics are all expressed in design through a suburban tradition of both residential and landscape architecture. Derived from the English concept of the picturesque, this tradition distinguishes the suburb both from the city and from the countryside and creates that aesthetic "marriage of town and country" which is the mark of the true suburb.

One need only contrast this definition with the realities of the eighteenth century city to see how radically suburbia contradicted the basic assumptions that organized the premodern city. Such cities were built up on the principle that the core was the only appropriate and honorific setting for the elite, and that the urban peripheries outside the walls were disreputable zones, shantytowns to which the poorest inhabitants and the most noisome manufactures were relegated.

In London—a typical premodern city in this respect and one with a special relevance to this study—income and social standing declined markedly as one moved from the center to the outskirts. These social distinctions were enshrined in the language itself. From its earliest usage in the fourteenth century until the mid eighteenth century, a "suburbe"—that is, a settlement on the urban fringe—meant (in the definition of the *Oxford English Dictionary*) a "place of inferior, debased, and especially licentious habits of life." The canon's yeoman in Chaucer's *Canterbury Tales* says of himself and his master, a crooked alchemist, that they live "in the suburbes of town. We lurk in corners and blind alleys where robbers and thieves instinctively huddle secretly and fearfully together... ."[2]

In Shakespeare's London so many houses of prostitution had moved to these disreputable outskirts that a whore was called "a suburb sinner," and to call a man a "suburbanite" was a serious insult.[3] One nineteenth century writer has described the inhabitants of the suburb of Cripplegate in the seventeenth century as

> a population of tanners and skinners, catgut makers, tallow melters, dealers in old clothes, receivers of stolen goods, charcoal sellers, makers of sham jewelry, coiners, clippers of coin and silver refiners, who kept their melting-pots ready day and night for any silver plate that might come to hand, toilers in noisome trades and dishonest dealers. ... Forgers of seals, of bills, of writs, professional pick-purses, sharpers and other thieves, conjurors, wizards and fortune tellers, beggars and harlots found a refuge here.[4]

If the modern suburb can be defined as a peripheral zone in which people of means choose to live, then such a district was literally unthinkable in the premodern city, a contradiction in the basic terms that defined urban structure.

Indeed, even the concept of a residential district from which commerce and industry had been excluded was inconceivable for the premodern city. The basic principle of a city like London before 1750 was that work and residence were naturally combined within each house. Almost all middle-class enterprises were extensions of the family, so that it was not only the Spitalfields weaver who lived with his loom or the grocer who lived above his shop. The banker conducted business in his parlor, the merchant stored his goods in his cellar, and both housed and fed their apprentices along with their families.

This intimate connection of work and residence explained the universal attraction of the wealthy bourgeoisie to the urban core. When workplace and residence are combined, the best location for transacting one's business determined the location of one's house. In a mercantile city this location was almost invariably the most crowded district of the urban core.

I should emphasize here that even the relatively wealthy core areas were never upper-class neighborhoods in the modern sense. Just as the idea of a district devoted to a single function—a residential district or a business district—was foreign to the premodern city, so too was a single-class district. John Strype describes the privileged parish of St. Giles in the Fields as possessing "a mixture of rich inhabitants, to wit, of the Nobility, Gentry, and Commonality, but, withal, filled with abundance of poor."[5]

The wealthy might, at best, occupy large townhouses that fronted on the principal streets. But the poor inevitably crowded into the narrow alleyways and courtyards that existed literally in the backyards of the rich. This "medley of neighborhood," as Strype put it, was accepted without question. The poor were often servants in nearby houses, or workers in the multitude of small workshops found throughout the city. As one eighteenth century writer observed, "Here lives a personage of high distinction; next door a butcher with his stinking shambles! A Tallow-chandler shall be seen from my Lord's nice Venetian window; and two or three brawny naked Curriers in their Pits shall face a fine Lady in her back Closet, and disturb her spiritual Thoughts."[6] Here indeed we find the "mixed uses" frequently romanticized by twentieth century "postsuburban" planners. These mixed uses often had a functional basis, as when workshops clustered around the homes of merchants who dealt in their products. Sometimes they seem bizarre, as when a notorious "crime district" called Alsatia could be found adjoining the Temple, the center of English law.[7] In any case, the basic principles of the modern suburb had no precedents in the premodern city.

The suburb as we know it, therefore, did not evolve smoothly or inevitably from the premodern city; still less did it evolve from those disreputable outlying districts which originally bore the name of "suburbes." The emergence of suburbia required a total transformation of urban values: not only a reversal in the meanings of core and periphery, but a separation of work and family life and the creation of new forms of urban space that would be both class-segregated and wholly residential.

Who then invented suburbia and why? To ask the question is to formulate a major thesis of this book, which is that suburbia was indeed a cultural creation, a conscious choice based on the economic structure and cultural values of the Anglo-American bourgeoisie. Suburbanization was not the automatic fate of the middle class in the "mature industrial city" or an inevitable response to the Industrial Revolution or the so-called transportation revolution.

Yet, if suburbia was an original creation, it was not the product of an architect of genius who conceived the modern suburb in a single vision, which then gradually inspired the design profession and eventually the middle class. Indeed, in this history of suburban design, professional architects and city planners play a remarkably limited role.

Suburbia, I believe, was the collective creation of the bourgeois elite in late eighteenth century London. It evolved gradually and anonymously by trial-and-error methods. Wealthy London bankers and merchants experimented with a variety of the traditional housing forms available to them to create an original synthesis that reflected their values. Suburbia was improvised, not designed. Its method of evolution paralleled that of the contemporaneous Industrial Revolution, then taking place in the north of England, which also proceeded by trial-and-error adaptation. In both cases one senses the power of a class with the resources and the self-confidence to reorder the material world to suit its needs.

The motives that inspired the creation of suburbia were complex [...]. Here I would emphasize only one, which seems to me the most crucial. The London bourgeoisie who invented suburbia were also experiencing a new form of family, which Lawrence Stone has called "the closed domesticated nuclear family." Inner-directed, united by strong and exclusive personal ties, characterized in Stone's phrase by "an emphasis on the boundary surrounding the nuclear unit," such families sought to separate themselves from the intrusions of the workplace and the city. This new family type created the emotional force that split middle-class work and residence.[8]

The bourgeois residence was now freed from traditional patterns to be redesigned as a wholly domestic environment—the home of a family that acted primarily as an emotional rather than an economic unit. This home, moreover, need not be restricted to the crowded districts of the urban core, as the logic of business location had formerly dictated. It was free to seek a more appropriate setting beyond the city in the picturesque villages that surrounded London. There, within easy commuting distance to the city by private carriage, these merchants and bankers could construct their "bourgeois utopia" of leisure, neighborliness, prosperity, and family life.

To this strong cultural impetus to suburbanization was soon added an equally strong economic motive. The suburban idea raised the possibility that land far beyond the previous range of metropolitan expansion could be transformed immediately from relatively cheap agricultural land to highly profitable building plots. This possibility provided the great engine that drove suburban expansion forward. For reasons that I hope to make clear in [...], builders in both England and the United States adapted more easily to the needs of suburban development than they did to the more difficult challenge of creating middle-class districts within the city. Suburbia proved to be a good investment as well as a good home.

Middle-class suburbanization thus entered into the structural logic of the expanding Anglo-American city. It formed an integral part of what Frederick Law Olmsted perceived to be "the most prominent characteristic of the present period of civilization ... the strong tendency of people to flock together in great towns."[9] Suburbia might appear to be a flight from the city but, seen in a larger, regional context, suburbanization was clearly the outer edge in a wider process of metropolitan growth and consolidation that was draining the rural areas and small towns of their population and concentrating people and production within what H. G. Wells called "the whirlpool cities."[10]

In 1800 only 17 percent of the English people lived in settlements larger than 20,000 people.[11] Cities were then places for highly specialized forms of consumption, manufacture, and trade. The real work of the world took place in the villages and in the countryside. By 1890, however, 72 percent of the English population lived in districts classified as "urbanized."[12] In the United States in 1800 less than 4 percent of the population lived in cities of 10,000 people or more; by 1890 that figure had reached 28 percent.[13] Behind these statistics lies a fundamental shift in the role of the modern city. Where premodern cities had been parasitic on the larger societies, the new industrial metropolis emerged as the most efficient and productive site for the most characteristic modern industries.[14]

As such "whirlpool cities" as London, Manchester, and New York came to dominate the world economy, their attraction grew ever more powerful. In these centers of exchange and information, crowding seemed to work; in other words, intense congestion led not to chaos and decline but to further expansion. In the nineteenth century the expression "urban crisis" referred to the explosive growth of the great cities, and to horrified critics it seemed that almost the whole population of modern nations would soon be sucked into the already crowded urban centers.[15]

Inevitably, these whirlpool cities had to expand physically, to break the barriers of size that had always constrained urban growth. The only question was if they would grow in the traditional manner, with the wealthy massed at the core and the poor pushed ever farther into the periphery; or if the middle class would use their wealth and resources to seize the unspoiled land at the urban fringe for their suburban "bourgeois utopia," forcing the working class into an intermediate "factory zone" sandwiched between the central business district and the suburbs.

Broadly speaking, continental and Latin American cities opted for the traditional structure, while British and North American cities followed the path of middle-class suburbanization. This distinction, still fundamental in so many of the world's great cities, had nothing to do with the supposed backwardness of continental cities as compared to their Anglo-American counterparts. Paris in the nineteenth century became far more intensively industrialized than London, and the French capital developed a network of omnibuses, streetcars, and railroads that matched the transportation facilities in any English or American city. Yet the Parisian middle class remained loyal to the central city; the transportation system in Paris was used to move Parisian industry and its workers to the suburbs, and every further advance in transportation and industry has meant moving factories and the working class even farther from the city while the Parisian middle class has solidified its hold on the urban core.

However "objective" the "industrial city" might appear in diagrams from the Chicago School of sociology, its form rests ultimately on the values and choices of the powerful groups within the city. The decision of the bourgeoisie in Manchester and the other early industrial cities in the 1840s to suburbanize created the basic structure of the Anglo-American industrial city, while the decision of the comparable group in Paris of the 1850s and 1860s (aided by considerable governmental aid and intervention) to live in apartment houses in the center created the modern continental-style city.

In both cases the key actor was that elite of the middle class, the bourgeoisie. By "bourgeoisie" I mean that part of the middle class which through its capital or its professional standing has attained an income level equal to the landed gentry, but whose daily work in urban offices ties it to a middle-class style of life. Their personal resources permit them to create new patterns of living, while the values they share with the rest of the middle class makes them the model for eventual emulation by the less prosperous. The history of suburbia must therefore be a cultural and social history of the Anglo-American bourgeoisie. They are the pioneers whose collective style and choices define the nature of suburbia for their era.

For these English and American bourgeois pioneers, the "frontier" was inevitably the urban periphery, with its relatively cheap, undeveloped land. In continental cities massive governmental intervention—the nineteenth century versions of urban renewal—opened the possibility of reshaping the urban core for bourgeois uses. In England and the United States, laissez-faire urban economics turned the core into a tangle of competing uses. Only the periphery was sufficiently undefined to permit innovation. Indeed, the fate of the periphery was ultimately decisive in defining the whole structure of the Anglo-American city. In this

Darwinian struggle for urban space, the bourgeoisie sought not only land for their commercial and industrial enterprises but also land for their dreams: their visions of the ideal middle-class home. These dreams are now deep in the structure of the twentieth century city.

This history of suburbia is thus a history of a vision—the bourgeois utopia—which has left its mark on thousands of individual suburbs, each with its own distinctive history. But I believe that all these communities can be linked to a single sub urban tradition of architectural and social history. In attempting to outline the principal stages in the evolution of this tradition, I have been forced to depart from the usual method of suburban history, which is to examine one community over time. No single suburb adequately represents all the stages of suburban evolution, so I have selected a series of communities that seem best to embody the suburban idea at each crucial point of innovation.

These suburbs are not typical of their time but rather exemplary. Built rapidly in periods of unusual growth and prosperity, they incorporate in their design a creative response to contemporary changes in the structure and economy of modern cities. Unconstrained by previous building, responding to new social and cultural forces, these communities are truly "of their time." Through a series of often uncoordinated decisions by developers, builders, and individuals, a new style arises, which is then copied in hundreds of other suburbs. These exemplary suburbs create the image that, at any particular time, defines the suburban tradition. This image then becomes an active force in urban history, shaping subsequent decisions by speculators and home buyers that transform the urban landscape.

READING 24: BOURGEOIS UTOPIAS

DISCUSSION QUESTIONS

- Fishman says that suburbs are defined by "a principle of exclusion." What is being excluded?
- Does it feel odd to think about suburban areas as a recent development? Why?

EXAMPLES TO THINK ABOUT

- Suburban planning and building codes

SECTION 8

EXAMPLES AND ISSUES:
ATTITUDES TOWARD SEX

Feminists for Porn

COUNTERPUNCH

By NINA HARTLEY

It was with a growing sense of outrage that I read Prof. Chyng Sun's report of her visit this past January to the Adult Entertainment Expo in Las Vegas. I couldn't help wondering it the author had done any prior research whatsoever into the active, twenty-year debate among women over the impact of pornography on their individual lives and their status as a gender. There's nothing new in her indignation, nothing fresh in her insights and nothing unfamiliar in her arguments. As a sex-worker and sex-worker advocate for over two decades, I've heard and read it all before.

The professor appears wholly unfamiliar with the work of accomplished, feminist women who reject her fundamental contentions about porn and sex-work. If she bothered to consider the writings of Nadine Strossen, Carol Queen, Pat Califia, Susie Bright, Wendy McElroy, Sallie Tisdale, Linda Williams, Annie Sprinkle, myself and others, her homework wasn't reflected in what she showed me. Clearly, testimony that failed to corroborate her pre-conceived notions of what porn is "really" about, or what it "really" means didn't register on her radar screen.

I am an R.N., a third-generation feminist and a First-Amendment activist as well as a porn performer with the longest continuous career in the history of the industry. I'm easy to find. In fact, I was in one place for four hours each day on the floor at AEE. She certainly found my husband, writer-director I.S. Levine, (whose videos and magazines appear under the name Ernest Greene). At her request, he granted her a two-hour, on-camera interview in good faith, hoping but not expecting to receive an open-minded hearing. Why did Professor Sun not speak to me? Could it be because she knew that my very existence argues against her core assertions? Where was the honest, fearless intellectual curiosity that is hallmark of the pioneering academic researcher?

Perhaps, like a number of anti-porn feminists these days, she chooses not to solicit the opinions of women engaged in or supportive of sex-work, rather than risk encountering a contrary-to-theory example.

Professor Sun's criticisms of pornography, though jazzed up with some contemporary media theory, are little different form those posed by the first round of anti-sex feminists I came across at the NOW conventions I attended the mid-1980's. The gender bias, anti-male hostility, neo-Victorian erotophobia and unacknowledged class prejudice are all too familiar. Having been told to my face, in the company of twelve other, like-minded women, that I was either a shill for or a victim of patriarchal domination, I know how powerful the angry denial of feminist porn-bashers can be.

And it is that very power that makes Professor Sun's generalizations and oversimplifications so dangerous. Though she begins her jeremiad with the obligatory disclaimer about opposing censorship, she and others of her persuasion cannot believe for a moment that their opinions are offered in a political vacuum.

For many years, right-wing ideologues have co-opted the language of feminism in their on-going, nefarious attempts to erase all forms of sexual choice. Prof. Sun plays into the hands of these enemies of women. Does she not know that making common cause with those whose most treasured ambition is the reversal of Roe v. Wade will always be suicidal? How is Prof. Sun different from Phyllis Schlafly? From Anita Bryant? From Beverly LaHaye? From Judith Reisman? From Lou Sheldon or Jerry Falwell? They all want to eliminate my choice in the disposition my body. If I have the right to choose abortion, then I have the right to choose to have sex for the camera. Sexual freedom is the flip side of the coin of reproductive choice. Make no mistake, Professor. When they've got rid of me, they're coming for you next.

Professor Sun's reportage dwells at length on the most distasteful aspects of what she saw and heard, but makes no mention of any attempt to establish direct communication with any of the women who work in the adult video industry. No wonder she finds it so effortless to ignore our opinions and dismiss our perceptions of our own lives. It's that much easier to characterize all female sex workers as degraded, humiliated and unhappy if you've never talked to any of us. That we might be involved in constructive, effective efforts to improve our own working conditions, and that our employers might take our concerns seriously, clearly doesn't fit Professor Sun's pre-cut template for who we are.

Likewise, none of the diversity of our vibrant, raucous and contentious creative culture seems to have attracted Professor Sun's notice. By focusing on one or two examples she finds particularly heinous, she obscures the broader truth, which is that the marketplace of sexual entertainment contains products for almost every taste and orientation, including material made by and for heterosexual women and couples, lesbians and gay men. It's not all Bang Bus, and by no means does all of it, or even most of it, conform to the author's notions of porn-as-expression-of-misogyny. For her to project her own, obviously conflicted, feelings regarding men and sex onto all of the incredibly broad medium we call pornography is intellectually indefensible.

Professor Sun defames male consumers of pornography with the same broad strokes used to stereotype the experiences of female performers. Does she really believe that the average man cannot tell the difference between a movie and real life? Does she really think that young people's difficult times with sex are more attributable to porn than to the enforced ignorance resulting from twenty years of abstinence-only "sex education" and anti-choice propaganda? Does anyone seriously harbor the idea that individual conceptions of intimacy and sexual pleasure are shaped more by exposure to pornography than by the examples parents set for their children?

A young person's self-image, ability to set boundaries, and attitude toward sex is formed long before his or her teen years, before he or she has encountered to the supposed "evils" of pornography. I have personally met, and looked into the eyes of, hundreds of thousands of fans over the past two decades, and precious few of them would fit Professor Sun's construction of the "typical" consumer.

And to confabulate the images on a screen, which are created performances, with the actual experience of the performers themselves, would be laughably literal-minded, were it not so profoundly insulting. Sex performers, like the products they make, vary greatly in taste and temperment. We are much more than the characters we play. Like it or not, many female performers enjoy what they do, including things Professor Sun finds repellent. If we are not to choose what forms of sexual expression we find appropriate for ourselves, who is to do the choosing for us, Professor Sun and her like-minded friends of the Christian Right?

Even those performers to whom work in porn is just a way to pay the bills don't need to be lectured by a tenured university professor regarding what work they may properly do, based on her interpretation of the gender politics of porn. Her essay pulsates with the unconscious classism that has contaminated feminist thought since I first encountered it. If I learned one thing when I started my career in 1983, myself the product of an ivory-tower upbringing in Berkeley, California, it was to rein in my received ideas about my fellow sex workers and to see them as individuals struggling with all kinds of situations. What does Professor Sun propose sex workers do instead of addressing their economic challenges with what resources they possess, go to Harvard? The real choices that present themselves in modern America to a young woman with a high school education and no class advantage are often far less appealing than sex work. Perhaps she thinks we should choose the dignity of minimum wage jobs, early pregnancies and abusive marriages over the relative autonomy we enjoy as independent tradespeople.

With what I've learned of Dr. Sun's views thus far, I can only await her film "documentary" with the usual weary apprehension. Knowing already what her conclusions will be, I'm only left to wonder who subsidizes her obviously well-funded labors and to what purpose. All I know at this point is that neither I nor anyone like me will be represented in her depiction of my world, or of any world anyone I know might recognize. To me, she's just one more exploiter, seeking to make her living from the attempt to deprive me of mine.

DISCUSSION QUESTIONS

- Hartley associates the choice to do porn with other choices championed by various forms of feminism. Do you agree?
- How "free" is the choice to do porn?

EXAMPLES TO THINK ABOUT

- Contemporary mainstream porn
- Feminist porn

Hard Core

Power, Pleasure, and the "Frenzy of the Visible"

SELECTIONS

By LINDA WILLIAMS

There are those who believe that the come shot, or, as some refer to it, "the money shot," is the most important element in the movie and that everything else (if necessary) should be sacrificed at its expense.

Of course, this depends on the outlook of the producer, but one thing is for sure: if you don't have the come shots, you don't have a porno picture. Plan on at least ten separate come shots.

Stephen Ziplow, *The Film Maker's Guide to Pornography*

Stephen Ziplow's manual of advice for the frugal pornographer asserts what had by 1977 become the sine qua non of the hard-core feature-length narrative: the necessity of showing external ejaculation of the penis as the ultimate climax—the sense of an ending—for each heterosexual sex act represented. Where the earlier short, silent stag films occasionally included spectacles of external ejaculation (in some cases inadvertently), it was not until the early seventies, with the rise of the hard-core feature, that the money shot assumed the narrative function of signaling the climax of a genital event. Previously, hard-core sequences tended to be organized as discontinuous, relatively nonlinear moments of genital show in meat shots offering visual evidence of penetration.

Each shot—"meat" or "money"—is emblematic of the different "climax" of its generic form. Each shot seeks maximum visibility in its representation but encounters the limits of visibility of its particular form. The stag film, seeking to learn more about the "wonders of the unseen world, " encounters its limits of visibility, as Gertrud Koch (forthcoming) notes, *ante portas* in penetration: for the male performer to penetrate the wonders is to make it nearly impossible for the viewer to see what is penetrated.

The money shot, however, succeeds in extending visibility to the next stage of representation of the heterosexual sex act: to the point of seeing climax. But this new visibility extends only to a knowledge of the hydraulics of male ejaculation, which, though certainly of interest, is a poor substitute for the knowledge of female wonders that the genre as a whole still seeks. The gynecological sense of the speculum that penetrates the female interior here really does give way to that of a self-reflecting mirror. While undeniably spectacular, the money shot is also hopelessly specular, it can only reflect back to the male gaze that purports to want knowledge of the woman's pleasure the man's own climax. This climax is now rendered in glorious Eastmancolor, sometimes even on a wide screen with optical or slow-motion effects, and accompanied by all the moans, groans, and cries, synchronized or post-synched, appropriate to such activity.

With all these changes, and especially with this late arrival of sound as a key element in the heightened explicitness of the genre, it is tempting to conclude that the feature-length pornographic film arrives at a truly realistic "hard core." In these films we seem to see not the representation of sex acts as such but, as the Meese Commission and others have put it, "sex itself," in living color and breathing sound. Yet we have only to read Ziplow's advice to porn producers and to observe with what regularity money shots are dispersed through hard-core films made in the decade after 1972 to realize the futility of assimilating hard core to a simple case of escalating verisimilitude. For obviously nothing could be more conventional than a money shot: like Diderot's speaking jewels, it is a rhetorical figure that permits the genre to speak in a certain way about sex.

This difference is, indeed, what the story of *Deep Throat* is all about. For all its silliness and obvious misogyny, this movie attempts to perceive the different "truth" of women's pleasure in ways unparalleled in previous film pornography. The movie's numerous money shots are posed as the answer to the female protagonist's dissatisfaction with her previous experiments of sex. The story is this: a young "swinging single" named Linda (played by Linda Lovelace) confesses to a more experienced woman friend that she finds sex pleasant—"a lot of little tingles"—but not earthshakingly orgasmic—no "bells ringing, dams bursting, or bombs going off." "Experiments" with numerous men in a variety of numbers confirm this fact. The emphasis in these experiments, it should be noted, is primarily on "meat" rather than "money."

We can already note an important difference between this scenario and that of the stag film. Whereas the one-reel stag gets down to its sexual business very quickly, assuming that the act (or show) of sex is significant or fulfilling in its own right, *Deep Throat* is typical of the new wave of post-1972 narrative hard core in that it problematizes satisfaction itself. For the difficulty that Linda confesses at the film's beginning is not the peccadillo of transgressive sexual adventure, as in *Les bijoux indiscrets,* but a much more shameful crime: the failure to find absolute fulfillment in these adventures.

The film thus begins with a premise that is quite rare in the stag film—the idea that sexual pleasure is not the same for everyone or, as Linda's older and wiser female friend puts it, the need for "diff'rent strokes for diff'rent folks." This well-known seventies cliché is an apt description of the new ethic of hard-core film, which sees itself as welcoming and encouraging a greater variety of sexual practice than could ever be represented in the short stag film. In the film's narrative the discovery of Linda's anatomical difference seems to stand symbolically for a male perception of the different sexual pleasure of women in general. This difference then becomes the motive for further experimentation.

Experimentation takes place under the auspices of therapy—yet another seventies cliché. In a clinical examination that involves a telescope in place of a speculum, Linda's sexologist doctor (the ubiquitous Harry Reems) informs her that she is different: she doesn't "have one." In a phallogocentric misunderstanding that Luce Irigaray would appreciate, Linda responds: "I'm a woman, I'm not supposed to have one." What is at stake in this film, however—and, I would argue, in much feature-length pornography of this period—is precisely the extent to which Irigaray's notion of the phallic "one" can be used to figure and then fix the "two" (or more) of feminine difference.

When the doctor finally locates Linda's clitoris in her throat, he reassures her that having "one" there is better than having "none at all." Her concern is with the freak status this lends her—"What if your balls were in your ears!" (His answer, "Then I could hear myself coming," is in keeping with the male obsession with measurable evidence of pleasure.) Physiotherapy soon comes to the rescue and, with much practice, beginning on the doctor himself, Linda learns the "deep throat" technique that leads to a climactic money shot—narratively presented as simultaneous with Linda's own long-awaited climax—that is enhanced by intercutting with fireworks, ringing bells, bursting bombs, and firing missiles.

The deep throat gimmick thus works to naturalize what in the stag film had always been the most photogenic of all sexual practices: fellatio. Fellatio—culminating in a money shot in which ejaculation occurs on the woman's face and mouth—becomes, in the wake of *Deep Throat's* enormous popularity, the privileged figure for the expression of climax and satisfaction (reaching, in fact, a kind of apotheosis in *Behind the Green Door,* made later that same year).

Satisfied for the first time in her life, Linda wants only to marry her doctor and be, as she says, his "slave." But the doctor has a more modern idea: she will become a physiotherapist. What follows is an extended parody of Masters and Johnson–style sex therapy in which Linda administers to various mildly kinky men while still undergoing "therapy" herself with the doctor. He soon lands in bed with a bandage around his exhausted penis, unable to meet her demands for more sex. Though comically treated, the specter of the insatiable woman has been shown to take its toll on more limited men. The final "gag" that ends the film "solves" this problem by introducing a bigger and better penis. In her work as a physiotherapist Linda encounters Wilbur, who likes to play the role of a sadistic burglar caught in the act of spying on her. Beneath this superficial kink, however, he is sweet and gentle, the man of her dreams. When he proposes to Linda, she insists that the man she marries must have a "nine-inch cock" to satisfy the demands of her "deep throat." Wilbur instantly calls the doctor, saying he is only four inches away from happiness. The doctor reassures him, and Wilbur turns to Linda with the news that his thirteen-inch penis can be cut down to any size she wants. Little Wilbur is thus her ideal man.

In just about every sense, *Deep Throat* can be said—for all its talk about the clitoris—visually to fetishize the penis. Yet as we have seen, the question of how to read this fetishization cannot be answered without recognizing the new importance of the clitoris. An oversimplistic feminist reading of this film might miss the sense in which the newly prominent clitoris has called for the money shot. It would only see the money shot as depriving women of "natural," organic pleasure by imposing on them the perversion not merely of fellatio, but of this particular degrading, gagging, "deep throat" variety [...]. Gloria Steinem (1986b, 275), for example, writes that Damiano, the film's director, invented a gimmick that was "second only to Freud's complete elimination of the clitoris as a proper source of female pleasure. ... Though his physiological fiction about *one* woman was far less ambitious than Freud's fiction about *all* women, his porn movie had a whammo audiovisual impact; a teaching device that Freudian theory had lacked." Thus the "millions of women" whose boyfriends, husbands, or pimps took them to the film were taught how to please a man by the example of this humiliating obeisance to the fetish.

In Steinem's interpretation, the woman is cast as Marx's savage fetishist who bows down and surrenders her own "proper source of female pleasure" to the power and pleasure of the phallus. The repeated ejaculations onto her face could thus be read as visual proof of her objectification and humiliation. Although there is a smile on that face, we read in Linda Lovelace (Marchiano's) autobiography that this smile was a lie masking terror and pain, that she was a sex slave to the man who was her pimp and manager, and that her entire life at this time was, like the title of this autobiography, an ordeal (Lovelace and McGrady 1980).

While I am inclined to believe Marchiano's allegations that she was coerced off screen to perform inauthentic pleasures on screen, and while I do not question the importance for feminists to reject as inauthentic the pleasures of women portrayed in such films, I do question the notion, strongly implied in Steinem's argument, that the film and, indeed, all pornography repress a "proper" female pleasure. I would argue instead that even though *Deep Throat* elides the visual representation of Linda Lovelace's clitoris, and even though its money shot fetish operates, in Gayatri Spivak's words, to "efface" that organ, its narrative is constantly soliciting and trying to find a visual equivalent for the invisible moments of clitoral orgasm. So if on the one hand the film tries to efface sexual difference through a gimmick that renders the practice of fellatio more "natural," on the other hand this very effacement could be said to allegorize the problem of difference by actually giving it Linda Lovelace's face.

All of the film's solicitous concern for the location of the clitoris thus needs to be seen in the context of the relatively new prominence this organ has received in other forms of the *scientia sexualis*. This new knowledge views the clitoris precisely not as a diminished or absent version of the penis—as in Freud's account of the phallic economy of the one—but as a new economy not reducible to that one: an economy of the *many*, of "diff'rent strokes for diff'rent folks." Even though the film's fetishization of the phallus attempts to disavow difference at the moment of orgasm and to model that orgasm on a decidedly phallic model of "bursting bombs," and even though the woman is portrayed as dependent for her pleasure on the "one" of the man, a contradictory subtext of plurality and difference is also registered. The very fact that the expanded narrative of the new feature-length hard-core film parodically joins with the scientific, Masters and Johnson–style quest for the "truth" of woman's difference indicates how fully the woman's invisible and unquantifiable pleasure has now been brought into frame, onto the scene of the obscene.

The paradox of contemporary feature-length pornography and its fetish of the money shot might therefore be described as follows: it is the obsessive attempt of a phallic visual economy to represent and "fix" the exact moment of the sexual act's involuntary convulsion of pleasure. The money shot utterly fails to represent the satisfaction of desire as involving a desire for, or of, the other; it can only figure satisfaction as failing to do what masculine sexual ideology frequently claims that the man does to the woman: to occupy, penetrate, possess her. Thus the solipsistic withdrawal from the other to the self paradoxically constructs another "memorial to lack" right where we might most expect to see presence and fullness. It would be wrong, however, to repeat Freud's misrecognition and to call this lack "castration." We might more properly call it a lack of relation to the other, a lack of ability to imagine a relation to the other in anything but the phallic terms of self.

Even though the money shot offers perhaps the clearest example of the phallic economy's failure to recognize difference, we must realize that it has been posed as a solution precisely because that economy is more aware of sexual difference and varying pleasures than it was in previous pornography. So rather than compare the phallic economy invoked by *Deep Throat* with that of Freud, as Steinem does, we might do better to contrast them. In Freud, fetishization is an obvious way for the male subject to maintain the phallic economy of the one. As we saw earlier, the Freudian fetishist attempts to preserve his own humanity at the expense of stressing the freakish inhumanity—the "horror"—of the female other. *Deep Throat* does not simply repeat this objectification of the female other; or, rather, if it does repeat it, it so blatantly puts the reigning "phallocracy" on display that we can glimpse, in the univocal limitations of its economy of the one, possible elaborations of economies of the many.

Foucault (1978, 48) writes that along with the incitement to sexuality contained in the modern age's proliferating discourses on the subject comes an increasing tendency to identify and address many different specialized sexual practices and in that process to "implant" these perversions. However absurd it may seem, I think one might say that the perverse implantation of the clitoris in *Deep Throat* represents something more than simple horror at the freakishness of female sexual "lack." It represents a phallic economy's highly ambivalent and contradictory attempt to count beyond the number one, to recognize, as the proliferating discourses of sexuality take hold, that there can no longer be any such thing as a fixed sexuality—male, female, or otherwise—that now there are proliferating sexualities. For if the "implantation of perversions" is, as Foucault says, an instrument *and* an effect of power, then as discourses of sexuality name, identify, and ultimately produce a bewildering array of pleasures and perversions, the very multiplicity of these pleasures and perversions inevitably works against the older idea of a single norm—an economy of the one—against which all else is measured.

NOTE

1. In her now-classic essay, Rubin (1979, 176) argues that the exchange of women is neither a definition of culture, as Lévi-Strauss says, nor a system in and of itself. A kinship system is an "imposition of social ends upon a part of the natural world. It is therefore 'production' ... a transformation of objects (in this case people) to and by a subjective purpose." Rubin's point is that the subordination of women should be seen as a product of the relationships by which sex and gender are organized. It is not a systematic given of all cultural arrangements but, rather, a product of them.

READING 26: HARD CORE

DISCUSSION QUESTIONS

- Williams argues that we should take a more historical approach to porn. What would that method entail?
- What can popular sexual fetishes show us about power relations?

EXAMPLES TO THINK ABOUT

- Historical porn
- Contemporary fetishes

Purity and Danger

An Analysis of the Concepts of Pollution and Taboo

SELECTIONS

By MARY DOUGLAS

INTRODUCTION

The nineteenth century saw in primitive religions two peculiarities which separated them as a block from the great religions of the world. One was that they were inspired by fear, the other that they were inextricably confused with defilement and hygiene. Almost any missionary's or traveller's account of a primitive religion talks about the fear, terror or dread in which its adherents live. The source is traced to beliefs in horrible disasters which overtake those who inadvertently cross some forbidden line or develop some impure condition. And as fear inhibits reason it can be held accountable for other peculiarities in primitive thought, notably the idea of defilement. As Ricoeur sums it up:

> 'La souillure elle-même est à peine une
> representation et celle-ci est noyée dans une
> peur spécifique qui bouche la réflexion; avec
> la souillure nous entrons au règne de la Terreur.'
> (p. 31)

But anthropologists who have ventured further into these primitive cultures find little trace of fear. Evans-Pritchard's study of witchcraft was made among the people who struck him as the most happy and carefree of the Sudan, the Azande. The feelings of an Azande man, on finding that he has been bewitched, are not terror, but hearty indignation as one of us might feel on finding himself the victim of embezzlement.

The Nuer, a deeply religious people, as the same authority points out, regard their God as a familiar friend. Audrey Richards, witnessing the girls' initiation rites of the Bemba, noted the casual, relaxed attitude of the performers. And so the tale goes on. The anthropologist sets out expecting to see rituals performed with reverence, to say the least. He finds himself in the role of the agnostic sightseer in St. Peter's, shocked at the disrespectful clatter of the adults and the children playing Roman shove halfpenny on the floor stones. So primitive religious fear, together with the idea that it blocks the functioning of the mind, seems to be a false trail for understanding these religions.

Hygiene, by contrast, turns out to be an excellent route, so long as we can follow it with some self-knowledge. As we know it, dirt is essentially disorder. There is no such thing as absolute dirt: it exists in the eye of the beholder. If we shun dirt, it is not because of craven fear, still less dread of holy terror. Nor do our ideas about disease account for the range of our behaviour in cleaning or avoiding dirt. Dirt offends against order. Eliminating it is not a negative movement, but a positive effort to organise the environment.

I am personally rather tolerant of disorder. But I always remember how unrelaxed I felt in a particular bathroom which was kept spotlessly clean in so far as the removal of grime and grease was concerned. It had been installed in an old house in a space created by the simple expedient of setting a door at each end of a corridor between two staircases. The decor remained unchanged: the engraved portrait of Vinogradoff, the books, the gardening tools, the row of gumboots. It all made good sense as the scene of a back corridor, but as a bathroom—the impression destroyed repose. I, who rarely feel the need to impose an idea of external reality, at least began to understand the activities of more sensitive friends. In chasing dirt, in papering, decorating, tidying we are not governed by anxiety to escape disease, but are positively re-ordering our environment, making it conform to an idea. There is nothing fearful or unreasoning in our dirt-avoidance: it is a creative movement, an attempt to relate form to function, to make unity of experience. If this is so with our separating, tidying and purifying, we should interpret primitive purification and prophylaxis in the same light.

In this book I have tried to show that rituals of purity and impurity create unity in experience. So far from being aberrations from the central project of religion, they are positive contributions to atonement. By their means, symbolic patterns are worked out and publicly displayed. Within these patterns disparate elements are related and disparate experience is given meaning.

Pollution ideas work in the life of society at two levels, one largely instrumental, one expressive. At the first level, the more obvious one, we find people trying to influence one another's behaviour. Beliefs reinforce social pressures: all the powers of the universe are called in to guarantee an old man's dying wish, a mother's dignity, the rights of the weak and innocent. Political power is usually held precariously and primitive rulers are no exception. So we find their legitimate pretensions backed by beliefs in extraordinary powers emanating from their persons, from the insignia of their office or from words they can utter. Similarly the ideal order of society is guarded by dangers which threaten transgressors. These danger-beliefs are as much threats which one man uses to coerce another as dangers which he himself fears to incur by his own lapses from righteousness. They are a strong language of mutual exhortation. At this level the laws of nature are dragged in to sanction the moral code: this kind of disease is caused by adultery, that by incest; this meteorological disaster is the effect of political disloyalty, that the effect of impiety. The whole universe is harnessed to men's attempts to force one another into good citizenship. Thus we find that certain moral values are upheld and certain social rules defined by beliefs in dangerous contagion, as when the glance or touch of an adulterer is held to bring illness to his neighbours or his children.

It is not difficult to see how pollution beliefs can be used in a dialogue of claims and counter-claims to status. But as we examine pollution beliefs we find that the kind of contacts which are thought dangerous also carry a symbolic load. This is a more interesting level at which pollution ideas relate to social life. I believe that some pollutions are used as analogies for expressing a general view of the social order. For example, there are beliefs that each sex is a danger to the other through contact with sexual fluids. According to other beliefs only one sex is endangered by contact with the other, usually males from females, but sometimes the reverse. Such patterns of sexual danger can be seen to express symmetry or hierarchy. It is implausible to interpret them as expressing something about the actual relation of the sexes. I suggest that many ideas about sexual dangers are better interpreted as symbols of the relation between parts of society, as mirroring designs of hierarchy or symmetry which apply in the larger social system. What goes for sex pollution also goes for bodily pollution. The two sexes can serve as a model for the collaboration and distinctiveness of social units. So also can the processes of ingestion portray political absorption. Sometimes bodily orifices seem to represent points of entry or exit to social units, or bodily perfection can symbolise an ideal theocracy.

Each primitive culture is a universe to itself. Following Franz Steiner's advice in *Taboo*, I start interpreting rules of uncleanness by placing them in the full context of the range of dangers possible in any given universe. Everything that can happen to a man in the way of disaster should be catalogued according to the active principles involved in the universe of his particular culture. Sometimes words trigger off cataclysms, sometimes acts, sometimes physical conditions. Some dangers are great and others small. We cannot start to compare primitive religions until we know the range of powers and dangers they recognise. Primitive society is an energised structure in the centre of its universe. Powers shoot out from its strong points, powers to prosper and dangerous powers to retaliate against attack. But the society does not exist in a neutral, uncharged vacuum. It is subject to external pressures; that which is not with it, part of it and subject to its laws, is potentially against it. In describing these pressures on boundaries and margins I admit to having made society sound more systematic than it really is. But just such an expressive oversystematising is necessary for interpreting the beliefs in question. For I believe that ideas about separating, purifying, demarcating and punishing transgressions have as their main function to impose system on an inherently untidy experience. It is only by exaggerating the difference between within and without, about and below, male and female, with and against, that a semblance of order is created. In this sense I am not afraid of the charge of having made the social structure seem over-rigid.

But in another sense I do not wish to suggest that the primitive cultures in which these ideas of contagion flourish are rigid, hide-bound and stagnant. No one knows how old are the ideas of purity and impurity in any non-literate culture: to members they must seem timeless and unchanging. But there is every reason to believe that they are sensitive to change. The same impulse to impose order which brings them into existence can be supposed to be continually modifying or enriching them. This is a very important point. For when I argue that the reaction to dirt is continuous with other reactions to ambiguity or anomaly, I am not reviving the nineteenth century hypothesis of fear in another guise. Ideas about contagion can certainly be traced to reaction to anomaly. But they are more than the disquiet of a laboratory rat who suddenly finds one of his familiar exits from the maze is blocked. And they are more than the discomfiture of the aquarium stickleback with an anomalous member of his species. The initial recognition of anomaly leads to anxiety and from there to suppression or avoidance; so far, so good. But we must look for a more energetic organising principle to do justice to the elaborate cosmologies which pollution symbols reveal.

The native of any culture naturally thinks of himself as receiving passively his ideas of power and danger in the universe, discounting any minor modifications he himself may have contributed. In the same way we think of ourselves as passively receiving our native language and discount our responsibility for shifts it undergoes in our life time. The anthropologist falls into the same trap if he thinks of a culture he is studying as a long established pattern of values. In this sense I emphatically deny that a proliferation of ideas about purity and contagion implies a rigid mental outlook or rigid social institutions. The contrary may be true.

It may seem that in a culture which is richly organised by ideas of contagion and purification the individual is in the grip of iron-hard categories of thought which are heavily safeguarded by rules of avoidance and by punishments. It may seem impossible for such a person to shake his own thought free of the protected habit-grooves of his culture. How can he turn round upon his own thought-process and contemplate its limitations? And yet if he cannot do this, how can his religion be compared with the great religions of the world?

The more we know about primitive religions the more clearly it appears that in their symbolic structures there is scope for meditation on the great mysteries of religion and philosophy. Reflection on dirt involves reflection on the relation of order to disorder, being to non-being, form to formlessness, life to death. Wherever ideas of dirt are highly structured their analysis discloses a play upon such profound themes. This is why an understanding of rules of purity is a sound entry to comparative religion. The Pauline antithesis of blood and water, nature and grace, freedom and necessity, or the Old Testament idea of Godhead can be illuminated by Polynesian or Central African treatment of closely related themes.

• • • •

THE SYSTEM AT WAR WITH ITSELF

When the community is attacked from outside at least the external danger fosters solidarity within. When it is attacked from within by wanton individuals, they can be punished and the structure publicly reaffirmed. But it is possible for the structure to be self-defeating. This has long been a familiar theme for anthropologists (see Gluckman, 1963). Perhaps all social systems are built on contradiction, in some sense at war with themselves. But in some cases the various ends which individuals are encouraged to pursue are more harmoniously related than in others.

Sexual collaboration is by nature fertile, constructive, the common basis of social life. But sometimes we find that instead of dependence and harmony, sexual institutions express rigid separation and violent antagonism. So far we have noted a kind of sex pollution which expresses a desire to keep the body (physical and social) intact. Its rules are phrased to control entrances and exits. Another kind of sex pollution arises from the desire to keep straight the internal lines of the social system. In the last chapter we noted how rules control individual contacts which destroy these lines, adulteries, incests and so forth. But these by no means exhaust the types of sexual pollution. A third type may arise from the conflict in the aims which can be proposed in the same culture.

In primitive cultures, almost by definition, the distinction of the sexes is the primary social distinction. This means that some important institutions always rest on the difference of sex. If the social structure were weakly organised, then men and women might still hope to follow their own fancies in choosing and discarding sexual partners, with no grievous consequences for society at large. But if the primitive social structure is strictly articulated, it is almost bound to impinge heavily on the relation between men and women. Then we find pollution ideas enlisted to bind men and women to their allotted roles, as we have shown in the last chapter.

There is one exception we should note at once. Sex is likely to be pollution-free in a society where sexual roles are enforced directly. In such a case anyone who threatened to deviate would be promptly punished with physical force. This supposes an administrative efficiency and consensus which are rare anywhere and especially in primitive societies. As an example we can consider the Walbiri of Central Australia, a people who unhesitatingly apply force to ensure that the sexual behaviour of individuals shall not undermine that part of the social structure which rests upon marital relations (Meggitt). As in the rest of Australia, a great part of the social system depends upon rules governing marriage. The Walbiri live in a hard desert environment. They are aware of the difficulty of community survival and their culture accepts as one of its objectives that all members of the community shall work and be cared for according to their ability and needs. This means that responsibility for the infirm and old falls upon the hale. A strict discipline is asserted throughout the community, young are subject to their seniors, and above all, women are subject to men. A married woman usually lives at a distance from her father and brothers. This means that though she has a theoretical claim to their protection, in practice it is null. She is in the control of her husband. As a general rule if the female sex were completely subject to the male, no problem would be posed by the principle of male dominance. It could be enforced ruthlessly and directly wherever it applied. This seems to be what happens among the Walbiri. For the least complaint or neglect of duty Walbiri women are beaten or speared. No blood compensation can be claimed for a wife killed by her husband, and no one has the right to intervene between husband and wife. Public opinion never reproaches the man who has violently, or even lethally, asserted his authority over his wife. Thus it is impossible for a woman to play off one man against another. However energetically they may try to seduce one another's wives the men are in perfect accord on one point. They are agreed that they should never allow their sexual desires to give an individual woman bargaining power or scope for intrigue.

These people have no beliefs concerning sex pollution. Even menstrual blood is not avoided, and there are no beliefs that contact with it brings danger. Although the definition of married status is important in their society it is protected by overt means. Here there is nothing precarious or contradictory about male dominance.

No constraints are imposed on individual Walbiri men. They seduce one another's women if they get a chance, without showing any special concern for the social structure based on marriage. The latter is preserved by the thorough-going subordination of women to men and by the recognised system of self-help. When a man poaches on another's sexual preserve he knows what he risks, a fight and possible death. The system is perfectly simple. There are conflicts between men, but not between principles. No moral judgment is evoked in one situation which is likely to be contradicted in another. People are held to these particular roles by the threat of physical violence. The previous chapter has suggested that when this threat is uninhibited we can expect the social system to persist without the support of pollution beliefs.

It is important to recognise that male dominance does not always flourish with such ruthless simplicity. In the last chapter we saw that when moral rules are obscure or contradictory there is a tendency for pollution beliefs to simplify or clarify the point at issue. The Walbiri case suggests a correlation. When male dominance is accepted as a central principle of social organisation and applied without inhibition and with full rights of physical coercion, beliefs in sex pollution are not likely to be highly developed. On the other hand, when the principle of male dominance is applied to the ordering of social life but is contradicted by other principles such as that of female independence, or the inherent right of women as the weaker sex to be more protected from violence than men, then sex pollution is likely to flourish. Before we take up this case there is another kind of exception to consider.

We find many societies in which individuals are not coerced or otherwise held strictly to their allotted sexual roles and yet the social structure is based upon the association of the sexes. In these cases a subtle, legalistic development of special institutions provides relief. Individuals can to some extent follow their personal whims, because the social structure is cushioned by fictions of one kind or another.

REFERENCES

Gluckman, M., 1962. *Essays on the Ritual of Social Relations.* Manchester.

Meggitt, M., 1962. *Desert People.* Sydney. 1964. 'Male–Female Relationships in the Highlands of Australian New Guinea.' *American Anthropologist,* 2. 66. 4. pp. 204–23.

Ricoeur, P., 1960. *Finitude et Culpabilité.* Paris.

Steiner, F., 1956. *Taboo.*

READING 27: PURITY AND DANGER

DISCUSSION QUESTIONS

- How does Douglas define "purity"?
- How is purity related to social structures?

EXAMPLES TO THINK ABOUT

- Purity balls, pledges, rings
- The metaphors used in abstinence-only education

Powers of Horror

An Essay on Abjection

EXCERPTS FROM: APPROACHING ABJECTION

By JULIA KRISTEVA

BEFORE THE BEGINNING: SEPARATION

The abject might then appear as the most *fragile* (from a synchronic point of view), the most *archaic* (from a diachronic one) sublimation of an "object" still inseparable from drives. The abject is that pseudo-object that is made up *before* but appears only *within* the gaps of secondary repression. *The abject would thus be the "object" of primal repression.*

But what is primal repression? Let us call it the ability of the speaking being, always already haunted by the Other, to divide, reject, repeat. Without *one* division, *one* separation, *one* subject/object having been constituted (not yet, or no longer yet). Why? Perhaps because of maternal anguish, unable to be satiated within the encompassing symbolic.

The abject confronts us, on the one hand, with those fragile states where man strays on the territories of *animal*. Thus, by way of abjection, primitive societies have marked out a precise area of their culture in order to remove it from the threatening world of animals or animalism, which were imagined as representatives of sex and murder.

The abject confronts us, on the other hand, and this time within our personal archeology, with our earliest attempts to release the hold of *maternal* entity even before existing outside of her, thanks to the autonomy of language. It is a violent, clumsy breaking away, with the constant risk of falling back under the sway of a power as securing as it is stifling. The difficulty a mother has in acknowledging (or being acknowledged by) the symbolic realm—in other words, the problem she has with the phallus that her father or her husband stands for—is not such as to help the future subject leave the natural mansion. The child can serve its mother as token of her own authentication; there is, however, hardly any reason for her to serve as go-between for it to become autonomous and authentic in its turn. In such close combat, the symbolic light that a third party, eventually the father, can contribute helps the future subject, the more so if it happens to be endowed with a robust supply of drive energy, in pursuing a reluctant struggle against what, having been the mother, will turn into an abject. Repelling, rejecting; repelling itself, rejecting itself. Abjecting.

In this struggle, which fashions the human being, the *mimesis*, by means of which he becomes homologous to another in order to become himself, is in short logically and chrono-logically secondary. Even before being *like*, "I" am not but do *separate, reject, abject*. Abjection, with a meaning broadened to take in subjective diachrony, *is a precondition of narcissism*. It is coexistent with it and causes it to be permanently brittle. The more or less beautiful image in which I behold or recognize myself rests upon an abjection that sunders it as soon as repression, the constant watchman, is relaxed.

DISCUSSION QUESTIONS

- Kristeva builds on Douglas's ideas by thinking about the impure or what she calls the "abject." What does she mean by the term and why would it be important to study?
- What is the relationship between the abject and the maternal?

EXAMPLES TO THINK ABOUT

- Purity balls, pledges, rings
- The metaphors used in abstinence-only education

SECTION 9

EXAMPLES AND ISSUES:
PARENTING

Of Woman Born

Motherhood as Experience and Institution

SELECTIONS

By ADRIENNE RICH

Childbirth is (or may be) one aspect of the entire process of a woman's life, beginning with her own expulsion from her mother's body, her own sensual suckling or being held by a woman, through her earliest sensations of clitoral eroticism and of the vulva as a source of pleasure, her growing sense of her own body and its strengths, her masturbation, her menses, her physical relationship to nature and to other human beings, her first and subsequent orgasmic experiences with another's body, her conception, pregnancy, to the moment of first holding her child. But that moment is still only a point in the process if we conceive it not according to patriarchal ideas of childbirth as a kind of production, but as part of female experience.

Beyond birth comes nursing and physical relationship with an infant, and these are enmeshed with sexuality, with the ebb and flow of ovulation and menses, of sexual desire. During pregnancy the entire pelvic area increases in its vascularity (the production of arteries and veins) thus increasing the capacity for sexual tension and greatly increasing the frequency and intensity of the orgasm. During pregnancy, the system is flooded with hormones which not only induce the growth of new blood vessels but increase clitoral responsiveness and strengthen the muscles effective in orgasm. A woman who has given birth has a biologically increased capacity for genital pleasure, unless her pelvic organs have been damaged obstetrically, as frequently happens. Many women experience orgasm for the first time after childbirth, or become erotically aroused while nursing. Frieda Fromm-Reichmann, Niles Newton, Masters and Johnson, and others have documented the erotic sensations experienced by women in actually giving birth. Since there are strong cultural forces which desexualize women as mothers, the orgasmic sensations felt in childbirth or while suckling infants have probably until recently been denied even by the women feeling them, or have evoked feelings of guilt. Yet, as Newton reminds us, "Women… have a more varied heritage of sexual enjoyment than men"; and the sociologist Alice Rossi observes,

> I suspect that the more male dominance characterizes a Western society, the greater is the dissociation between sexuality and maternalism. It is to men's sexual advantage to restrict women's sexual gratification to heterosexual coitus, though the price for the woman and a child may be a less psychologically and physically rewarding relationship.

The divisions of labor and allocations of power in patriarchy demand not merely a suffering Mother, but one divested of sexuality: the Virgin Mary, *virgo intacta*, perfectly chaste. Women are permitted to be sexual only at a certain time of life, and the sensuality of mature—and certainly of aging—women has been perceived as grotesque, threatening, and inappropriate.

If motherhood and sexuality were not wedged resolutely apart by male culture, if we could *choose* both the forms of our sexuality and the terms of our motherhood or nonmotherhood freely, women might achieve genuine sexual autonomy (as opposed to "sexual liberation"). The mother should be able to choose the means of conception (biological, artificial, or parthenogenetic), the place of birth, her own style of giving birth, and her birth-attendants: midwife or doctor as she wishes, a man she loves and trusts, women and men friends or kin, her other children. There is no reason why it should not be an "Amazon expedition" if she so desires, in which she is supported by women only, the midwife with whom she has worked throughout pregnancy, and women who simply love her. (At present, the father is the only nonmedical person legally admitted to the labor and delivery room in American hospitals, and even the biological father can be legally excluded over the mother's decision to have him there.)

But taking birth out of the hospital does not mean simply shifting it into the home or into maternity clinics. Birth is not an isolated event. If there were local centers to which all women could go for contraceptive and abortion counseling, pregnancy testing, prenatal care, labor classes, films about pregnancy and birth, routine gynecological examinations, therapeutic and counseling groups through and after pregnancy, including a well-baby clinic, women could begin to think, read about, and discuss the entire process of conceiving, gestating, bearing, nursing their children, about the alternatives to motherhood, and about the wholeness of their lives. Birth might then become one event in the unfolding of our diverse and polymorphous sexuality: not a necessary consequence of sex, but one experience of liberating ourselves from fear, passivity, and alienation from our bodies.

♦ ♦ ♦ ♦

I am a woman giving birth to myself. In that psychic process, too, there is a "transition period" when energy flags, the effort seems endless, and we feel spiritually and even physically "nauseous and chilled to the bone." In such periods, turning to doctors for help and support, thousands of women have been made into consumers of pain-numbing medication, which may quell anxiety or desperation at the price of cutting the woman off from her own necessary process. Unfortunately, there are too few trained, experienced psychic midwives for this kind of parturition; and the psycho-obstetricians, the pill-pushers, those who would keep us in a psychological lithotomy position, still dominate the psychotherapeutic profession.

There is a difference between crying out for help and asking to be "put under"; and women—both in psychic and physical labor—need to understand the extremity and the meaning of the "transition stage," to learn to demand active care and support, not "Twilight Sleep" or numbing. As long as birth—metaphorically or literally—remains an experience of passively handing over our minds and our bodies to male authority and technology, other kinds of social change can only minimally change our relationship to ourselves, to power, and to the world outside our bodies.

NOTES

1. Mary Jane Sherfey, *The Nature and Evolution of Female Sexuality* (New York: Vintage, 1973), pp. 100–101.
2. Niles Newton, "The Trebly Sensuous Woman," *Psychology Today*, issue on "The Female Experience," 1973.
3. Alice Rossi, "Maternalism, Sexuality and the New Feminism," in *Contemporary Sexual Behavior: Critical Issues in the 1970's*, ed. J. Zubin and J. Money (Baltimore: Johns Hopkins University Press, 1973), pp. 145–71.
4. Kathy Linck, "Legalizing a Woman's Right to Choose," in *Proceedings of the First International Childbirth Conference*, 1973, New Moon Communications, Box 3488, Ridgeway Station, Stamford, Conn. 06905.

DISCUSSION QUESTIONS

- What does it mean to call motherhood an "institution"?
- How is a mother "supposed" to behave?

EXAMPLES TO THINK ABOUT

- *What to Expect When You're Expecting*
- *The Business of Being Born*
- Attachment parenting

The History of Research on Father Involvement

MARRIAGE & FAMILY REVIEW, VOL. 29, ISSUE 2–3

By MICHAEL E. LAMB

A BRIEF HISTORY OF FATHERHOOD

Within the sprawling literature on the social (as opposed to the biological or procreative) aspect of fatherhood, one can discern at least three broad and widely recognized dimensions of fatherhood. First of all, current concerns about fatherlessness and "deadbeat dads" highlight the implicit equation of responsible fatherhood with successful provisioning or bread-winning. Second, some scholars (especially developmental psychologists) have focused on the direct interactions between fathers and children in the provision of care, discipline, coaching, education, companionship, play, and supervision. A third set of writings have focused on the relationships between fathers and mothers—a primary determinant of the family climate which, in turn, affects child development and adjustment in profound ways. These three aspects of fatherhood are all of central importance. However, both researchers and theorists have tended to restrict their focus to individual components of fatherhood, ignoring or paying minimal attention to the interactions among multiple roles and the ways in which a broader and more inclusive conception of fatherhood might both enrich and change our analysis and understanding. This narrow or restrictive conception of fatherhood, rather than a more inclusive and complex portrait, reflects, in part, the changing ways in which fatherhood has been viewed within the broader society which social scientists shape and by which they are simultaneously shaped.

The available data are obviously limited, but social historians argue that much can be learned by examining letters (even though admittedly few of our forebears wrote letters, and even fewer thought to preserve them for posterity) and the literature or popular writing during particular eras in the past. The sequence of changes in popular concerns identified by scholars such as La Rossa (1988) and others who have analyzed such historical materials (LaRossa, Gordon, Wilson, Bairan, & Jaret, 1991; Mintz, 1998; Pleck & Pleck, 1997; Rotundo, 1993; Demos, 1982; 1986), are of interest not only because they help articulate our past, but also because they may help us understand the contemporary concern with and confusion about fatherhood. According to Pleck (1984), one can actually discern four phases or periods over the last two centuries of American social history. In each of these, a different dominant motif became prominent in writing to or about fathers, making other aspects of the complex, multifaceted role seem much less important by comparison.

The Moral Teacher or Guide

The earliest phase was one that extended from Puritan times through the Colonial period into early Republican times. During this lengthy period, the father's role was predominately defined by responsibility for moral oversight and moral teaching. By popular consensus, fathers were deemed primarily responsible for ensuring that their children grew up with an appropriate sense of values, acquired primarily from the study of religious materials like the Bible. To the extent that a broader role was defined, fathers assumed responsibility for the education of children—not necessarily because education and literacy were valued in their own right (although they might have been so evaluated by some), but because children had to be literate to read the Scriptures. Helping children become literate served to advance the father's role as moral guardian by ensuring that children were academically equipped to adopt and maintain Christian ways. In their more detailed and thorough reviews, both Demos (1982) and Pleck (1984) pointed out that, during this era, good fathers were defined as men who provided a model of good Christian living and whose children were well versed in the Scriptures.

The Breadwinner

Around the time of centralized industrialization, however, a shift occurred in the dominant conceptualization of the father's role (Pleck, 1984). Instead of being defined in terms of moral teaching, fathers came to be defined largely by their responsibility for breadwinning. This almost uni-dimensional conceptualization of the father endured from the mid-nineteenth century through the Great Depression (Pleck, 1984). An analysis of the then-popular literature and of letters written between fathers and children during that period confirms the dominant conception of fathers as breadwinners. This is not to say that other aspects of the father's role, such as the presumed responsibility for moral guardianship, had disappeared. Nor does this focus imply that, before industrialization, breadwinning had been insignificant. However, prior to industrialization, mothers and fathers had clearly shared the responsibility of provisioning. After industrializaton, the reduction in the importance of subsistence agriculture and home industry forced a separation between in-and out-of-home work. With industrialization, breadwinning became the most important and defining characteristic of fatherhood—*the* criterion by which "good fathers" were appraised.

The Sex-Role Model

Perhaps as a result of the disruption and dislocation brought about in rapid succession by the Great Depression, the New Deal, and the Second World War, the 1940s brought to prominence a new conceptualization of fatherhood, manifested primarily in a literature focused on the inadequacy of many fathers. Although breadwinning and moral guardianship remained important, focus shifted in the 1930s and early 1940s to the father's function as a sex-role model, especially for his sons (Pleck, 1981). Many books and articles in the professional and popular literature focused on the need for strong sex-role models, with many professionals concluding that fathers were clearly not doing a good job in this regard (e.g., Levy, 1943; Strecker, 1946; Wylie, 1942). Their alleged or apparent inadequacies were underscored in dramatic works such as *Rebel Without a Cause,* and were ridiculed in such comedies and cartoons as *Blondie* and *All in the Family* (Ehrenreich & English, 1979).

The New Nurturant Father

Around the mid-1970s a fourth stage emerged. For the first time, many writers and commentators emphasized that fathers could and should be nurturant parents who were actively involved in the day-to-day care of their children. Active parenting was defined as the central component of fatherhood and was implicitly (sometimes even explicitly) portrayed as the yardstick by which "good fathers" might be assessed. This redefinition of successful fatherhood was popularized in fictional works such as *Kramer vs. Kramer* and *The World According to Garp,* but professional interest in "the new fatherhood" soon followed. As Griswold (1995) noted, fathers had been exhorted to be more involved in the care of their children since early in the century, but the 1970s marked a change in the relative and defining importance of such behavior.

◆ ◆ ◆ ◆

Although mothers are associated with caretaking and fathers with play, we cannot assume that fathers are less capable of child care. A number of researchers have attempted to investigate the relative competencies of mothers and fathers with respect to caretaking and parenting functions, and the results of these studies are fairly clear (Lamb, 1981a; 1997a; Lamb & Goldberg, 1982). First, they show that, during the newborn period, there are no differences in competence between mothers and fathers–both parents can do equally well (or equally poorly). Contrary to the notion of a maternal instinct, parenting skills are usually acquired "on the job" by both mothers and fathers. However, mothers are "on the job" more than fathers, and not surprisingly, mothers become more sensitive to their children, more in tune with them, and more aware of each child's characteristics and needs. By virtue of their lack of experience, fathers become correspondingly less sensitive and come to feel less confidence in their parenting abilities. Fathers thus continue to defer to and cede responsibility to mothers, whereas mothers increasingly assume responsibility. In this way, the imbalanced distribution of parental responsibility discussed earlier is consolidated. The crucial question thus becomes: What explains the different motivations or commitments of mothers and fathers?

Motivation

Obviously, different conceptions or definitions of fatherhood are associated with different sets of motivations. Whether or not biological drives or tendencies impel men in general, conceptions of fatherhood, as well as the extent to which individual fathers are motivated to behave accordingly, appear to be determined by the men's socio-cultural background, their current social circumstances, and their earlier experiences, particularly the behavior of their own parents. Therefore, instead of trying to rank motivations in order of importance or associate them with particular functions, it may be more productive to enumerate the most important motivational or explanatory categories that have been hypothesized. We must acknowledge, however, that empirical research in this area is, at best, scanty.

Sociobiologists emphasize that both men and women strive to maximize the representation of their genes in future generations (Trivers, 1972). Several implications flow from their observation that males (unlike females) can be biologically involved in many pregnancies simultaneously and do not need to make major physiological contributions to the physical survival of their offspring after insemination. The "down side," according to these same theorists, is that men can never really be sure of paternity, and thus always face the risk of investing resources in someone else's children (genes). Several predictions flow from these simple (if controversial) observations:

1. Men invest less in individual offspring because the costs of not investing are so much lower and the risks of mis-investment are so much higher than they are for women.
2. Men support their partners and offspring economically and socially (rather than physiologically).

3. Biologically determined differences in male and female investment may continue after delivery.

4. Like mothers, fathers invest time in the care and rearing of their children in order to bring children to reproductive maturity. Unlike mothers, their behavior does not appear to be hormonally facilitated.

5. The more men invest in partners and their children, the more they want to be sure of paternity; the extent to which they provide economic and socio-emotional support may affect the extent to which their partners' later children have the same fathers.

6. The fewer the children, the greater the motivation to invest time and resources in the success of each.

The clarity of some of these predictions is offset by the fact that the motivations are unconscious and must therefore be studied. Subsequent investigations must proceed, therefore, not by probing attitudes and values in interviews, but by studying the effects, often at the level of population groups rather than individuals. Fortunately, the desire to be a father is not driven solely (or even consciously) by the desire to propagate one's genes, and sociobiological explanations in terms of ultimate causes involve a different level of analysis than psychological and sociological explanations.

Being a father denotes maturity and confers status in many societies and subcultures, while participation in shaping the growth and development of another person brings fulfillment to many men and women. Such participation is hard to quantify empirically, but time-use measures come closest, especially when they illuminate both *what* and *how much* fathers do for or with their children. No large-scale studies measure *how well* fathers perform these roles or tasks–rather, that is the focus of smaller scale studies that are informed by direct observation.

Likewise, social status attaches to those whose partners and children are well-provisioned and successful (for example, as denoted by school performance, sports achievement, college admissions, and career attainment). Attitude surveys may indicate the relative, if not absolute importance of these motivations, as well as differing perceptions of the ways in which these desired outcomes can best be hastened (by coaching, supervision, warmth, play, physical provisioning, etc.). The type and extent of individual involvement in fathering may also be affected by recollections of the fathering experienced by men as children. Some men, particularly those who embrace hands-on involvement and avoid being defined solely as breadwinners, are motivated to emulate the behavior of their fathers. In contrast other men who behave in this way are apparently driven by a desire to be better fathers than were their own fathers. Finally, although spending time with children may or may not be an important aspect of fatherhood to the individuals concerned, the time diary studies have shown that the amount of time fathers spend with, and the amount of responsibility fathers assume for their children is associated with several factors. Specifically, we refer to socioeconomic class membership (lower class fathers tend to spend more time with their children), child's age (fathers spend more time with younger than with older children), child's gender (fathers spend more time with boys than with girls), and maternal employment status (fathers assume more responsibility when their partners are employed).

•••••

REFERENCES

Demos, J. (1982). The changing faces of fatherhood. In S. H. Cath, A. R. Gurwitt, & J. M. Ross (Eds.), *Father and child: Developmental and clinical perspectives* (pp. 425–445). Boston, MA: Little Brown.

Demos, J. (1986). *Past, present, and personal: The family and the life course in the nineteenth century.* New York: Oxford University Press.

Enrenreich, B. & English, D. (1979). *For her own good.* New York: Anchor Books.

Griswold, R. L. (1995). *Fatherhood in America: A history.* New York: Basic Books.

Lamb, M. E. (1981a). The development of father-infant relationships. In M. E. Lamb (Ed.), *The role of the father in child development* (Revised edition, pp. 459–488). New York: Wiley.

Lamb, M. E. (1997a). The development of father-infant relationships. In M. E. Lamb (Ed.), *The role of the father in child development* (Third edition; pp. 104–120; 332–342). New York: Wiley.

Lamb, M. E., & Goldberg, W. A. (1982). The father-child relationship: A synthesis of biological, evolutionary and social perspectives. In L. W. Hoffman, R. Gandelman, & H. R. Schiffman (Eds.), *Parenting: Its causes and consequences* (pp. 55–73). Hillsdale, N.J.: Lawrence Erlbaum Associates.

LaRossa, R. (1988). Fatherhood and social change. *Family Relations, 36,* 451–458.

LaRossa, R., Gordon, B. A., Wilson, R. J., Bairan, A., & Jaret, C. (1991). The fluctuating image of the 20th century American father. *Journal of Marriage and the Family, 53,* 987–997.

Levy, D. (1943). *Maternal overprotection.* New York: Columbia University Press.

Mintz, S. (1998). From patriarchy to androgyny and other myths: Placing men's family roles in historical perspective. In A. Booth and N. Crouter (Eds.), *Men in families: When do they get involved? What difference does it make?* (pp. 3–30). Mahwah, NJ: Erlbaum.

Pleck, E. H., & Pleck, J. H. (1997). Fatherhood ideals in the United States: Historical dimensions. In M. E. Lamb (Ed.), *The role of the father in child development* (Third edition; pp. 33–48). New York: Wiley.

Pleck, J. H. (1981). *The myth of masculinity.* Cambridge, MA: MIT Press.

Pleck, J. H. (1984). *Changing fatherhood.* Unpublished manuscript, Wellesley, MA: Wellesley College Center for Research on Women.

Rotundo, A. (1993). *American manhood: Transformations in masculinity from the revolution to the modern era.* New York: Basic Books.

Strecker, E. (1946). *Their mothers' sons: The psychiatrist examines an American problem.* Philadelphia: Lippincott.

Trivers, R. L. (1972). Parental investment and sexual selection. In. B. G. Campbell (Ed.), *Sexual selection and the descent of man: 1871–1971* (pp. 136–179). Chicago: Aldine.

Wylie, P. (1942). *A generation of vipers.* New York: Rinehart.

READING 30: THE HISTORY OF RESEARCH ON FATHER INVOLVEMENT

DISCUSSION QUESTIONS

- Lamb describes a series of changes to ideas about fatherhood. Can you outline them?
- What is responsibility? Is it divided equally amongst parents?

EXAMPLES TO THINK ABOUT

- *Modern Dads*
- Fatherhood advice guides
- *Mad Men*

SECTION 10

EXAMPLES AND ISSUES:
SCIENCE

Unbearable Weight

Feminism, Western Culture, and the Body

EXCERPTS FROM: READING THE SLENDER BODY

By SUSAN BORDO

SLENDERNESS AND THE SOCIAL BODY

Mary Douglas, looking on the body as a system of "natural symbols" that reproduce social categories and concerns, has argued that anxiety about the maintenance of rigid bodily boundaries (manifested, for example, in rituals and prohibitions concerning excreta, saliva, and the strict delineation of "inside" and "outside") is most evident and intense in societies whose external boundaries are under attack.[17] Let me hypothesize, similarly, that preoccupation with the "internal" management of the body (that is, management of its desires) is produced by instabilities in what could be called the macro-regulation of desire within the system of the social body.

In advanced consumer capitalism, as Robert Crawford has elegantly argued, an unstable, agonistic construction of personality is produced by the contradictory structure of economic life.[18] On the one hand, as producers of goods and services we must sublimate, delay, repress desires for immediate gratification; we must cultivate the work ethic. On the other hand, as consumers we must display a boundless capacity to capitulate to desire and indulge in impulse; we must hunger for constant and immediate satisfaction.

The regulation of desire thus becomes an ongoing problem, as we find ourselves continually besieged by temptation, while socially condemned for overindulgence. (Of course, those who cannot afford to indulge their desires as consumers, teased and frustrated by the culture, face a much harsher dilemma.)

Food and diet are central arenas for the expression of these contradictions. On television and in popular magazines, with a flip of the page or barely a pause between commercials, images of luscious foods and the rhetoric of craving and desire are replaced by advertisements for grapefruit diets, low-calorie recipes, and exercise equipment. Even more disquieting than these manifest oppositions, however, are the constant attempts by advertisers to mystify them, suggesting that the contradiction doesn't really exist, that one can "have it all." Diets and exercise programs are accordingly presented with the imagery of instant gratification ("From Fat to Fabulous in 21 Days," "Size 22 to Size 10 in No Time Flat," "Six Minutes to an Olympic-Class Stomach") and effortlessness ("3,000 Sit-Ups Without Moving an Inch ... 10 Miles of Jogging Lying Flat on Your Back" [Figure 31-1], "85 Pounds Without Dieting," and even, shamelessly, "Exercise Without Exercise"). In reality, however, the opposition is not so easily reconciled. Rather, it presents a classic double bind, in which the self is torn in two mutually incompatible directions. The contradiction is not an abstract one but stems from the specific historical construction of a "consuming passion" from which all inclinations toward balance, moderation, rationality, and foresight have been excluded.

Conditioned to lose control at the mere sight of desirable products, we can master our desires only by creating rigid defenses against them. The slender body codes the tantalizing ideal of a well-managed self in which all is kept in order despite the contradictions of consumer culture. Thus, whether or not the struggle is played out in terms of food and diet, many of us may find our lives vacillating between a daytime rigidly ruled by the "performance principle" and nights and weekends that capitulate to unconscious "letting go" (food, shopping, liquor, television, and other addictive drugs). In this way, the central contradiction of the system inscribes itself on our bodies, and bulimia emerges as a characteristic modern personality construction. For bulimia precisely and explicitly expresses the extreme development of the hunger for unrestrained consumption (exhibited in the bulimic's uncontrollable food binges) existing in unstable tension alongside the requirement that we sober up, "clean up our act," get back in firm control on Monday morning (the necessity for purge—exhibited in the bulimic's vomiting, compulsive exercising, and laxative purges).

The same structural contradiction is inscribed in what has been termed (incorrectly) the "paradox" that we have an "epidemic" of anorexia nervosa in this country "despite the fact that we have an overweight majority."[19] Far from paradoxical, the coexistence of anorexia and obesity reveals the instability of the contemporary personality construction, the difficulty of finding homeostasis between the producer and the consumer sides of the self. Bulimia embodies the unstable double bind of consumer capitalism, while anorexia and obesity embody an attempted resolution of that double bind. Anorexia could thus be seen as an extreme development of the capacity for self-denial and repression of desire (the work ethic

FIGURE 31-1

in absolute control); obesity, as an extreme capacity to capitulate to desire (consumerism in control). Both are rooted in the same consumer-culture construction of desire as overwhelming and overtaking the self. Given that construction, we can only respond either with total submission or rigid defense.

Neither anorexia nor obesity is accepted by the culture as an appropriate response. The absolute conquest of hunger and desire (even in symbolic form) can never be tolerated by a consumer system—even if the Christian dualism of our culture also predisposes us to be dazzled by the anorectic's ability seemingly to transcend the flesh. Anorectics are proud of this ability, but, as the disorder progresses, they usually feel the need to hide their skeletal bodies from those around them. If cultural attitudes toward the anorectic are ambivalent, however, reactions to the obese are not. As Marcia Millman documents in *Such a Pretty Face,* the obese elicit blinding rage and disgust in our culture and are often viewed in terms that suggest an infant sucking hungrily, unconsciously at its mother's breast: greedy, self-absorbed, lazy, without self-control or willpower.[20] People avoid sitting next to the obese (even when the space they take up is not intrusive); comics feel no need to restrain their cruelty; socially, they are considered unacceptable at public functions (one man wrote to "Dear Abby," saying that he was planning to replace his brother and sister-in-law as honor attendants at his wedding, because "they are both quite overweight"). Significantly, the part of the obese anatomy most often targeted for vicious attack, and most despised by the obese themselves, is the stomach, symbol of consumption (in the case of the obese, unrestrained consumption taking over the organism; one of Marcia Millman's interviewees recalls how the husband of a friend called hers "an awful, cancerous-looking growth").[21]

SLENDERNESS, SELF-MANAGEMENT, AND NORMALIZATION

Self-management in consumer culture, I have been arguing, becomes more elusive as it becomes more pressing. The attainment of an acceptable body is extremely difficult for those who do not come by it "naturally" (whether aided by genetics, metabolism, or high activity-level) and as the ideal becomes firmer and tauter it begins to exclude more and more people. Constant watchfulness over appetite and strenuous work on the body itself are required to conform to this ideal, while the most popular means of "correction"—dieting—often insures its own failure, as the experience of deprivation leads to compensatory binging, with its attendant feelings of defeat, worthlessness, and loss of hope. Between the media images of self-containment and self-mastery and the reality of constant, everyday stress and anxiety about one's appearance lies the chasm that produces bodies habituated to self-monitoring and self-normalization.

Ultimately, the body (besides being evaluated for its success or failure at getting itself in order) is seen as demonstrating correct or incorrect attitudes toward the demands of normalization itself. The obese and anorectic are therefore disturbing partly because they embody resistance to cultural norms. Bulimics, by contrast, typically strive for the conventionally attractive body shape dictated by their more "normative" pattern of managing desire. In the case of the obese, in particular, what is perceived as their defiant rebellion against normalization appears to be a source of the hostility they inspire. The anorectic at least pays homage to dominant cultural values, outdoing them in their own terms:

I wanted people to look at me and see something special. I wanted to look in the face of a stranger and see admiration, so that I would know that I accomplished something that was just about impossible for most people, especially in our society. ... From what I've seen, more people fail at losing weight than at any other single goal. I found out how to do what everyone else couldn't: I could lose as much or as little weight as I wanted. And that meant I was better than everyone else.[22]

The anorectic thus strives to stand above the crowd by excelling at its own rules; in so doing, however, she exposes the hidden penalties. But the obese—particularly those who claim to be happy although overweight—are perceived as not playing by the rules at all. If the rest of us are struggling to be acceptable and "normal," we cannot allow them to get away with it; they must be put in their place, be humiliated and defeated.

A number of talk shows have made this abundantly clear. On one, much of the audience reaction was given over to disbelief and to the attempt to prove to one obese woman that she was *not* happy: "I can't believe you don't want to be slim and beautiful, I just can't believe it." "I heard you talk a lot about how you feel good about yourself and you like yourself, but I really think you're kidding yourself." "It's hard for me to believe that Mary Jane is really happy ... you don't fit into chairs, it's hard to get through the doorway. My God, on the subway, forget it." When Mary Jane persisted in her assertion that she was happy, she was warned, in a viciously self-righteous tone, that it would not last: "Mary Jane, to be the way you are today, you had better start going on a diet soon, because if you don't you're going to get bigger and bigger and bigger. It's true."[23] On another show, in an effort to subdue an increasingly hostile and offensive audience one of the doctor-guests kept trying to reassure them that the "fat and happy" target of their attacks did not *really* mean that she didn't *want* to lose weight; rather, she was simply tired of trying and failing. This construction allows people to give their sympathy to the obese, assuming as it does the obese person's acknowledgment that to be "normal" is the most desired goal, elusive only because of personal inadequacy. Those who are willing to present themselves as pitiable, in pain, and conscious of their own unattractiveness—often demonstrated, on these shows, by self-admissions about intimate physical difficulties, orgies of self-hate, or descriptions of gross consumption of food, win the sympathy and concern of the audience.

SLENDERNESS AND GENDER

It has been amply documented that women in our culture are more tyrannized by the contemporary slenderness ideal than men are, as they typically have been by beauty ideals in general. It is far more important to men than to women that their partner be slim.[24] Women are much more prone than men to perceive themselves as too fat.[25] And, as is by now well known,

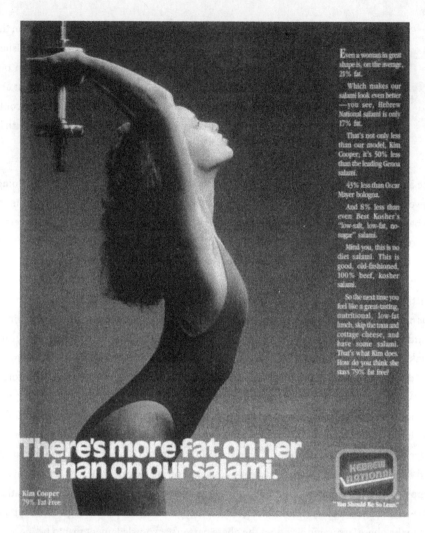

Even a woman in great
shape is, on the average,
23% fat.

Which makes our
salami look even better
—you see, Hebrew
National salami is only
17% fat.

That's not only less
than our model, Kim
Cooper; it's 50% less
than the leading Genoa
salami.

43% less than Oscar
Mayer bologna.

And 8% less than
even Best Kosher's
"low-salt, low-fat, no-
sugar" salami.

Mind you, this is no
diet salami. This is
good, old-fashioned,
100% beef, kosher
salami.

So the next time you
feel like a great-tasting,
nutritional, low-fat
lunch, skip the tuna and
cottage cheese, and
have some salami.
That's what Kim does.
How do you think she
stays 79% fat free?

There's more fat on her than on our salami.

Kim Cooper
79% Fat Free

"You Should Be So Lean."

FIGURE 31-2

girls and women are more likely to engage in crash dieting, laxative abuse, and compulsive exercising and are far more vulnerable to eating disorders than males. But eating disorders are not only "about" slenderness, any more than (as I have been arguing) slenderness is only—or even chiefly—about being physically thin. My aim in this section, therefore, is not to "explain" facts about which so much has now been written from historical, psychological, and sociological points of view. Rather, I want to remain with the image of the slender body, confronting it now both as a gendered body (the slender body as female body—the usual form in which the image is displayed) (Figure 31-2) and as a body whose gender meaning is never neutral. This layer of gender-coded signification, suffusing other meanings, overdetermines slenderness as a contemporary ideal of specifically *female* attractiveness.

The exploration of contemporary slenderness as a metaphor for the correct management of desire must take into account the fact that throughout dominant Western religious and philosophical traditions, the capacity for self-management is decisively coded as male. By contrast, all those bodily spontaneities—hunger, sexuality, the emotions—seen as needful of containment and control have been culturally constructed and coded as female.[26] The management of specifically female desire, therefore, is in phallocentric cultures a doubly freighted problem. Women's desires are by their very nature excessive, irrational, threatening to erupt and challenge the patriarchal order.

Some writers have argued that female hunger (as a code for female desire) is especially problematized during periods of disruption and change in established gender-relations and in the position of women. In such periods (of which our own is arguably one), nightmare images of what Bram Dijkstra has called "the consuming woman" theme proliferate in art and literature (images representing female desire unleashed), while dominant constructions of the female body become more sylphlike—unlike the body of a fully developed woman, more like that of an adolescent or boy (images that might be called female desire unborn). Dijkstra argues such a case concerning the late nineteenth century, pointing to the devouring sphinxes and bloodsucking vampires of *fin-de-siècle* art, and the accompanying vogue for elongated, "sublimely emaciated" female bodies.[27] A commentator of the time vividly describes the emergence of a new body-style, not very unlike our own:

> Women can change the cut of their clothes at will, but how can they change the cut of their anatomies? And yet, they have done just this thing. Their shoulders have become narrow and slightly sloping, their throats more slender, their hips smaller and their arms and legs elongated to an extent that suggest that bed, upon which the robber, Procrustes, used to stretch his victims.[28]

The fact that our own era has witnessed a comparable shift (from the hourglass figure of the fifties to the androgynous, increasingly elongated, slender look that has developed over the past decade) cries out for interpretation. This shift, however, needs to be interpreted not only from the standpoint of male anxiety over women's desires (Dijkstra's analysis, while crucial, is only half the story) but also from the standpoint of the women who embrace the "new look." For them it may have a very different meaning; it may symbolize, not so much the containment of female desire, as its liberation from a domestic, reproductive destiny. The fact that the slender female body can carry both these seemingly contradictory meanings is one reason, I would suggest, for its compelling attraction in periods of gender change.[29]

To elaborate this argument in more detail: earlier, I presented some quotations from interviews with eating-disordered women in which they describe their revulsion to breasts, stomachs, and all other bodily bulges. At that point I subjected these quotations to a gender-neutral reading. While not rescinding that interpretation, I want to overlay it now with another reading, which I present in "Anorexia Nervosa: Psychopathology as the Crystallization of

YOU DO NOT HAVE TO BE YOUR MOTHER UNLESS SHE IS WHO YOU WANT TO BE. YOU DO NOT HAVE TO BE YOUR MOTHER'S MOTHER, OR YOUR MOTHER'S MOTHER'S MOTHER, OR EVEN YOUR GRANDMOTHER'S MOTHER ON YOUR FATHER'S SIDE. YOU MAY INHERIT THEIR CHINS OR THEIR HIPS OR THEIR EYES, BUT YOU ARE NOT DESTINED TO BECOME THE WOMEN WHO CAME BEFORE YOU. YOU ARE NOT DESTINED TO LIVE THEIR LIVES. SO IF YOU INHERIT SOMETHING, INHERIT THEIR STRENGTH. IF YOU INHERIT SOMETHING, IN-HERIT THEIR RESILIENCE. BECAUSE THE ONLY PERSON YOU ARE DESTINED TO BECOME IS THE PERSON YOU DECIDE TO BE.

FIGURE 31-3

Culture." There, I suggest that the characteristic anorexic revulsion toward hips, stomach, and breasts (often accompanied by disgust at menstruation and relief at amenorrhoea) might be viewed as expressing rebellion against maternal, domestic femininity—a femininity that represents both the suffocating control the anorectic experiences her own mother as having had over her, *and* the mother's actual lack of position and authority outside the domestic arena. (A Nike ad [Figure 31-3] embodies both these elements, as the "strength" of the mother is depicted in the containing arm that encircles her small daughter, while young women reading the ad are reassured that they can exercise *their* strength in other, non- maternal ways.) Here we encounter another reason for anxiety over soft, protuberant body-parts. They evoke helpless infancy and symbolize maternal femininity as it has been constructed over the past hundred years in the West. That femininity, as Dorothy Dinnerstein has argued, is perceived as both frighteningly powerful and, as the child comes increasingly to recognize the hierarchical nature of the sexual division of labor, utterly powerless.[30]

The most literal symbolic form of maternal femininity is represented by the nineteenth-century hourglass figure, emphasizing breasts and hips—the markers of reproductive femaleness—against a fragile wasp waist.[31] It is not until the post-World War II period, with its relocation of middle-class women from factory to home and its coercive bourgeois dualism of the happy homemaker-mother and the responsible, provider-father, that such clear bodily demarcation of "male" and "female" spheres surfaces again. The era of the cinch belt, the pushup bra, and Marilyn Monroe could be viewed, for the body, as an era of "resurgent Victorianism."[32] It was also the last coercively normalizing body-ideal to reign before boyish slenderness began its ascendancy in the mid-1960s.

From this perspective, one might speculate that the boys who reacted with disgust or anxiety to fleshy female parts were reacting to evocations of maternal power, newly threatening in an age when women are making their way into arenas traditionally reserved for men: law, business, higher education, politics, and so forth.[33] The buxom Sophia Loren was a sex goddess in an era when women were encouraged to define their deepest desires in terms of service to home, husband, and family. Today, it is required of female desire, loose in the male world, to be normalized according to the professional (and male) standards of that world; female bodies, accordingly, must be stripped of all psychic resonances with maternal power. From the standpoint of male anxiety, the lean body of the career businesswoman today may symbolize such a neutralization. With her body and her dress she declares symbolic allegiance to the professional, white, male world along with her lack of intention to subvert that arena with alternative "female values." At the same time, insofar as she is clearly "dressing up," *playing* male (almost always with a "softening" fashion touch to establish traditional feminine decorativeness, and continually cautioned against the dire consequences of allotting success higher priority than her looks), she represents no serious competition (symbolically, that is) to the real men of the workplace (Figures 31-4 and 31-5).

For many women, however, disidentification with the maternal body, far from symbolizing reduced power, may symbolize (as it did in the 1890s and 1920s) freedom from a reproductive destiny and a construction of femininity seen as constraining and suffocating.

FIGURE 31-4

FIGURE 31-5

Correspondingly, taking on the accoutrements of the white, male world may be experienced as empowerment by women themselves, and as their chance to embody qualities—detachment, self-containment, self-mastery, control—that are highly valued in our culture. The slender body, as I have argued earlier, symbolizes such qualities. "It was about power," says Kim Morgan, speaking in the documentary *The Waist Land* of the obsession with slenderness that led to her anorexia, "that was the big thing ... something I could throw in people's faces, and they would look at me and I'd only weigh this much, but I was strong and in control, and

FIGURE 31-6

hey *you're* sloppy."[34] The taking on of "male" power as self-mastery is another locus where, for all their surface dissimilarities, the shedding of weight and the development of muscles intersect. Appropriately, the new "Joy of Cooking" takes place in the gym, in one advertisement that shamelessly exploits the associations of female body-building with liberation from a traditional, domestic destiny (Figure 31-6).

In the intersection of these gender issues and more general cultural dilemmas concerning the management of desire, we see how the tightly managed body—whether demonstrated through sleek, minimalist lines or firmly developed muscles—has been overdetermined as a contemporary ideal of specifically female attractiveness. The axis of consumption/production is gender-overlaid, as I have argued, by the hierarchical dualism that constructs a dangerous, appetitive, bodily "female principle" in opposition to a masterful "male" will. We would thus expect that when the regulation of desire becomes especially problematic (as it is in advanced consumer cultures), women and their bodies will pay the greatest symbolic and material toll. When such a situation is compounded by anxiety about *women's* desires in periods when traditional forms of gender organization are being challenged, this toll is multiplied. It would be wrong to suppose, however, that it is exacted through the simple *repression* of female hunger. Rather, here as elsewhere, power works also "from below," as women associate slenderness with self-management, by way of the experience of newfound freedom (from a domestic destiny) and empowerment in the public arena. In this connection we might note the difference between contemporary ideals of slenderness, coded in terms of self-mastery and expressed through traditionally "male" body symbolism, and mid-Victorian ideals of female slenderness, which symbolically emphasized reproductive femininity corseted under tight "external" constraints. But whether externally bound or internally managed, no body can escape either the imprint of culture or its gendered meanings.

DISCUSSION QUESTIONS

- According to Bordo, what is the relationship between contemporary capitalism and advice about dieting?
- Bordo suggests that women's appetites are often understood as convey ideas about women's desire. Do you agree?

EXAMPLES TO THINK ABOUT

- The visual culture of diet programs
- Laura Aguilar's photographs
- Plus-sized clothing

A Cyborg Manifesto

Science, Technology, and Socialist-Feminism in the
Late Twentieth Century

SELECTIONS

By DONNA HARAWAY

AN IRONIC DREAM OF A COMMON LANGUAGE FOR WOMEN IN THE INTEGRATED CIRCUIT

This [selection] is an effort to build an ironic political myth faithful to feminism, socialism, and materialism. Perhaps more faithful as blasphemy is faithful, than as reverent worship and identification. Blasphemy has always seemed to require taking things very seriously. I know no better stance to adopt from within the secular-religious, evangelical traditions of United States politics, including the politics of socialist feminism. Blasphemy protects one from the moral majority within, while still insisting on the need for community. Blasphemy is not apostasy. Irony is about contradictions that do not resolve into larger wholes, even dialectically, about the tension of holding. Incompatible things together because both or all are necessary and true. Irony is about humour and serious play. It is also a rhetorical strategy and a political method one I would like to see more honoured within socialist-feminism. At the centre of my ironic faith, my blasphemy, is the image of the cyborg.

A cyborg is a cybernetic organism, a hybrid of machine and organism, a creature of social reality as well as a creature of fiction. Social reality is lived social relations our most important political construction, a world-changing fiction. The international women's movements have constructed 'women's experience,' as well as uncovered or discovered this crucial collective object. This experience is a fiction and fact of the most crucial, political kind. Liberation rests on the construction of the consciousness, the imaginative apprehension of oppression, and so of possibility. The cyborg is a matter of fiction and lived experience that changes what counts as women's experience in the late twentieth century. This is a struggle over life and death, but the boundary between science fiction and social reality is an optical illusion.

Contemporary science fiction is full of cyborgs—creatures simultaneously animal and machine, who populate worlds ambiguously natural and crafted. Modern medicine is also full of cyborgs, of couplings between organism and machine, each conceived as coded devices, in an intimacy and with a power that was not generated in the history of sexuality. Cyborg 'sex' restores some of the lovely replicative baroque of ferns and invertebrates (such nice organic prophylactics against heterosexism). Cyborg replication is uncoupled from organic reproduction. Modern production seems like a dream of cyborg, colonization work, a dream that makes the nightmare of Taylorism seem idyllic. And modern war is a cyborg orgy, coded by C^3I, command-control-communication-intelligence, an $84 billion item in 1984's US defence budget. I am making an argument for the cyborg as a fiction mapping our social and bodily realty and as an imaginative resource suggesting some very fruitful couplings. Michael Foucault's biopolitics is a flaccid premonition of cyborg politics, a very open field.

By the late twentieth century, our time, a mythic time, we are all chimeras, theorized and fabricated hybrids of machine and organism; in short, we are cyborgs. The cyborg is our ontology; it gives us our politics. The cyborg is a condensed image of both imagination and material reality, the two joined centres structuring any possibility of historical transformation. In the traditions of Western' science and politics—the tradition of racist, male-dominant capitalism; the tradition of progress; the tradition of the appropriation of nature as resource for the productions of culture; the tradition of reproduction of the self from the reflections of the other—the relation between organism and machine has been a border war. The stakes in the border war have been the territories of production reproductions and imagination. This [selection] is an argument for *pleasure* in the confusion of boundaries and for *responsibility* in their construction. It is also an effort to contribute to socialist-feminist culture and theory in a postmodernist non-naturalist mode and in the utopian tradition of imagining a world without gender, which is perhaps a world without genesis, but maybe also a world without end. The cyborg incarnation is outside salvation history. Nor does it mark time on an oedipal calendar, attempting to heal the terrible cleavages of gender in an oral symbiotic utopia or post-oedipal apocalypse. As Zoe Sofoulis argues in her unpublished manuscript on Jacques Lacan, Melanie Klein, and nuclear culture, *Lacklein,* the most terrible and perhaps the most promising monsters in cyborg worlds are embodied in non-oedipal narratives with a different logic of repression, which we need to understand for our survival.

The cyborg is a creature in a post-gender world; it has no truck with bisexuality, pre-oedipal symbiosis unalienated labour, or other seductions to organic wholeness through a final appropriation of all the powers of the parts into a higher unity. In a sense, the cyborg has no origin story in the Western sense—a 'final' irony since the cyborg is also the awful apocalyptic *telos* of the 'West's' escalating dominations of abstract individuation, an ultimate self untied at last from all dependency, a man in space. An origin story in the 'Western,' humanist sense depends on the myth of original unity, fullness, bliss and terror, represented by the phallic mother from whom all humans must separate, the task of individual development and of history, the twin potent myths inscribed most powerfully for us in psychoanalysis and Marxism. Hilary Klein has argued that both Marxism and psychoanalysis, in their concepts of labour and of individuation and gender formation, depend on the plot of original unity out of which difference must be produced and enlisted in a drama of escalating domination of woman/nature. The cyborg skips the step of original unity, of identification with nature in the Western sense. This is its illegitimate promise that might lead to subversion of its teleology as star wars.

The cyborg is resolutely committed to partiality, irony, intimacy, and perversity. It is oppositional, Utopian, and completely without innocence. No longer structured by the polarity of public and private, the cyborg defines a technological polis based partly on a revolution of social relations in the *oikos*, the household. Nature and culture are reworked; the one can no longer be the resource for appropriation or incorporation by the other. The relationships for forming wholes from parts, including those of polarity and hierarchical domination, are at issue in the cyborg world. Unlike the hopes of Frankenstein's monster, the cyborg does not expect its father to save it through a restoration of the garden; that is, through the fabrication of a heterosexual mate, through its completion in a finished whole, a city and cosmos. The cyborg does not dream of community on the model of the organic family, this time without the oedipal project. The cyborg would not recognize the Garden of Eden; it is not made of mud and cannot dream of returning to dust. Perhaps that is why I want to see if cyborgs can subvert the apocalypse of returning to nuclear dust in the manic compulsion to name the Enemy. Cyborgs are not reverent; they do not remember the cosmos. They are wary of holism, but needy for connection—they seem to have a natural feel for united front politics, but without the vanguard party. The main trouble with cyborgs, of course, is that they are the illegitimate offspring of militarism and patriarchal capitalism, not to mention state socialism. But illegitimate offspring are often exceedingly unfaithful to their origins. Their fathers, after all, are inessential.

◆ ◆ ◆ ◆

So my cyborg myth is about transgressed boundaries, potent fusions, and dangerous possibilities which progressive people might explore as one part of needed political work. [...]

From one perspective, a cyborg world is about the final imposition of a grid of control on the planet, about the final abstraction embodied in a Star Wars apocalypse waged in the name of defence, about the final appropriation of women's bodies in a masculinist orgy of war (Sofia, 1984). From another perspective, a cyborg world might be about lived social and bodily realities in which people are not afraid of their joint kinship with animals and machines, not afraid of permanently partial identities and contradictory standpoints. The political straggle is to see from both perspectives at once because each reveals both dominations and possibilities unimaginable from the other vantage point. Single vision produces worse illusions than double vision or many-headed monsters. Cyborg unities are monstrous and illegitimate; in our present political circumstances, we could hardly hope for more potent myths for resistance and recoupling. I like to imagine LAG, the Livermore Action Group, as a kind of cyborg society, dedicated to realistically converting the laboratories that most fiercely embody and spew out the tools of technological apocalypse, and committed to building a political form that actually manages to hold together witches, engineers, elders, perverts, Christians, mothers, and Leninists long enough to disarm the state. Fission Impossible is the name of the affinity group in my town. (Affinity: related not by blood but by choice, the appeal of one chemical nuclear group for another, avidity.)

FRACTURED IDENTITIES

It has become difficult to name one's feminism by a single adjective—or even to insist in every circumstance upon the noun. Consciousness of exclusion through naming is acute. Identities seem contradictory, partial, and strategic. With the hard-won recognition of their social and historical constitution, gender, race, and class cannot provide the basis for belief in 'essential' unity. There is nothing about being 'female' that naturally binds women. There is not even such a state as 'being' female, itself a highly complex category constructed in contested sexual scientific discourses and other social practices. Gender, race, or class consciousness is an achievement forced on us by the terrible historical experience of the contradictory social realities of patriarchy, colonialism, and capitalism. And who counts as 'us' in my own rhetoric? Which identities are available to ground such a potent political myth called 'us,' and what could motivate enlistment in this collectivity? Painful fragmentation among feminists (not to mention among women) along every possible fault line has made the concept of *woman* elusive, an excuse for the matrix of women's dominations of each other. For me—and for many who share a similar historical location in white, professional middle-class, female, radical, North American, mid-adult bodies—the sources of a crisis in political identity are legion. The recent history for much of the US left and US feminism has been a response to this kind of crisis by endless splitting and searches for a new essential unity. But there has also been a growing recognition of another response through coalition—affinity, not identity.

◆ ◆ ◆ ◆

* A practice at once both spiritual and political that linked guards and arrested anti-nuclear demonstrators in the Alameda County jail in California in the early 1980s.

Monsters have always defined the limits of community in Western imaginations. The Centaurs and Amazons of ancient Greece established the limits of the centred polis of the Greek male human by their disruption of marriage and boundary pollutions of the warrior with animality and woman. Unseparated twins and hermaphrodites were the confused human material in early modern France who grounded discourse on the natural and supernatural, medical and legal, portents and diseases—all crucial to establishing modern identity.[30] The evolutionary and behavioural sciences of monkeys and apes have marked the multiple boundaries of late twentieth-century industrial identities. Cyborg monsters in feminist science fiction define quite different political possibilities and limits from those proposed by the mundane fiction of Man and Woman.

There are several consequences to taking seriously the imagery of cyborgs as other than our enemies. Our bodies, ourselves; bodies are maps of power and identity. Cyborgs are no exception. A cyborg body is not innocent; it was not born in a garden; it does not seek unitary identity and so generate antagonistic dualisms without end (or until the world ends); it takes irony for granted. One is too few, and two is only one possibility. Intense pleasure in skill, machine skill, ceases to be a sin, but an aspect of embodiment. The machine is not an *it* to be animated, worshipped, and dominated. The machine is us, our processes, an aspect of our embodiment. We can be responsible for machines; *they* do not dominate or threaten us. We are responsible for boundaries; we are they. Up till now (once upon a time), female embodiment seemed to be given, organic, necessary; and female embodiment seemed to mean skill in mothering and its metaphoric extensions. Only by being out of place could we take intense pleasure in machines, and then with excuses that this was organic activity after all, appropriate to females. Cyborgs might consider more seriously the partial, fluid, sometimes aspect of sex and sexual embodiment. Gender might not be global identity after all, even if it has profound historical breadth and depth.

The ideologically charged question of what counts as daily activity, as experience, can be approached by exploiting the cyborg image. Feminists have recently claimed that women are given to dailiness, that women more than men somehow sustain daily life, and so have a privileged epistemologicai position potentially. There is a compelling aspect to this claim, one that makes visible unvalued female activity and names it. as the ground of life. But *the* ground of life? What about all the ignorance of women, all the exclusions and failures of knowledge and skill? What about men's access to daily competence, to knowing how to build things, to take them apart, to play? What about other embodiments? Cyborg gender is a local possibility taking a global vengeance. Race, gender, and capital require a cyborg theory of wholes and parts. There is no drive in cyborgs to produce total theory, but there is an intimate experience of boundaries, their construction and deconstruction. There is a myth system waiting to become a political language to ground one way of looking at science and technology and challenging the informatics of domination—in order to act potently.

One last image: organisms and organismic, holistic politics depend on metaphors of rebirth and invariably call on the resources of reproductive sex. I would suggest that cyborgs have more to do with regeneration and are suspicious of the reproductive matrix and of most birthing. For salamanders, regeneration after injury, such as the loss of a limb, involves regrowth of structure and restoration of function with the constant possibility of twinning or other odd topographical productions at the site of former injury. The regrown limb can be monstrous, duplicated, potent. We have all been injured, profoundly. We require regeneration, not rebirth, and the possibilities for our reconstitution include the Utopian dream of the hope for a monstrous world without gender.

Cyborg imagery can help express two crucial arguments in this essay: first, the production of universal, totalizing theory is a major mistake that misses most of reality, probably always, but certainly now; and second, taking responsibility for the social relations of science and technology means refusing an anti-science metaphysics, a demonology of technology, and so means embracing the skilful task of reconstructing the boundaries of daily life, in partial connection with others, in communication with all of our parts. It is not just that science and technology are possible means of great human satisfaction, as well as a matrix of complex dominations. Cyborg imagery can suggest a way out of the maze of dualisms in which we have explained our bodies and our tools to ourselves. This is a dream not of a common language, but of a powerful infidel heteroglossia. It is an imagination of a feminist speaking in tongues to strike fear into the circuits of the super-savers of the new right. It means both building and destroying machines, identities, categories, relationships, space stories. Though both are bound in the spiral dance, I would rather be a cyborg than a goddess.

NOTES

1. For ethnographic accounts and political evaluations, see Epstein (forthcoming), Sturgeon (1986). Without explicit irony, adopting the spaceship earth/whole earth logo of the planet photographed from space, set off by the slogan 'Love Your Mother', the May 1987 Mothers and Others Day action at the nuclear weapons testing facility in Nevada none the less took account of the tragic contradictions of views of the earth. Demonstrators applied for official permits to be on the land from officers of the Western Shoshone tribe, whose territory was invaded by the US government when it built the nuclear weapons test ground in the 1950s. Arrested for trespassing, the demonstrators argued that the police and weapons facility personnel, without authorization from the proper officials, were the trespassers. One affinity group at the women's action called themselves the Surrogate Others; and in solidarity with the creatures forced to tunnel in the same ground with the bomb, they enacted a cyborgian emergence from the constructed body of a large, non-heterosexual desert worm.

2. Powerful developments of coalition politics emerge from 'Third World' speakers, speaking from nowhere, the displaced centre of the universe, earth: 'We live on the third planet from the sun'—Sun Poem by Jamaican writer, Edward Kamau Braithwaite, review by Mackey (1984). Contributors to Smith (1983) ironically subvert naturalized identities precisely while constructing a place from which to speak called home. See especially Reagon (in Smith, 1983, pp. 356–68). Trinh T. Minh-ha (1986–87).

3. hooks (1981, 1984); Hull *et al.* (1982). Bambara (1981) wrote an extraordinary novel in which the women of colour theatre group, The Seven Sisters, explores a form of unity. See analysis by Butler-Evans (1987).

4. On orientalism in feminist works and elsewhere, see Lowe (1986); Said (1978); Mohanty (1984); *Many Voices, One Chant: Black Feminist Perspectives* (1984).

5. Katie King (1986, 1987a) has developed a theoretically sensitive treatment of the workings of feminist taxonomies as genealogies of power in feminist ideology and polemic. King examines Jaggar's (1983) problematic example of taxonomizing feminisms to make a little machine producing the desired final position. My caricature here of socialist and radical feminism is also an example.

6. DuBois (1982), Daston and Park (n.d.), Park and Daston (1981). The noun *monster* shares its root with the verb *to demonstrate*.

REFERENCES

Bambara, Toni Cade (1981) *The Salt Eaters.* New York: Vintage/Random House.

Butler-Evans, Elliott (1987) 'Race, gender and desire: narrative strategies and the production of ideology in the fiction of Toni Cade Bambara, Toni Morrison and Alice Walker', University of California at Santa Cruz, PhD thesis.

Daston, Lorraine and Park, Katherine (n.d.) 'Hermaphrodites in Renaissance France', unpublished paper.

DuBois, Page (1982) *Centaurs and Amazons.* Ann Arbor: University of Michigan Press.

Epstein, Barbara (forthcoming) *Political Protest and Cultural Revolution: Nonviolent Direct Action in the Seventies and Eighties.* Berkeley: University of California Press.

hooks, bell (1981) *Ain't I a Woman.* Boston: South End.

———. (1984) *Feminist Theory: From Margin to Center.* Boston: South End.

Hull, Gloria, Scott, Patricia Bell, and Smith, Barbara, eds (1982) *All the Women Are White, All the Men Are Black, But Some of Us Are Brave.* Old Westbury: The Feminist Press.

Jaggar, Alison (1983) *Feminist Politics and Human Nature.* Totowa, NJ: Roman & Allenheld.

King, Katie (1986) 'The situation of lesbianism as feminism's magical sign: contests for meaning and the U.S. women's movement, 1968–72', *Communication* 9(1): 65–92.

———. (1987a) 'Canons without innocence', University of California at Santa Cruz, PhD thesis.

Lowe, Lisa (1986) 'French literary Orientalism: The representation of "others" in the texts of Montesquieu, Flaubert, and Kristeva', University of California at Santa Cruz, PhD thesis.

Mackey, Nathaniel (1984) 'Review', *Sulfur* 2: 200–5.

Many Voices, One Chant: Black Feminist Perspectives (1984) *Feminist Review* 17, special issue.

Marcuse, Herbert (1964) *One-Dimensional Man: Studies in the Ideology of Advanced Industrial Society*. Boston: Beacon.

Merchant, Carolyn (1980) *The Death of Nature: Women, Ecology, and the Scientific Revolution*. New York: Harper & Row.

Mohanty, Chandra Talpade (1984) 'Under western eyes: feminist scholarship and colonial discourse', *Boundary 2*, 3 (12/13): 333–58.

Park, Katherine and Daston, Lorraine J. (1981) 'Unnatural conceptions: the study of monsters in sixteenth- and seventeenth-century France and England', *Past and Present* 92: 20–54.

Said, Edward (1978) *Orientalism*. New York: Pantheon.

Sandoval, Chela (1984) 'Disillusionment and the poetry of the future: the making of oppositional consciousness', University of California at Santa Cruz, PhD qualifying essay.

Smith, Barbara., ed. (1983) *Home Girls: A Black Feminist Anthology*. New York: Kitchen Table, Women of Color Press.

Sofia, Zoe (also Zoe Sofoulis) (1984) 'Exterminating fetuses: abortion, disarmament, and the sexo-semiotics of extra-terrestrialism', *Diacritics* 14(2): 47–59.

Sofoulis, Zoe (1987) 'Lacklein', University of California at Santa Cruz, unpublished essay.

Sturgeon, Noel (1986) 'Feminism, anarchism, and non-violent direct action politics', University of California at Santa Cruz, PhD qualifying essay.

Trinh T. Minh-ha (1986–7) 'Introduction', and 'Difference: "a special third world women issue"', *Discourse: Journal for Theoretical Studies in Media and Culture* 8: 3–38.

DISCUSSION QUESTIONS

- According to Haraway, you are a cyborg. What does she mean by that term and do you agree?

- How to cyborgs relate to identity politics?

EXAMPLES TO THINK ABOUT

- Plastic surgery
- Fitness trackers, cell phones

Testo Junkie
Sex, Drugs and Biopolitics in the Pharmacopornographic Era

SELECTIONS

By PAUL B. PRECIADO

INTRODUCTION

This book is not a memoir. This book is a testosteronebased, voluntary intoxication protocol, which concerns the body and affects of BP. A body-essay. Fiction, actually. If things must be pushed to the extreme, this is a somatopolitical fiction, a theory of the self, or self-theory. During the time period covered by this essay, two external transformations follow on each other in the context of the experimental body, the impact of which couldn't be calculated beforehand and cannot be taken into account as a function of the study; but it created the limits around which writing was incorporated. First of all, there is the death of GD, the human distillation of a vanishing epoch, an icon, and the ultimate French representative of a form of written sexual insurrection; almost simultaneously, there is the tropism of BP's body in the direction of VD's body, an opportunity for perfection—and for ruin. This is a record of physiological and political micromutations provoked in BPs body by testosterone, as well as the theoretical and physical changes incited in that body by loss, desire, elation, failure, or renouncement. I'm not interested in my emotions insomuch as their being mine, belonging only, uniquely, to me. I'm not interested in their individual aspects, only in how they are traversed by what isn't mine. In what emanates from our planet's history, the evolution of living species, the flux of economics, remnants of technological innovations, preparation for wars, the trafficking of organic slaves and commodities, the creation of hierarchies, institutions of punishment and repression, networks of communication and surveillance, the random overlapping of market research groups, techniques and blocs of opinion, the biochemical transformation of feeling, the production and distribution of pornographic images. Some will read this text as a manual for a kind of gender bioterrorism on a molecular scale. Others will see in it a single point in a cartography of extinction. In this text, the reader won't come to any definitive conclusion about the truth of my sex, or predictions about the world to come. I present these pages as an account of theoretical junctions, molecules, affects, in order to leave a trace of a political experiment that lasted 236 days and nights and that continues today under other forms. If the reader sees this text as an uninterrupted series of philosophical reflections, accounts of hormone administration, and detailed records of sexual practices without the solutions provided by continuity, it is simply because this is the mode on which subjectivity is constructed and deconstructed.

◆ ◆ ◆ ◆

The preceding and following days are marked by my ritual of testosterone administration. It's a home protocol; it would even be a secret and private one if each of these administrations weren't being filmed and sent anonymously to an Internet page on which hundreds of transgender, mutating bodies all over the planet are exchanging techniques and know-how. On this audiovisual network, my face is immaterial, my name of no significance. Only the strict relationship between my body and the substance is a cult object, an object of surveillance. I spread the gel over my shoulders. First instant: the feeling of a light slap on the skin. The feeling changes into one of coldness before it disappears. Then, nothing for a day or two. Nothing. Waiting. Then, an extraordinary lucidity settles in, gradually, accompanied by an explosion of the desire to fuck, walk, go out everywhere in the city. This is the climax in which the spiritual force of the testosterone mixing with my blood takes to the fore. Absolutely all the unpleasant sensations disappear. Unlike speed, the movement going on inside has nothing to do with agitation, noise. It's simply the feeling of being in perfect harmony with the rhythm of the city. Unlike with coke, there is no distortion in the perception of self, no logorrhea or any feeling of superiority. Nothing but the feeling of strength reflecting the increased capacity of my muscles, my brain. My body is present to itself. Unlike with speed and coke, there is no immediate comedown. A few days go by, and the movement inside calms, but the feeling of strength, like a pyramid revealed by a sandstorm, remains.

How can I explain what is happening to me? What can I do about my desire for transformation? What can I do about all the years I defined myself as a feminist? What kind of feminist am I today: a feminist hooked on testosterone, or a transgender body hooked on feminism? I have no other alternative but to revise my classics, to subject those theories to the shock that was provoked in me by the practice of taking testosterone. To accept the fact that the change happening in me is the metamorphosis of an era.

◆ ◆ ◆ ◆

Contemporary society is inhabited by toxic-pornographic subjectivities: subjectivities defined by the sub-stance (or substances) that supply their metabolism, by the cybernetic prostheses and various types of pharma-copornographic desires that feed the subject's actions and through which they turn into agents. So we will speak of Prozac subjects, cannabis subjects, cocaine subjects, alcohol subjects, Ritalin subjects, cortisone subjects, silicone subjects, heterovaginal subjects, double-penetration subjects, Viagra subjects, $ subjects …

There is nothing to discover in nature; there is no hidden secret. We live in a punk hypermodernity: it is no longer about discovering the hidden truth in nature; it is about the necessity to specify the cultural, political, and technological processes through which the body as artifact acquires natural status. The oncomouse,[1] the laboratory mouse biotechnologically designed to carry a carcinogenic gene, eats Heidegger. Buffy kills the vampire of Simone de Beauvoir. The dildo, a synthetic extension of sex to produce pleasure and identity, eats Rocco Sififredi's cock. There is nothing to discover in sex or in sexual identity; there is no *inside*. The truth about sex is not a disclosure; it is *sexdesign*. Pharmacopornographic biocapitalism does not produce *things*.

It produces mobile ideas, living organs, symbols, desires, chemical reactions, and conditions of the soul. In biotechnology and in pornocommunication there is no object to be produced. The pharmacopornographic business is the *invention of a subject* and then its global reproduction.

NOTE

1. See Donna J. Hamway, "When Man™ is on the Menu," in *Incorporations (Zone 6),* eds. Jonathan Crary and Sanford K. Winter (New York: Zone Books, 1992), 38–43.

READING 33: TESTO JUNKIE

DISCUSSION QUESTIONS

• Can you define "pharmacopornographic capitalism"?
• Why would someone take testosterone recreationally?

EXAMPLES TO THINK ABOUT

• Chemical birth control
• Synthetic hormones

SECTION 11

CONCLUSION: REACTIONS TO FEMINISM

Interrogating PostFeminism

Gender and the Politics of Popular Culture

SELECTIONS

By YVONNE TASKER AND DIANE NEGRA

INTRODUCTION

Feminist Politics and Postfeminist Culture

Postfeminism broadly encompasses a set of assumptions, widely disseminated within popular media forms, having to do with the "pastness" of feminism, whether that supposed pastness is merely noted, mourned, or celebrated. Crucially for us, postfeminism suggests a more complex relationship between culture, politics, and feminism than the more familiar framing concept of "backlash" allows. Feminist activism has long met with strategies of resistance, negotiation, and containment, processes that a model of backlash—with its implication of achievements won and then subsequently lost—cannot effectively incorporate within the linear chronology of social change on which it seems to be premised. What appears distinctive about contemporary postfeminist culture is precisely the extent to which a selectively defined feminism has been so overtly "taken into account," as Angela McRobbie has noted, albeit in order "to emphasize that it is no longer needed."[1]

The limits of the kind of gender equality enacted within contemporary popular media culture are profound: they are marked by the valorization of female achievement within traditionally male working environments and the celebration of surgical and other disciplinary techniques that "enable" (i.e., require) women to maintain a youthful appearance and attitude in later life.[2] As the essays in this collection demonstrate, such a limited vision of gender equality as both achieved and yet still unsatisfactory underlines the class, age, and racial exclusions that define postfeminism and its characteristic assumption that the themes, pleasures, values, and lifestyles with which it is associated are somehow universally shared and, perhaps more significant, universally accessible. If, as bell hooks writes, "feminism is for everybody," postfeminism is in many ways antithetical to the notion of an open society in which all members are valued in accordance with their distinct identities.[3] Postfeminist culture's centralization of an affluent elite certainly entails an emphatic individualism, but this formulation tends to confuse self-interest with individuality and elevates consumption as a strategy for healing those dissatisfactions that might alternatively be understood in terms of social ills and discontents. Indeed, as hooks and others note, the limited inclusion of certain women within privileged educational, professional, and other work contexts results as much from the demands of a consumer-led capitalism (for both new forms of labor and new forms of consumption) as from a thoroughgoing response to the demands of feminist activism.[4]

Postfeminist culture works in part to incorporate, assume, or naturalize aspects of feminism; crucially, it also works to commodify feminism via the figure of woman as empowered consumer. Thus, postfeminist culture emphasizes educational and professional opportunities for women and girls; freedom of choice with respect to work, domesticity, and parenting; and physical and particularly sexual empowerment. Assuming full economic freedom for women, postfeminist culture also (even insistently) enacts the possibility that women might *choose* to retreat from the public world of work. Postfeminist fictions frequently set aside both evident economic disparities and the fact that the majority of women approach paid labor as an economic necessity rather than a "choice." As this suggests, postfeminism is white and middle class by default, anchored in consumption as a strategy (and leisure as a site) for the production of the self. It is thus also a strategy by which other kinds of social difference are glossed over. The limits of this construction and the challenges it poses for feminist scholarship are questions we return to below.

Postfeminism does not always offer a logically coherent account of gender and power, but through structures of forceful articulation and synergistic reiteration across media forms it has emerged as a dominating discursive system. It generates and draws strength, for instance, from a rhetorical field that produces buzzwords and slogans to express visions of energetic personal empowerment (the borrowed African American idiom "You go, girl!" the phrase "girl power," etc.). Meanwhile postfeminism draws on and sustains an invented social memory of feminist language as inevitably shrill, bellicose, and parsimonious. Thus, while feminism is constituted as an unwelcome, implicitly censorious presence, it is precisely *feminist* concerns that are silenced within postfeminist culture. Reference to "the F word" underscores the status of feminism as unspeakable within contemporary popular culture.[5]

The demand for content to fulfill diverse delivery systems continues to drive contemporary popular media, drawing in the process, as McRobbie suggests, on the talents of young women (and men) conversant with feminist critiques of representation. Recent books such as those by Kim Akass and Janet McCabe (2004) and Ariel Levy (2005) exemplify the emergence of popularized feminist scholarship. While Levy, a journalist, explores the formulaic female sexualities of a culture in which (most often young) women enthusiastically perform patriarchal stereotypes of sexual servility in the name of empowerment, Akass and McCabe, who are both academics, have produced an anthology that mixes fan-style appreciations of *Sex and the City* with feminist critique. Publications of this kind mark a new space of convergence between journalism, popular fiction, and academic analysis.[6] Despite the emergence of accessible accounts such as these, postfeminism nevertheless works to invalidate systemic critique. As McRobbie writes in her influential essay, reprinted here, "The new female subject is, despite her freedom, called upon to be silent, to withhold critique, to count as a modern sophisticated girl, or indeed this withholding of critique is a condition of her freedom."[7]

In line with this peculiarly silent visibility, postfeminism also perpetuates woman as pinup, the enduring linchpin of commercial beauty culture. In fact, it has offered new rationales for guilt-free consumerism, substantially reenergizing beauty culture (primarily for women but sometimes also for men through new archetypes such as the seemingly ubiquitous "metrosexual") and presiding over an aggressive mainstreaming of elaborate and expensive beauty treatments to the middle class. Nicely evocative of the positive embrace of consumer-led beauty culture and the new freedom to disassociate from the "burdens" of feminism is B. Ruby Rich's anecdote about body hair: "Passing by a shop that did waxing one day with my then-girlfriend, we whimsically decided to go in and put an end, for no apparent reason, to a decade of ideological attachment."[8] Here is feminism "taken into account" in a somewhat different, though related, fashion to that identified by McRobbie; for Rich, this anecdote points to the complex intersection of feminist politics, appearance, and consumption and to the ways in which living with feminism and living as a feminist have changed over the last few decades.

If postfeminist popular culture celebrates female agency and women's powers of consumption, it also anxiously raises the possible consequences of female independence, crudely: emotional isolation for women (a preoccupation that neatly sidesteps questions of women's economic instability); and loss of power for men (again, a formulation premised on the somewhat tenuous assumption that all men previously occupied equally elevated positions of social and economic power). For us, postfeminism signals more than a simple evolutionary process whereby aspects of feminism have been incorporated into popular culture—and thereby naturalized as popular feminism. It also simultaneously involves an "othering" of feminism (even as women are more centralized), its construction as extreme, difficult, and unpleasurable. Kathleen Karlyn has shrewdly observed that one of the biggest challenges for feminism in the academy involves coming to grips with generational impasses at a time when "feminism itself seems most evident as a 'structuring absence' for middle class young women."[9] As teachers and researchers committed to producing feminist work in an antifeminist context (whether that of academic institutions, themselves increasingly led by a student-consumer model, or the wider political culture), we find postfeminist culture to be provocative in all the senses of that term: it is troubling and yet at the same time compelling.

◆ ◆ ◆ ◆

While it has been argued that aspects of postfeminism appeared in popular media as far back as the early 1980s, it was during the 1990s that the term became concretized, both as a discursive phenomenon and as a buzzword of U.S. and U.K. journalism. Since the 1990s, popular culture in those countries has also been characterized by a dramatically heightened address to women consumers. The construction of women as both subjects and consumers, or perhaps as subjects only to the extent that we are able and willing to consume, is one of the contradictions at the core of postfeminist culture. Postfeminism is, we contend, inherently contradictory, characterized by a double discourse that works to construct feminism as a phenomenon of the past, traces of which can be found (and sometimes even valued) in the present; postfeminism suggests that it is the very success of feminism that produces its irrelevance for contemporary culture. In fact, the question is more complex than this since, as Sarah Projansky makes clear, postfeminist discourse deploys a variety of positions with respect to feminism, at times celebratory and at times laying blame for contemporary anxieties at the door of a past politics now felt to be misconceived.[10] What the many discursive postfeminisms identified by Projansky share is their relationship to the pastness of feminism, a feature commented on earlier; herein lies a suggestion that social change with respect to gender norms has been experienced, concretized even, through the passage of time.

Indeed, one of postfeminism's key functions is to negotiate the failure of contemporary institutions and the prospect of social death. Postfeminism frequently imagines femininity as a state of vitality in opposition to the symbolically deathly social and economic fields of contemporary Western cultures, and the highest-profile forms of postfeminist femininity are empowered to recharge a culture defined by exhaustion, uncertainty, and moral ambiguity. Thus, the postfeminist heroine is vital, youthful, and playful while her opposite number, the "bad" female professional, is repressive, deceptive, and deadly. In the romantic comedy *13 Going on 30* (2004), the distinctions drawn between Jenna and Lucy, who have known each other since childhood and are now editors at the same women's magazine, starkly illustrate this dynamic. When the magazine is challenged to reconceptualize itself (to undergo, in effect, a makeover), Jenna's youthful enthusiasm takes center stage. Making her presentation of a high school graduation concept for the magazine while wearing a bright pink ensemble and holding a pink balloon, she declares that she "wants to put life back into the magazine,"

FIGURE 34-1   13 Going on 30 structures an operative contrast between Jenna's (Jennifer Garner) girlish enthusiasm and her rival's calculation.

underscoring the importance of remembering "what's good." By contrast, while her colleagues shudder and cringe, the manipulative and scheming Lucy envisions a "deadly serious" redesign concept she deems "fashion suicide," featuring gaunt, unhappy-looking women in dark clothing. Jenna's proposal narratively inverts but ideologically extends the film's broader focus on the retention of youth. Her concept showcases the ritual of high school graduation, symbolically deaging the magazine's female subjects and reinforcing the film's plot, for Jenna has, in fact, magically time traveled to the physical age of thirty though her psychology remains that of an adolescent. Near the close of the film, she will gratefully return to adolescence after having endured romantic, creative, and professional disappointment as an adult woman.

As this example suggests, many postfeminist texts combine a deep uncertainty about existing options for women with an idealized, essentialized femininity that symbolically evades or transcends institutional and social problem spots. In concert with this, as many of the essays in the volume show, postfeminism evidences a distinct preoccupation with the temporal. Women's lives are regularly conceived of as time starved; women themselves are overworked, rushed, harassed, subject to their "biological clocks," and so on to such a degree that female adulthood is defined as a state of chronic temporal crisis. *13 Going on 30* is only one of a number of media texts that specialize in time-shifting fantasies that conflate youthfulness and the past. In this context of beset contemporary femininity, it is perhaps unsurprising that so many of the contributors to this anthology draw examples from the broad categories of lifestyle programming and reality television, with several essays focusing on the significance of the makeover as a recurrent trope of postfeminist media.[11] With its particular capacity to articulate the ordinary, reality TV provides a rich nexus of the desire for transformation, the yearning to achieve perfection in one's physical self and/or domestic environment, and the need to avoid at all costs a politicized understanding of these dynamics.[12]

Moreover, the makeover, whether of body or lived environment, enacts, as Sadie Wearing demonstrates in this volume, a particular form of temporality in which youth is fetishized and change accelerated or even presented as instantaneous. This accelerated temporality is characteristic of postmodern culture more broadly, as is the presentation of consumption itself as both therapeutic and transformative. Like daytime talk shows, makeovers trade in the vulnerability and resilience of their participants, functioning as simultaneously exploitative, sentimental, and compelling. Thus, the makeover mobilizes familiar tropes. As Brenda R. Weber writes of ABC's *Extreme Makeover*, "The story it tells—one of suffering and transformation, of desperation and joy—is as old as narrative itself."[13] But it does so in a contemporary context that aligns female consumption with freedom in a fashion that is (perversely perhaps) informed by feminism, even as that feminism is firmly "posted." Similarly, as Kimberly Springer notes in this volume, while reality TV is more than willing to make use of the "angry black woman" as a type, the question of why she might be angry remains unspoken. And, as Paul Gilroy writes with respect to the domestic makeover so central to British television schedules, "By exploring the process of changing private space and refining the ability to act there, these shows offer an implicit justification of the refusal to act elsewhere." In articulating rapid transformations, the makeover format works to suggest that "taste and lifestyle preference are much more important elements of identity than ethnicity, class, or regional ties could ever be."[14]

Postfeminism in all its guises posits the contemporary as surpassing feminism, leaving it behind. In doing so, it implicitly draws strength from the anxiety of aging at work in so many of its texts. Postfeminist representational culture is, of course, acutely age conscious; a variety of "chick" fictions from *Bridget Jones's Diary* (2001) and *How Stella Got Her Groove Back* (1998) to *Sex and the City* (1998–2004) and *13 Going on 30* have shown themselves to be exceedingly precise about the ages of their female protagonists. Meanwhile, the cult of youth is being technologically facilitated on a variety of fronts; myriad forms of reality TV, for example, dedicate themselves to staging rejuvenating transformations and the fantasy that aging can be managed away. The ambivalence about aging that strongly characterizes such fictions is also extended to feminism itself. As postfeminism has raised the premium on youthfulness, it has installed an image of feminism as "old" (and by extension moribund).

◆ ◆ ◆ ◆

We are not in the business of simply celebrating icons of postfeminist culture: the self as a project; kick-ass, working-out women as expressions of agency; or freedom as the freedom to shop or have cosmetic surgery. Our responsibility as feminist critics is to approach the popular with a skeptical eye, questioning whether identity politics inevitably generates a politics of the self, culminating in the "self as project" so characteristic of postfeminism. Equally, however, we are not engaged in interrogating or understanding postfeminist culture simply as a forerunner to rejecting it. The images and icons of postfeminism *are* compelling; the women and girls who (literally) buy into this visual and narrational repertoire are not simply dupes. As an idiom, postfeminism popularizes (as much as it caricatures) a feminism it simultaneously evokes and rejects. Thus, many of the essays in this collection aim to explore the address postfeminist culture makes to female spectators while acknowledging its limitations.

Within the broad field of media studies, critical commentary continues to pose questions about the meaning of popular texts in either-or terms. Thus, texts from *Buffy* to Britney are either progressive or regressive, liberating or containing. Underpinning this anthology is a reservation as to how far such a model can take us. Can it ever, we ask, reflect the complexity and ambivalence of popular culture or postfeminism? Postfeminist culture is evidently postmodern in character, its self-reflexivity mobilizing the terms of its own critique. Postfeminist culture does not allow us to make straightforward distinctions between progressive and regressive texts. Nevertheless, it urgently requires us to develop new reading strategies to counteract the popularized feminism, figurations of female agency, and canny neutralization of traditional feminist critiques in its texts.

Feminism challenges us to critique relations of power, to imagine the world as other than it is, to conceive of different patterns of work, life, and leisure. Postfeminist culture enacts fantasies of regeneration and transformation that also speak to a desire for change. Clearly, however, it is unhelpful to mistake one for the other. The challenges facing feminist media critics of an earlier era centered on the need to make women visible, to denaturalize the construction of women's culture as inherently trivial or banal. The contemporary challenges that postfeminist culture poses for feminist media studies are rather different. Postfeminism displaces older forms of trivialization, generating a sense of newness, yet it also refreshes long familiar themes of gendered representation, demonstrating the ongoing urgency of speaking feminist critique.

NOTES

1. McRobbie, "Post-feminism and Popular Culture," 254. McRobbie's seminal essay is reprinted in this volume.
2. In the United Kingdom, supermodel Claudia Schiffer ends a current television advertisement for an antiaging product with the telling phrase, uttered straight to camera in a blandly reassuring tone, "Let surgery wait." Cosmetic surgery is here invoked, in a quite taken for granted manner, as compulsory rather than optional, although consumers can postpone the inevitable, perhaps suggesting the unpalatable aspects of such invasive procedures. For a discussion of the plastic surgery industry and contemporary body politics, see Blum, *Flesh Wounds*.
3. hooks, *Feminism Is for Everybody*.

4. Ibid., 50.

5. Ironic references to feminism as "the F word" are a familiar feature of popular media culture in the United Kingdom.

6. Levy, *Female Chauvinist Pigs: Women and the Rise of Raunch Culture*; McCabe and Akass, *Reading "Sex and the City."* In the British context, it is also relevant to note the visibility of feminist scholars as public intellectuals with commentators such as Germaine Greer disseminating their ideas through print journalism and other media forms in addition to traditional publication techniques.

7. McRobbie, "Post-feminism and Popular Culture," 260.

8. Projansky, *Watching Rape*, 67.

9. This is also in line with the amount of scholarly work relating to reality tv. Two recent collections stand out in this regard: Oullette and Murray, *Reality TV*; and Holmes and Jermyn, *Understanding Reality Television*.

10. For analyses of another category of postfeminist Anglo-American transit text, the nanny series (in which British child-raising experts train American families to deal with their recalcitrant children), see Kim, "Elevating Servants, Elevating American Families"; and Ouellette, "Nanny tv."

11. Weber, "Beauty, Desire, and Anxiety."

12. Gilroy, *Postcolonial Melancholia*, 119. Although Gilroy refers to British shows such as *Changing Rooms* and *Ground Force*, the evacuation of the potential for social change is also dramatically (even excessively) foregrounded in the ABC series *Extreme Makeover: Home Edition*, which mobilizes commerce and communities in the service of consumption.

13. For a discussion of the complex interdependencies between first-world women employers and their third-world women employees see Ehrenreich and Hochschild, *Global Woman*.

14. Joanne Hollows's discussion of the downshifting narrative in recent British popular culture addresses the compartmentalization of domesticity in feminist scholarship and feminist lives and asks probing questions about the fantasy of reclaimed (often rural) domesticity that has proved so saleable in print fiction, reality television, and the celebrity personae of domestic sensualists such as Nigella Lawson. See Hollows's "Can I Go Home Yet?"

15. Negra, "Girls Who Go Home."

16. One sign of the political estrangement of American women is to be found in the fact that 22 of the 45 million single women in the United States in 2000 did not cast a vote in the 2000 presidential election. See Loth, "Women Who Vote, and Those That Don't." The particular terms within which women can achieve political success are evident with respect to Condoleezza Rice in Kimberly Springer's essay in this volume. In a somewhat earlier British context, several of the representational tropes identified by Springer with respect to Rice featured in responses to Margaret Thatcher, who was styled as sexless on the one hand (the "iron lady") and as caught in illicit passion with then U.S. president Ronald Reagan on the other. Jacqueline Rose discusses Thatcher as an icon of fearful femininity in "Margaret Thatcher and Ruth Ellis."

17. Sturkin, "Masculinity, Courage and Sacrifice," 444.

18. Karlyn, "Feminism and Its Discontents."

19. Of course, some of these texts may present themselves as globally generic and be culturally protective at the same time. For instance, in the *Bridget Jones* novel and its sequel the British hero rescues Bridget after she has been victimized by the actions of a foreign male. In addition, culturally specific postfeminist franchises still flourish. One example is the series of novels *Five Go Mad in...*, which relies on British traditions of same-sex groups taking vacations together that would probably not be as clear and resonant to a reader without this cultural frame of reference.

20. The extent to which regional differences are also at issue is an aspect that we acknowledge but do not have the space to address here.

21. Tania Modleski's pathbreaking study *Feminism without Women: Culture and Criticism in a "Postfeminist" Era* confronts directly the ways in which the centrality of "new" men and "new" masculinities in American culture are achieved at the expense of women.

22. Battema and Sewell, "Trading in Masculinity," 261.

23. Some of the scholarship on the celebrity talk show host and postfeminist icon Oprah Winfrey has begun to move in this direction. See in particular Illouz, *Oprah Winfrey and the Glamour of Misery*. Illouz offers a commentary on Winfrey's selective engagement with the problematics of race, noting, for instance, that she "consistently twists political categories and transforms them into ethical and spiritual ones" (24).

REFERENCES

Blum, V. *Flesh Wounds: The Culture of Cosmetic Surgery.* Berkeley: University of California Press, 2005.

Gilroy, P. *Postcolonial Melancholia.* New York: Columbia University Press, 2005.

Holmes, S. and Deborah, J., eds. *Understanding Reality Television.* London: Rout-ledge, 2004.

hooks, b. *Feminism Is for Everybody: Passionate Politics.* London: Pluto, 2000.

Karlyn, K. R. "*Scream*, Popular Culture, and Feminism's Third Wave: 'I'm Not My Mother.'" *Genders OnLine Journal* 38 (2003), http://www.genders.org/g38/g38_rowe_karlyn.html.

Kim, L. S. "Elevating Servants, Elevating American Families." *Flow* 1:12 (2005).

Levy, A. *Female Chauvinist Pigs: Women and the Rise of Raunch Culture.* New York: Free Press, 2005.

McCabe, J. and Kim A. *Reading "Sex and the City."* London: I. B. Tauris, 2004.

McRobbie, A. "Post-feminism and Popular Culture." *Feminist Media Studies* 4:3 (2004): 255–64.

Ouellette, L. "Nanny TV." *Flow* 1:11 (2005).

Ouellette, L. and Susan Murray, eds. *Reality TV: Remaking Television Culture.* New York: New York University Press, 2004.

Projansky, S. *Watching Rape: Film and Television in Postfeminist Culture*. New York: New York University Press, 2001.

Rich, B. R. *Chick Flicks: Theories and Memories of the Feminist Film Movement*. Durham: Duke University Press, 1998.

Weber, B. R. "Beauty, Desire, and Anxiety: The Economy of Sameness in ABC's *Extreme Makeover*." *Genders Online Journal* 41 (2005), http://www.genders.org/g41/g41_weber.html.

DISCUSSION QUESTIONS

- What does "post-feminism" mean? Is it a good characterization of today's culture?
- What are the limits of women's freedom in post-feminist culture?

EXAMPLES TO THINK ABOUT

- Beyoncé
- Taylor Swift

"LAD FLICKS"

Discursive Reconstructions of Masculinity in Popular Film

By *DAVID HANSEN-MILLER AND ROSALIND GILL*

INTRODUCTION

The aim of this chapter is to discuss an emerging genre of films that we call "lad flicks" or "lad movies." Lad flicks can be thought of as a hybrid of "buddy movies," romantic comedies, and "chick flicks" that center on the trials and tribulations of a young man or men as they grow up and make their way in the world (usually in North America or the United Kingdom). What distinguishes this popular and expanding genre from other coming of-age movies, or movies featuring traditional male comic leads, is that *masculinity itself* is the central object. The source of dramatic tension and humor is the protagonists' struggle with competing definitions of what it means to be a man and their own ability to live up to that category. In what strikes us as a significant shift in popular discourses concerning masculinity these films are increasingly confident in treating masculinity as an object of humor.

Lad flicks came to prominence in the late 1990s against the backdrop of anxieties about a "crisis in masculinity," and the proliferation of a number of other "lad productions" in different sites across popular culture: for example, radio, television, and "lad magazines." Unlike other popular forms, however, lad movies have gone relatively unnoticed as a culturally significant genre of films and have received little scholarly attention.[1]

In this chapter, we will set out to analyze dominant features of the genre and focus our discussion on two prominent examples: *The 40-Year-Old Virgin* (Judd Apatow, 2005). and *Role Models* (David Wain. 2008). Lad flicks arc compelling texts for film theorists as they signal movement away from the subjective pleasures of masculine identification and towards examination of objectified masculinity as a troubled cultural category. While the films deploy classical techniques of scopic pleasure and identification they also fall within more recent trends in popular films and rely heavily on a knowing gaze and irony. As discourse analysts, our interest is to explore "lad flicks" as historical and culturally specific gendered, racialized, and classed texts, which enunciate distinctive constructions of contemporary masculinity. We are primarily interested in analyzing these cultural texts in an effort to illuminate contemporary changes in, and understandings of, gender relations in the early twenty-first century.

The chapter is divided into four sections. We start by contextualizing lad flicks within wider social and cultural transformations and the emergence of the figure of the "new lad." We then chart the growth of lad flicks and explore some of their generic features. In the following section we consider the films in more detail, focusing on some distinctive features: their constructions of unheroic, fallible masculinities, their structural dependence upon a dynamic of homosociality and homophobia, and (connected to this) the representations of women within the movies. In the final, concluding section of the chapter we critically interrogate the narrative resolutions offered by the films in which growing up or coming of age is framed in terms of individuated, heterosexual monogamy.

THE RISE OF LADDISM

The figure of the "new lad" has been a feature of popular culture in the United Kingdom, United States, and elsewhere since the early 1990s. He materialized as a new and distinctive articulation of masculinity, across a variety of cultural sites including "zoo" radio, quiz shows, sitcoms, "ladvertising," and popular fiction. Primarily, the new lad gained visibility in a new generation of magazines launched (or relaunched) in the mid-1990s. The so-called "lad mags" moved away from depictions of the egalitarian "new man," born of feminist demands for equality in the home and workplace, and towards a more "assertive articulation of the post-permissive masculine heterosexual script."[2] The new lad was a cultural figure organized around homosocial bonding and predatory and objectifying attitudes towards women. Lad mags offered a hedonistic, apparently shameless celebration of masculinity, constructed around men's assumed obsessions with drinking, foot ball, and (heterosexual) sex.

There have been a variety of attempts to understand the cultural ascendance of the figure of the "new lad." Most relate it to ongoing social and economic transformations in post-industrial societies, including the decline of manufacturing and traditionally valued "male" laboring jobs, the "downsizing" of management roles through the mergers and acquisitions of the 1980s and 1990s, the ological displacement of well-paid administrative positions, the rise of "ferminized" service sector work, as well as broader associated changes in the position of women.[3] However, these more recent changes constituting the "new lad" also fall into the line of older discourses concerning perceived threats to men culinity.

Michel Foucault has explained the manner in which repressive forms of social control were historically displaced by the modern profusion of regulatory, "bio-political" discourses and their demand for increasing self discipline.[4] This meant that "private" spaces such as the family home and the intimate processes of rearing children increasingly became the object of state intervention. Through such processes women were increasingly invested with forms of social responsibility and authority that were historically reserved for men. As such powers became manifest so did cultural anxieties about the condition of men and masculinity. Signs of such insecurity were apparent as early as the late nineteenth century when men sought to imaginatively and practically disassociate themselves from the arenas of women's authority— what the historian John Tosh refers to as "the flight from domesticity."[5] The Victorian era saw a rapid growth in social and sporting clubs where men could escape into all-male environs, while the early twentieth century saw rising popularity in rugged all-male sports such as hunting and fishing.[6]

The "crisis" in masculinity consistently re-emerged over the twentieth century. Barbara Ehrenreich explores the unexpected success of *Playboy Magazine* in 1954, and the masculine bachelor lifestyle it advocated, by contextualizing it within the demanding conformity of the postwar American corporate world.[7] Men of the era faced considerable pressure towards marriage and family life such that those who resisted could find their sexuality under suspicion. *Playboy* turned the tables by mocking and deriding marriage as an arrangement where parasitic women sapped men's virility. From its start, *Playboy* combined the unapologetic enjoyment of urban consumer culture (fine clothing, the arts, expensive cars) with an unabashedly heterosexual hedonism. As the pages of *Playboy* dripped with sexuality they served to re-signify historically suspect pursuits as prime evidence of manly virility.

The late 1990s saw a proliferation of discourses about boys' poor educational performance relative to girls', young men's increasing "body anxieties" and associated disorders, as well as general concerns—amplified by small but vocal men's rights organizations—that men were becoming the new victims as they lost out to women in divorce courts, workplaces, and elsewhere. By the start of the twenty-first century, the word "masculinity" was rarely heard unless quickly followed by "crisis." As Beynon put it: "'masculinity' and 'crisis' have become so closely associated in some sectors of the media that they are in danger of becoming synonymous."[8] While scholars remain skeptical about the notion of masculinity being in crisis there is no doubt about the significance of "crisis talk" in opening up a discursive space in which the figure of the "new lad" could flourish.[9]

What marks laddism out as distinct from the "traditional" or "unreconstructed" versions of masculinity associated with a pre-feminist era is its self-consciously *postfeminist* style.[10]

"New laddism" is not ignorant but entirely aware about how it offends against contemporary norms of probity, good taste and "reasonable" attitudes towards women. This is captured in *Loaded* magazine's strapline: "For men who should know better." The implication is that they do indeed know better, but take pleasure in not caring. Defiance is melded with a general ethos of "not taking things too seriously." More broadly, the affective tone of lad texts is anti-aspirational, smart, detached, ironic, and "deeply shallow."[11] Imelda Whelehan has argued that the new lad is "a nostalgic revival of old patriarchy; a direct challenge to feminism's call for social transformation, by reaffirming albeit ironically—the unchanging nature of gender relations and sexual roles."[12] For others, he is better regarded as a response to the figure of the "new man," a more caring, sharing, and egalitarian version of masculinity which achieved a certain media prominence in the 1980s. Ben Crewe claims that lad culture emerged out of contempt for the "miserable liberal guilt" of the new man and his "hesitant and question-ing stands on sexual relations."[13] The new man was condemned as unappealing, narcissistic, and above all inauthentic. Against this, lad culture is depicted as libidinous and refreshingly honest.

LAD CULTURE GOES TO THE MOVIES

The "lad flick" emerges and resides within this history as well as collectively indicating ongoing transformations in popular understandings of laddishness and contemporary masculinity. The films do not simply depict laddishness but meditate upon it. Where the "chick flick" historically targeted and commercially constituted female audiences through a focus on women and contemporary interpersonal relationships, any parallel cinematic focus on men and interpersonal relationships was traditionally subsumed under the banner of humanistic universality and therefore assumed to hold general relevance, not linked to one gender. For instance, while westerns and war movies drew predominantly male audiences this was not accomplished through an explicit attempt to engage with masculinity as such. A more direct engagement with masculinity did emerge in the 1980s with the popular American "buddy movie." Such films often paired black and white men, and therefore marked masculine differences, together for comedic and dramatic effect, as well as a more general cultural renegotiation of racial difference.[14] The contemporary "lad flick" combines different genre elements to focus specifically on the interpersonal difficulties facing contemporary masculinity. As we will detail, a predominantly white, entirely heterosexual, and generally lower-middle-class masculinity emerges as the significant point of crisis within these films.

While early films within the genre wedded humor with elements of melodrama, like the looming threat of Fiona's suicide in *About A Boy* (Chris Weitz, 2002), and so appeared to be sincere about the difficulties of a masculine adulthood, the genre has evolved to suggest that laddishness, new or old, is problematic and unsustainable.

DISCUSSION QUESTIONS

- Can you describe New Laddism or Bro Culture?
- Are we supposed to take the statements and actions of New Lads seriously?

EXAMPLES TO THINK ABOUT

- Totalfratmove.com, barstoolsports.com, and similar sites
- Dick Pics

9 781516 549979